# Translation of the

# Belchatow Yizkor Book

Dedicated To The Memory Of

A

Vanished Jewish Town In Poland

———

Original Yizkor Book Published by
The Central Federation Of Polish Jews In Argentina
Together With The
Belchatow Society In Argentina, Brazil, And South America
Buenos Aires, 1951

**Published by JewishGen**

**An Affiliate of the Museum of Jewish Heritage—A Living Memorial to the Holocaust
New York**

Translation of: Belchatow yizker-bukh
Translation of Belchatow Memorial Book (Bełchatów, Poland)

Translation Project Coordinator: Roni Seibel Liebowitz
Editors: Mark Tarkov and Abraham Mittleberg
Layout: Donni Magid
Cover Design: Nina Schwartz, Impulse Graphics, LLC. artstop@impulsegraphics.com
Name Indexing: Bena Shklyanoy

Published by JewishGen, Inc.
An Affiliate of the Museum of Jewish Heritage
A Living Memorial to the Holocaust
36 Battery Place, New York, NY 10280

JewishGen, Inc. is not responsible for inaccuracies or omissions in the original work and makes no representations regarding the accuracy of this translation. Digital images of the original book's contents can be seen online at the New York Public Library website.

The mission of the JewishGen organization is to produce a translation of the original work, and we cannot verify the accuracy of statements or alter facts cited.

Printed in the United States of America by Lightning Source, Inc.

Library of Congress Control Number (LCCN): 2020935351
ISBN: 978-1-939561-49-7
(Hard cover: 486 pages, alk. paper)

Cover photograph: Front cover photo: Blatt and Warszawski families at unveiling for Sura Necha Warszawski Blatt, Fall 1932. Photo courtesy of Claudia Weiss Greve, Rona Weiss and Carlton Greve.

(The headstone reads: Here lies buried Sarah Necha, a woman of valor, a crown to her husband, a modest and G-d-fearing woman, daughter of Yehiel of blessed memory, wife of Reb Zvi Levi Blatt, may his light shine. 25 Shevat 5692. Mr. Blatt, standing next to the headstone, sent this photo to his daughter Rose in New Jersey, with the note: Dear Daughter Feige Rochel, A memory from your mother and your dear father to wish you and your children—May you be inscribed for a good year.)

1915 Map: Courtesy of Map Archive of Wojskowy Instytut Geograficzny

Back Cover Credit: Jewish textile workers at a Bełchatów factory, late 1920s, Tojwie Zysman Przybylski shown in first row,s econd from left. Courtesy of Sofia Przybylski Andel.

# JewishGen and the Yizkor Books in Print Project

This book has been published by the **Yizkor Books in Print Project**, as part of the **Yizkor Book Project** of JewishGen, Inc.

**JewishGen, Inc.** is a non-profit organization founded in 1987 as a resource for Jewish genealogy. Its website [www.jewishgen.org] serves as an international clearinghouse and resource center to assist individuals who are researching the history of their Jewish families and the places where they lived. JewishGen provides databases, facilitates discussion groups, and coordinates projects relating to Jewish genealogy and the history of the Jewish people. In 2003, JewishGen became an affiliate of the **Museum of Jewish Heritage—A Living Memorial to the Holocaust** in New York.

The **JewishGen Yizkor Book Project** was organized to make more widely known the existence of Yizkor (Memorial) Books written by survivors and former residents of various Jewish communities throughout the world. Later, volunteers connected to the different destroyed communities began cooperating to have these books translated from the original language—usually Hebrew or Yiddish—into English, thus enabling a wider audience to have access to the valuable information contained within them. As each chapter of these books was translated, it was posted on the JewishGen website and made available to the general public.

The **Yizkor Books in Print Project** began in 2011 as an initiative to print and publish Yizkor Books that had been fully translated, so that hard copies would be available for purchase by the descendants of these communities and also by scholars, universities, synagogues, libraries, and museums.

These Yizkor books have been produced almost entirely through the volunteer effort of researchers from around the world, assisted by donations from private individuals. The books are printed and sold at near cost, so as to make them as affordable as possible. Our goal is to make this important genre of Jewish literature and history available in English in book form, so that people can have the personal histories of their ancestral towns on their bookshelves for themselves and for their children and grandchildren.

A list of all published translated Yizkor Books in the project with prices and ordering information can be found at:
http://www.jewishgen.org/Yizkor/ybip.html

*Binny Lewis, Yizkor Book Project Manager*
*Joel Alpert, Yizkor-Book-in-Print Project Coordinator*

# JewishGen
# Yizkor Book Project

This book is presented by the
Yizkor Books in Print Project
Project Coordinator: Joel Alpert

Part of the
Yizkor Books Project of JewishGen, Inc.
Project Manager: Lance Ackerfeld

These books have been produced solely through volunteer effort
of individuals from around the world. The books are printed and
sold at near cost, so as to make them as affordable as possible.

Our goal is to make this history and important genre of Jewish
literature available in English in book form so that people can have
the near-personal histories of their ancestral towns on their bookshelves for themselves and for their children and grandchildren.

Any donations to the Yizkor Books Project are appreciated.

Please send donations to:
Yizkor Book Project
JewishGen
36 Battery Place
New York, NY 10280

JewishGen, Inc. is an affiliate of the
Museum of Jewish Heritage
A Living Memorial to the Holocaust

# Notes to the Reader:

We apologize ahead of time for the poor quality of images in the book. Often these images had been scanned from the original Yizkor books which were of poor quality to begin with, being copies of old photographs. Each transfer results in loss of quality. We have done the best we could, given the original material and the resources and technology at hand. Even though images often appear of higher quality on computer screens, that does not transfer to high quality images in print. A reader can view the original scans on the web sites listed below.

Within the text the reader will note "{34}" standing ahead of a paragraph. This indicates that the material translated below was on page 34 of the original book. However, when a paragraph was split between two pages in the original book, the marker is placed in this book after the end of the paragraph for ease of reading.

Also please note that all references within the text of the book to page numbers, refer to the page numbers of the original Yizkor Book.

The original book can be seen online at the New York Public Library site:

https://digitalcollections.nypl.org/items/4e04b840-4f50-0133-0a27-00505686d14e#/?uuid=4f96a260-4f50-0133-7b13-00505686d14e

or at the Yiddish Book Center web site:

https://www.yiddishbookcenter.org/collections/yizkor-books/yzk-nybc313685/belkhatov

In order to obtain a list of all Shoah victims from Belchatow, the reader should access the Yad Vashem web site listed below; one can also search for specific family names using family name option. These lists are continually updated by Yad Vashem, so it is worthwhile to periodically search these lists.

There is much valuable information available on this web site, including the Pages of Testimony, etc.
http://yvng.yadvashem.org

A list of this book and all books available in the Yizkor-Book-In-Print Project along with prices is available at:
http://www.jewishgen.org/Yizkor/ybip.html

# Geopolitical Information:

Bełchatów, Poland is located at 51°22' N 19°23' E, 92 miles SW of Warszawa

Alternate names for the town are: Bełchatów [Pol], Belchatov [Yid], Belkhatuv [Rus], Belkhatov
Russian: Белхатув. Yiddish: בעלכאָטאָוו

| Period | Town | District | Province | Country |
|--------|------|----------|----------|---------|
| Before WWI (c. 1900): | Bełchatów | Piotrków | Piotrków | Russian Empire |
| Between the wars (c. 1930): | Bełchatów | Piotrków | Łódż | Poland |
| After WWII (c. 1950): | Bełchatów | | | Poland |
| Today (c. 2000): | Bełchatów | | | Poland |

Jewish Population in 1900: 2,987

**Nearby Jewish Communities:**
   Bełchatów 2 miles NNE
   Wola Krzysztoporska 9 miles E
   Kamieńsk 10 miles SE
   Szczerców 11 miles W
   Zelów 11 miles NNW
   Rozprza 12 miles E
   Sulmierzyce 13 miles SW
   Gorzkowice 13 miles SE
   Piotrków Trybunalski 14 miles ENE
   Radomsko 19 miles SSE
   Nowa Brzeźnica 19 miles SSW
   Widawa 19 miles WNW
   Łask 20 miles NNW
   Tuszyn 20 miles NNE
   Pajęczno 20 miles SW
   Sulejów 22 miles E
   Pabianice 23 miles N
   Wolbórz 23 miles ENE
   Rzgów 24 miles NNE
   Będków 24 miles NE
   Pławno 25 miles S
   Osjaków 25 miles W

BALTIC SEA                    LITHUANIA

RUSSIA                Vilnius ●

POLAND                              BELARUS

GERMANY

● Poznan            Warsaw ●

● Lodz
●Belchatow

● Prague                            UKRAINE

CZECH REPUBLIC            ● Krakow

SLOVAKIA

250 miles

POLAND - Current Borders

0

0            250 Km            500 Km

Belchatow located in Poland

Yiddish Title Page of Yizkor Book

Translation of the Title Page of Original Yizkor Book

# BELCHATOW

## YIZKOR BOOK

DEDICATED TO THE MEMORY OF A
VANISHED JEWISH TOWN IN POLAND
—
Published by
**THE CENTRAL FEDERATION OF POLISH JEWS IN ARGENTINA**

together with the
**BELCHATOW SOCIETY IN ARGENTINA, BRAZIL, AND SOUTH**

**AMERICA**

**BUENOS AIRES, 1951**

[The above title page was translated from the Yiddish
by Dr. Khane-Feygl (Anita) Turtletaub]

# בעלכאַטאָוו

## יזכור־בוך

געווידמעט דעם אַנדענק פֿון אַ
פֿאַרשווונדן ייִדיש שטעטל אין פּוילן

★

אַרויסגעגעבן דורכן

**צענטראַל־פֿאַרבאַנד פֿון פּוילישע ייִדן אין אַרגענטינע**
צוזאַמען מיט די
בעלכאַטאָווער לאַנדסלייט־פֿאַראיינען אין אַרגענטינע, בראַזיל
און צפֿון־אַמעריקע

בוענאָס איירעס, 1951

# Table of Contents

## IV. The Destruction of Belchatow

*[Page 2]*

ביבליאָ-סעריע

דאָס פּוילישע יידנטום

**80**

רעדאַקטאָר:
מאַרק טורקאָוו

פֿאַרלאַגס-לייטער:
אברהם מיטלבערג

די רשימה פֿון דערשינענע ביכער — צום סוף פֿונעם בוך

Book Series
Polish Jewry

# Vol. 80

Editor:
Mark Turkov and Abraham Mittleberg

**Translation of the above title page by Dr. Khane-Feygl (Anita) Turtletaub**
**(Translation donated by Sharon and Samuel Shattan and Shmuel Shottan)**

The list of titles already published -- at the end of the volume

———

[Page 5]

# BELCHATOW

## YIZKOR BOOK

DEDICATED TO THE MEMORY OF A
VANISHED JEWISH TOWN IN POLAND

—

Published by
**THE CENTRAL FEDERATION OF POLISH JEWS IN ARGENTINA**

together with the
**BELCHATOW SOCIETY IN ARGENTINA, BRAZIL, AND SOUTH AMERICA**

**BUENOS AIRES, 1951**

[The above title page was translated from the Yiddish
by Dr. Khane-Feygl (Anita) Turtletaub]

———

*[Pages 9-10]*

# FROM THE EDITOR

## Translation from the Yiddish by Dr. Khane-Feygl (Anita) Turtletaub (Translation donated by Sharon and Samuel Shattan and Shmuel Shottan)

This volume, the 80th in the book series "Polish Jewry" is an anthology of research work, memoirs, documents and pictures of a vanished town in Poland: it is the Yizkor Book of the town of Belchatow.

With this volume we begin a new cycle of important works in our book series. Although many of the books that have been published to date are Yizkor Books, although a many of the books have been dedicated to the history, struggle and demise of various towns and villages, they were always written by one author and therefore had to have one point of view representing the personal feelings and thoughts of one individual.

This present volume contains the works of a variety of authors, some of them professional scholars and writers. The majority, however, are informal describers and portrayers of the world which they experienced in their town. [They write of] the times of great changes in Jewish societal, political, social and cultural life as well as the difficult years of struggle and death.

It is an eternal monument, a monument to the history of the Yiddish shtetl in living Yiddish words, an eternal reminder of all our dear ones who were martyred, a Yizkor Book to the memory of Jewish life that was destroyed.

It is possible that in the individual chapters of memoirs written by individual authors, which are presented in this Yizkor Book, there are facts, episodes, events which are repeated. But these repetitions are the result of various points of view and various worldviews, and therefore, bring out more clearly the coloring of the described period, showing all the aspects of the pulsating Jewish life of the erstwhile Belchatow.

The Society of Belchatowers in Buenos-Aires, with the help of other Belchatowers living elsewhere in the world, in Israel, Poland, South America, Brazil, Australia and everywhere they happened to find themselves dispersed in the world, felt the great debt that they owed their deceased brothers and sisters and the town of their birth, and they assisted morally and materially in the publishing of this Yizkor Book. By means of this Yizkor Book, the people of

Belchatow have erected an eternal memorial in Jewish history in general and in Polish Jewish history specifically to their town that disappeared.

The editors of the book series "Polish Jewry" feels an obligation to acknowledge the Belchatower Society, the Yizkor Book Publication Committee, and especially the members of the Editorial Committee, Avraham Laib, Zainwel Przedborski, and Hershl Goldminc, for their valuable and companionable assistance, so that this book will fulfill the intentions and objectives that we had set for ourselves.

Buenos Aires, July 1951

———

*[Pages 11-13]*

# A Word to the Reader

### Translation from the Yiddish by Dr. Khane-Feygl (Anita) Turtletaub (Translation donated by Sharon and Samuel Shattan and Shmuel Shottan)

The Publishing Committee of this Yizkor Book, dedicated to our hometown of Belchatow, feels an obligation to provide its readers with a short explanation

As soon as the Second World War ended, the Assistance Union was created to help the refugees of our town, which were dispersed in other lands and in camps. And the thought was born that, together with those who has remained alive, the people of Belchatow should create a work that would memorialize those who had been martyred, those who had died during the Holocaust. We wanted to honor our dear departed and at the same time erect a monument to our dear town of Belchatow, the site of our early years, of our struggles, hopes and strivings.

We will indeed mention our friends who first brought up the idea of publishing a Yizkor Book, and the officials of our Belchatow Society, who undertook and carried out this initiative. This was in the year 1946, and the officials at that time were the following:

| | |
|---|---|
| President | Avraham Laib |
| Vice-President | Yosef Gliksman |
| Secretary | Zainwel Przedborski |
| Vice-Secretary | Hershl Goldminc |
| Treasurer | Leybl Hecht |
| Vice-Treasurer | Yakov-Yosef Zilberszac |
| Workers | Fayvl Wilhelm |
| " | Rochl-Leya Szimkowicz |
| " | Motl Laib |
| " | Naftali Huberman |
| " | Shloyme Zhitnitsky |
| " | Yankl-Meyer Pukacz |
| " | Dovid Zilberglat |
| " | Shimshom Dzienczarski |
| " | Yankl Elbinger |
| " | Alter Rozental |

Toybe Przybilski, Leyzer Huberman,
Fishl Szmulewicz, Chaim Grunwald

Those who helped financially should also be mentioned. We received [funds] from our fellow Belchatowers in Brazil and in South America. We want to especially recognize and give thanks to our fellow Belchatowers Zisl and Berl Laib for their financial contribution to this book in honor of the memory of their unforgettable daughter Sarah Leah , who was torn from them in the blossom of her youth and who was always a paradigm of willingness to help those Belchatowers who remained alive after the Holocaust. We remember her here with great honor to her memory.

We thank all the coworkers on this Yizkor Book: the professional writers Dr. Philip Fridman, Yakov Botoshansky and F. Wald for their assistance. [We also thank] all the other Belchatowers both in this country and outside it who through their memoirs, documents and pictures had a part in actualizing our efforts.

It gives us special satisfaction that this Yizkor Book, dedicated to the town of Belchatow, is part of the series of books entitled "Polish Jewry," which the Central Federation of Polish Jews in Argentina publishes and which has attained such importance in the world of Jewish culture.

It is understandable and quite possible that there would be some errors in some of the articles in which facts and people are mentioned, so we ask your forgiveness in advance.

Our only intention in publishing this Yizkor Book was to give a complete picture of our town -- [to show it] as everyone saw it, to show the Belchatower Jews in their pain and in their joy, in their struggles and strivings up to the time of their demise.

With this Yizkor Book we wanted to erect a memorial on the unknown graves of our martyrs and to create an eternal monument to commemorate our town Belchatow.

*The Yizkor Book Committee of the People of Belchatow*
Buenos Aires, July 1951

———

[Page 14]

# Dedicated to
# Our Unforgettable
# Sarah - Leah
# [by] Berl and Zisl Laib

**Translation from the Yiddish by Dr. Khane-Feygl (Anita) Turtletaub (Translation donated by Sharon and Samuel Shattan and Shmuel Shottan)**

----

[Page 15]

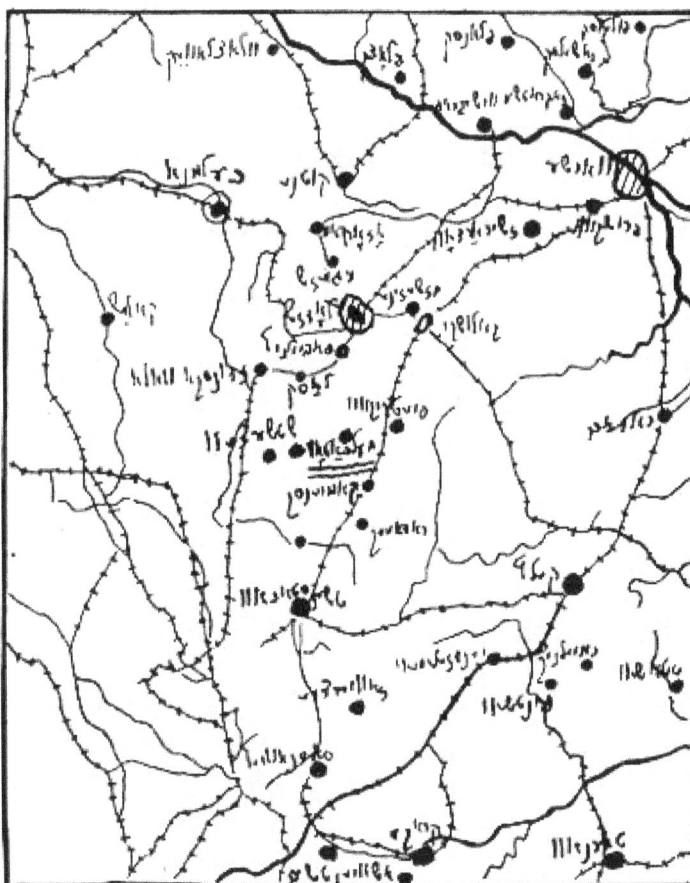

**Belchatow on the Geographic Map of Poland**

----

*[Page 16]*

**The Seal of the Belchatower Municipal Government**

*[Page 19]*

# I.

# "The History of the Jewish People in Belchatow"

### by Dr. Ph. Fridman

**Translated from the Yiddish by Hiller and Phyllis Bell (Belchatowski) (President and Secretary of the New York Independent Belchatower Benevolent Association)**

**With editing by Martin Bornstein**

### 1. The Story of the Beginning

Belchatow is a Polish Shtetl in the vicinity of Piotrkow. It was a feudal shtetl (small town). In the 19th century it belonged to the Kaczkowski family. Like the majority of feudal cities Belchatow also had no limitations for Jews. They could settle there free and did not need to live in a separate ghetto. It seems that until the 18th century the shtetl did not have the pulling power for Jews because of economic reasons.

In general it is hard to determine when the first Jews settled in Belchatow. The old Jewish cemetery that was located in the new market (Polish

"Targowiska"), did not have any head stones left at the beginning of the 20th century. This was an open space grown with trees. The old cemetery was, it seems, not used any more since the year 1860.

From the old Shul (synagogue) we can also learn nothing about the history of the Belchatower Jews. By the end of the 19th century the old wooden Shul (synagogue) was rotten. It was completely renovated by the year 1893. The old Mikva (ritual bath), not far from the new Mikva, in the backyard of the Bes Medrish (study house), was a broken down place to the end of the 19th century.

The only place that we could find out anything about the first Jewish people from Belchatow was the official statistics that only gave us dry numbers. The first information came from the census of the Jewish people that took place in the year 1764 through the Polish government. These statistics mention that there were only seven (7) Jews in Belchatow.

The second statistic took place in the time of the Warsaw Large Principality (Furstentum), in the year 1808. At this count there were seventeen (17) Jews in Belchatow already. It seems that at that time there lived no more than two or three Jewish families in Belchatow.

This Shtetl first came alive during the time of the congress of Poland, (This is after 1815). It started intensive industrialization during the Kingdom of Poland (Konigreich), with the help and under strong stimulus from the Polish government that wanted to pick up the backward country in the economic center.

In the Piotrkower and Kalisza counties (Gubernias) bursting with activity, were a few small sleepy shtetlach (small towns) and settlements awakening to a new intensive economic development, and among these small and larger cities were Lodz, Alexandrow, Zgierz, Zdunska Wola, Ozorkow and others.

Everywhere weaving looms started to knock. Factory chimneys were smoking, middlemen, sellers and businessmen started to get busy. Large horse drawn wagons were coming in loaded with materials. New inhabitants from far away and colonies sometimes with immigrants and specialists from other countries were also coming in. The main industry that stimulated the fast and hurried development in that region was the textile industry. Coming to life everywhere were spinning, weaving, coloring and making woolen and yarn goods. Later lining, padding and silk goods were made. Some manufacturers made tallisim (prayer shawls) and so on.

Belchatow was also brought into the same fast industrial development. It's true that Belchatow did not achieve the fast development tempo as the larger industrial centers, but in comparison with the 18th century the city was also growing fast and big. The population multiplied ten times in a short time. The numbers from the beginning of the 19th century, seventeen (17) Jews, to the end of the century were three thousand (3,000) Jews, are truly not to be compared (in quantity).

## 2. The Belchatower Textile Industry

The decisive time for this development begins in the first 20 years of the19th century. The Polish government had just started to develop the textile industry. In the beginning of the year 1827 Belchatow had 35 houses and numbered 365 inhabitants. Among them were 262 Jews, a majority.

In the year 1859 the city already had 101 houses (among them 26 made of brick) and the population was 1526 people. Of this there were 1100 Jews. From this we can see that the main role in the development of the city was the Jewish element. This made up over 70% of the population. The main income in the city came from the textile industry. There were also (in the same year 1859) ten small working weaving outlets with 101 workers, with a yearly production of 36,000 rubles (Russian currency), and fourteen cotton mills with 103 workers and a 17,200 ruble yearly production.

We have still more precise statistics from the Belchatower textile industry from the year 1867. Then Belchatow numbered 15 small wool and cotton textile factories. Of the two wool factories, one was Jewish and of the thirteen cotton factories twelve (or eleven) belonged to Jews. Besides this, there were also three small factories making large shawls and knit materials and those did not belong to Jews. The production from the Jewish factories in the year 1867 amounted to about 40,000 rubles.

According to the information that we received from a friend, Zalman Pudlowski, this enabled us to put together a list of the more important Jewish manufacturers who worked in Belchatow to the end of the 19th century. They are as follows:

1. Chaim Tusk and Family

2. Peretz Freitag, one of the biggest manufacturers in Belchatow

3. Chaia Faivish (Shraga) and sons and son-in-laws

4. Avrom Mendel Warszawski

5. Yosef Warszawski

6. Nisn Warszawski

7. Ruguzsinski

8. Abraham Yacov Goldshtein

9. Schloima Ribenbach

10. Wadislawsky (from Lodz)

11. Michael Vigdor Pitowsky (later settled in Lodz)

12. Chaim Mendel Wislicki

13. Dzalowski and his whole family

14. Kasow (a Lodzer firm)

15. Moishe Eliezer Pudlowski

16. Aaron Lieb, and others.

It would be a mistake to picture the Belchatower factories like an industrial unit undertaking, where workers worked at machines in a mechanized production process. Until the beginning of the 20th century there were not, in general, any mechanized machinery or factories in Belchatow. The whole production was established by handwork. There were no spinning machines. All of Belchatow and vicinity were working on hand textile machines.

The Belchatower manufacturers were actually jobbers (farlagar) or (livarantn), as they used to call manufacturers without factories. They were, in essence, dependent on the Lodz manufacturers, from whom they took the raw material and delivered ready-made goods. The jobber very seldom had the weaving machines in his own house or factory. The organization of the production was very interesting.

Again, the jobber (farlager) gave out to his employed weavers (chalupnikas in Polish) the raw material and also a part of the necessary tools with which they had to work (the "comb" to hold threads in place for weaving and the "sheet" [blat]). The weaver took all this home and started to work on it together with his whole family, wife and children, and partly also with hired workers and apprentices. Even the younger children helped out to accomplish this primitive work, for instance handing over, cleaning, sweeping and so on. For all this hard work the weaver used to make an average of two to three rubles a week.

**The building of the Freitag Factory**

Among the weavers were faster workers who could move very fast back and forth from one side of the machine to the other and whose work earned a little more. This was a very small income. The hired workers and the apprentices with some knowledge earned still less. For all this the work was not secured.

In a bad season a lot of weavers were unemployed. However, in a good season it was also not so good. The manufacturer usually paid out the salary for the weavers on Friday afternoon when he came back from Lodz, where he delivered his goods. Many times it happened that he came back from Lodz without money, or in general, didn't come back to Belchatow at all for the Sabbath. Then the wife used to tell the weaver "Her husband didn't come back," although he was back and didn't show up and the weavers used to be left without any money for the Sabbath.

Another trouble was the voucher system. A lot of manufacturers used to pay out the hired weavers not with money, but only with vouchers to a store. The storeowner gave the worker goods on account of the vouchers such as food, household goods, also clothing and so on. It is logical in this case that the storeowner could dictate the prices and the quality as he wanted, and the worker had no choice. This same voucher system, which was spread among the whole Polish wage industry (called the "trok system" in Polish) made a lot of bad blood.

The wages were not the same in all branches of the industry. The higher ups among the workers were the "sharers". (This is those who make the "prepared yarns" (ketn) for the weaving machines) The sharers worked mostly in the homes of the manufacturers and did not take out the work to their own homes. The lowest category of paid workers was the "spinners" ("tribarins") (women who spun the yarn for the sharers). Their salaries were pennywise.

A constant pressure to make the wages yet lower came from the farmers living in the vicinity in the small villages. The farmers took home all kinds of work for the long winter nights, (mostly spinners and weavers). Since this was a side income for them they could compete with the regular workers.

In this way many thousands of people worked in Belchatow and vicinity, among them a large number of Jews. In Belchatow itself, around the year 1895, there were 925 Jewish weaving workers.

Since the wages were so low that they couldn't make ends meet, they found all kinds of half legal and illegal ways to increase their income. The most half legal practice was to "matzen". The word matzen comes it seems from the Hebrew rashi tuvut-mutrut tzmr. This means left over remnants of wool. When the manufacturer gave out the wool to the worker he weighed it and wrote down the weight. The worker had to give back the ready made material with the same weight that he received, but the weaver always had a way to save a little raw material for himself. For this purpose he put the ready material in the basement so that it would soak in moisture, and then it would weigh the same. The little saved up raw material (the matz) the worker brought to the dealers (called the matzers), who bought the stuff from them and the dealers then used to sell this same material back to the manufacturers. Similar ways started to develop in other branches of the weaving trade. For instance, the spinners took flour to stiffen the yarn, so they saved a part of the flour for themselves for their household needs.

However, all these actions did not help to improve the situation of the wage weavers. Their lot became more critical. The weavers used to get together Saturday afternoon in the bes-medrish (house of study) and they discussed what to do about their bad situation. They had ideas of having a strike, but nobody had the will to be the first.

At the beginning of the 20th century the situation worsened so badly that it came to the first open conflict. In one day the weavers decided to take back beams, (a part of the weaving machine) on what the material was made from. All the workers put down all these instruments at the manufacturers door. Around 1903 or 1904 there was a larger demonstration yet. The Gurer rabbi was very sick at that time and the Gerer Chasidim (among the manufacturers were a lot of Chasidim), congregated in shul and recited "tihillim" ("psalms" – recited when someone is gravely ill). Coming out from shul a young group of weavers confronted them and badly beat them up. They were not satisfied with only doing this, they went to the houses of the manufacturers who had not been in shul and beat them up also.

New troubles and conflicts came out when the Belchatower industry began to change from hand weaving to mechanized production. According to Zalman Pudlowski, the first mechanized factories in Belchatow came at the beginning of the 20th century. The first pioneer in this field was Peretz Freitag. His factory employed about two hundred (200) workers. The factory of Mayer Zsuchowski (together with the firm "Adler Zsuchowski" in Lodz) also had two hundred workers and they also employed about two hundred workers in Lodz. There were also other mechanized factories like Velvel Farshtar, Joseph Warszawski's son, the brothers Epstein, the family of Dzialowski, the Szmulewicz Brothers, Borach Starowinski, Yankel Klug, Herzkah Tusk and Shloima Kowal. In total there were about twelve mechanized Jewish factories and one factory belonging to a German by the name of Baran.

With the creation of mechanized factories there came new problems. First the mechanized factories needed less workers than with hand production.

Secondly, it turned out that even with many fewer working places, the Jewish workers still couldn't hold a job. The largest number of Jewish workers was employed in the factory of Zsuchowski. A certain number of Jews were also employed in the factories of Warszawski, Farshtar, Epstein and others.

The main excuse from the Jewish manufacturers was that the Jewish workers could not work on the Sabbath and the Jewish holidays and the factories will suffer from it. The Jewish factories worked on the Sabbath and some of them (for instance Freitag's factory) even on Rosh Hashanah and Yom Kippur. This called for strong protests from the religious circles in the city. Another deeper reason that was not brought to light was that the manufacturers preferred to have unenlightened people, the farmers from the villages, who would listen to the boss better than the enlightened Jewish workers, among whom revolutionary opinions started to show, and socialistic ideologies.

### 3. On the Threshold of a New Epoch.
### (In the beginning of the 20th century)

In the first few decades of the 20th century a lot changed in the Jewish environment. The time of the naïve demonstrations "like bringing back the beams" and "fights in front of the shul" were over.

At the end of the 19th and the beginning of the 20th century the town grew very much in the economic and social structure. It became more differentiated. In the year 1897 Belchatow numbered 3859 residents, among them 2987 Jews. In the year 1909 there were 3849 Jews. In the year 1917 there were 4922 Jews. The first years after the First World War a large number of Jews came in to Belchatow. In 1921 Belchatow now had 369 houses and 6249 inhabitants, among them 3788 Jews. The Jews at this time made up only 60% of the cities inhabitants. The reasons for this change were in large measure connected to the suffering from the time of the First World War. During the war the Belchatower industry and commerce suffered a lot. The worsened economic situation along with (and also for) a number of individual reasons, compelled a lot of Belchatow Jews to migrate. A number of them moved to Lodz and other Polish cities, but a lot of them emigrated further to Germany, Austria and also some to America. As it is said in the last decades of the 19th century the economic life of the Belchatower Jews was a lot more variegated. The farmers until 1864 played a small role as consumers and purchasers as long as they were enslaved to their feudal masters.

Because of the Agrarian reform, the farmers in the year 1870, were brought into the modern financial economy and in small measure became consumers and buyers. The farmers used to come into the town to make business with Jews, selling their products and buying what they needed. The business in the towns brought everything to life. On market days (Belchatow had two market days a week) the farmers used to come into town in the hundreds. A part of the Polish youth started to settle in the town, some of them as workers in the mechanical factories and some (this happened in independent Poland) as students and hired hands and so on. In 1921 Belchatow already had over 2500 Christian inhabitants in comparison to less than 1000 in the year of 1897 and 450 in the year 1857. In ratio few Poles got involved in business. A larger amount of the Christian population were involved in home work. In general, the sphere of consumers from the Jewish businessmen, storekeepers, and home workers much increased. This was because of the increase from the town itself and also because of the larger consumption from the surrounding villages. The Jewish business in the homework situation grew very much. On the other hand the Jewish population lost their absolute numerical numbers in the town and started to feel with the time (in particular in independent Poland) ever-stronger Polish competition in homework and business. In Jewish life there started to show more concrete groups and economic and social classes. The richest in the town were the manufacturers. There were also rich businessmen and property owners. There started to develop a middle class in the town. Again, store owners, market stall owners who sold foodstuffs, hardware and so on. Some of the storeowners had connections with the manufacturers and sold merchandise to their wage weavers with vouchers instead of money. A more mobile element was the peddlers. They used to put up their stands in different towns on market days. There were also Jewish workers such as tailors, shoemakers, hat makers, metal workers and so on. They had their own stands in the market and sold their own production.

The large masses of Jewish weavers and other wage workers employed in the textile industry slowly started to lose their numerical power, although it was always the strongest and largest part of the Jewish population. The activity and devotion to business and the industry necessitated (caused a need for) a lot of transportation. Until the end of the 19th century the whole transportation business was in the hands of the Jewish shippers. These people had a special place in the life of the city. They, together with the horse dealers, butchers and so on, were the strongest, and many times you could hear of their unbelievable deeds in the city.

On the eve of Yom Kippur (possibly at the end of the 19th century) there were rumors in the town (Shtetl) that the Polish farmers were preparing to make a pogrom in the city. The strong ones didn't hesitate long. They waited for the farmers to come into town and beat them up right away.

It happened many times that drunk army recruits from the surrounding villages decided to make trouble in the city, before they went into the army. In many instances these came to big confrontations between them and the strong men and the Jews prevailed.

Zalman Pudlowski told an interesting story of what happened at the beginning of the Twentieth Century. In Szczercow there lived a Jewish vagrant who was a thief and also set fires, by the name of David Pfeifer. With his deeds he enraged the Polish butchers and they killed him. The Belchatower Jewish strong men paid them back for the killing. When these Szczercow butchers once came to Belchatow to a market, to sell their goods, the Jewish strong men beat them up.

Belchatow also had bad people. They were the delinquents who stole horses, people who made all kinds of tricks and card players. They made their living on market days by fooling and tricking the farmers. Another type were the Jews who extorted money from Jewish boys by pretending that the girl the boy went around with was their girl, and therefore they wanted and got money from the frightened young men.

## 4. The Social and Cultural Life of the Jews

Until the end of the 19th century the different social classes never organized in separate social organizations or in party groups. The organized societies in Jewish life expressed itself in religious forms and institutions. The rich landlords, the respected Jews, the clergy, the manufacturers, and the rich businessmen. organized themselves around the religious places there were in the town (the different Chasidic study houses). There were in the town Gurer Chasidim, Radziner, Alexander, and others, but the most influential were the Gerers. Almost all of the manufacturers belonged to the Gerer Chasidim. The

Gerer Chasidim influenced the whole Jewish community life in the town, though the community budget was modest. The yearly budget was 270 Rubles in the time between 1846 – 1854 and 370 Rubles in later years.

The poorer Jews mostly gathered at the synagogue or Bes-Medrish, like the shoemakers, weavers and poor business people (and were called "shul [synogogue] Jews or "Bes Medrish Jews").

The young people strived for something different. They were eager for something new that would break the monotony of provincial life. One group of young people founded an association for young men. This group spent their time together and prayed together and on Saturday afternoons debated topics. However, since they did not have a concrete agenda, the whole group slowly fell apart.

Right after this there came into being another group of young men. They also prayed together and decided to make membership dues. With this money they brought reforms to the town. They built up a brick fence for the synagogue, made a wedding for a poor couple, wrote a Torah, and in honor of the Torah made a big gathering in the Shtetl. During this parade they disguised themselves as feudals and Cossacks and rode on horses. They awoke the whole town.

Another group went even further. It was called a "Maskilim" ("Enlightened Men") group. The head of this group was Joel Leib Goldsztejn and his brother, also Shier Langnas and Berel Waldman and others. Joel Leib Goldsztejn was the only romantic writer that Belchatow produced.

He debuted with a story on the topic "The Last Man". After this, in Warsaw, he issued a thick book (of 1200 pages) called "The Breakdown or Rebuilding". He then wrote a book of stories called "With the Face to the Mirror" and at the end a utopian fantasy "1960" written in a territorial way.

Another young literary talent in the same "Maskilim" group was Meyer Zussman. He was a leather worker. During the years 1910 and 1911 he wrote a number of Yiddish songs with a partly social radical content. Later on other Belchatower started to become interested in literary activities. Schmuel Chaim Kalman, a Poalei Zionist workers activist, wrote stories. Peretz Freitag was a steady correspondent for the Polish socialist newspaper in Warsaw called "Robotnik" ("The Worker"). Zalman Pudlowski was the correspondent of the

Peterburger (St. Petersburg) "Zeit" ("Times") and later on in the bundist papers like "Lebensfragen" ("Lifes Question") and "Folkszeitung" ("Peoples Newspaper"), in Warsaw. In these papers (between the two world wars) were articles about Belchatow written by Henry Ehrlisch, Chmurnar, Yankiv Pat, Barach Scheffner and others.

Some of the previously mentioned literary circle later started to create the first "Zarei-Zion" group in Belchatow. They were Chaskell Shotten , Feffer (a young man from Lodz), Weissblat (a private teacher to the Potockis) and others.

Still another group from the Bes Medrish young men, used to get together in the Bes Medrish and read about the Yiddish and Hebrew modern literature and have discussions about philosophy and literature. To this group belonged Ali Twardowski, the brothers Moishe and Shimon Szmulewicz, Aaron Pinchus Bornstein, Zalman Pudlowski, Abraham and Hanach Lieberman, Hanach Pegula and Hanach Grushka (the last four names belonged to the Radzinar Chasidim). One Saturday this group was caught by another group of Chasidim in the Bes Medrish (motzeieh Passover 1913) and a scandal broke out in the town because of these nonbelievers.

All the different groups in town had wars among themselves. All the wars in the religious circles were for mostly two reasons, regarding the rabbis and for ritual slaughtering. At the end of the 19th century the Rebbe Kanshtam passed away. He was a Gurer Chasid. It should be understood that the Gerer Chasidim wanted to have their own rabbi again. However, their enemies, the Alexander Chasidim, didn't like it. The Alexander united with the common Jews (Bes Medrish Jews). The leader of the plain Jews was Moshka Dozar. His surname came from the word Dozar, meaning commissioner. He was a member of the local committee and did good things for the town. Because of his deeds the new shul was erected, though the Gerer Chasidim campaigned against it. The arguments became more aggressive, but in the end Moshka Dozar, together with the Alexander Chasidim, prevailed and they brought down to Belchatow their own candidate for rabbi, Reb Moishe Ali Bierenbaum. The whole deal however was not plain and straight. It seems that the Gerer Chasidim could not do anything about it so they started to split the united front from the inside. For their own purpose they managed to persuade the leader of the united front, Moshka Dozar, to come to their side. Right after this they started a propaganda campaign against the rabbi. They spread rumors and innuendos. One of the heaviest arguments against him in the eyes of the Gerer Chasidim was the fact that he sympathized with the Zionist movement. In the end Rabbi Bierenbaum got fed up living in Belchatow with the atmosphere of a permanent Gerer agitation against him. It seems that he himself resigned from the position and went to Lodz. He was one of the most important leaders of the Mizrachi until he went to Palestine.

The new Rabbi was Rebbe Shmuel-Shloima Braun recommended and supported by the Gerer Chasidim. He was known in town as "Der Lukovar Rebbe". He built a large Yeshiva in Belchatow and many young men from other towns also studied there. The Yeshiva was the pride of the Belchatower Jews. Although the material situation of a lot of Belchatower middle class Jews was not a good one, they whole-heartedly helped to feed these Yeshiva students in spite of this. The Lukovar Rebbe had a big influence in Belchatow and also had a very good name himself. His strong service couldn't however, divert from Belchatow the new free winds coming from all sides.

In the years 1904-1905 when Belchatow was full of demonstrations, strikes and new discussions, the Rabbi made big speeches in Shul against the non-believers who were against the good Jews, the King, Jewishness in general and thundered against the non-believers and violators (transgressors) of Israel (Jewish People). When all this did not help and the world went its own way, the Lukovar Rabbi resigned and left Belchatow (possibly about 1905-1906).

A new fight broke out for a new Rabbi. The Gerer Chasidim (supported by the Radziner Chasidim) opposed the coalition of the common Jews with the Walbarszer and Alexander Chasidim. The coalition won the fight and Rabbi Zmach David Tornheim, the Walbarszer Rabbi's son, got the job. The Yeshiva that the Lukovar Rabbi managed was not in existence any more in Rabbi Tornheim's time. Rabbi Zmach David Tornheim held the post in Belchatow until he died, a few years before the Second World War. In the infighting in the Jewish community he was always on the side of the Mizrachi and against agudas Israel. Fights also broke out between the religious slaughtering and slaughterers in the town. The Gerer Chasidim in general had their own slaughterers and went so far as not to eat the meat slaughtered by somebody else. This was particularly at the time they were fighting (struggling) against Rabbi Zmach David Tornheim, but the controversies and arguments between the orthodox religious groups slowly ceased to be the central events in the

Jewish life of the town. In the twentieth century new ideologies came to life. New organizations and institutions came into being from branches of political parties. They organized workers unions and all these events brought out a new social life in Belchatow.

The events of 1904-1905 brought changes to Jewish life in Belchatow. This was a deep radical revolution that entirely changed the future of the social and cultural face of Jewish life in Belchatow. In 1904-1905 Belchatow was shook up by a series of strikes and demonstrations. The economic strikes were as a result of the tragic situation of the Belchatower wageworkers. There were several political strikes (the first of May strike, the January Strike after the bloody suppression of the (Gapons) demonstration in St. Petersburg the 9th of January 1905) and also a solidarity strike (at the time of the great Lodzer street fight at the end of June 1905 ). In the demonstrations of 1905 there showed up an armed Jewish militia in the streets of Belchatow.

It is really unbelievable how it was possible in Belchatow to organize such a complicated and hard working event with strikes and demonstrations with their own militia, since we know that until 1904-1905 there were not any working organizations in Belchatow. Professional unions only started to organize at that time (around 1904-1905). These professional unions were the wage weavers union, the sharers union, and the professional textile union.

The wage weavers and sharers unions did not come out with any professional or political activities. The professional textile union took in the poorest and most oppressed portions of the workers. For instance, the apprentices and young children who had to learn the trade and who worked by the wage weavers, the needle workers, the knitters and others.

The textile union was organized and led through the leaders of the Bund and was a part of the Bundist party organization. A charismatic fact that happened in the year 1905 gives us a sample of the connections that the Belchatower workers had in those days with the Jewish revolutionary parties outside of Belchatow.

When the strikes and demonstrations broke out, the frightened landlords and Gerer Chasidim looked for a power that could break the working class. They looked to the transport workers to break down this working class power as they had some influence with them. They wanted them to be the counter revolutionaries. The transport workers together with other strong people started to interfere with the workers meetings, but then a warning came from the leaders of the Lodzer Bund and this helped to quiet down the transport workers. From this we can see that the existence of the Belchatower Bundist organization started from these events of 1904-1905.

At the same time the counter-revolution in Russia succeeded and Belchatow started to feel the new iron hand of the reactionaries.

In the year 1906 the Czarist government, without any reason, sent a detachment of ten Cossacks in to Belchatow. They had nothing to do in this little sleepy town so they were always drinking and dancing and having a good time, until this quiet little town played a trick on them. In the year 1907 the horse thieves, at the suggestion of the Jewish organizations, broke into the Cossack quarters at a time when they were away drinking and partying in the town, dressed themselves up in the Cossack uniforms, took away the armor, then mounted the horses and galloped out from the town. They killed some of the horses and led the others to the forest and tied them up. The Cossacks could not stand this indignity. One of them committed suicide and the others were arrested and sent out of Belchatow. A new detachment of Cossacks then came to Belchatow, but they were already very careful and stable.

In the meantime the government found out that there were subversive elements in Belchatow, and it seems they decided with a strong hand to make an end to these activities. On January 30th, 1908, they all of a sudden arrested twenty-three young people with the claim that they were leading an illegal Bundist activity. In truth, only some of these people arrested belong to the Bundist organization. They put these people in jail in Piotrkow and later in Siedlec. They never had a trial but sent them administratively to Siberia, some of them for four years, and the rest from two to three years. By these arrests the Bund organization was destroyed. However, the police, being in such a hurry, left the entire library, the first social library in Belchatow that was created a few years before. Still, there was no one left to manage the library and little by little the books disappeared.

It did not take long until by a coincidence this group of people organized again and started to lead an even larger and greater activity. In the spring of 1913 there came into Belchatow a textile worker named Gershon Percal. Percal was from the city of Lodz. He had been arrested in Lodz in 1912 and kept in jail for eight months. After he was released the Czarist regime exiled him to live in the small town of Zdunska Wola. Percal ran away from Zdunska Wola and came to Belchatow to live. He organized an active Bund organization again. They had discussions, made speeches and once more created a small library.

They brought in progressive Jewish papers from Petersburg and Warsaw. This work was led by a committee consisting of Percal, Zalman Pudlowski (secretary), Hainach Lieberman and others. Meetings and smaller gatherings used to take place on the new road on the "Berzia" ("Gathering Place"), or at the mountains near the town. Later, they also met in the café of Shloima Midlosz. Percal himself, after a short time, left Belchatow because his place of exile was in Zdunska Wola. It seems he became concerned that the Czarist police might arrest him because he left his forced living town ("Wisedlenia"), and he disappeared from Belchatow. Later on, after a short while, he again returned to Belchatow.

## 5. Between Two World Wars

The Zionist movement started to organize in Belchatow, part of the Maskilim united with the Zairei-Zion group that came into being in 1914. In the group were Moishe Freitag, Meyer Warszawski and others. Their first legal activity was to start a library in Belchatow. Later on they started a club by the name of Moishe Ostrowski, the son of Yankel Ostrowski, who had just died. They brought the teacher Menachim to Belchatow and started Hebrew classes for adults and later on a Hebrew school. They also had activities in the drama club of the organization.

The Zionist movement changed with the times. The Mizrachi Organization had a big influence in Belchatow. This organization did not rely solely on its own membership, which was not very big, but relied mostly on rich individuals and rich landlords who belonged to the organization. Beside this the Mizrachi influenced the Jewish "Folkes-Bank" ("Peoples Bank) in Belchatow to a large extent. This gave them much power. They also tried to open a school for their own children (Yavneh school).

The Zionist Socialist organization from the political right had less influence in Belchatow. They also founded a club for young people called "Freiheit" ("Freedom") the sport club "Hapoal" and also had Hebrew lectures.

The political left called the "Poalei-Zion" was a weaker group in Belchatow. Also weak were the extreme right faction in the Zionist movement (revisionists).

Around 1921-1922 there started to develop a communist party. They were fighting strongly against the bund and also the professional textile union, and the culture society. They also tried to create their own legal organization, their own library, an I.L Peretz club and a sport club affiliated with the Agro-Yid. Some of them were convicted by the Polish courts and sent to jail. Others, in the later years, were sent to a concentration camp called "Bereze Kartuska." After the First World War a strong political power developed called "Agudas Israel." However, before the First World War and during the time of the war, there appeared a group of religious young people in Belchatow who created an organization called "Tiferes Buchurim" (Young peoples group). This was a loose group without a crystal clear program. They had long discussions about world events and political questions. After a while this group split up. Some of them went to the "Zarei-Zion" organization and the rest created the base of "Agudas Israel."

For the first time the Agudas took part in the stormy election to the "Sejm" (Parliament) in 1918. At this time the Aguda managed the largest amount of the Jewish vote on her side. The second largest vote in this election was for the Bund. After the persecution in the Czarist times, the Bund came out into the open for the first time at the time of the Austrian occupation (around the year 1914).

The Bund created not only a strong political organization and had a big influence in the professional organization, (the professional organization embraced Jewish and Polish workers); the representative of the bund also led a wide active work in the legislation of the city of Belchatow, and also in the health department. They also, in general, had a large part in the Jewish life in Belchatow. They created a library (of 1,000 books), a club, the young workers organization "Kultur" ("Culture"), the young organization "Zukunft," ("The Future") the sport club "Morgenstern" ("The Morning Star") and a childrens' school to which they brought the teacher Aharon Bergman from Lodz.

From time to time at special events they gave out a periodical from Belchatow called "Veker" ("Alarm Clock"). They also created a dramatic club and brought in from Lodz and Warsaw as guests the famous Jewish actors the

(Turkow Kaminska Vilna Troupe). In general, Belchatow was a cultured town. Almost every organization had a dramatic club, their own choir and music classes. Among the local theatre people, the previously mentioned writer, Joel Leib Goldsztejn directed and led the dramatic club and also gave music lessons.

Until 1925 Belchatow was considered a market shtetl or a settlement (in Polish: osada). It did not have the full municipal right. In 1925 Belchatow was again elevated to the rank of a city. After Belchatow regained status as a city a municipal election took place for the first time in 1925. They elected 24 councilmen, among them 13 Jews. Besides the councilmen the city also had an executive of 5 people, one mayor, one vice mayor and three commissioners. Two of the commissioners were Jews: Mayer Warszawski (a Zionist) and Shmuel Jacubowicz (representative of the self-employed). In the year 1927 at the second municipal elections only seven Jews were elected among the twenty-four councilmen, two Bundist, one Zarei-Zionist, two from the business organization and two from the self-employed. In the executive was commissioner Noach Lieberman (from Agudas Israel).

In the city council there were always strong arguments about political, national and social questions right from the first celebrated meeting of the council. The Jewish councilman reminded everybody about their Jewishness. Councilman Zalman Pudlowski, in his welcoming speech to the councilmen and government guest, spoke in Yiddish. In one of the later meetings, the Bunds councilman suggested changing Pabianicer Street to I.L. Peretz (a famous Yiddish author) Street. This suggestion was accepted after a vigorous fight.

Belchatow went through hard economic and political changes between the two world wars. The mechanized factories developed rapidly (in the year 1939 they employed more than 1000 workers) and the situation of the hand weavers became more critical. From time to time there were strikes. The hardest and longest strike in the Belchatow industry broke out in 1932. It lasted for six months. Besides economic strikes there were also political strikes. A separate impressive strike and demonstrations took place in Belchatow after the pogrom in "Przytik."

## 6. The Tragedy of Belchatow

### a) In the first years of the German occupation (until 1942)

On September 1st, 1939 the war started between Nazi Germany and Poland. On September 5th, 1939 the Germans were already in Belchatow. The German offensive was made with lightning speed and only a few Jews managed to escape. Many Jews started to leave on the road to the east in order to save themselves, but were overtaken by the motorized German units and after the cessation of the war operations of the moment, most of them returned to Belchatow. With the Germans entering this was the last tragic hour for the Belchatow Jewish community. The number of Jews in Nazi occupied Belchatow was greater than ever before. The Germans had accurate statistics of the population and the new German commissar diligently sent these numbers to his boss, the German commission of the Lask rural district., who resided in the city of Pabianice. According to this information the number of the population in Belchatow was:

| Date | Total | Jews |
|---|---|---|
| August 16, 1940 | 10,951 | 5,371 |
| July 3, 1941 | 10,955 | 4,874 |
| August 1941 | 10,324 | 4,874 |
| January 1942 | 11,064 | 5,560 |
| March 1942 | 11,070 | 5,460 |
| December 14, 1942 | 5,379 | 0 |

As we can see, the number of Jews was not stable even in comparatively quiet first period of the German occupation. In the time between July and August of 1941, 450 Jews disappeared from Belchatow. These were the unfortunate victims who were sent away to German work camps in the Posner vicinity from where they never came back.

In the last few months of 1942 the population of Belchatow again grew by 700 people. At the same time, according to an estimation from an underground leader, the Jewish population grew even more, to about 6,000 people. This was as a result of the resettlement policy of the Germans that they activated in the vicinity of Belchatow. They liquidated many smaller settlements like Grocholic, Szczercow, Widawa, Klesciw, Chabialic, Gurszkowic, Orzekow, Parzniwic, and others. They brought in part of these people to Belchatow, part to Lodz or to other cities and work camps. This way the Jewish population in Belchatow was enlarged during the three tragic years from September 1939 until August 1942.

They were constant victims of German brutalities until the tragic end of Belchatow.

When the Germans came, one third of Belchatow was burned as a result of the war activities. As soon as the soldiers came into town, they started wild activities against the Jews with the help of the local Germans. In Belchatow, like in other industrial cities in the vicinity of Lodz, in the 19th century a certain number of German specialists, mostly textile engineers, settled in the town. With time some of them became integrated but most of them stayed with the German language and with the Lutheran church. Now, all the Germans, even those that were integrated, reminded themselves of their Teutonic background.

The German authorities relied strongly on the folk Germans (Volks Deutsch) (those born in Poland). They brought them into all the Nazi organizations. They were supposed to play a large role in the Nazi plan to Germanize the occupied Polish land, especially the parts that were integrated into the German Reich.

For a short time in the beginning, Belchatow had belonged to the general government, but right after this it was incorporated in the part of west Poland, which was incorporated again into the Third Reich under the name "Wartegau" ("District Watch"). The Gauleiter (District Manager) in Vater Land

(Fatherland) was the famous tragic Jewish enemy and Jewish murderer Arthur Greiser, who resided in the city of Poznan. .

It seems that the folk Germans, who became Nazis overnight, were also big anti-Semites and tried at every step to show their great enthusiasm by being trustworthy to the Nazi idea on account of the Jews. Because of the pressure of the Nazi occupants and because of the good example of the local German leaders, the local party of the folk Germans in Belchatow was constantly growing.

The official German statistics gave the following numbers: In August 1940, 1106 Germans in Belchatow. In July 1941, 1447 and in March 1942, 1458.

The Folk Germans together with the German soldiers made plenty of trouble for the Jews in Belchatow right from the beginning. The Germans right away nominated a Folk German mayor and vice mayor, the bricklayer Wolf and Otto Frei, who previously was a worker in Epstein's factory. It seems that the Pastor, Jacob Gerhardt, had a large but not a good influence on the fate of the Jewish population. He was a fanatic Nazi and had already been arrested before the war for his pro nazi political activities. The Germans freed him from jail immediately and gave him back his post as an evangelical pastor. He also functioned for a short time as the mayor.

The new German (Folk German) city government right away gave out anti-Semitic ordinances. For instance:

Jews are not allowed to walk on the sidewalk. They have to go in the middle of the road where the horses and wagons go.

Jews have to report for forced labor to clean up all kinds of debris and also the trenches.

Later on they came out with an ordinance that Jews have to wear the yellow star and are not allowed to walk in the streets in the evenings and so on.

At the same time they started to make holdups and murder Jews. The German soldiers and SS men were walking around in Jewish homes under the pretext of looking for armaments. They took away jewelry, gold, money and beat up the people in a terrible way. The folk Germans helped them out a lot in this respect as well. Every member of the local party was allotted a few

Jewish homes. German women and children also helped to search these Jewish homes. They took out everything they could, loaded it up on wagons and took it to their homes or officially to the warehouse, which they made from the confiscated house of Mendel Feld, (""Schutzen-haus" [shooting-range/guard house] in Polish "Strzelco") ") where the German gendarmes made their headquarters. They also brought Jews to this same house to beat them up and get out every penny they could from them.

The forced labor was also only a pretext to torment Jews. Let me give you one example: according to a report from an eyewitness, a group of Jews went out with brooms to the Market Square to clean up the horse manure there. They were under the command of the Folk German "Wiler." Before the war he worked as a weaving loom fixer in a Jewish factory. He told them to collect the garbage with their hands and put it in their own pockets and caps and do it at a faster and faster tempo. In his hand he had a little leather whip with a woven piece of iron through it and hit them without any reason. After this he told them to make a big circle around the water well and told them to sing Jewish prayers, zmires and songs. Then he finished with a speech saying that it is the Jews fault that the war broke out and in all the world's troubles the fault is only the Jews.

At such forced labor places Jews were beaten up terribly. The first victim of these beatings was Mayer Zieslawsky.

In order to belittle the Jews even more in the eyes of the non-Jewish population, the Germans made all kinds of mock masquerades with the Jews, especially at the time of the Jewish holidays. They dressed them in prayer shawls, told them to climb on ladders and were carried around the city and then threw the ladder together with the Jews on it, off a bridge, till they had beaten / bruised their head and bones. They also painted their faces and told them to dance in the streets and photographed them in these situations. The Germans behaved especially wild on the Jewish holiday of Yom Kippur in 1939. They told the Jewish people to go out into the streets and throw out all their Jewish religious and other books. They again made mock parades in the center (Market Square) of the city and at the end told them to burn the books and dance around this bonfire upon spread out Torah scrolls. These wild events only stopped when the new German administration stabilized in Belchatow. To the post of commissar of Belchatow they selected the German named "Talmer". Belchatow belonged to the vicinity of Lask and the commissar resided in Pabianice.

New legal events of robberies and economic pressure started up. They took away the best houses and apartments from the Jews. From other living places the Germans took out the best furniture and put German commissars into Jewish businesses. Jewish manufacturing materials and machines were confiscated and sent out of Belchatow. According to figures from a Polish underground report, the losses that the Jews sustained at that time came to more than a half million Zlotys (Polish currency).

The Jewish population all at once fell into an abyss of economic poverty and became very depressed. The hunger was everywhere in Jewish homes (streets). The Jewish committee (Judenrat) made a soup kitchen in the Bes Medrish, where they served about one thousand meals a day. Frau (Mrs.) Rottenberg led the kitchen with a lot of devotion, but in 1940 the Folk Germans destroyed the Bes Medrish.

As a result of having its way with hunger, need, and lack of housing the disease typhus came (a typhus epidemic broke out). In Belchatow there were very few Jewish doctors as some of these doctors managed to run away before the Germans came in. Of the remaining doctors, Dr. Baran was right away liquidated (killed) by the Germans. The second Jewish doctor in the city, Dr. Basiar, fought the epidemic with the help of a "Feldsher" someone with medical training (an old time barber surgeon) named Abe Warszawski, who immediately became a victim of this epidemic.

It seems that the epidemic was stronger than the Jewish medical capabilities of the town. The Lodzer Jewish committee (Judenrat) also sent in a Jewish doctor to fight the Typhus (outbreak). The community at that time still had a small Jewish hospital at her disposition. Dr Basiar remained still at his medical post until the liquidation of the Belchatower Ghetto, when he, together with a truck full of Jewish children, was sent to be (annihilated) killed.

It seems the epidemic possibly returned in 1942, because in March 1942 the local German commissar demanded that the Jewish doctor, Dr. Haber from Turig (Turik), be sent to Belchatow.

A hard event for the Jewish population in Belchatow was the transport for forced labor to "Poizner" (Poznan) and vicinity. In 1940 they first took Poles for forced labor and in 1941 they registered all Jews in Belchatow from the age of 16 years to 50 years, for forced labor. Since not everyone registered and not all of those that were registered came to be taken for forced labor, they made searches to find these people. Some categories of the committee (Judenrat) and specialists in the important war industry were exempted from the forced labor. Beside this, if you had money, you could free yourself by paying from 50 to 200 Reich marks (German currency of the Third Reich) of buy-out money. In the end there was a transport of about 450 young people, mostly workers and poor people, who were sent out to the Poznan camps to work. Right away tragic reports started to come in from the camps. Hunger, cold and hard work destroyed the workers. Almost no one came back from these camps. (There is available an exhaustive work about the Jewish working camps in Vater Land (Fatherland), written by the master of arts (Yishaiha) Isaiah Trunk.) (The name is called "Pages for History", volume 1, number 1, pages 114-169, and number 2, pages 14-45) When it came to a second registration in Belchatow, for the forced labor camps, no one went to register anymore. The Germans conducted a search all over the city that lasted for two days. They caught a number of people (about 200 people according to one source) and sent them out to the camps.

A separate ghetto did not exist in Belchatow. The Germans only decided where the Jews had to live, it was carried out in principal (they made a law) that Jews and Aryans, especially Germans, are not allowed to live in the same apartment houses. The fact that a ghetto did not exist in Belchatow made it a lot easier for the economic situation. A lot of Jews started to make illegal business (in manufactured goods and money) and to smuggle. Smuggling of manufactured goods and money was widespread in general in the occupied countries by Jews and non-Jews as it was a form of economic struggle against the occupation and also sabotage of their robber politics.

In Belchatow the illegal business was concentrated in the bazaar, and the illegal materials were delivered by the Germans and Folk Germans (so called patriots) or through the peasants (farmers). Besides the local illegal business there was also a widespread black market from the Vaterland (Fatherland) through Belchatow. Over the "green border" they took all kinds of material, which were found in the general government, manufactured goods, jewelry, money and medicines to Piotrkow. The main traffickers stood out especially in this black market. There was Winter, Flakowicz, Lieberman and others. These black marketers worked together with the German middlemen. They paid off the German officials and gendarmes (soldiers), drank together with them and developed their own dark underworld morals. From this mutual business with the Germans, it was not too far from collaboration with them in other fields.

The already mentioned Winter, they called the "king of Belchatow". The anti-Semitic Poles used to say that in Belchatow there are two governments, one German and one Jewish. A similar role was also played by another so-called Jewish "Macher" doer (arranger of slightly illegal transactions "mover and shaker") Peretz Altman, who had been a leather stitcher (Shtepper – makes leather shoe tops, pocketbooks, and other items) and in the leather business. A characteristic type of collaborator besides the already mentioned Winter, was the one time mentioned Szmuel Jakubowicz. He was also a so called "Macher" doer / arranger, even before the war, under the Austrian occupation of 1914-1918 in the first world war, when he lived in friendly conditions with the Austrian occupation and exploited it for his own personal needs.

Later on he opened a barbershop in Belchatow and created a union of (artisans) self-employed businessmen. With the support of this union he managed to be elected to the city government in 1925. Due to various off-colour activities, that he carried out (illegal business activities), he was arrested, and after this went to live in the city of Lodz.

In the year of 1939 he came back to Belchatow and was again elected to the city government as a representative of the artisans (self-employed union). For a man of this type the German occupation was the right time again to play a role in Jewish life. He started (bought up) all kinds of connections and acquaintances with the Germans and tried with their help to put his hand on the Jewish social life. He became the "Gray Excellency" (an untrustworthy man), who stood behind the scenes of various secret crisis of Jewish life in the Jewish community of Belchatow.

The speculators in the war, smugglers, the "Machers" doers / arrangers, and the black marketers were only a small part of the Jewish population. The main Jewish people, the workers, the self-employed and the former business people and shopkeepers found themselves in a worse situation. The self-employed businesses that were almost all in Jewish hands, were registered and controlled strongly by the city hall. Jewish self-employed were not allowed to accept direct orders from customers but only through the middlemen of the magistrate. The magistrate set the prices and the customer had to pay in the money to the magistrate, of which 50% went to the Jewish businessman and the balance was shared between the magistrate and the Jewish committee (Judenrat). They often made searches of the workers and artisans and if they found a piece of work not registered by the magistrate they confiscated the goods and heavily fined the worker (tradesman) and the one who ordered.

The Jewish workers worked in the commissar led factories for a very small wage. They worked almost for nothing. This is because they wanted to avoid a greater disaster of being sent out (transported) to forced labor camps or to be "deported".

In still a worse situation were office workers, religious people and all kinds of free professionals. For them there was no way to get work unless by physical labor, as there wasn't any qualified work. They sold everything they owned and possessed. Some of them looked for work in the professional institutions, which were the only places available to the (intellectual) Jews, the Jewish committee (Judenrat), the Jewish police and the Jewish work organizations and so on. This was a slippery road to take, especially for people of weak character. It is possible that a lot of them did not figure (judge and calculate) out the moral conflict and ethical decline this could bring them (resolve) to. Very few of these people were left (in-tact) uncorrupted in this rotten atmosphere of corruption and violence. They thought they had bought their secure existence for the price of betrayal. Still less had the strength and courage to get out of this spellbound circle. Because of these factors, the abyss between the plain Jewish people and the intelligent ones grew deeper than it would be.

There were a few free professions where the Jews could stay longer, because they could not be replaced by others. For instance, the Jewish medical personnel. In the beginning there were only a few individuals involved, and this was also temporary. Characteristically this was the case of the Jewish dentists in Belchatow. In the Polish cities this profession was almost monopolized in Jewish hands. In Belchatow as well almost all the dentists were Jews. They were Berta Regirar, Channa or Anna Bugdanska, M. Jakubowicz, Janina Obolewska and the tooth technician Shlomo Laskowski, also one Polish woman Olszewska. Right from the beginning there was an extensive correspondence between the German institutions on how to limit or prohibit the Jewish dentists from doing their work, although they did not have any non-Jews "aryans" to replace them. In June of 1941 the high German authorities told the Belchatower commissar Talmer to "Sicherstellen" (This means to confiscate) (put in safe keeping) the dentists' cabinets of the Jews for the future German dentists, who will come into practice after the war in Belchatow. Little by little they took away all the working instruments from the Jewish Dentists and forbid them from working any more. There was only one Jewish dentist left, Anna Bugdanska. Even this the Germans didn't leave in peace. In April of 1942 a German official report writer lamented that Bugdanska had a large clientele,-- even customs officials, gendarmes (German soldiers), and (German) Reich civilians were coming to her because she was good and cheap. This difficult problem eventually solved itself. After the atrocities that happened in March and the summer of 1942 (see below), a big calamity befell the Jewish people in Belchatow. Everyone tried to save themselves. They tried to escape the extermination action that hovered over the heads of the Jews in Belchatow. In Belchatow they thought that the action would only take out (encompass) the Jews in the Fatherland (Vaterland) and whoever would go out (escape) to the general government would be saved. The Jews started to illegally cross ("smuggle") the border to the general government. Anna Bugdanska and her family also tried to save themselves by taking the same road, but they were caught in the middle of June 1942 by the Gestapo, when crossing the border ("blackening the border"). Their fate was doomed. The whole family, among them her husband the lawyer Bugdanski and her brother Shlomo Laskowski were taken away to the Radogoszczer jail near Lodz, and from there to an extermination camp.

In order to avoid the German forced labor and the terrible transports to the work camps the Belchatow Jews created a needle factory that in the beginning worked for the German military orders. Sometimes a few hundred workers were employed in the sewing shop. It should be understood that all these people were not professional tailors. A lot of unemployed among the Jewish intelligence and rich young people from Jewish homes tried through influential people to get jobs as workers in the shop and in this way avoid the forced labor camps and transports.

After a certain amount of time the orders from the Germans stopped coming in and the number of workers was severely reduced. At the beginning of 1942 the number of workers in the shop was only 200, they made only cheap civilian clothes (men's suits). The workers, of course, never received real wages for their work. Of the money that came in from the goods that were delivered, the workers received very little money (advance), but even that came to an end. Their only "reward" was the so to say protection from the German round ups and transports. The leaders of this factory were: Shloima Szmulewicz, Sucher Przybylski, and a certain Pelcman who was there, during the time of the war, in Belchatow.

Besides this there also existed a shoe factory. This was not as large as the needle factory. In this factory worked more specialized men than in the needle factory, mostly qualified leather stitchers and shoemakers. More than 100 Jews worked here. The leader of this shoe shop was Peretz Altman.

## b) Jewish Committee (Judenrat)

In the desperate struggle of life and death with the barbaric occupant, the Jewish population could not expect any help or support from the only Jewish institution that could exist under the German terror, the Judenrat. In order for the Germans to manipulate and destroy the Jews they created the "Judenrat". Concerning the role of the Judenrat, their function, during the dark Nazi time period, as the Germans envisioned it and carried out their plan, to use out the said, so to say autonomous Jewish institution, almost to fool and exterminate the Jewish people. Concerning all of this, this is not the place to write at length about it. This is a problem that needs to be widely historically and sociologically investigated. This small amount of information that we have regarding the Belchatow (Judenrat) committee will also help contribute in general, in a wider way, to find out the problems of other Jewish committees in other parts of the Nazi occupied lands.

Regarding the Belchatower committee we have information from two sources. First from Jewish witnesses who survived and second the German and Polish sources. The Jewish sources of information allow us to penetrate deeper into the lives of the Belchatower Jews. The Polish and in particular the German sources of information only gave the formal circumstances of the development of the Jewish committee (Judenrat).

Right after the Germans came into Belchatow there came into being a social committee that wanted to be in the leadership of Jewish life and see to the security of the population through intervention with the authorities. They had a very naïve belief about the German Nazi government methods and believed in the effect of parliamentary methods and democratic peoples representation with regard to the occupiers. Right after the first German activities they lost all their illusions. Besides this, a few Machers (doers / arrangers of slightly illegal activities) penetrated this social committee like Shmuel Jakubowicz and others. Seeing their methods, the other responsible Jewish activists decided to get out right away and give up on this committee.

In the meantime the German government organizations began to be organized in the town, they were instructed to create a (Judenrat) Jewish committee. The Judenrat (was established) whose members were nominated by the German police and gendarme authorities in accordance with communication with the German mayor. This committee did not always have the same number of members on it. The smallest number was three and the largest were twelve Judenretler (Judenrat members). Originally there were twelve people on the Judenrat. In March of 1940 this number was drastically reduced through the gendarmerie to three persons. Upon the intervention of the mayor the number was raised to five. On October 18th, 1940 all the members of the committee were dismissed and in their place they put in five new people. A few days later on October 23rd, 1940 the new president was arrested and in his place another new person was put in. The new committee was in power for almost a whole year. On August 2nd, 1941 they put in a new leader (Judeneltster – Elder of the Jews). This one was like a dictator with only two other people to advise him and six "resortleiters". This committee didn't have much longevity. On September 24th, 1941, the "resortleiters" were changed. Only the president and the two other members were left in their place. That's how things happened. As you can see from these dry examples, heated fights were occurring around the G-d like thrones of (Judenretler) members of the Jewish committee. All kinds of Machers (movers and shakers) and cliques tried to get into the Judenrat. By this they looked for security from the German persecution, they searched for power, money, and "prestige" ("honor").

No eminent and social-minded people were involved in this clique competition. In the beginning a few responsible leaders did try to have an influence at least on certain aspects of the Jewish committee (for instance (social security and social help)) but seeing the real face of the activities of the (Judenrat) committee they right away pulled back. The fights among the cliques were very hot and reckless (ruthless)(rucksichtslos). In a lot of cases they used the help of the corrupt German government authorities and brought them into these quarrels. In one case, the mayor, also pursuant to information given to him by the Jewish machers (movers and shakers), who squealed on the president of the Judenrat committee saying he was in contact with a band of Jewish smugglers, and the Elder of the Jews was arrested.

Who were these Judenrat leaders and what do the surviving Jews know to tell about them?

We don't know much about the exact composition of the first social committee. Besides this, as we remind you, it did not have much longevity.

The first individual nominated by the Germans to the Judenrat was Michal Jakubowicz. He was a former commissioner. After him a young lawyer named Bugdanski became president of the Judenrat. (This was the husband of the dentist Anna Bugdanska) He tried to bring in to the Judenrat Jews with a social background. On this commission of the social security were Haskell Birenzweig, Mendel Lipman, Meilech Galster and so on. One Yankel Flakowicz refused to become a member of this commission. Birenzweig also pulled out right away under the pretext that he had heart trouble. Identically it right away became apparent that the Judenrat was going down a slippery road. Shmuel Jakubowicz had a big influence in the Judenrat and from this time on was in all later Judenrats. This new Judenrat made new ordinances that shook up the Jewish Population. They started to lash people as punishment for not executing the orders of the Judenrat. Strong protests came into the Judenrat through courageous Jewish representatives and the shameful punishments by whipping were officially abolished. In fact however, the Jewish militia in a quiet way continued to beat up and murder Jews who committed the crime of not obeying the Judenrat.

At the head of the third Judenrat was the bank employee and Mizrachi leader Yankel Ehrlich. He was "mild to the Jews" according to the depiction of a survivor in Belchatow. In March 1942, he together with nine other Jews, were hung by the Germans in Belchatow. At this time he was no longer the Judenrat president His successor was Shloima Hersh Topolowicz. Perhaps lashing about on a report (denunciation) against him the Germans carried out a search of his home and immediately shot him.

The last Judenrat president (Elder of the Jews) was Yakov Schier Szmulewicz, nobody spoke evil (badly) against him. This is the only scarce information and characteristics we have regarding the Judenrat members. We know still less about the activities of the Judenrat. The so-called wide autonomy that the Germans gave to the Judenrat was only an unashamed fiction and a cover for the criminal extermination plans. In the frame work of this autonomous fiction the Judenrat had unlimited power (rule) over the Jewish population.

For this purpose it had built up a large bureaucracy. The Judenrat had about fifty employed members in Belchatow besides the Jewish militia. Some of them were paid (between fifty and one hundred twenty marks a month). Others worked for nothing, just to enjoy the feeling of security, of course, this proved to be completely worthless right away. We don't know about the budget of the Judenrat. We have only scant information of their expenses. Until 1940 the Judenrat gave out about one thousand free meals daily. The expenses for social help at the beginning of 1942 came to two thousand marks a month. The same amount was spent monthly for administrative expenses. The largest expense of each Judenrat was the colossal sums of money used to bribe the German authorities in order to avoid all kinds of (cursed) ordinances. These sums, of course, were not registered.

The income from the Judenrat came from all kinds of sources, direct and indirect taxes, buyout money that came in to the work division, repayments from the artesans, and from all sorts of economic undertakings, that the Judenrat carried out. The Judenrat had the whole distribution of foodstuffs and coal and wood for the Jewish people in their hands, it (also) carried out various workshops. They also collected contributions for the German government that were levied on the Jews, special repayments and larger taxes.

### c.) The Destruction (Extermination)

The most tragic year in the history of the Belchatower Jews was 1942. It began with the official decision of the tragic famous "gauleiter das vaterlands," (District Leader of the Fatherlands) Artur (Arthur) Greiser, dated January 2nd 1942. In this official document he informed everyone under his administration that it has been decided that "The Un-Jewing of the Wartegaus (Administrative

Regions)" that means that the land was to be free of Jews. In the German Nazi language this meant expulsion and destroying them. It should be understood that the Nazis kept this (decision) quiet and a secret from the local people especially the Jews. However, this information regarding the terrible things that were going to happen to the Jews, little by little did spread among the Jewish population. Among the Jews a tragic panic grew from day to day. The first sign of the Nazi politic against the Jews was in the Vaterland (Fatherland). They made "execution spectacles" that were organized by the Germans in the months of February, March and April of 1942. In many cities the Nazis selected a Jewish group of ten people (a minyan) and hanged them publicly with set ceremonies. This repeated itself in every city. The gruesome public gallows were in the following cities of the Fatherland:

| Place | Date | Jews |
| --- | --- | --- |
| Wloin | February 1942 | 10 |
| Bresin | February 28, 1942 | 10 |
| Zdunska Wola | March 3, 1942 (Purim) | 10 |
| Lecycz (Lentshutz) | March 10, 1942 | 10 |
| Podembia | March 10, 1942 | 10 |
| Belchatow | March 10, 1942 | 10 |
| Piontek | April 10, 1942 | 2 |
| Ozorkow | April 10, 1942 | 8 |
| Naj-Czecholic (Neu-Tzecholitz) | April 17, 1942 | 10 |

The purpose of this it seems was to terrorize the Jewish population and break its moral power of resistance. It was also to prove to the Germans and Poles the feeling that the Jews are unprotected and guilty of all crimes and therefore deserved this punishment at the hands of the Germans. With it they also used the opportunity to squeeze out money from the Jews. How this devilish scheme of psychological and physical terror, also blackmail (szantaz) and killings worked we can see clearly by their methods in the Belchatow "Murder Spectacle".

At the beginning of March the Germans arrested 15 to 17 Jews from different social spheres in Belchatow and started to build gallows in the main market square. A fear befell the Jewish people. With the intervention of the German mayor Talmer, they succeeded in asking him to agree to a big money contribution instead, in order to buy out the hostages. A special contribution commission started to collect money, jewelry, gold, and silver from the Jews. At the contribution place Jews were standing in line in order to pay this money and jewelry to redeem the captives. The Belchatower Jewish population (made an effort beyond their strength) worked hard to make this money available (to save these Jews), but when this money and the boxes of gold and jewelry were brought to the Germans they declared in a cynical way that this was not enough to buy out all the arrested Jews and ten of them will be hanged. All the Polish and German population from Belchatow and vicinity were invited to this execution. Jews had to appear dressed nicely and were not allowed to cry or shriek. The Germans first took the Jewish hostages out from the jail, took them to the Shul and told them to pray "vidui" (confessional) and after this they took them to the gallows.

The Judenrat leader Topolowicz had to read a long accusation papers, against the 10 "criminals", written in the known Nazi style, (before they were hanged). A Jewish militiaman named Goldberg was forced, under threat of death, to carry out the execution by hanging.

Those condemned to death were as follows: Yankel Ehrlich, former bank employee and member of the Judenrat, Mendel Feld, a manufacturer, Chaim Shapiro, a business man, Moishe Wolfowicz, a butcher, Leibl Pelcman, a butcher (yidl), Moishe Lazerowicz, also a butcher, Moishe Aaron Taub, a fisherman, Yerachmiel Baum, a weaver, Yitzchok Eliahu Greenbaum, a business man and Leibish Michal Landau, a weaver.

The condemned kept themselves very quiet. Some of them at the last minute managed to say something. To comfort their families and the Jews gathered there one of them said "soon will come the defeat of Hitler and the right trial for the Nazi hangmen and called on them to take revenge."

Since the executions in March, tragic events took place at a breath-taking tempo. In the month of May or June 1942 the barbaric selection of the Jewish population came in the building of the Talmud Torah. They told all the Jews to march naked before the Nazi commission, and they were divided into three categories. Every category was marked with a different stamp on their papers. Later on this selection did not have any great practical meaning, but in the meantime the fear was great among the Jewish people.

At the same time in different cities there started the expulsions. Over 10,000 people from different towns and communities were driven into the Lodz Ghetto in the month of July. Among them was also a group of Belchatower. Some of them were taken to work on the land at Mariszin (near Lodz), which was governed by the Judenrat of Lodz. Another group the Germans sent to (forced) labor and later killed.

In the neighboring towns there were constantly many expulsions, deportations, and bloody liquidations. The bitter fate came upon Belchatow on August 11th, 1942. The Germans collected the Jewish people in the (marketplace) main square and carried out selections. A group of about one thousand young and strong people from the ages of 16 to 45 was taken away to Lodz. The remaining people were chased into the Shul (synagogue) and a Catholic church, kept there under inhumane conditions and then sent to the liquidation camp at Chelmno (Ingerman-Kulmhof) near Lodz to be gassed. The Chelmno killing factory is well known through a lot of written literature and it is not necessary to repeat it here.

In the meantime, mayor Talmer started to collect all that remained from the Jews' possessions (fortune). He bought up from the Nazi ghetto authorities in Litzmannstadt (Lodz) all the furniture and everything else from the houses of the killed Jewish people of Belchatow. (This was the official German committee for Jewish possessions in Lodz and the surrounding towns with Hans Bibow at its head). He then resold it for dirt cheap prices to the Germans and Folk Germans who lived there.

The Belchatower Jews who came into the Lodzer ghetto tried to create a committee to help other Belchatowers. A Belchatow help committee was created especially through the representatives of the workers organizations.

Some Belchatower representatives also went into the Zionist committees to help. Other Belchatowers were active in the Bundist organization. Some Belchatower with leftist leanings went into the Agudah young peoples organization in the Lodz Ghetto. The Belchatower in Lodz went through the same tragic fate as the rest of the Lodzer Jews.

In August of 1944 they were sent out to Auschwitz and other German concentration camps, where the majority of them perished. Only a small number of Belchatower Jews had the opportunity and luck to stand up and face the enemy with arms in their hands.

We know all kinds of particulars, about a small group of Belchatower who turned up in Bialystok at the beginning of the Polish – German war and lived there or in the vicinity in 1941 when the Germans came in. These Belchatow Jewish youth are: Moishe, Hinda and Chaim Kon (Kohn) and their brother-in-law Leib Pudlowski. They already understood what a German transport meant. They jumped down from a German transport train taking them to a concentration camp and left around October of 1942 to join a partisan group called "forward". There they fought heroically against the Nazis. Chaim Kon (Kohn) fell in the fight of August 18th, 1943, in a village near Bialystok. Moishe and Hinda Kon (Kohn) are now living in Poland. Leib Pudlowski went to Israel. The 3 men Chaim Kon (Kohn) (already after his death), Moishe Kon (Kohn), and Leib Pudlowski were decorated by the Polish government with the Heros' Cross "Krzyz Walecznosc" (medal).

Besides this we don't have any sure information about a fight that took place in Belchatow itself. At the time of a German search there came about a shooting between a group of Jewish young men and the German gendarmes. One of the young men, Moishe Lev, was wounded and fell into German hands. Through a large bribe they managed to get him out of jail and after this he went to the forest, where it seems he joined up with a group of partisans. Later he was again caught by the Germans, they sent him to Oswiecim (Auschwitz) where he perished.

We also know about a Belchatower tailor by the name of Josef Reich. He was also in a partisan group in the "Stolpczer" vicinity. He now lives in Australia.

The number of Belchatower survivors is hard to determine. In the year 1939 about one hundred Belchatower Jews saved themselves from the

German hands by going to Russia. Some of them died in the wartime over there. The rest came back later to Poland. The number of Jews who immediately appeared back in Belchatow in 1945 and 1946 after the war was very small, about twenty families. Slowly others started to come back -- from Russia, those saved from the German concentration camps, from the bunkers and from hideouts, from the forests, and from the partisans, and from those that survived on false "Aryan papers". They did not stay in Poland for long. They migrated further to Germany and D.P. camps and from there waited for an opportunity to migrate to Israel or America. The number of Belchatower Jews in the German D.P. camps in 1946 and 1947 was estimated to be about 250 people. By now, most of them have already left Germany. In total the number of Belchatower survivors is estimated to be about 300 to 350 people. This means less than 1% of the previous flourishing Jewish community in Belchatow.

*[Page 61]*

# II.

# Belchatow in struggle, work and art

*[Pages 63-80]*

## The Beginning and the End

### By Yisroel Pitowski

**Translated from the Yiddish by Dr. Khane-Feygl (Anita) Turtletaub**

[with footnotes at end of chapter]

**Edited by Gloria Berkenstat Freund**

[with comments in brackets]

**(Translation donated by Sharon and Samuel Shattan and Shmuel Shottan)**

On the outside, Belchatow was not much different than the neighboring towns, like Szczercow, Kamiensk, and so on. It was somewhat larger in size. It had two or three thousand more inhabitants than the above mentioned towns. However, in the area of culture and society, the lives of both the individuals and of people in general were on a higher level than that of people in the surrounding towns. The people from Belchatow did not look as if they came from the provinces. They did not have the provincial small-mindedness nor the penny-pinching, shopkeeper's ideas. A person from Belchatow always had a sense of the problems of the world, both in the political and cultural and communal arenas.

Even before the end of the previous century [the 19th century], Jewish communal life began, mainly among the young people. First small brochures appeared about class problems, about [political] parties and ideological questions. This was the interesting time of my life during the years 1897-1914. These were years of economic and spiritual ascension. Serious literary works by Yiddish and Hebrew writers were brought into Belchatow, as well as translations of world literature. Agitators for unions began to appear, Bundists (they were called "Akhdusnikes" [unionizers][1]), Poalei-Zionists [Workers for Zionism], and general Zionist speakers.

**Yisroel Pitowski**

Before my eyes I see the first Zionist messenger[2], or preacher (that is what they were called at that time) who came to our town. A tall, thin Jew, with the appearance of an ascetic, he had a long beard, sidecurls; he spoke with genuine chasidish fervor. He told ardent tales of morality; crackled with insights into the Torah, the prophets, and the Talmud. He spoke about Dr. Herzl as if he had been sent from G-d, although he was [of] German [descent] and wore a short jacket and fedora. The synagogue was full of Jewish artisans, shopkeepers, and chasidim. He kept them all enthralled. The next day, Jews began to organize meetings, to start Zionist groups. The more affluent Jews in every small synagogue did the same in their way. However, this did not go on for very long.

The rabbis took a very negative position regarding Zionism and that cooled off the chasidim's [fervor]. There remained only a small number of affluent Jews who were interested and later the more religious among them formed the Mizrachi [an Orthodox Zionist movement], which carried on satisfactory activity.

The "Bund" [the Jewish Labor Organization of Poland] was the most active organization among the young people at that time. Of course, all of these activities were illegal. The leaders of the Belchatower "Bund" at that time (the ones that I can still remember) were: Leybush's son, Yitzhakl Ire, his friend Pitze Dritshe (that was his nickname), Fishl Meyer Weis (who later immigrated to America), Leybush Mikhl Landau. Later – Avraham Szmulewicz, Plawner's son, Hershl, one of Jakubowicz's grandchildren. This [latter] was a young man, who was very learned in world literature. [He was] a follower of Nietzsche and enthusiastic about his Zarathustran philosophy. [He was] knowledgeable about Tolstoy and Dostoyevsky and an ardent follower of Karl Marx.

There were a lot of religious young men among the Bundists, children of Chasidic parents. I am reminded of the figure of a young religious boy, whom I used to meet often on the berze[3], (a special meeting place in front of the Catholic church or along the new road). He strolled around holding the hand of a boy 14-15 years old, while teaching him Marxist theories. It was a remarkable picture: the young tall man bent over the boy, swaying back and forth as he walked, pulling at his peyos [side curls] – and with a Gemara melody[4] explaining to the boy that there did not need to be rich people and poor people, that everyone must work equally and live the same...

Much earlier than in other – even larger – cities, Belchatow began to experience the fervor and the agitation of illegal gatherings, terrible proclamations, calls for economic strikes, and so on.

There was a reason for the early development: several years earlier there had been a textile factory in Belchatow. [It was] only hand-weaving until the end of the 90s, but later – also machine weaving. To a certain extent, the fact that Belchatow was also a summer vacation spot for the surrounding cities was also important.

According to historical Polish sources, during the Napoleonic Wars there were a total of three hundred people living in Belchatow. There were no weaving factories at all at that time, only tailors, shoemakers, and most important – potters, who stamped the city coat of arms into their clay pots: the Garden of Eden with a tree with a snake wrapped around it, and near the tree – Adam and Eve. Perhaps it was this Garden of Eden stamp that drew the young people from the surrounding towns, but it is a fact that during the summer young people from Lodz and other large cities used to come to us and [they] brought urbanity to Belchatow.

As mentioned, until the Napoleonic era, there were no weaving factories in Belchatow. But, immediately thereafter, Germans began to settle here, and they started the cottage weaving. They produced cotton cloth and later woolen material as well, which was at that time called tukh. They spun the wool themselves, carded it themselves, and finished it themselves; with only the means that they had at home. The Polish weavers learned their trade from the Germans.

In the seventies of the previous century [18th century] (and perhaps even earlier), there was a mechanical wool spinner. Horses were used as a source of power, with a "carrot," which the peasant farmers still use to this day [to drive] their threshing machines. This [early] weaving plant was in the building in which my father-in-law, Peretz Freitag, later built the first mechanized weaving plant. In the nearby areas there was a dyeing plant. For as long as I can remember, there has not been a trace of any of this.

In 1888 or 1889, when I came to Belchatow from the village of Parzniewice (where my parents lived) in order to study with the Gemara teacher, Reb Notele, and later with Reb Yeshaye Eksztajn, that building had been turned into a residence, and only the older Jews saw signs in the neighboring places of there having ever been a dyeing plant and an repair center.

I do not know when Jews began to take part in the weaving industry in Belchatow. Polish history is also silent about this. Perhaps it was noted in the pinkas[5] of the Jewish community in Belchatow. The first weaver I knew in my early childhood years was my grandfather, Moyshe Fatersman. About him it used to be said that he had come to Belchatow as a young man from some German town or other close to the Polish border and got married here. He was, it is said, a specialist in finishing, dyeing, and repairing woolen fabric. At that time this was called bostn. (In Belchatow, my grandfather was indeed called Moyshe Boster.)

It would be good here to write a few words about my grandfather Moyshe Fatersman, of blessed memory. I remember him from the time that I was five or six years old. He was an old man of 70 even then: a tall man with a nice, white beard. He wore "German" clothes: a short, cut-off jacket, no black cap on his head, as was worn at that time, but a hat in the German fashion. When I was a grown up young man, older Jews used to tell me, both surprised and upset, that he possessed a full closet of religious texts and many non-Yiddish books (probably German). He was a heretic, did not much believe in certain customs, like kapores-shlogn[6], and so on. He was a wise man and good with people.

I can only give actual information about the general development of the textile industry in our town and with the Jews in particular from the year 1889. That was when I came to town from my village in order to study with teachers and in school. It is worthwhile to mention that there was already a Jewish school and a Jewish teacher in Belchatow at that time. I do not remember his last name, but his first name was Abner. I remember him well. [He was] a very pleasant man, handsome, with a fine beard, wore a short jacket and a fedora. He was very friendly to his students. He was much respected in town.

At that time there were already many Jewish weavers in Belchatow and several Jewish manufacturers and contractors: Chaim Tusk, Faywish Shrage, Yakov Huberman, Feiwel Leyb (Feiwel Amberduks), and so on. At that time, light twill-like fabric was produced, woolen flannel, satin, wool shawls and scarves. From 80 to 90 percent of these articles were produced by Jewish weavers. Other less expensive items such as: molton [an opaque cotton fabric], all kinds of cotton fabrics, pinafores, bed linens, and the like were produced in the surrounding villages.

Machine work was also starting to develop in Belchatow at the time. Before that, fabric was produced by [machines run by] foot treadles: from two for flannel and from four, six, or ten treadles for satin. They made better fabrics on electric machines: combed- wool and woolen cheviot[7] articles. Machine work was started in Belchatow, or rather in the nearby Kolonia Koldunow, by a German named Shultz. He was the first to bring such a machine from Pabianice, where machine work developed quickly, as it also did in the neighboring colonies of Koldunow, Zawardow, Belchatowek, and so on.

Chaim Tusk and Yeshaye Shrage were the first to turn to machine work. The Jewish weavers resisted using mechanical looms. Around 1892-1893, my brother-in-law, Peretz Freitag, came to Belchatow and settled in Koldunow. He became the partner of the German, Shultz. I must comment here that my brother, Shimshon Pitowski, who at that time was a manufacturer of better combed wool fabric in Lodz, was also instrumental in the production of better combed wool material in Belchatow by sending his material to us to be worked on in town. My brother-in-law, Peretz, was in Koldunow for two years and later, in 1894, settled in Belchatow, where he began to employ a large number of handlooms.

I should take this opportunity to mention my part in the development of machine work among the Jewish weavers and later leading Jewish workers to mechanized machine work. And later yet, in the years 1912-1913, [I would like to mention] the work of Jewish weavers on mechanized looms.

In 1895, when I had already completed my training as a weaver with my father, Hershl Weis, I worked as an apprentice to Feiwel Leyb.

In relation to Feiwel Leyb, it is worthwhile to mention several details, which will characterize the relationship at that time of the manufacturers to the workers or apprentices.

Feiwel Leyb had a factory of 10-12 handlooms, which produced woolen scarves and kerchiefs. Big, grown young men worked in that small factory as apprentices: Shmuel Zuken Choinacki and his brother, Yakov Szuster, Ayzik's son Moyshe, who had already done his military service, and so on. Reb Feiwel used to come to Belchatow from Lodz every Friday to spend the Sabbath there. When he came into the factory, he would look through the finished material and never stinted in his criticism, whenever he noticed defects in the work. I remember, one time he came over to my loom, looked at my work and suddenly he screamed: "You impudent fellows, come over here to this little one and learn how to do a good piece of work." (I was the youngest of the workers.)

Electric machine weaving started to develop for Jews in Belchatow during the years 1897-1898. At that time they were producing an article, which they called r.v. [possibly reine veberay – fine woven fabric]. It was woven in two procedures: a diagonal, with two above [the diagonal] and two futer-shus[8] [mechanical term used in weaving – a double-stitch of sorts]. One did not earn very much by producing this article. The second article was satin binding made with one above [the diagonal] and two futer-shus. Much more was earned from this article. I brought this article to the Jewish weavers. Then other Belchatow manufacturers brought in machine looms and began to make this same article. They would give out the work to be woven in the villages, where the wages were significantly lower, and in this way they harmed the interests of the weavers of Belchatow. This led to the formation of a weavers' guild, which opposed, in any way it could, the farming out of the work to the villages.

It is worthwhile to dedicate several words to this weavers' guild. I only remember several of the founders' names and [the names] of those who were active members of this guild. They were: Sh. Chojnacki, Ch. Sh. Szpigelman, Z. Machabanski, and others. The guild was limited purely to economic interests. It stood in the way, as mentioned above, of the manufacturers sending the work out to the villages, and it organized strikes to attain higher wages. The guild made sure that during a strike the village workers did not bring their merchandise to town, and it did not permit any raw material to go to the villages. In order to achieve this goal, pickets were set up at the edge of town. More than once, the guild arranged "occupation strikes" against the more stubborn manufacturers. A large number of weavers would go into the home of the factory owner and sit there until he conceded to their stated demands.

This guild did not have any cultural activities. The members of the guild did form a quorum of ten men so that they could pray together on the Sabbath and on holidays. On those occasions, they drank a keg of beer and socialized with one another.

The guild ended in a tragic way: In 1908, the police and the militia attacked the homes of the leaders of the guild. (I only remember the names

Chaim Szpigelman, Shmuel Zuken Chojnacki). They were sentenced to two years in prison; others got four years. In town, it was strongly suspected that they had been denounced by the manufacturers, but there was no real proof of this. My brother-in-law, Yakov Ostrowski, was also arrested and sent to Siberia. Although he himself did not belong to the guild, they did hold their meetings in his house.

In either 1898 or 1900, the first mechanized weaving plant began to operate in Belchatow. It belonged to my brother-in-law, Peretz Freitag, and I managed it.

As I mentioned previously, I had the privilege of being the first to introduce the Jewish workers of Belchatow to mechanized machine work. Certain jobs in the weaving plants had already been performed by Jewish workers, both male and female, even in the mechanized factories. These were the warp thread setters and stitchers. This was a kind of monopoly for the Jewish workers. In the first years of mechanized weaving in Belchatow, warp threads were cut by hand shears, and because the cutting trade had been in Jewish hands for many years, the Jews automatically got the first jobs as cutters in the mechanized factories.

I hired the first Jewish bobbin winders and spoolers to run the mechanized machines in the years 1901-1902. In doing so I ran into two difficult barriers: First of all, no Jewish woman at that time wanted to work on the Sabbath, and even if one had wanted to – the Orthodox Jews would have stoned us. So every Friday afternoon[9], I had to send for Christian bobbin winders and spoolers, who were unemployed at that time, to run the machines and get them to prepare spools to be cut for the Jewish cutters, who worked on Sunday. The second barrier was the fear of class-consciousness on the part of the Jewish workers, of the "akhdusnikes" [unionizers], "buntovshteshikes" [insurgents], that they would call a strike. This fear on the part of the Jewish manufacturer was actually based on fact. In 1913 and later, other Jewish weaving plants were founded in Belchatow like: Dzialowski, Epsztajn Brothers, later Ferszter and Warszawski.

Until after the First World War, there were no Jewish bobbin winders or spoolers in the mechanized weaving plants, except perhaps for individual cases that I did not know about.

In the year 1910, the first mechanized Konus cutting machine was built in Belchatow. I taught my brother-in-law, Shmuel Goldberg, to operate that machine and that later became his job.

In 1912, I brought ten of my own carding machines back from Germany.

At that time Jewish community activists in Lodz had already started to bring Jewish workers into the mechanized weaving plants. The Jewish manufacturers, the religious ones as well as the nationalists [non-religious], tried with all their might to oppose this action. In this instance, there were also obstacles relating to the Christian workers, who went on strike more than once when the Jewish manufacturers wanted to hire Jewish workers in their mechanized weaving plants.

When I became the owner of my own ten machines, I decided to hire Jewish workers to run them. My first attempt was not successful, although the wages made from running my carding machines were much higher than could be made at two English looms. Instead of five rubles a week at two English machines, a worker at one of my carding machines earned between eight and 10 rubles a week – a very nice wage for that time.

I made my first attempt with a relative of mine – a young man, who was working at a business in Lodz. He was an idealist, who belonged to the Social-Democratic Party and always strove to be more productive at work. I hired him and placed him near a Polish weaver. I told the Pole that my relative wanted to be a weaver in a different country and wanted to learn the basics of weaving here (otherwise the Pole would not have agreed to teach him). I paid the Pole for his instruction, and my relative, Danski was his name, stayed with me until he learned the trade. I later gave him a loom to work on. He worked fairly well for several weeks but later, not being used to physical work, he tired very quickly. Work in the factory would start at six in the morning, but Danski came at eight o'clock. I could not let him work on the Sabbath in Belchatow, although he actually did want to. This gave the Poles an opportunity to laugh at the Jewish "noble worker" as they called him. The [other] Jewish manufacturers ridiculed me [saying]: "Here you have an example of a Jewish factory worker."

I began to argue with Danski: "You know what I wanted to achieve by bringing you in. And you see that with your work [habits] you have given the

Jewish manufacturers a good excuse not to give Jewish workers a chance. So from now on, you must work five normal[10] days a week or leave the factory.

He chose the latter and went to Germany. When I later saw him in Berlin, he was a member of the Communist Party. In 1933, when Hitler took power, he escaped to Russia, and I heard no more from him.

My second attempt was with a Chasidic young man. After working two weeks normally, he, like Danski, started to come to work at eight o'clock. I explained to him that he was setting a bad example and frightening off other manufacturers.[11] I gave him a choice: either he work regular hours or he teach the trade to another Jew, who could replace him at the machine.

Avraham Naparstek took his place, and this was my first successful attempt to show that a Jewish worker was no worse than a Polish worker, even at carding. Naparstek did his job very responsibly. He worked only five days a week (except for the Friday nights that he worked "stealthily"), and he did not produce 16-17 percent less than Polish workers, only 5 or 6 percent less. This was a big accomplishment, something that I could use to counter the complaints of the Jewish manufacturers. The truth is that these arguments did not accomplish much, because the manufacturers' fears were caused by something else: Jewish workers were considered agitators, strikers, rabble-rousers. This was a natural phenomenon, because the Jewish worker was more conscious, and – as a resident of the city – had greater needs than the Polish workers, who mostly came from the villages.

In this regard, the situation of the Jewish workers was "not so good." Actually a friend of Naparstek's, Zalman Pudlowski, pointed this out to me. One day Naparstek told me that he wanted to teach this trade to his friend, Zalman Pudlowski. Pudlowski was at that time the leader of the "Bund" in Belchatow.

I agreed. Why should there not be another Jewish worker at the carding machine? However, Comrade Pudlowski went right to "work." He began to convince the workers to strike. And not only my workers... This activity did not remain a secret for long. Polish workers told me sarcastically: "There you have your Jewish weavers." I received an even worse reaction from the Jewish factory owners.

I turned to Comrade Pudlowski with "weighty" arguments: "What do you mean? First – my workers earn double that of English workers. Second – why did you not organize the Polish workers? You are ruining all my efforts to bring Jewish workers into mechanized weaving."

It was useless to talk to an "akhdusnik" [unionizer]. He had his own arguments: that bringing Jewish workers into the factory was not for their own good... My telling him that rather than exploit a Jewish worker five days a week, it would have been better for me to have a Polish worker, who worked six days a week did not help. The outbreak of World War I brought an end to our discussion...

I want to add that before this, I had brought my mechanized threading machine with 240 spindles from Lodz to Belchatow and had employed two girls to run it: Ruchel Eksztajn and Miriam Borzykowski. Both of them were excellent workers.

In total, before the First World War, I had placed thirty Jewish workers in the mechanized factories: bobbin winders, spoolers, threaders, one Jewish cutter and one weaver. I did not make any more efforts in this area until 1932, when I once again made a similar effort involving a greater number of Jewish weavers.

**Peretz Freitag**

In 1931, after a hiatus of over 17 years, during which time I lived in Lodz, my brother-in-law, Peretz Freitag, came to me with the suggestion that I again take over the management of his factory. Until then the factory had been leased by Szukowski and Adler. My two cousins, Shimek and Nachum (both of them were killed by the Nazis) were still too young too manage the factory. Their father, Peretz Freitag, was already ailing (he actually died soon thereafter). On his suggestion, I started to come three times a week from Lodz to Belchatow on factory business. With satisfaction I insisted that a certain number of Jewish workers be employed at motorized looms. At that time, there were not only "akhdusnikes" [unionists] and Bundists working in the factory, but also respectable [Jewish] children. The economic situation of the Jewish middle class in Poland was already bad at that time. The Polish government did everything in its power to expel Jewish shopkeepers from their positions. The young people felt that they had to seek new paths and began to stream into the factories to the extent they were able, considering the given conditions. The Jewish population's relationship to factory work changed radically. It was no longer a disgrace to be a worker. Pukacz, Szczekocki, Davidowicz and others all worked in the factory.

In 1932, when I came to Belchatow and organized the factory, we – Shimek, Nachum, and I – brought in a number of Jewish workers, who had previous experience working on mechanized weaving machines. I also took on several apprentices, who later worked on these machines. In addition, all the bobbin winders and spoolers were Jewish girls and women. Five Jewish cutters also worked at the power machines that set warp arms.

It was my bitter fate to see every single Jew that I had tried so hard to bring in thrown out of the factory. This was the beginning of the Second World War.

## Meir Szukowski's factory

Starting in 1936, the factory was run by my sister's children, the sons and sons-in-law of Peretz Freitag. Three weeks after the start of the Second World War, on the 21st of September 1939, Peretz and Hertske, Dovid Freitag's sons, came to see me in Lodz. They told me that a mob in Belchatow had stolen the raw materials from all the factories, and the Germans prevented the looting of fabric and raw materials in only one factory – ours. The asked me, therefore, to come to Belchatow and try to make some order in the factory.

It was already dangerous to be on the roads, but I made an effort. I arrived in Belchatow on the 22nd of September. Several dozen workers were waiting and happily welcomed me. The local Germans, who already had the keys to the factory and to the warehouses, turned the keys over to me and even the several thousand zlotys, which they had earned from the sale of merchandise. I paid the workers and the foremen – in cash and in merchandise – and started to put the factory back on its feet. This was the only factory, where workers could still earn a living, and, in the beginning, where manufacturers could bring their merchandise to be worked. At that time, the Germans had not yet set up a civil government in Belchatow, and in comparison to the civil government set up later, the military regime was, at the beginning, much less restrictive.

I was called to City Hall first thing in the morning on Yom Kippur, 1939. The Mayor, Frei, a local German, explained to me that I must immediately restart the factory, because they had to show the occupying power that the factory was operating normally. He also warned me that if I did not keep the factory running, I would be taking on a heavy responsibility[12], because this was the only factory that could – because of its condition and its supply of raw materials – be left operational.

Even at that time, in the City Hall premises, I experienced a moment of terrible horror: it took a long time to take care of the various formalities. At around 10 o'clock, I noticed that the Germans were pushing their way to the windows and that the younger ones were choking back laughter. Then I also went over to the window, and I was appalled at what I saw. Jews were being chased from all sides. Some fell while they were carrying Torah scrolls and religious books in their hands. They were being chased, beaten, and kicked. Opposite the windows of the City Hall, the Germans had made a big bonfire, and the Jews had to throw their religious books and the Torah scrolls into the fire. They were being kicked the entire time, and some Jews were badly burned, as a result of having been pushed into the fire. From the window of his house, which was right across from the City Hall, the Rabbi of Belchatow, Rabbi Shmuel Yehoshua [Horowicz], of blessed memory, was made to throw down his religious book. Later, the Germans dragged him down and forced him to carry those books to the fire.

When I left the City Hall, two local Germans, who had accompanied me on the way to the City Hall, were waiting for me. We had to wait for a third German, who had gone to bring a certain amount of money to me. The two Germans, who were standing with me, watching this hellish scene, comforted me with their heads down: they kept on repeating, "This is truly horrible. This should not be happening." They promised that they would do everything [they could] so that such scenes would not be repeated. I, however, thought to myself: Even if they are sincere, they will also not be able to withstand this dark power.

On the way back, we passed the store of our baker, a German. His wife called me over and said: "I am telling you, Mr. Pitowsky, that because of these murderous acts, the Germans will lose the war... But, we, the local Germans, cannot oppose them." The three Germans who accompanied me agreed. Her prophecy did come true, but too late!

I permitted the continued operation of the factory, and I managed it for several weeks. The Germans did not interfere. I hired all the Jewish workers who applied. And quite a lot applied, because in addition to the salary, the factory had another positive attribute; [being employed there] meant that the workers were released from forced labor, at which they were cruelly beaten.

In November 1939, I was visited by a whole group of upper-level staff officers from Piotrkow, led by their chief officer. There was also a civilian, who the chief appointed as the so-called "trustee," that is, the manager of the factory. In the morning, I turned over the money to this German, went over the accounts, and wanted to return to Lodz, but the new manager did not let me go – he did not have the slightest idea about weaving.

I was actually very pleased about the possibility of remaining, because I could give back to the Jews the material that they gave to the factory to be worked on. We also had the opportunity to help many Jews who had their raw material in Lodz, and enable them to bring their merchandise to Belchatow, along with the raw material, which we brought to the factory. At that time, this saved many Jewish families from starvation, because they could sell the merchandise they brought [to Belchatow] in an unofficial way.

In addition to the "trustee," a Belchatower German professional weaver also came to the factory. This is a person who had been fired from our factory in 1937, because he could not work. Now he had the opportunity to get back at his former bosses.

As soon as he arrived in the factory, he began to dismiss the Jewish workers and to put Germans in their places. We tried to influence the "trustee," to convince him that the new worker, the German, did not understand the first thing about this work. It did not do a bit of good. Paljaczek, the new worker, complained to the party, which said that we should do exactly as he ordered.

I remained at the factory until May of 1940. During this time, I had to witness many horrible persecutions that the Jews had to endure. Others, however, will write about this, comrades who escaped the murderous hands of the Hitler thugs.

I was once again in Belchatow in 1946. I did not see a single living Jew there.

So I went to see the cemetery. I wanted to see the place where those closest to us were resting. I walked around the place several times, where I knew that the cemetery had been long ago; there was nothing I could recognize. Then a gentile acquaintance assured me that this was indeed where the cemetery had been.

I stood there for a very long time, and I left the cemetery with a heavy heart.

This was the beginning and this was the tragic end of Jewish life in Belchatow.

**A group of Jewish women workers in
Freitag's factory in the year 1913:**

Mindl Benczkowski, Freydl N. Borszikowski, Machabanski,
Gele Benczkowski, Tsipor Goldblum, Miriam Eksztajn, Blime
Sherman, Chaye Blime Jakubowicz, Itke Spiegel, Sore Ite
Sztatlender, Miriam Borszikowski, and Gitl Eksztajn

**Translator's footnotes:**

1. Literally, "those for unity."
2. Sent from Israel.
3. This word means "stock market" in Yiddish, but here it is used metaphorically as a marketplace of ideas.
4. A sing-song melody used in the learning of Gemara.
5. The official history and record journal of a town.
6. Waving a live chicken over one's head before Yom Kippur as atonement for one's sins. This could also be done with a fish or money.
7. A woolen fabric in a coarse twill weave.
8. The word in Yiddish, futer-shus, refers to a plush fabric, like velvet or any other fabric with a pile.
9. The Jewish Sabbath starts at sundown Friday night.
10. That is, keeping regular hours.
11. From hiring Jewish workers.
12. There would be heavy reprisals.

[Page 81]

# "The Belchatow Revolutionary"

## by Lucian Rudnitzky (Lucjan Rudniczki)

## Translated from the Yiddish by Martin Bornstein

*Our Friend M. Klenowski sent us from Lodz an interesting fragment that is taken from the volume of memoirs from the known Polish Revolutionary fighter and writer Lucjan Rudniczki, dedicated to the Belchatow Jewish revolutionary Moshe Goldfish.*

At the end of October[1] there arrived a new group of prisoners from all corners of the Piotrkower industrial region. Also from Belchatow there was found a revolutionary in the personage of the shoemaker's apprentice Moshe Goldfish. He was placed in a cell, in captivity, together with me, and all those "honored" members, that was in those days set aside for political prisoners. The guards from the prison however were not acquainted (in agreement) with the ideology (concepts) of the prison administrator and were ready to deal out (bless) discipline, as Moshe now became acquainted with, as a political prisoner. The prison commander and his helpers avoided encountering him (the guard) and when they had to meet up with him, they closed their eyes or turned around. The smaller prison administrators were often not able to control things and because of that there constantly came about (events of) social friction.

Goldfish proud came to express himself to Ambultzin, when he used to go through the long corridor on a walk or on an exploration. The guard(s) didn't tolerate his bad walk (gate), with slow steps, and constantly pushed him to move faster. On (receiving) not correct (fair) notices Moshe answered with a grand lordly manner of indifference.

One of the guards, wanting to use strength to compel Goldfish to carry out his will, gave him a slap. We heard the struggle and the cry from Moshe: "Slave! How are you guarding? I am a political (prisoner)!" Hearing and partly seeing the conflict, I began to beat with a bench on the door of my cell. Upon (hearing) the echo of the beating sound, other guards came running. Moshe, the person making a stand, was pushed in by his stomach into his cell, but then his door also began to thunder. The (prison) commander was called along with one of his helpers, the so called by us "horses-head", had called for the military. Several minutes later the guards came into the cell and took out all the valuable things. At the same moment a resounding sound was made in the whole prison. These were the remaining friends, numbering 30 men, proceeding to (the) assault.

When Moshe had been dragged into the dark punishment cell, he screamed to them:

- Friends they are beating Political (prisoners)!

The atmosphere was very strained, because upon the call from Moshe all the prisoners simultaneously began to demonstrate. Early the next day the prisoners began a hunger strike.

With the understanding (accordance) of the other friends I demanded the immediate release of our friend Goldfish from the dungeon, as well as the resignation of the (prison) commander and of the section (division) guard. I paint here (for you) the proud stance of Goldfish, as a Jew and Revolutionary. While fighting against oppression of people and social suppression, Moshe Goldfish simultaneously fought against racial discrimination.

Goldfish wore a long frock, from his face shined forth pride. So much attention and self importance did he have, that the pitiful long cloth coat, looked on him like a mantel of a Roman Patrician. . .

---

1.  In the year 1903

*[Pages 83-101]*

This chapter is translated in Memory of

**PEREC HAFT (1918-2000)**
a Holocaust survivor from Belchatow

# Belchatow in the Year 1898

**by P. Wald**

**Translated from the Yiddish
in parts by
Arthur Haft, Rosa Rynski Haft, David Haft
and by Martin Bornstein
In Honor of his mother Dora Bornstein,
a Holocaust survivor from Belchatow
and by Gloria Berkenstat Freund**

**Edited by Gloria Berkenstat Freund and Jerry Liebowitz**

[with comments in brackets]

There was a road from Piotrkow. It went through fields, forests and villages that spread out between the Vistula and Warta Rivers to Prussia. The road led to Belchatow.

It was spring. The small fields around the shtetl [town] were in bloom. Potatoes and rye were growing; barley and oats grew. As in the shtetl, gardens and orchards were wedged in; cattle, calves, goats and chickens could be heard in the surrounding yards.

The houses on the main street of the shtetl, wooden and brick, for the most part small, low with pointy roofs, covered with grey wooden shingles, on which grew moss and others that were covered with tar paper and smeared with tar, were hung with shutters in which the shamas [synagogue caretaker] of the synagogue banged [to let people know it was time] to go to the synagogue; they stood in the front of a large open courtyard and the courtyard ran out into the fields.

The main street was not the only one, because there was one more. It ran crosswise from where the main street ended at the marketplace. The other street, which like the first one had no name, was located on one side in the Jewish shtetl and on the other side went out toward the highway.

The other street passed the beer brewery, merged into the highway, which began on the other side of the shtetl, and went further over gorgeous Polish, noble estates and across green meadows and forests of evergreens that held the sky on their heads.

* * *

The shtetl in Poland, the [part of] Poland that was allocated to the Russian Empire, was populated by Jews. The few Polish Christians who were there were Shabbos-goyim [Sabbath Gentiles who performed work that the Jews were prohibited from doing on the Sabbath]. They very much liked the Shabbos fish that was cooked by the Jewish women only for Shabbos. The Shabbos-goy very willingly took the metal candlesticks off the table and made a fire for a piece of gefilte fish [stuffed fish – originally the ground fish was stuffed into fish skins and cooked].

* * *

As a shtetl in Russian-Poland, it did not have any freedom, any human rights and it was entirely subject to the rule of the autocracy of the Russian emperor, the tsar and despot of the Romanov dynasty.

**Pictures of the old market**

We did not know of books, of newspapers, of periodicals. The only things that were printed with Yiddish letters were the old written religious prayers and seforim [religious books], which kept the Jews in fear, in dejection, in submission. No one thought of a change; they believed themselves as inferior and they did not feel the humiliation. Thus they dragged the yoke, just to survive the wretched years here on earth.

Jews whispered in the synagogue ... somewhere in far Russia, noblemen had created a plan of action against the emperor ... this reached to the real Petersburg ... They had already shot at "him." ... There were further rumors about the revolutionary movement of the Narodna Volya [People's Will – left-wing organization responsible for the assassination of Alexander II], which went through the small synagogue of the Jewish shtetl in Poland, but the town Jews had no feelings or thoughts about this. A "blessing" was said in the synagogue for the Russian emperor on Shabbos before reading the Torah and – done.

\* \* \*

Of the mighty Greater Russian Empire to which the shtetl belonged – its political regime, its government, its laws, its institutions – who in the Jewish shtetl knew of this? They did not even know yet that they lived in a ghetto, a large ghetto, which consisted of all of Russian Poland, White Russia, Lithuania, Bessarabia, to part of Ukraine, but – a ghetto of the largest part of the land, where Jews were not supposed to live, unless a merchant of the first gilde [merchant's guild], which Belchatow did not have. Who even thought of political regimes? Of democracy and freedom, of culture, of citizen's rights, of human rights, of protest, of opposition, struggle, revolution? These were terribly strange, "alien" words for a Jewish shtetl into which they had not yet entered and whose meanings were unknown. In their own, only natural mother tongue, Yiddish, which they were not even taught, these words, worldly and expressive of secular things, were entirely absent.

The shtetl was open on all sides, but the world did not enter. And the Jews with "consciousness" of the great "we must not" for everything, absorbed it into themselves with all their strength, and saw to it with all their power that they did not transgress against "we must not" – that they not, God forbid, rebel against the lack of rights, and so they lived shut in their own ghetto.

\* \* \*

They actually traveled. They did not make a yetsies [going-out/exodus], no exodus, no emigration – God forbid; they traveled to fairs; they traveled to Piotrkow and to Lodz to purchase goods, took their goods and in return brought new fibers for the Belchatow cloth weavers; they traveled to arrange marriages for their children, because matches were made with those in other places; they traveled to weddings with the bridegrooms when the brides, who did not know their matches and whom they did not see until under the khupah [wedding canopy] (if they did see them under khupah [the bride was veiled and the pair may not have seen each other until after the wedding ceremony]), lived in other towns with their parents who were marrying off their daughters; and they also traveled to look for apprentices who were taken on for four years; they also searched for yahr-yinglekh [year boys]. These were [young men] who had just finished their studies and had not yet been taken on as apprentices for a term and they also looked for journeymen.

Hershl Bliacharsz's young wife, who was the house owner and the supplier of everything, made a trip that year to no less than Tamoszow, to bring an entire troika [three workers] for herself. In Piotrkow, she barely got a yahr-yingl; she brought an apprentice from Tomaszow, but she did not get a journeyman. It was after Pesach [Passover], spring, when the men who were hired khol-hamoed [intervening days of holiday, when work is permitted] for a period of time were already busy and the Bliacharszes were pelted with work.

* * *

The shtetl had six weekdays: from Shabbas night after Havdalah [the closing Shabbos prayer] until Friday night before blessing the candles when the Shamas went through the streets and called aloud: "Jews, go into the synagogue!"

The weekdays were filled with work. They worked so much, just as if life in the world had been sentenced to work, or as if the work took up all of their interest and all of their enjoyment in life. Eating, sleeping were in order to be able to work; even a son-in-law oyf kest [the expenses of a young man who was engaged in religious study were paid for by his father-in-law] also worked ... day and night he sat over the Gemara [Talmudic commentary]. They would also have worked on Shabbos and on holidays if it had not been a sin, but the prohibition against working on Shabbos and on holidays was still in essence only because of the work. To be a little rested for it.

* * *

[Spending time in] the shtetl's large yeshiva [religious school for young men] with a large number of young yeshiva men was thought of as a profession that consisted of learning Torah, in praying for the shtetl, holy work for which one is rewarded with essen teg [daily meals provided for students in the local homes] with the shtetl middleclass.

And with the exception of the cloth makers, all trades worked first for the benefit of the shtetl itself; one worked for another, all worked for everyone and each worked for everyone.

If the cloth makers, the weavers, worked through Lodz, for the interior market, from which the shtetl also had to buy goods to dress itself, through the earnings for their work they were then able to pay for the production in the shtetl for their needs and to provide through this the opportunity for the shtetl to import what it needed.

All trades had enough to do [to meet the] needs of the town itself.

The population grew. At 15 one became a bride and at 18 a groom and such a couple gave the shtetl a child every year. Wealthy men, powerful men, also had children, less in number, but they had. One would not not have [children]. All of the Jews in the shtetl were pious, even the wealthy men were pious. And Jews had religious divorces after 10 years of not having children. Who knew of methods to not have children? This life did not choose child murder, not before [birth] and not after. If the rich, after they also were granted the mitzvah [commandment] of having children, carried out a certain control over their further fruitfulness and reproduction, this was not the case of the poor who were rich in this regard. And there were few rich Jews in the shtetl, while there were many poor, almost all.

They always had to build: molding clay and carrying bricks; erecting walls and covering roofs; sawing wood and making furniture; providing shoes and boots (made entirely by hand), dressing with long, wide dresses to cover the sinful bodies and covering the heads of the women with caps and sheitln [wigs worn by married women] and the heads of the males with yarmulkes [skull caps], hats with low crowns, shtreimlekh [fur hats worn by many married Hasidic men].

Talisim [prayer shawls], tefilin [phylacteries], tsitis [garment with fringes on four corners worn by observant men], mezuzahs [small boxes containing the Shema prayer placed on every doorpost in a house], sidurim [prayer books], sforim [religious books] and other holy articles were imported; however, Shabbos candles, havdalah candles and wedding candles and soap to wash clothing were fabricated by the Jews in the shtetl. Also from our shtetl: the shoykhetim [ritual slaughterers] did the ritual slaughter; the moyhelim [ritual circumcisers] – the circumcisions, and there also were several klezmorim [musicians] for the weddings. Today they work in the mikvah [ritual bath] and the cemetery.

All of this required a great deal of work; in addition, the synagogue was completed at that time on the street of the beis-medrash [house of prayer] and where the yeshiva was located.

However, the shtetl also worked for the gentiles, for the Polish male peasants and female peasants who would come in their village horse-drawn carriages and would also come on foot in their colorful clothing and the men in four-cornered hats and the women in red and white striped, pleated dresses, hanging from the head down. They came to the town market that was [held] once a week and they brought their goods to the market: bundles of bark straw for straw mattresses and for beds, bundles of wood to burn, young calves for slaughter, eggs and poultry, green branches for Sukkos [Feast of Tabernacles – the branches are used as a roof for the sukkah – the hut in which meals are eaten]; butter wrapped in cabbage leaves and baskets of black and red berries and of mushrooms.

However, they did not remove any rubbed off three-kopek pieces from the shtetl. Tables with brand-new colorful peasant dresses, stiff belts, aprons, boots, laced gaiters with bootlegs; cakes and candies; sparkling tin utensils, lanterns and lamps; whips, horse-collars and reins and wagon grease; cut-goods, ribbons and rosaries, of which the Jewish artisans and shopkeepers knew the tastes of the Polish peasants – these were displayed so attractively and drew the male and female peasants and very often a peasant couple left a few gildn in the shtetl that they had brought from the village wrapped in a knot of a kerchief.

Hershl Bliacharsz also stood at a table at the market, a Jew, a member of the shtetl middleclass, an influential man, a boor who gave slaps rather than talking to those who were stubborn at conflicts about synagogue matters, about the rabbi in the shtetl, the purity of the ritual bath, about maftir [person reading the Haftorah – reading from the Prophets at the Sabbath service] and the 613 mitzvos [commandments].

Hershl Bliacharsz was a resolute Jew with a black beard that looked as if it had been trimmed and which grew up around his lips and on the cheeks of a fleshy face with a low forehead, from under which looked out a pair of hot black eyes as if they were filled with the tar with which Hershl Bliacharsz smeared the tar paper roofs – in general, he did what he was permitted to do rather than that which was forbidden.

His feet were wrapped with squares of cloth and placed in a pair of light black boots that were smeared with castor oil every erev Shabbos [Sabbath eve] and erev yom-tov [holiday eve]; [he wore] a wide talis-koten [four cornered tasseled garment worn under a pious man's clothing] that hung from his shoulders down beneath his stomach and four-tied up, white tsitsis [fringes] dangled to his knees and [he wore] a wide kaftan with long, wide sleeves that covered him, and, as he walked and stood, only a nose appeared in the middle of an overgrown face under a black, shallow and round Jewish-Polish hat – yet Hershl Bliacharsz exuded a passion for everything.

Hershl Bliacharsz had to cover the roof of the new synagogue with black tin and to make the cornices, the gutters and the pipes of zinc-tin; he had a great deal to do in finishing the spires, towers and cupola of the local church, which stood with its front to the main street and with its back to an orchard of plums, raspberries, gooseberries, currants, grapes, pears and apples that teased the appetite and that were not forbidden fruit for those who worked there. Hershl Bliacharsz worked on the municipal brick buildings; there were not many, but those that were, were his. He also had work at the surrounding aristocratic courts. In addition to this he was involved with the forest, where gentiles, who rented from Hershl Bliacharsz, cut grown pine, oak and white birch trees; they hewed, sawed into blocks, into posts and into boards for construction. If this was too little, he also placed a table at the market. He did not stand at the table, only his wife; she was a better seller. However, Hershl Bliacharsz also stood at a table, not because he had to do so, but that was the way of a shtetl Jew, an artisan, a middleclass man, to not let anything fall through that could provide a gildn of income and because Hershl Bliacharsz, actually [it was] she more than he, had a "hidden" tavern on Shabbos after a nap and on holidays in the afternoon, because the apprentices rolled a barrel of beer from the brewery on Friday night. They did not, God forbid, sell [beer] for money on Shabbos, and did not write down [who owed money], but kept it in their heads that someone had treated someone and what one had requested he be given, allowing them in for this through the back door.

Regarding illness, it was the habit of the shtetl Jew not to immediately run for the doctor when he did not feel right; first he used all of his own remedies: a wet handkerchief for a headache; wolfberry for vomiting; fenchel [fennel] tea and castor oil for stomach aches; garlic and pepper and ground horse teeth on burned coals – for toothaches. And when it was not better, they went to the apothecary, he should give them something and then when leeches and cupping glasses needed to be applied or a tooth had to be pulled, they called the feldsher [barber-surgeon] who on the way took along a scissors in case a Jew wanted to have a haircut, and then, finally, after a remedy against the evil eye had been said and the women also were in the synagogue and pleaded in front of the open ark for a complete cure, the doctor was called.

The shtetl had its merchants, shopkeepers and booths that provided the daily needs of the shtetl. However, there were mainly trades – weaving and tailoring, shoemaking and hatmaking, baking and retailing, building and blacksmithing – and as was the custom, the family's residence was part of the [artisan's workshop] and the home life of the family was carried out alongside the apprenticeships and the professional life.

The teaching of the trade began with the boy as an apprentice. These were years of pure slavery.

Only the "apprentice boy" and not the "apprentice girl," because Jewish girls did not learn a trade, they did work in the home, the housekeeping, also helped in the trade work in the house, helped in the shop and, in the very poor families, they became servants for those who were richer.

The apprentice, usually 13 years old when he was rented out, was hired, based on a promise, for four years. It is understandable that one takes an apprentice [by agreeing to provide] food and sleep and clothing. What kind of food, what kind of bed and what kind of clothing was not recorded anywhere. The little bit of food for the apprentice was just [enough] to maintain him. Sleep, the several hours at night on some sort of bed, was in the workshop where they also ate. When the clothing, which the apprentice usually wore, fell apart, it was changed completely, so that it would not be said that with Moshe-Meir the carpenter, or with Dovid Khackl the gaiter maker, the apprentice wore torn clothing. But all in all, the clothing for the apprentice cost the "foreman," as the boss, the artisan was called, only a few rubles in the course of all four years.

However, this, which the "foreman" gave as a donation to the apprentice, was a matter of secondary importance. The same with the instruction, which the boy stole, more than received. It was mainly this, that the apprentice had to do things for the "foreman" (master craftsman), for his wife, for their children and even for the half and full men or journeymen. The so-called apprentice was completely subject to the boss. The apprentice had to do unskilled work, dirty work, heavy work and even work that was not related to the trade [to which he was apprenticed]. He had to be slavishly obedient, obey everyone and follow everything, as well as the whims and making fun of him and the insults. He was beaten for not obeying something, showing resentment, transgressing, committing such a crime as stealing a piece of bread; everyone in the "foreman's" household could always hit the apprentice; he could be beaten for a reason and he also could be beaten without a reason. The apprentice had no one to whom he could complain; he could only run away. Several did so, although the apprentice could not [make things better for himself] because it was the same with all of the "foremen."

And the apprentice was the servant for the mistress of the house; he had to be this. It was the routine of being an apprentice; every servant did everything that he was asked for every mistress of the house. And if the "foreman" had older children, the apprentice also had to serve them, and where there were men hired for allotted times, journeymen, the apprentice had to serve them. Very little time remained for the apprentice after so much service that had nothing to do with the trade. Therefore, the apprenticeship period for the four years was one in which the apprentice stole and nibbled more learning than was given to him and in the end he barely had any mastery when he finished the four years of slavery and an apprenticeship of hard labor.

The apprentice went to yearly work after finishing with the apprenticeship; more to learn the trade; he was a boy employed by the year.

The apprentice who emerged from his apprenticeship through four years of slavery could earn as a year-boy for another year with the same "foreman" with whom he had been for his apprenticeship, but as patriarchal as it was in the Jewish artisan-house in the shtetl (as well as in the city), the apprentice who had finished [his apprenticeship] wanted to be freed from the house where he been a slave for four interminable years and he rented himself or he was rented to another "foreman" of the same trade. One served for a year, from Pesach to Pesach, or from Sukkos [the Feast of Tabernacles] to Sukkos, with food and a place to sleep, but without clothing. However, for a wage that reached up to 25 rubles for the entire year.

The patriarchy or the slavery continued. The difference between an apprentice and a year-boy was that the apprentice was a servant and also was used in the trade and the year-boy worked in the trade and he also was used as a servant. This was not done with the purpose that the apprentice perfect his technique in the trade, but because it was so worthwhile for the income of the boss. The apprentice, under the supervision of the journeyman, or of the "foreman," almost did the work of a "man," or a journeyman or the "foreman" himself.

The work was put away every Friday night, when the shamas went through the shtetl and cried out that it was time for Shabbos, until Shabbos ended with Havdalah, which was observed as soon as the stars appeared in the sky. A pause also was made in the work – which did not have any time limit and during which we were forbidden to look at the watch – because of the Jewish holidays: Pesach, Shavuos, even Tisha B'Av is also a holiday. In addition, Rosh Hashanah, Yom Kippur, Sukkos. It was a shame for the boy employed for a year that Chanukah was not a holiday and that Purim only was a one-day holiday, after having fasted on the fast of Esther.

Ending the year after the apprenticeship, the year-boy became a journeyman. Then he rented himself out not for only one year, but for a term, for a half year, from Pesach to Sukkos or from Sukkos to Pesach. They earned food and a place to sleep as usual and a wage of 30 rubles for the term, which became higher with each future term with the same "foreman" or with another one and they reached up to 60 rubles for the last term when the journeyman married and he became a "boss" himself, an artisan, a boss with or without "men."

The hope of the journeyman, who became fit for marriage as soon as he became a journeyman, was to marry and to become a "boss."

The artisans usually married later, later than a "Talmudic student," than a young man in a yeshiva, or the child of a merchant. Firstly, no one chased after an artisan, a young tailor, a young weaver, a young baker, and, secondly, one had to have the means to create a workshop. One anticipated a dowry. Or what does one do if the dowry was only a promised one? No matter, one got married and then [there was no dowry]. They swore that the dowry had been deposited with such and such valid businessman and that it would be settled right after the wedding. What was not done for the mitzvah [commandment] of [arranging] a marriage for a Jewish daughter?

Not sure of the dowry, the journeyman was sure that a match would be made with the draft. He would not make a mistake with the match. And if he needed to serve Russia and be sent to the devil, he would not wait for the match [to be completed] but would go out into the world.

The accumulation [of money] during the terms [of employment] was used for a workshop because there would not be a divorce over not being able to agree on the promised dowry. And yet getting married, becoming a husband was connected to the hope of becoming a "boss" oneself, a small businessman, with wealth: a wife, children, "employees," a household, furniture, a workshop, shelves of ones own manufactured good, or with woven "skeins of yarn," sent with the large wagons to Lodz...

He became a "master," a boss; he no longer worked for someone; he worked for himself; he no longer had to obey anyone. He had to be obeyed and he was the one who asked, the one who gave orders, the one who bullied his "men" and the one who hit, the one who slapped if he was not obeyed, it someone sinned with something, or when he wanted to show who was the boss.

The boss himself did not know of freedom, of any rights, of any human dignity: he lived in fear of God the all powerful, of the strong gentile and of the brass buttons of the policeman with his whip, sword and "pistol" representing the Czar in the shtetl, the brutal, the "God-anointed" Czarist regime from which nothing good was expected.

* * *

Jewish trade in Belchatow, the commerce, the business, was a special thing; [the opportunities for] a trade and income were small and very limited. This does not match the anti-Semitic idea that Jews only were involved in trade, but this was the reality in Belchatow. The great majority of Belchatow Jews were employed in productive work. This was not because of a principle, not a preference, not an ideal. They were involved with productive work because of income. This was always the result of productive work; but with trade this was not the case.

At that time, at the end of the preceding century [19th century], all of the necessary productive work was done by the Jews. There were very few gentiles in the shtetl. There were no excess workers. There was a shortage of workers. It even resulted in writing or traveling to Piotrkow, to Tomaszow [to look for] workers and it was difficult to get them because if they left home, they went from the smaller city to a larger one.

And the artisans, the craft workers commercialized their production. They were the shopkeepers, the merchants of the things that they themselves had made. No one went to a shop to buy bread, but one went to a baker for bread; one went to a shoemaker for boots, gaiters, slippers or loafers. Whoever needed a long man's coat, a pair of pants, a hat, a cap, a shtreiml [fur hat worn by Hasidim], a fur – went to a tailor, to a hat-maker, and to a furrier.

And if someone wanted to buy a watch, a remedy, a teapot – one went to a watchmaker, to an apothecary, who sold soda water and honey as a remedy. They were dissuaded from being a cloth weaver, which was the main trade in the shtetl, both in number and in importance, in size and in security and who did not have anything to sell. The large rolls of goods that they manufactured were taken to Lodz on large wagons. Middle class women and their daughters created several items for their own use, or as gifts; they made "sacred items," although the "sacred" considered them as sinful and they belittled and insulted them, saying: it is ritually unclean for an old man to touch a woman. At prayer in the hall of the synagogue into which no woman was supposed to enter, the old man said: "...for not making me a woman," which is thanks to God that one was not created as a woman ... yet she sewed bags for tefillin [phylacteries], bags for talisim [prayer shawls] and cloaks for the Torah scrolls.

Something also remained for commerce: goods that the shtetl did not produce itself: Havdalah [ceremony ending the Sabbath] spices, raisins and almonds, herring, sugar, kasha [buckwheat groats], millet, rice, chicory or sacred things such as talisim, tefillin, tsitsis [four corned garment with fringes worn by pious men], sedorim [prayer books], makhzorim [prayer book for the Days of Awe], or haberdashery and dry goods, needles, threads, buttons, combs, so that there was some retail and even intermediate trade, but very restricted, so it did not play the same role in the economic life of the shtetl as the great role played by the crafts, the productive work, whose concert of creation was always heard in the streets of the shtetl, except on the Sabbath and on holidays.

* * *

The chorale of the gemara [oral law] melody in the yeshiva that was located in the house of study on the main street of the shtetl, across from the new synagogue which stood almost completed, covered with a black tin roof, painted red with a high window and colored window panes and in which there already was prayer, also joined the concert of Jewish productive work in the shtetl, in which was heard the pain of slavery, the groan of weariness and dejection, of pain and suffering.

The yeshiva pushed its way into its own ghetto, in the old house of study, between the thick, grey old walls hung with spider webs, from which emanated an odor.

A mass of yeshiva students. Not one from the shtetl itself; all arrive from near and far and always remain strangers here. They are still young, but their faces are darkened, their foreheads wrinkled and they look much older than they are. Small hairs first begin to sprout on the older ones, on the chin, under the nose and on the jaws, from which hand curled peyos [side curls] that grow from under the creased, dirtied velvet hats that are never taken off, not day or night; not in sleep and not when awake, once-black kapotes [long coats] looking as if they have turned green hang on the body like a sack.

He [the yeshiva student] lives in the old house of study. The furniture of the yeshiva students' residence – long, heavy tables covered with the wax drippings from the candles, with burned in old black stains, and long, hard benches worn out from sitting. He sleeps in the old house of study on the hard bench or on the floor and he eats teg [meals provided each day by residents of the shtetl]: one day a week with one head of a household in the shtetl and another day with a second head of a household. He must provide for the seven days of eating at seven heads of a household. And if he is left with one day not provided for – he goes hungry for the day. No one is forced to give food for a teg. One does it of his own will; it is considered a mitzvah to maintain the soul of a yeshiva student, for his spending day and night studying the Torah, which to the simple Jew was considered to be serving God, that is, doing a sacred work that everyone is obliged to do, but which not everyone can.

The yeshiva thus was maintained in the old house of study with needs, without funds and without concerns about living. And the yeshiva students sat at the tables covered with tallow from dawn until into the night, day in and day out and wrinkled their brows and racked their brains over the yellowed and creased pages of the large gemaras and an anguished song was heard like a touchingly sincere cry from a group that longs for, that suffers, that tortures itself, that torments itself and that struggles and that cries in a chorus with a haunting melody and which resounds from the city's symphony of labor:

"May ko mashme lon?" – What does this teach me?...

The yeshiva student only crawls out of the house of study to eat from the teg. He does not speak to anyone while eating; he does not look at anyone. He sits at the table and yet he is not there; where is he? What does he do in life? Does he go anywhere? What will be the purpose? Perhaps he will marry? Become a son-in-law oyf kest [financial support given while he studies Torah]. He will see the bride on the day of the wedding, after fasting, after the khuppah [wedding ceremony]... Who will be his in-laws? His father-in-law? How long will he be oyf kest?... Belchatow is a shtetl of artisans. A local head of a household would rather have his daughter's husband with a ready trade; what will be his fate?...

* * *

The life of a child, of childhood, of the young – how did it seem?

It is difficult, very difficult to remember something that almost never was. If the child was a girl, from behind the environment of her mother's apron she only heard, "It is forbidden" and she was frightened, held constantly in fear of a gentile, of a corpse, of a "legendary monster" and of God and she was frightened of all kinds of punishments. If it was a boy, that is, a little Jew, he had to endure the kheder during his childhood years.

The kheder – this was the primitive residence of the melamed [religious primary school teacher], where hygiene had no entry and which was a prison for the child in which he was held from the morning until night. Thus, day after day, week after week, year after year, the melamed appeared before one's eyes in the form of a flogger.

The melamed took to the teaching profession because he did not have anything else, because he did not want to do something else; because he knew that this was a trade that he did not have to know, or because he wanted to be employed with a sacred thing, with prayer and he knew that all that was need was a pointer made of fish bone and mainly a small whip with thick leather straps that would cause pain when it slapped, and the melamed, who the children had to call "rebbe," loved, had pleasure from whipping bare flesh.

They did not learn Yiddish, no Hebrew; they did not learn to write, to read, to do arithmetic; they did not learn any history, no geography, no natural science and God protected them from astronomy... The kheder did not know of any education, and, besides the kheder, the Jewish child did not go anywhere. They "crammed" Hebrew with "diacritic marks for pronunciation" in the kheder. They learned "the Holy language" [the Hebrew of the Torah] which the "rebbe" often did not himself know. This was cramming words that they did not understand, just as the praying, the other prayers and the sections of the khumash [Torah] that they "learned" in the same way, in which the subject was not understood and because of which the child was transformed into a little Jew, languishing his childhood years in the kheder.

The shtetl did not know of childhood. A childhood did not have where, when and how to be expressed. The young ones (there was no such concept then) left for an apprenticeship during which his young years were blackened and he became embittered. In a few cases, the young boys continued their education with a gemara-melamed, but there is no childhood for the boy before and after his bar mitzvah in learning gemara, and when his father blesses him with the "Borukh she-ptornai" [Blessed be He who has freed me], he himself now has to carry on his back the 613 mitzvos [commandments].

There was no time for "childhood sins." During the week, after 18-hour workdays, one fell down asleep, dead tired. On Shabbos and on holidays a considerable part of the day passed at meals at which there also was singing and the recitation of Psalms. Only during the several Shabbos afternoon hours, a small portion of the Jewish male young people, the so-called young weavers, young tailors, young blacksmiths and other such young people amused themselves at the open places around the shtetl in primitive, naïve play, or went to the surrounding meadows, into the forests, picked fruits in the orchard, or fought with the gentile boys.

* * *

The piety, the fanaticism and the entire ghetto-Jewish way of life, the [fact] that the poor only spoke "jargon" [derogatory description of Yiddish], were religious, did not subscribe to any culture – there was no word and no concept of it [culture] in the Jewish shtetl at that time and [no culture] to write about here at this time.

There was no education in modernity, in the free, objective and worldly sense; there was no school and there was no sort of education. There dared not be; the religious way of life prohibited it. There was no literature and there was no press; there was no theater system, except at Purim and there were no concerts, except the playing by the klezmer [traditional Jewish musicians], who only played at weddings.

Yet Belchatow, as a Jewish working shtetl, as was the neighboring shtetele Grocholice, was not culturally backwards compared to the Jewish shtetl of Poland, but stood with a forward step facing the rise of a new Jewish life in a Poland of earlier times.

With the arrival of our century, the 20th, that our amiable Belchatow also did not escape, the Jewish shtetl removed its own ghetto, opened its windows to the world; stood up and joined in the new life that came with the revolutionary movement of the Jewish worker and intelligentsia in Poland, in step with the general movement for freedom.

———

[Page 102]

# Belchatow that Lives in My Memory

## by Yosef Reich

## Translated from the Yiddish by the late Morris Horowitz

## Translation donated by Lisa Webne-Behrman

Belchatow which lives in my memory, Belchatow was distinguished from its surrounding towns in several ways. However, one of its most distinguished characteristics, wherein it is different from cities like Stetzov, Vidava, Tilev, Zeler, Piotrikow, was that Belchatow was more Jewish. It is quite noteworthy that most of the non-Jews of the city communicated with the Jewish people in Yiddish. Therefore most of the Jews of Belchatow were poor conversers in Polish.

The Jews of Belchatow lived in peace with their non-Jewish neighbors, but it was not at the expense of unwarranted expediencies - like refraining from reacting against injustices, lest it displease their non-Jewish neighbors. The Belchatow Jews were proud Jews conscious of their rights and of their status of being first class citizens.

There are some events which are deeply impressed upon my memory and I wish to record several of them, especially those which show how the Jews of Belchatow stood up for their human dignity.

The story which I am about to tell I heard when I was yet a small child.

The Chief Officer of our town (equivalent to an American mayor) was replaced by a harsh Russian. This new officer was from Siberia. He clung relentlessly to the harshest interpretation of the municipal ordinances. He was very stubborn and all negotiations to divert him from issuing his strict edicts had failed. In order to show his authority this Siberian despot made life for the Jewish inhabitants of Belchatow extremely difficult. In their effort to free themselves from near bondage, the Jews of Belchatow had devised a resourceful idea in combating their dictator.

Once on a dark evening some strong hands got a hold of their oppressor, there was a sack over his head and dragged him down to a deep well which was near the mikvah, the Jewish ritual bath house. There they told him as follows: "if you change your tactics and become more human, you will lack nothing among the Jewish people, you will have plenty of vodka, gifillte fish, chicken soup and chicken necks, but if you persist to remain as brutal as ever,

you will be thrown into this well and no one will ever know your whereabouts."

After this lesson this man became as soft as butter and Belchatow lived in peace.

In 1905 Belchatow was all shaken by the revolutionary spirit which prevailed in Russia at that time. Strikes street demonstrations and the display of red flags were common occurrences of the day. Jewish youngsters were prominent participants in the revolutionary movement. Carrying loaded guns they would shoot at government officials. The police were in mortal fear of these revolutionaries and instead of resisting them, they were hiding.

I distinctly remember one such revolutionary demonstration. I was then a child attending cheder. My teacher was Berish the Melamed. What I am about to tell happened several months past the holiday of Sukkoth, when the days are short and the nights are long. We used to Judy in cheder, by the light of small kerosene lamps. One day my regular teacher became sick and his substitute was his son, Elie, who had a self-inflicted chopped off tip of his right thumb. He did it in order to avoid service in the Russian army. Yet with this disfigured thumb he would nick us whenever we dared to look out of the window instead of looking into our books.

When on that day I came home for lunch from cheder, my brother Shmuel told me that a demonstration would take place in that same day. Shmuel was a member of the P. P. S. and he never moved any place without a loaded revolver.

It was evident that on that day I had not been at peace in cheder. I kept looking out of the window to see whether the demonstration had started. It was already pitch dark and the kerosene lamp was burning and spreading its dim light at the open books of the Talmud in which some of the students were absorbed. I found an alibi and asked to be excused from the rest of the students. All of a sudden I began to notice lights of lanterns approaching, it was indeed a demonstration, a sensuous and a quick one with flags draped in black. When I saw that, I hastily opened the door of the cheder and announced in great excitement, "they are coming." My rabbi did not like my actions at all. On the following day I was severely punished and received a torrid slap on my face.

This is how Belchatow had taken part in the revolution. Belchatow was one of the cities high on the list of the insurrectionists and had, therefore, been singled out for suppression. From time to time the government would send into Belchatow about 15 selected Cossacks, who would roam the streets on their swift horses and with heavy clubs in their hands would beat up all suspicious people. This evil practice was especially executed on Friday evenings when young Jewish people would go out for walks.

I remember that on one Friday evening they arrived drunk and ordered all to raise their hands and they began to beat them brutally with their clubs. The streets were then quickly evacuated and people began to hide in their homes, locking the doors behind them and looking through the crevices of the closed shutters outside.

While this was happening a sixteen-year-old weaver was walking on the sidewalk erect and unafraid, facing the Cossacks. When the Cossacks saw the young man they began to scream wildly ordering him to raise his hands, but the teenager whose name was Moishe, did not mind them and kept on walking with his hands in his pockets. He cursed them and looked them straight in their eyes and exclaimed "I am not going to raise my hands." The people who saw and heard this, while looking through the crevices of their shutters, were mortally afraid. What was going to happen to Moishe they wondered fearfully. But before the Cossacks were able to do anything to Moishe, he got mixed up with the crowd in the street and the Cossacks were not able to find him.

Yitzchak Uri, the son of Leibush, also a weaver was not that lucky. One day the Cossacks spotted him and ordered him to raise his hands, but he defied them and showed them his behind. The Cossacks caught him, they beat him up brutally and then they exiled him to Siberia.

However, this heroic and fearless resistance of the young weavers, instilled some heroics in the hearts of the rank and file who also began to rebel against their merciless task masters. It raised the morale of the people, the authority of the oppressors was downgraded and this is what had eventually happened:

During one night when the Cossacks had ostensibly slept in peace in Kasteletzkis' house - a group of fearless revolutionaries overpowered the guard on duty. Another group broke into the house and took away the uniforms of the sleeping Cossacks and also their arms. The young revolutionaries then got dressed in the cossack's clothes and ran away riding on their horses. When the Cossacks awakened they found themselves without clothes, horses or arms.

Belchatow had no river, unlike its neighboring town Sterzer, but close to Belchatow there is the village, Binkoff. There, there is a clean transparent lake. In this lake young people used to bathe and learn to swim. On Friday afternoon elderly Jews would come to the lake to bathe in honor of the Sabbath.

The gentiles of the village did not like it and had tried many times to chase us away from there. As a result, many battles ensued between the Jews and the gentiles. We received blows and we landed blows, but they were not able to chase us away.

"New Way" was one of the widest and most beautiful streets of Belchatow. It was surrounded by grass and trees. Summer evenings and on Sabbaths the young generation used to constantly walk on this street, girls separately and boys separately. One could, however, notice the exchange of winks and hear some suggestive words between the boys and girls. When it became dark the males and females began to mix with one another.

Many of the anti-Semitic Poles could not stand our well-being of those pleasant evenings. One day a group of chauvinistic Poles from a nearby village attacked the hikers of the "New Way," some of them attacked with pointed knives. One young boy by the name of Meyer did not seem to be frightened. He faced one of the hooligans who threatened him with a knife, skillfully dispossessed him of the knife and stabbed him with his own knife, wounding him seriously,

A trial was held in Petrikoff and Meyer was exonerated. The court had ruled that Meyer acted in self-defense and was therefore freed. From that day on the hikes on "New Way" continued with much less intervention.

In the year 1911, Belchatow was captured by the Austrians. Prior to the entry of the Austrians, Belchatow was for awhile without a government. No harm was done to anyone, although there was no one to preserve order in the city.

However, this ideal situation did not last very long. Many idle goyim and drunks had felt that this was ---a good opportunity to plunder Jewish possessions. So they let out on such a course with the Chief of the Firemen at the head. His name was Nagurski. This "citizen militia" began to terrorize the Jewish Community in an effort to extort money from them. As time went on they became more intolerant. They arrested many Jews, they made their own laws, and they made it difficult for Jewish merchants to do business.

These gangsters grew more confident after their initial successes. The hooligans took the Jewish patience as a weakness. They became bolder with every passing day. Their motto was "beat the Jews".

At first Jewish leaders tried to intercede. Among them were a few aged and respected Jews. They were Kalman Skarpes and Tzemach, the Rabbis of Belchatow. They were able to somewhat appease "the rulers of the mob" and cool their heated tempers.

Rabbi Tzemach was the son of the Rabbi of Walbish and he caused some conflicts in the city when he took over the mantle of the rabbinate. The Hassidim of Ger had it against him because he did not get married through a matchmaker, but got married through love, just like the goyim. They never forgave him for that. Rabbi Tzemach was a tall, well, and healthily built person with powerful shoulders. He got a hold of the chief of the mob and shook him up like a lulav. Although the mob was more numerous than the Jews congregated, they nevertheless began to withdraw while Rabbi Tzemach held onto their chief. One of the mob even began to beg the Rabbi to let the chief go, but the Rabbi held on to Mr. Nagurski, the chief, and continually rebuked him for the evil which he had been doing to innocent people.

On that very evening a meeting was held in the field near the river. The meeting consisted of mostly young people. They decided to make an end to the wicked rule of the self-proclaimed militia.

All vowed that they would not go home until all the arrested Jewswere freed from prison. Hence, a march toward the doors of the prison began when they approached the gate of the prison. They ordered the guard to open the doors, but he refused. However, among the group was the strong Shimon, the cake-baker. He took hold of the guard, lifted him up high and warned him "either you open the doors or you will be thrown to the ground with your head down". The guard became immediately submissive, he opened the doors and all prisoners were freed.

Hence we lived up to our vow. The prisoners came home and the militia went out of existence.

[Page 110]

# On the Border of Two Centuries

### by By Zalman Pudlowski

### Translated from the Yiddish by Gloria Berkenstat Freund

[with comments in brackets]

On the border of two centuries, the 19th and 20th, when Jewish life in Eastern Europe was marked by strong national and social storms - something began to stir in the standing swamps that had been unresponsive to Jewish need and poverty in Belchatow.

Those dominant in shtetl [town] life wanted to be (and often were) the influential ones in the Gerer shtibl [small, usually one room prayer house]. They were mostly manufacturers and their assistants. The largest majority of the manufacturers in the shtetl prayed in the Gerer shtibl. Two families simply flooded the shtetl with manufacturers. Chaim Tusk, one of the esteemed Gerer Hasidim, raised a generation of manufacturers. Each son - a manufacturer, each daughter - a manufacturer, grandsons and great grandsons - all manufacturers. Another generation of manufacturers was raised by Yeshayahu Szrage. The two families had a say about the appearance of Jewish life in Belchatow through the Gerer shtibl. The Gerer shtibl had many others among them, manufacturers, merchants, teachers and Hasidic kest [1] sons-in-law.

Working people were rarely found in the shtibl. There was felt among the Gerer a certain scorn for the men who worked for a living. For matches for their daughters, the Gerer chose the greatest ne'er-do-wells before a working man. The poorest of the Gerer endeavored to ensure that their children not become workers. In the spiritual-religious sense, the Gerer were truly much higher. There were many great scholars among them, shrewd people, zealots who were successful over the years in making a siyum-haShas [celebration for the conclusion of the seven-year cycle of Talmud study]. In the morning and in the evenings many Hasidim sat and studied. And the praying had an entirely different sense. At best, it mirrored the Days of Awe [from Rosh Hashanah to Yom Kippur]. Those who stood in front of the pulpit did not excel in vocal music, but the praying had a particular zest. When Alter Bresler (Alter the shoykhet [ritual slaughterer]), who recited the Shacharit [morning prayers], began with HaMelekh [the King] it really touched one. Yeshayahu Szrage, who recited the Musaf prayers [the prayer service on Shabbos added to the morning prayers], prayed with sweetness. A specific mood reigned in the shtib on Erev Yom Kippur [the eve of Yom Kippur] at Kol Nidre ["All vows" - the opening Yom Kippur prayer] and the next day at Ne'ilah [concluding Yom Kippur prayer]. It truly felt as if we were standing for a very important spiritual mission. It was not that they wanted to ask for or secure their lives, health, income and other good things; this could have been fulfilled with prayer in the synagogue and beis-hamedrash [house of prayer], in other shtiblekh and groups. Something higher, mystical lay in the Gerer shtibl during the Days of Awe and hovered in the air.

The Gerer wanted to impose their stamp on Jewish life. The most important Jewish problems in the shtetl, around which quarrels would take place, were religious, such as: the Rabbi, shoykhet [ritual slaughterer], synagogue, khevre-kadishe [burial society] and the like.

The necessity of building a new synagogue was felt in the shtetl in the second half of the 19th century. The old, wooden synagogue was in such a condition that it was impossible to continue to use it. The synagogue was sealed by the police. Those praying in the synagogue had to move to the beis-hamedrash. The beis-hamedrash could not accommodate all of the synagogue worshippers. Therefore, some had to go to the [prayer houses] of societies. Or prevail upon Hasidic shtiblekh. It was worse for the women who did not have the option of taking part in prayer when the synagogue was sealed. Some of them, the very pious, prayed under the open sky, under the beis-hamedrash windows.

A movement to build a new, solid brick synagogue was created in the shtetl. The Jewish population approached the synagogue building plan with enthusiasm. The Gerer Hasidim were opposed. Why this was so was impossible to imagine. They hindered the carrying out of the plan with significant means, by refusing to assess themselves for the building fund although they were the wealthiest segment of the Jewish population. They also lay stones in the road in other ways. However, they did not succeed. The idea of building the synagogue gripped all of Jewish Belchatow. At the head of the movement stood the very energetic dozor [synagogue warden], Moshke Grynberg. He moved heaven and earth to realize the plan. Significant help came from the side of Shmuel Zylberstang (Shmuel Kliker); wood for the synagogue came from the Kliker Forests. In addition to all of the wood, which he gave for the building and the internal accommodations, he also gave a significant sum of money as an assessment.

**The Talmud Torah**

**The Belchatow Synagogue**

The fire from the quarrels had not yet cooled and new struggles were underway. The old Rabbi Konsztajn died. Who should be his successor? Who should occupy the rabbinical throne? The Gerer strongly wanted him to be one of their own from the Gerer circles, but the Aleksanderer Hasidim - the Gerers' eternal opponent - said, absolutely not! The Aleksanderer Hasidim surely could not have competed with the Gerer without the help that they received from the synagogue Jews and Jews from the House of Prayer and from the dozor, Moshke Grynberg. [2]

The coalition of the Gerer opponents was victorious; Moshe Eli Birnbaum, not a Gerer follower, came to Belchatow as rabbi. However, the Gerer did not lay down their weapons; they did everything to annoy the rabbi. They did not recognize him. They did not address him with the title rabbi, but called him by his name, Moshe Eli. All of this would not have mattered if the Gerer had not bent and brought into their circle the dozor, Moshe Grynberg. They simply reconciled with him. Then they spread rumors about the rabbi about immoral conduct that is not appropriate for a rabbi and the rabbi ran away from Belchatow.

The new Rabbi, Shlomo Baron (the noble Braun), known as the Lukower Rabbi, was already taken to heart by the Gerer. The rabbi excelled in several areas. He erected a large yeshiva with many young men who came from various areas of Poland.

Learning was heard from the yeshiva students from morning until late at night. The gemara melody that came from the small beis-hamedrash alley carried across the shtetl. The melody was sung automatically in speaking, in arguing; the melody was used as well while trading. The melody was even absorbed by the peasants when they came into contact with Jews. Scores of young men filled the house of prayer and the religious court, sitting around a table and studying aloud and rocking non-stop back and forth. The Belchatow poor fed the young men by giving them food for "teg," although they themselves were hungry. [3] They took from their own mouths and gave the yeshiva students food. This was the result of the rabbi's work. The rabbi also tried to influence Jewish religious life by other means. He sought to restrain the young. He would very often give moralizing sermons in the house of prayer. This would take place Shabbos after the midday nap. Jews would enter the house of prayer and the rabbi would give his moralizing sermon on the platform. In special cases, the Jews were called to the synagogue and the rabbi spoke to men and women.

When the rabbi left Belchatow, new quarrels appeared on the horizon.

It was not long before the quarrel started. Aleksanderer and Wolborzer Hasidim and a large number of those who prayed in the synagogue and house of prayer (or as they were called, "simple Jews") decided to bring the Wolborzer Rebbe's son, Zemach Tornheim, as the rabbi in Belchatow. That alone, that the candidate proposed as the new rabbi was so disliked by the Gerer coalition in all likelihood had to provoke the Gerers' opposition. To justify their opposition, the Gerer sent two scholars to question the rabbi. As the questioning established, the candidate for the rabbinical seat was too weak in learning. The Gerer decided that in no case would they permit the Wolborzer Rebbe's son to take the Belchatow rabbinical seat.

Nevertheless, the son of the Wolborzer Rebbe became rabbi and the Wolborzer Rebbe himself brought him [to Belchatow]. The old Wolborzer Rebbe, who came along to settle his son on the Belchatow rabbinical throne, practiced Hasidus, "gefirt tish" [4] and covered the expenses, it should be understood, by accepting kvitlekh [notes asking for prayers for good health, children, etc.] with payments for advice. His followers arranged parades in honor of the rebbe. It was crowded at the entryway to the rebbe. People came to the rebbe from neighboring shtetlekh and villages. Belchatow was then in turmoil. The Gerer mocked the parade and the pushing toward the rebbe with kvitlekh.

The rabbi remained and the Gerer Hasidim had a longer and embittered quarrel as their goal. The Gerer separated themselves as a separate religious group, with its own rabbi, shoykhet and butcher shops. Everything on the other side was declared unkosher. They became enemies and did not go to each other's celebrations. Women at the head of their homes could not bring pots to their neighbors who belonged to the other side. Many comic situations occurred, particularly when in-laws belonged to the opposing sides.

The Gerer obtained permission from the regime allowing birth, marriage and death events to also be recorded by their rabbi. Belchatow's shtarke [strong ones, connotes tough guys], who stood on the rabbi's side in the struggle, also had a say and several Gerer had their bones broken.

The struggle was a very long one; it appeared that the war would last forever, but in time the crowd grew tired. Only a few extreme, stubborn Gerer Hasidim did not want to give up the struggle. When Berl the shoykhet [ritual slaughterer - shoykhetim is the plural form] had to stop slaughtering because of his age, new fights began about shoykhetim. The same when Hershl the shoykhet had to lay down his khalef [slaughtering knife]. The struggle rarely stopped. The Gerer were always more firm, spiritual, in the religious sense, much higher and they all stood on principled ground in the quarrels.

After the earlier years, the young Jewish people in Belchatow were unsatisfied with the monotony of their lives. They wanted something new. This found its expression in the creation of a "society" of young men [khevre bokhurim]. The society of young men did not do any great things and nothing especially new took place in their lives. Yet, just praying separately and sometimes spending time together was something new.

Hasidic young men did not group themselves in the society - they were as if forged to the Gerer shtibl. The young artisans also were grouped in the society; Yisroel Moshe Benczkowski, Manele Piotrkowski and others from this segment were particularly active. The society did not show any great activity and, therefore, it could not have a long life. It finally fell apart.

The above mentioned khevre bokhurim was followed by a second khevre bokhurim that was similar to the first. The new khevre bokhurim, just as the first, prayed together and spent time together. However, they tried to be more active and bring innovations to the young. First of all, the group began to carry out an organizational life. Joining the group, one had to pay a registration fee as well as a monthly payment. The program of the group was to help those suffering from need. A large undertaking that gave the group esteem was the group arranging the marriage of a begging couple. The couple was dressed and given shoes; a wedding was arranged with music and a wedding meal. The entire shtetl, kith and kin, rejoiced. Organizing the wedding was a great event in the shtetl at that time. But the achievement in which the group took pride was the building of a fence for the recently built synagogue. All of the activities were not enough to keep the group in existence. New winds were already in the air. It was too little for the storms of the time. Active in this group were: Lipman Benczkowski, Josef Gliksman, Itshe Piotrkowski and others.

Belchatow also had few shtarke who were respected and who also began to be [socially] aware. These were the wagon drivers, butchers and so on. Very often they would have wars among themselves, usually for competitive reasons. It also occurred that their physical strength had general uses. Thus once they got even with groups of peasants who, led by a dark hand, on an erev Yom Kippur [eve of Yom Kippur] at the end of the last century [19th century], came to the shtetl intending to go on a spree. They waited outside the shtetl for the peasants who were well battered.

There was a case when the Szczercow Poles carried out a "familiar" judgment on one Dovid Feiffer. They murdered him because he was supposed to have set fire to peasant stables. As revenge, the Belchatow butchers and wagon drivers got even with the Szczerców Polish butchers who came to the market in Belchatow. It could also occur on a market day that peasants would want to create a scandal, particularly with horse trading. All such attempts were suppressed and often bruised peasants were driven home.

On the eve of the army conscription times, the village and city Polish young people, being tipsy, wanted to go on a spree. Once, when such conscripts attacked Yeshayahu Szimkewicz (Misziker's), scores of Poles were beaten by Jewish butchers.

There were also cases of non-ethical conduct on the part of the "strong ones," such as takers of pretenzie-gelt [demands of money], lewdness, denunciations - but this was on such a small scale that it was not apparent.

Obtaining money through cheating in the throwing of three cards occupied a large spot. The victims were mainly peasants. This chiefly took place on market days.

A small number of workers were drawn into not so nice deeds. Without doubt it was a result of the bitter economic situation in which a large number of Belchatowers found themselves.

The economic situation of the Belchatow Jews was not so very good. Several dozen competing food shops were located in the shtetl; the owners of a few shops were relatives of the manufacturers, and they received workers with notes from the manufacturers as customers and had better luck. There were also several large shops whose owners brought goods in large quantities from Piotrkow and Lodz. The merchants sold to other smaller shops as well as directly to the customers. There were also grain merchants, cloth shops, iron shops, haberdashery businesses, bakeries, butchers and others.

There were also market merchants who would sell their goods at the market twice a week: Monday and Friday. A number of the market merchants went to the surrounding shtetlekh when there were market days in those shtetlekh.

All kinds of goods were arranged in the market: baked goods and roasted meats to herring and other articles of food, as well as sweets, various manufactured goods, all kinds of men's and women's clothing, linens, hats, shoes, leather, dishes, furniture, horses, cattle, pigs, poultry, eggs and other things.

The much larger segment of the Jewish merchants was not wealthy and lived labored lives. Commerce mainly was done on credit; payments were made with promissory notes. The entire life of an average Belchatow merchant consisted of seeking loans, loans with very little interest from the loan fund of Doctor Radczewicz, later from the loan fund of Alter Bornsztajn (the fat Alter). They were also forced to take money from private usurers who would discount promissory notes.

Many of the merchants went bankrupt. But this did not mean that he stopped doing his business. It took a little time until such a merchant came to terms with his creditors to pay a part of his debts in installment payments. The remaining [debts] were cancelled and trade further continued.

There were also artisans who worked principally for the city population. These were: tailors, seamstresses, underwear seamstresses, shoemakers, quilters and other trades. But these were not the main sources from which the Belchatow population drew its livelihood. The main employment of the shtetl and partly in the surrounding area, was work in the textile industry.

In the greater number of houses of Belchatow Jews, and not only Jews, the noise of the banging weaving stools reigned from early morning until very late into the night. People at the weaving stools did not only work with their hands and feet, but their entire body quivered - all of their limbs worked. The earnings for a weaver were from two to three rubles a week. There were weavers who earned more, but these were exceptions. Usually a weaving house was filled with weaving stools. When they wanted to go to sleep, it was necessary to crawl through the stools to the bed. If there was work, everyone in the house, from small to large, worked. The family members, who did not work as weavers, spooled or drove a small wheel.

There also would be apprentices employed in the weaving factory. These were in large part young men from other places. They were extraordinarily exploited. Matz [a taste] was a supplement to a weaver's earnings. This was legal robbery. The manufacturers knew of this very well. The weaver would remove a certain amount of thread from the spool (gengl) as well as some from the loom and sell to merchants who were called Matzar. Buyers of mats would often present material to the manufacturer that had originated with the same manufacturer. The weaver lived from all of this in indescribable poverty.

In addition to the weavers there were still others who were employed around the weaving factories. First of all, the wagon drivers. This was a group of men who had their own goods wagons and horses and they also hired people to work for them. Twice a week the wagon drivers would load spun yarn in Lodz and bring it to Belchatow and twice a week the same wagon drivers would load the finished goods in Belchatow and return it to Lodz.

The dyer or the bleacher would take the wool that was brought from Lodz. Dozens of packs of yarn, which would first be cooked, were thrown into large boilers; then dyed or bleached.

The yarn was taken from the dyers by the treyberin [women who carried the yarn]. These were [known as] the Belchatow parier [outcasts]. Usually a worker in the textile industry earned little. A Belchatower earned even less. The refiners earned the least; their earnings were so picayune that it had almost no influence on the price of the goods. It was mostly village women who carried the yarn. The treyberin would also have a "taste," or taking off a little of the wool. The "taste" compensated a little for the very poorly paid work. The refiners had to starch the thread to strengthen it. The manufacturer gave flour, paraffin and clay to the refiners for this purpose. It is self evident that the refiners took some of the flour for themselves. The manufacturers waged a struggle against the "thefts" by the refiners and they sprinkled the flour with kerosene so that the refiners could not use it.

The cutters represented their own uncharacteristic group. These were respected men of whom many were Hasidim; some even worshipped in the Gerer shtibl. Cutting was not considered an ordinary trade. Although the work was physical, it was given respect. The cutters were the "aristocrats" of occupations. The work was better paid, not only in Belchatow, but in the entire Lodz textile area. There were two categories of cutters in Belchatow: there was a primary cutter with each manufacturer who usually was a relative of the manufacturer or a close friend. The remaining second class [cutters] worked for less money and the primary cutter received the difference. Not all of those in the second category received the same amount. The wage was regulated separately for each. The cutters, who received from the carriers goods spun for the weavers, examined them in the manufacturer's special cutting room. The tools, such as pattern holders, spools of thread to spin, spool sticks, cutting boards and the like, belonged to the manufacturers. The cutters were the manufacturers' trusted men. They did not only inform the manufacturer about the length of the thread on the wound spools which the refiners had brought, they also told of the mood among the weavers. Almost all of the cutters were Jewish. Jews also were the product inspectors and winders. The work of the product inspectors took place in their own houses. The product inspectors had helpers who received very little for their work. The product inspectors also dealt with containers and pages. Each product inspector had his manufacturer who gave him work.

The work was only partly carried out in Belchatow. The thread was spun and finished in the apreton [place with the process was completed] in Lodz. The greater number of Belchatow manufacturers were that in name only because in truth they were only middlemen or jobbers (contractors). Some were partners in Lodz enterprises. The Belchatow manufacturers were, except for individual exceptions, all Jews. Chaim Tusk and his sons and daughters, Yeshayahu Szrage, Henekh Szrage, Mendl Wolfowicz, Welwl Ferszter, Gruber [fat] Shaul, Meir Moshe Fajwisz, Avraham Mendl and Josl Warszawski, Peretz Freitag, Ragodzinski, Shwartser [dark or black] Shlomo, Makawer, Mikhal Dozor, Chaim Mendl Wiszlicki, Mikhal Avigdor Pitowski, Shmuel Yankl Kaszub, Ahron Flacek Tomaszower, Feywel Ambordiks and others.

Another hardship made things difficult for the Belchatow weavers. This was the payment for the work. They had to pay on Friday afternoon. The weavers worked all of Thursday night in order to supply the merchandise and receive the paid out wages. The workers assembled at the manufacturer's on Friday afternoon waiting for his arrival from Lodz with money for payments. It often happened that the manufacturer was late or did not come at all for Shabbos. It also happened that the manufacturer came without money. Also, more than once, the manufacturer hid and his wife said that her husband had not come. The worker went home without money after waiting hours. The worker's family was desperate because they were in debt over their heads; not receiving payment meant a catastrophe. In addition to the baker, butcher and storekeeper not giving any more credit, they would be abusive, too. Such Shabbosim [Shabbats] were transformed into sad days. However, this was only half the trouble.

The other half was the receipt system. The manufacturer paid for work with a receipt for a certain shop instead of with money. Often the merchant was a relative of the manufacturer. The products [bought with] a receipt were expensive and worse. In general the worker was forced to take the goods that the storekeeper had. The weavers were dissatisfied with the receipts; the weavers' wives particularly hated the receipts. However, the merchant who had a large number of customers profited and earned a nice living. The manufacturer also profited. He usually paid the storekeeper with a promissory note when taking the receipts. Paying with receipts was illegal. The history of receipts even reached court, manufacturers were threatened with jail, but the existing order did not cause too much trouble for the manufacturers, even the Jewish ones. The police, the bailiff, even the judge, looked away. All offenses were washed clean with bribes.

The bad economic situation, the inhuman living conditions had to awaken feelings of protest. The voices found an echo in the beis-hamedrash where weavers would come to pray. Between Minkhah-Maariv [afternoon and evening prayers] the weavers spoke to each other from their hearts. It was even more so on Shabbos after the midday sleep. Then the other group of weavers gathered in the beis-hamedrash. At the same time they would talk about the dark luck of the weavers and, in speaking, the idea of a strike occurred. A large number seized on [the idea]. But at home, in the dark weaving rooms, the enthusiasm for the strike evaporated. The wives argued: from where will we get what we need to maintain the soul? But the miserable conditions meant that such a protest would come and it actually was decided in the beis-hamedrash. On a beautiful early morning, spinning wheels being carried with the tools dangling and finished goods wrapped around them were seen everywhere. Whole trees were laid down in front of the doors of the manufacturers. The impact of the protest was very strong. Everyone in the city admitted that the weavers were correct. But the situation did not improve as a result. The workers were to return to work with the same sorrowful conditions because of their severe need. A second act of protest - a stronger one - was carried out by the weavers against the manufacturers, when the Gerer rebbe, the author of Sfas Emes [The Language of Truth], was ill. The Belchatow Jews were then called to the synagogue to pray for the health and the life of the rebbe. The synagogue was packed with Jews, among whom were found many manufacturers. Upon leaving the synagogue, a number of manufacturers were attacked by young weavers who considerably beat the manufacturers. Only those who had behaved brutally in relation to the workers received blows. The workers were dissatisfied not only with the manufacturers who were in the synagogue; they also went to the houses of those who were not in the synagogue and beat them in their own homes.

Attempts were made to disrupt the distribution of the work to the village by dousing the material with vitriol [sulfuric acid]. When the manufacturers gave out the material quietly so that the Jewish weavers would not notice, there were shearers who made it known when such village weavers came for material. The manufacturers then turned to the regime. An investigative commission of police and court representatives came from Piotrkow.

The Jewish weavers, who were under suspicion of using vitriol to burn the material which the village weavers were taking from the city, were summoned to the commission. But nothing came of this. The arrival of a stormy time was felt in the air. At that time a Wage Weavers Union arose in Belchatow. Political, revolutionary work began among the young.

One of those who were the first to be infected with revolutionary ideas was Mikhal Josef's son, Chaim Shlomo, a young man, a weaver. As young as he was he had already had the opportunity to have a conflict with the Lukower Rabbi on a Shabbos daybreak. It was at Uzer Czuchowski (Migac), near the beis-hamedrash, and the rabbi and young people would meet, spending time together sometimes with a glass of whiskey and snacks. Once the rabbi appeared and began to scold the youths; why are they not praying. Chaim Shlomo was not afraid and boldly answered the rabbi's shouting.

Chaim Shlomo did not let Belchatow rest. He was drawn to Chojny, Rokicie, Lodz. In Lodz he came into a Bundist environment; there he became acquainted with a young man, a weaver, whose name was Berl Binem, with whom he became a friend. In a conversation, Chaim Shlomo told Berl Binem about the situation in Belchatow. They agreed to go to Belchatow to do something to better the situation of the Belchatow worker. Both came to Belchatow and began to spread Bundist ideas. They had quick success. Supporters were acquired and the group grew. The meetings took place in private houses, sometimes on the Neyem Weg [New Road] or in other places.

Among the first occupied by revolutionary activity were Avraham Machabajnski (Yeshaya's son, later names: Shwartser [black] Avraham, Avraham Black), Fishl Meir Weiss (Perl of Bosterin's son), as well as his sister, the Gela [blond] Chana took part. Moshe Bornsztajn (Kaiser), Avraham Yankl Przybylski (Sabran), Avraham Szmulewicz (Prowiser), Chona Itsik (Tsalikl's [son]) and still others.

A two-fold program of activities was undertaken. Political and economic struggle. With the several strasznikes [guards] who were in the shtetl we could do even more than we wanted. For a small payment we could bribe the police and all of the clerks.

The second form of struggle - the economic or professional movement, seized everyone who lived through their work. Everyone wanted to better their economic situation. Better living conditions was the call to which everyone responded. A Bundist organization was created and a textile union that was led by a Bundist.

The activity of the organizations was very popular and it was possible to feel this. All of the working young were drawn into the organizations. The apprentices were also drawn into the "small Bund." Moshe Kopl, a young man who was a relative of Yoske Melamed [teacher], led the apprentices. Besides verbal propaganda at the birzhe [market], on the Neyem Weg and still other places, they began to use the printed word.

Newspapers, journals, brochures, appeals began to appear in Belchatow, as well as the establishment of a library.

The textile union took demands to the manufacturers about the situation of the weavers. The union organized strikes, which did not please the manufacturers.

Two intermediaries made attempts to disrupt the political and, mainly, the professional activities of the Bundists; this was the rabbi and the foremen.

The rabbi gave fiery sermons against those who wanted to destroy the world. Against the non-religious, who denied God's Torah and stood against God's will; they were going to war with God, with the Czar and with the rich Jews. The rabbi threatened excommunication for the shkotzim [5] and brats.

He particularly came out publicly against Chaim Shlomo Sztatlender and Berl Binem. The latter was then forced to leave the shtetl.

Another power, a more real one, came to help the manufacturers. This was the wagon drivers. Men of physical strength, who would have wars among themselves, now began to use their strength against the young men from the weaving stools. Slaps from the work-hardened wagon driver fists fell on the young enthusiasts who took as their goal the betterment of the living conditions of the Belchatow weavers.

The rabbi's droshus [sermons] were of no help. Berl Binem did leave Belchatow, but the organization was strengthened. And the wagon drivers were forced to stop bothering the Bundists. They received a message from the

Lodz organization and the wagon drivers were warned not to disturb the Belchatow workers and such a message was carried out without reservation at that time. On the contrary, they submitted to the demands of the Belchatow Bundists when they were called upon not to pack goods to take to Lodz.

There were various strikes then: economic, political and strikes of solidarity. A given number of the economic strikes were successful. Jewish weavers constantly had work and received better pay for the work. The situation for the journeymen and apprentices also became significantly better.

Political strikes were connected to political actions such as the 1st of May, 9th of January [6], Constitution [Day - 3rd of May] and many other cases. During a political strike, in addition to ceasing work, the stores were also closed. It looked like Shabbos in the shtetl, both Jews and Christians were forced to rest.

The strike of solidarity took place principally when there were strikes in Lodz and the Belchatow workers were called to show solidarity. Then work stopped in Belchatow and even the goods wagons did not circulate.

The Belchatow organization had other tasks in the area of solidarity. When a comrade who had been severely persecuted by the police in Lodz or in other cities announced in a letter to the organization that he was coming to Belchatow, he was provided with an apartment, work and everything he needed.

Delegates and speakers from Lodz, Piotrkow and other places used to come from time to time to help lead the political-communal activities. Many times large meetings were arranged with the help of the outside delegates. Sometimes they were on the normal exchange on the Neyem Weg or in the forest. Meetings also took place in the Gerer shtibl, the prayer house, the synagogue or other places.

Public demonstrations would also take place under the Bundist flag. Such a flag was painted by Shmuel Reich, the headstone carver. The flag was stretched out on the exchange many times. There were a few street demonstrations. The street demonstrations would march protected by an armed militia. An accident once happened during a demonstration. Leibush Makhel Landau, the militia man shot and wounded Josef Leib Feld. Turmoil arose that was immediately silenced. The wounded one was taken to receive medical help and the demonstration went on according to the planned program.

Weapons were then often demonstrated. Weapons were shown at every opportunity. Both at demonstrations and at large meetings, weapons were always seen, although outwardly it gave the impression of children's play.

The authority of the organization grew. Its effect spread beyond the ranks of its members and supporters. Very many wronged people would turn to the organization to take their part in their grievances. The organization did not always think it necessary to get involved. In many cases the organization did intervene with success.

The organization would also save young workers who entangled themselves in the underworld. Little by little organization members began to combat the underworld. Unnoticed, the young worker element began to change. An interest in political-communal problems began. The want of a book, a newspaper grew. The feeling of being politically active grew. Personal attitudes became more cultured.

Other organizations arose that were influenced by the times, which had as their purpose the support of workers' interests. A wage-weaver's union was thus created. This was an organization of weavers who had their own looms in their homes. They worked with their families and employed journeymen and apprentices. The wage-weaver's union demanded various improvements from the manufacturers. The union also defended [the weavers] against the journeymen and apprentices, who belonged to the textile unions. However, no struggles between the wage-weaver's union and the textile union took place. On the contrary, the textile union would use the premises of the wage-weavers union. But the manufacturers preferred to deal with the representatives of the wage-weaver's union. They would also pray at the wage-weaver's union. Meir and Shmuel Zaken Chajnacki, Chaim Shlomo Szpigelman, Moshe, Yisroelke's son, Mendl Piusker and others led the wage-weaver's union.

A cutters' union with its own premises, where they prayed and even studied Mishnius [Talmudic commentary] on Shabbos, also existed at the same time. The cutters unions demanded that there be only one category of cutters, that the deduction of a percentage for the first cutter be abolished. Also, the clipping of the remnants should be ended or special payment should be given for it. Notice of the account should be given every six months. The union requested that the cutters should be given an account every week. The union also demanded that the wage should be the same as the Zdunska Wola wage. The chief leaders of the union were Yakov [and] Beynis, Markewicz's children.

* * *

The changes in the communal life of Belchatow were no different than those in all the other places in Poland. Particularly, those populated by the working elements. A stormy wave was carried against everything that oppressed and repressed. The political regime was shaken. The manufacturers, the rabbi, just as the priest, did not feel it was for the best. The representatives of the regime in the shtetl were so pitiful that they were completely lost. The several "guards" did everything so that they would not be noticed. It was as if they had gone into the earth. It could be thought that they did not exist. The manufacturers also tried everything possible not to pick a fight with the workers.

In 1906 the storms that carried the wave grew weaker. Everything was as it was before. There were celebrations on the 1st of May. The only mechanized weaving factory - Freitag's factory, stopped. The marketplace [of ideas] and circles functioned normally. Yet, a small change took place - 10 Cossacks arrived in Belchatow and they requisitioned a stable from Klink. The Cossacks did not carry out any struggles in the city. They only raised their voices alongside the manufacturers.

The political and professional activity did not weaken. Only a little cautiousness was apparent in order not to give the Cossacks an opportunity to carouse. It was impossible to protect oneself completely. Once Yitzhak Zilberszac was severely beaten by the Cossacks. Moshe Kopl was arrested on the 1st of May 1907 for going through the stores asking that they close. A group of young people, among whom was Alter Naparstek, had to spend a month in Piotrkow detention A police-judicial commission came to Belchatow in connection with the forced cessation of Freitag's mechanized factory. Many Bundists and activists from the wage weaver's union were called to an investigation. They were threatened with repression.

Belchatowers, who were active in Lodz, began to feel the intensified activities of the police. Khona Yitzhak Pelcer was arrested. He was delivered to the military. After serving, he was arrested and exiled, but he escaped abroad.

Chaim Shlomo Sztatlender sat in jail in Lodz under suspicion of burning the eyes of a high police official with vitriol. Chaim Shlomo was freed under bail until his trial. However, he did not appear at his trial. He forfeited the bail and went abroad.

On a dark winter night, at the end of January 1908, large wagons of police and gendarmes arrived in Belchatow. Bunikowski, a former old watchman came with them. On the same night, searches were carried out in dozens of houses and 23 Jewish young people were arrested: 1) Yissakhar Szilklaper, 2) Shlomo Szilklaper, 3) Chaim Shlomo Szpigelman, 4) Moshe Zorekh Belchatowski, 5) Lipman Benczkowski, 6) Avraham Machabajnski, 7) Avraham Szmulewicz, 8) Meir Zilberszac, 9) Yisroel Dovid Zilberszac, 10) Meir Machabajnski, 11) Avraham Landau, 12) Shmuel Landau, 13) Dovid Belchatowski, 14) Yekl Ostrowski, 15) Alter Naparstek, 16) Josef Rajnharc, 17) Hershl Goldberg, 18) Moshe Bornsztajn, 19) Shmuel Zaken Chojnacki, 20) Tuvya Dzenczarski, 21) Mendl Flamholtz, 22) Moshe Asher Laskowski, 23) Zaken Machabajnski. The arrestees were placed in the Belchatow jailhouse (prison). The unexpected arrests incited the shtetl. It was clear that the men were arrested according to precise instructions; that a denouncer had shown whom to arrest. Efforts were made to find out who could have made the denunciations, but they never learned [who it was]. Some parents searched for ways to free their sons. They wanted the rabbi to intercede. Nothing was of help. In the afternoon, the same wagons took away the locked up men to Piotrkow and they were placed in jail there.

The number of arrestees in the Piotrkow jail grew constantly and it became so crowded that many arrestees had to be taken to other jails. The Belchatower arrestees also were taken from Piotrkow after sitting several months and they were again placed in jail in Siedlce. After spending two months in Siedlce, all of the Belchatowers were sent under guard to Siberia.

During the time they sat in Piotrkow and Siedlce, they were investigated several times. No trial was held. The sentence was an administrative one. Five received up to four years exile, three received up to three years exile and the remaining ones up to two years exile - all for belonging to the Bund, although a number of them had no connection to the Bund.

The Bund became an underground organization in the largest cities, too. In general, communal life was not obliterated. The proletarian organizations carried out activities, although in a different way than previously. It became as quiet as a cemetery in Belchatow. There was no sign that there was once something. In the Polish national camp, in which there was a little movement, it also became absolutely quiet. Several Polish intellectuals were also arrested and exiled. There was no socialistic or organizational activity visible among the Polish workers.

**Alter Naparstek, Moshe Bornsztajn (Kajzer) and Yakov Ostrowski**
**[referred to above as Yekl], three Belchatower revolutionaries,**
**who were exiled to Siberia where this photograph was taken**

\* \* \*

The appearance of Belchatow changed systematically. One by one the streets were bricked over; instead of the open wells, pumps were installed. New brick houses appeared, a mechanical mill and, also, mechanical weaving factories. If Jewish workers and other Jews left Belchatow, Christian workers took their place, and even merchants.

The Jewish communal life, which lost its proletarian face, took on a local form.

After a large fire beyond the bridge (on the road to Szczercow and Kamiensk), during which a large number of houses were burned, there was a movement among the young men to become stroszh (firemen). Other Jewish firemen, such as Mikhal Yakubowicz (Dizurnik [Russian word for "on duty" - here it is used as a nickname]), Nisen Freitag, Meir and Daniel Warszawski and so on, joined Hershl Cines, the regular stroszhak, for whom belonging to the firemen was an ideal. There were those who belonged to the firemen passively. They did not wear firemen's uniforms and the brass hats, did not take part in "practices." They helped only in the event of a fire. Yehezkiel Szotten was one of them.

Young Jews also formed groups around the Bikor-Khoylem [society to help the sick poor]. This was an old institution that grew from the Mashorim Khoylem [Guardians of the Sick], another institution. The Mashorim Khoylem was created by Hershl Shoykhet [ritual slaughterer], Shaya Yoskowicz, Yankl Warszawski and so on. The Mashorim Khoylem, and later the Bikor-Khoylem, was one of the sides in a dispute with Yankl Warszawski, a feldsher [barber surgeon] in Belchatow. The institutions were a means for the competition among the feldshers in the city.

There was always the feldsher, Meir Lewkowicz, who worked as a doctor because not everyone could afford to have a doctor. There were those who had to come to him at the time of the military draft, or a girl because of "an unpermitted love." In general, he practiced as a doctor, in addition to working as a hairdresser.

There was another feldsher who worked as a hairdresser - Yehiel Warszawski. He principally practiced by hakn bankes [placing cupping glasses used to draw blood to the skin] or shteln piawkes [placing of leeches on the skin] on the village population on market days.

The third feldsher was a son of Yehiel Warszawski, the young Yankl Warszawski. He studied to be a feldsher at a school and later served in the Russian military as a feldsher. The population had more trust in Yankl

Feldsher; he was trusted no less than Doctor Rodziewicz. Yankl Warszawski helped many of the sick poor through the Bikor-Khoylem.

Yankl Warszawski's children had an inclination to communal activities and with their friends helped to create funds for a Bikor-Khoylem. Thus, they once hired a Polish theatrical troupe, which starred in Belchatow. Yehezkiel Szotten and Nisan Freitag went around selling tickets to the performance. Later, an amateur troupe under the direction of Yoel Leib Goldsztajn (Yankl Warszawski's son-in-law) carried out their own Yiddish theatrical performances in behalf of Bikor-Khoylem.

**Reb Yankl Warszawski**

Yankl Warszawski's house belonged to the so-called "free houses," in which young boys and girls would spend time. Yankl Warszawski himself kept the religious precepts, it can be said, pious, as much as a feldsher in general can maintain piety. But the family was much freer. There were five sons and four daughters in the house and young people spent time there very often. One could find there one Meir Zisman, who was a tanner - not a fragrant trade - but he was a success with the Belchatow young people of that time. He was a maskil [follower of the Enlightenment], wrote songs about love, about the relationship of the madams to the servants and on other themes. He also read beautifully, so he was willingly seen in the community of the young people.

One could also meet the Lichtenfeld sisters, Mendl Grocholicer's daughters, there. Ruchl, the older one was active in the Bund.

Perl, the Bosterin's house also was a "free" one. Young boys and girls would come together; they would jointly read books and they would sing songs. There were four daughters in the house. One of them, the gela Chana was active in the Bund.

In addition to the "free houses," there were also kavalerkes [places where young people, gentlemen came together]. One such room for young men was in Yankl Ostrowski's house. One Feffer, the son of a banker, who came to learn to draw patterns at Freitag's, lived in a small room. There, Moshe Freitag and several sisters, Nisen Freitag, Yehezkiel Szotten, Yankl Warszawski's children, Fela Rozenblum, Dobski's son and daughter, Yankl Elbinger, and others came together. Attempts were made there to establish a dramatic circle. A small lending library existed there. They sang there. Feffer, himself, had a very beautiful voice and, in general, they enjoyed themselves there.

Yoel Leib Goldsztajn also had a kavalerke. This was in Abish's on Piotrkow Street. A select community entered there. Goldsztajn tried to create a music lovers' group. Yoel Leib, himself, one of the most distinguished Belchatow communal workers, a writer, who wrote several books, such as: Der Letster Mentsch [The Last Man], Tsuzamenbrukh oder Iberboy [Collapse or Rebuild] (a novel in two volumes of more than 1,200 pages), a volume of short stories, Mitn Punim Tsum Shpigel [With the Face to the Mirror]. The last one was named, 1960. There were rumors that he had written many more than had been published. Among the Belchatow masklim [plural of maskil] were also Welwel Goldsztajn, Shaya Langnas, Yehiel Meir Krawicki, Yehiel Meir Jakubowicz, Dovid Luszczanowski, Berl Waldman and others. They did not develop any communal activities that were visible in the shtetl.

Yankl Elbinger had a small lending library where one received books to read. Morris Freitag also had Yiddish books and through the mediation of Morris' cousin, Arke Freitag, one could sometimes borrow a book to read without any payment. In 1911-1912, a group of young men in the beis-hamedrash were engaged in reading Yiddish books. Ahron Pinkhas Bornsztajn, Eli Twordowski, Moshe Szmulewicz and the writer of these lines belonged to the group. The obtaining of a book to read was very difficult. In addition to reading, they discussed the books that were read. They also discussed communal problems. When quarrels began between Heynt [Today] and Moment around the suspicion that Hillel Ceytlin had eaten non-kosher food in a train station, the group of young men from the beis-hamedrash sent a protest against the suspicion. The shortage of reading material gave the young men the idea of buying books. A discussion arose, which books should be bought, Yiddish or Hebrew? In the end, they came to a compromise - they bought both Yiddish and Hebrew.

The group of young men grew. At first, three Redziner, children of Redziner Hasidim, were added: Avraham Liberman, Henekh Liberman and Henekh Pigula. Later, Henekh Groszke and Shimele Szmulewicz joined.

Young men from the group often read in the beis-hamedrash, as long as they could sometimes sit with a gemara and thereby read a book. It once happened that the rabbi, Shmuel Shaya, caught them reading Abraham Mapu's Ahavat Zion [The Love of Zion]. However, he did not make a great fuss about it.

**Reb Yakov Elbinger during his young years**

Around Passover 1913, an incident happened that enraged the shtetl. One of the young men had borrowed Sholem Aleichem's Mabl [In the Storm] from Morris Freitag's library through the involvement of Arke Freitag. The book could only be kept for several days. Several of the young men came together and at the end of the holiday sat in a corner of the beis-hamedrash and were engrossed in reading Mabl at a candle. A group of Hasidim, who were passing by and noticed that there was light in the beis-hamedrash, entered. The young men were engrossed in reading and first realized it when the Hasidim began to shout. The shtetl was buzzing for several days. There was agitation everywhere Jews came together. In the shtiblekh [one room prayer houses] and other houses of prayer, even in the mikvah [ritual bathhouse] - Jews were agitated. My father, Moshe Eliezer Pudlowski, protested the most. He stormed against the young men. The rabbi also interested himself in the incident. Ahron Pinkhas, who was close to of the rabbi, was called to him. The rabbi chastised him, not letting him say anything in order to explain or to clarify. I was also called to the rabbi. Here the rabbi was milder. "Although your father is an enemy of mine, still it does not please me." With that the rabbi began to reproach me.

**A group of young activists from the Culture Union**

One could always find an older, poor and shabbily dressed young man in the beis-hamedrash. They called him "Itshe the Rebbitzin's [son of the rabbi's wife]." This was a son of the old rabbi. He was never called by another name. He would be occupied with buying "antique" religious book. He had read a great deal of the modern literature; he was a learned man. He also loved to speculate on communal and religious problems.

In the spring of 1913, a young ma, who drew the attention of everyone who met him appeared in Belchatow. The unknown one had a bleached out face enclosed with a small black beard; he wore a loose coat with a pair of boots. It was a strange way of dress even for Belchatow. He worked in Shlomo Kowal's small factory. Young workers, who would usually come together mainly on Shabbos with a keg of beer where they danced, sang, carried on love affairs, grouped around him

The unknown young man spent Shabbosim with them in the woods and endeavored to organize them. His lectures for the young jobless were very successful. Apparently because the young man met on appreciative terrain. The speeches were entwined with Yiddish worker and folk songs. The young people were very satisfied with spending time in the woods and the number of those taking part greatly increased.

The name of the young man was Gershon Perkal. He was a Lodz weaver. He lived with his mother and his four brothers in a very small room on Dworske Street (Balut). There was great poverty in the house. Once on a winter night, the house was surrounded by police and gendarmes, who broke into the house and after a vigorous, precise search took along Gershon to jail. After sitting in a Lodz jail for eight months, he received a visilka [expulsion order] to Zdunska Wola. There, he had to be under police supervision. He escaped from Zdunska Wola and came to Belchatow.

He immediately took to the work. In addition to meetings with the young workers, he also established contact with other groups of young men and interested them with his lectures.

When switching work to Uzer Czuchowski, Gershon Perkal had a room of his own. One could always meet visitors in the room. Gershon offered a library in the small room. [He] subscribed to a number of copies of Die Tseit [The Time], the Bundist weekly publication that was published in Petersburg. His closest helper was the writer of these lines, who took care of Perkal's entire written or secretarial work. Gershon was the only one who led the meetings. He made speeches, answered questions and even gave the note for singing the folk songs. Gershon was not educated. His knowledge came from the Bundist circles and from reading books.

The Bundist movement, which was cut short during the first months of 1908, now, after five years, began to grow anew. True, Gershon did not propose any official Bundist organization. But his campaigning and entire work was in the Bundist spirit. He also subscribed to various Bundist publications in addition to the Bundish weekly, Die Tseit, from Petersburg. The movement that lasted an entire summer finally began to draw the attention of the police, who sought to learn the particulars about Gershon. He felt it was getting hot under his feet and one evening he left the shtetl not saying one word to anyone.

**Gershon Perkal**

In the morning a group of those closest to Gershon first learned of it and regretted his disappearance. No one thought that it was bad that he had left before they were able to catch him. Almost everyone felt that with his departure, ended contact - meeting. Everyone really regretted this, but did not despair. They removed the books and all of the material from Uzer Czuchowski's house and meanwhile placed it in another place. They also brought together a larger group, which would decide what to undertake. The conference took place at night, erev [on the eve] of Yom-Kippur. It was a Kol-Nidre [opening prayer on the eve of the Day of Atonement] conference in the meadows beyond the Belchatow bridge. Two dozen young people came together, among whom were: Henekh Liberman, Avraham Mendl Jakubowicz, A. Leib, Yehiel Leibish Goldberg, Moshe Ostrowski, the writer of these lines and others. A very large number of those mentioned took part in the debate.

That such a group could come together on a Kol-Nidre night at that time showed that Gershon's work had sunk its roots. It was further decided to go on with Gershon's original work. While it was not possible to have speeches, we should read books, brochures and from Die Tseit. The address of the group was made that of the writer of these lines. It was decided to rent a small room as a kavalerke; a library would be there and we would meet on the wintry Shabbosim. We also decided that I would travel to Lodz and get instructions from Gershon.

All of the decisions of the Kol-Nidre meeting were carried out. After a short interruption, Die Tseit reappeared. The library functioned normally. We came together on the Shabbosim in the small room where the library was located. We read from books and sang folk songs. On the evenings in the middle of the week, a group could be found at Shlomo Midliacz's and in the confectioners' store.

On International Woman's Day, Die Tseit published reports from various provincial cities about the situation of the women workers. There were reports from four cities and one of them was Belchatow. In this report the Belchatower women workers were discussed, illustrated with facts from particular factories.

On the 1st of May, a small group gathered in the woods. They discussed Belchatow matters.

Just before the First World War, the group carried out a meeting on behalf of the striking Baku kerosene workers. The money collected (around five rubles) was sent to the address of the Tseit in Petersburg just before the outbreak of war.

The work of the Bundist group also pushed other groups to become active communally. In addition it affected those who did not fit into the Bundist environment. There also were those who were disposed to Zionism, so a short time before the outbreak of the First World War another library arose in Belchatow. The books probably came from Yankl Elbinger's and Morris Freitag's library. The second library was much richer in books and had good bookcases, and the premises were more comfortable. This was in Yankl Ostrowski's house.

However, it was not long before not only communal life in the shtetl ceased. Great changes occurred in the economic life of the shtetl; the First World War broke out, which began a new chapter in our history.

**The first "TSISHO" [Central Yiddish School Organization] School in Belchatow. The children together with Zalman Pudlowski and the woman teacher, Rozenband.**

**Teachers and students of the first Yiddish secular school**

**Yavne [religious Zionist] School with teacher**

**Jewish children of the general Folks-Shul [public school]**

## Translator's Footnotes

1. Kest is the practice through which a father-in-law supports his daughter's husband so that the son-in-law can study Torah.

2. The author refers to the dozor with both the diminutive, Moshke, and his given name, Moshe.

3. teg = day. Families provided individual yeshiva students their meals for a day.

4. "Gefirt tish" = "Led a table" - Hasidic rabbis held discussions and provided commentary on the Torah to their followers at meals, often at the Shabbos lunchtime meal.

5. Sheygets - plural Shkotzim - is a derogatory word for a gentile boy or young man. It can also mean a boy or young man who is impudent.

6. On January 9, 1905, according to the Julian Calendar, the Russian Revolution of 1905 began when Russian workers marched on the Winter Palace ending with Bloody Sunday - the massacre of workers by Tsarist troops.

[Page 144]

# This is How We Began

## by Levi Herzkowicz

## Translated from the Yiddish by Hanka Wajsberg Gliksman

## Edited by Martin Bornstein and Jerry Liebowitz

After 25 years living in Israel, I can still picture, swimming around in my mind, the images of my town Belchatow, just as it would have been like yesterday, when I left it. The town has burned itself into my heart and soul, so that it is always near to me and that is why it is so hard to forget.

**The leaders of the Tzeirei-Zion Organization in the year 1913**

Belchatow has been a town with so much Jewish culture, even when a large part of the Jewish population was poor.

Who of us does not remember the peaceful atmosphere on Fridays, late in the afternoon, when it was close to Shabbat, and the "Shamis" [the synagogue's caretaker], knocked on the Jewish doors and with a special unique tune called out to the Jews, that it is time to go to pray.

To the working class youth, it didn't matter to them how tired they were after a day's work. They still used every spare second to read books, newspapers and study to increase their knowledge.

But straight after Shabbat, in the evening, you could see how the new weekly work begins. The non-Jewish workers do their deliveries to the Jewish factories with the materials on their backs. The kerosene lamps were lit up and the new weekly work began again. The noise of the weaving machines began. You could hear workers' songs, folk songs, and Chasidic tunes being sung by the workers.

From the beginning of the century, the working class started to organise meetings in clubs. A lot of Belchatow's youth showed great interest and ability.

They started off with secret meetings at the homes of sympathisers of the "Bund" [organization] and also at the homes of Zionists youths.

I still remember until today the first secret Zionist meeting, which took place on the new road, on a beautiful full moon night in the summer of 1905 or 1906. A representative speaker from another town gave us a lecture about Zionism. A. Majer, Fygel and Nache Warszawski, S. Langsam, M. Freitag, N. Freitag, J.L. Goldstein, and I, plus a few other people were there. Soon after, we formed the first provisional Zionist committee in Belchatow, and secretly we started the Zionist organization for ourselves and others. Later we managed to organise a legitimate library at a time in Poland when only a few Jewish libraries existed. Mr. M.A. Pitowski was the man who worked very hard and spent a lot of time and effort to bring the library to a successful standard.

Also at this time other new parties were formed in Belchatow –The "Bund," S.S., the Polish Socialists Party (P.P.S.) – and we had different discussions about the parties and programs.

Our group had started to sell Shekels – memberships [in the Zionist party]. Every one of us tried to sell as many Shekels as possible, so a large section of the Jewish population would become members of the Zionist Party.

It reminds me of when I wanted to sell a Shekel to Abraham Frizirer Szmulewitch. I had to have quite a long discussion with him about the goals and aims of Zionism, but I wasn't successful in convincing him of its importance. I was successful with somebody else, the matzeva [tombstone] mason's son, Szmuel Reich. After a long talk, I persuaded him to join the party and purchase the first Shekel. It was very important for us to draw the intellectual and better class of people from our town to our group.

Little by little we expanded our activities. We formed a club which provided Hebrew classes & a drama section AD"GL. The center of our activities were at Jakob Elbingern's and Yoel Goldstein's places.

When I left Belchatow in 1917 there already existed well branched out Zionist activities, various movements had evolved, and all of them encountered the possibility for work and development.

**A group of teachers and schoolchildren from the evening courses by Tzeirei-Zion in the year 1915, with the teacher Menachem Brash**

**A group (for) Zionist matters**

[Pages 148-199]

# Belchatow 1914 – 1922

## By Avraham Laib

### Translated from the Yiddish by Gloria Berkenstat Freund

[with comments in brackets]

I do not remember if there was ever a census in Belchatow, only that by all estimates, the population of Belchatow was 10,000: there were 6,000 Jews and the other 4,000 were Poles and Germans. Because of the proximity of the German border (55 kilometers in all), and perhaps for other reasons, there were many Germans among us.

As we see, of the Belchatow population, Jews totaled 60 percent, but the activity of the Jews gave everyone the impression that it was a 100 percent Jewish shtetl [town]. All of the businesses and shops, except for the whiskey and pork shops, as well as the apothecary, belonged to Jews. It was the same with the factories: of the dozens of factories located in the shtetl, only one belonged to a German baron, and the owners of all of those remaining were Jews.

Belchatow is located a little apart from the larger world because it does not have a direct railway line. The closest railway line for the shtetl is Piotrkow, 24 kilometers from Belchatow, and at that time the trip to Piotrkow by ox lasted three or four hours and, in order to reach Lodz, it was an additional four hours. A trip by automobile that now takes one hour then took eight hours under the best circumstances. And Lodz, as we will later see, was very necessary for the people of Belchatow, because Belchatow actually lived off Lodz.

There were two aspects to the character of Belchatow, and as paradoxical as it may sound, two extremes: on one side were the Hasidim and on the other side, the proletariat. Compared to other cities and shtetlekh [towns] of the same size or even those with a much larger population, and compared to all of the neighboring shtetlekh, our shtetl found itself at a much higher level of development.

If we speak about the development of the shtetl, we must also be sure to remember the names of several people who are very much "to blame" for the fact that those from Belchatow were and remain educated, conscious of their status and cultured, a situation that might not have existed without these people. These are the Messrs. Gershon Perkal, Menachem (I do not remember his second name) and Ahron, Ahron the beloved, the dear Ahron Bergman. It should be remembered here that none of the three listed friends were from Belchatow. They only lived in and had an effect on Belchatow at various times, some less and some more. Later an entire range of comrades arose who affected everyone in their time and in their way. Comrades Zalman Pudlowski and Yehezkeil Birencwajg distinguished themselves and reached the level of local leaders and teachers.

Belchatow, in contrast with other small Jewish shtetlekh in Poland, did not live from the air, but from hard toil. Belchatow was a factory town, a weaving town. And almost all – the largest number directly and the smaller number indirectly – lived from weaving. There were a dozen larger and smaller mechanized factories in which almost exclusively all of those who worked were Christian workers. And although the factories belonged to Jews, it was very difficult for a Jewish worker to gain employment in these factories. As most of the manufacturers were pious Jews, they did not want to cause Jewish workers to desecrate the Sabbath and they believed that if Jewish workers could work only five days a week, it would not be worthwhile for the manufacturers. Therefore, the Jewish weavers were forced to work on handlooms and each Jewish worker's home was a small factory of two, three or four stools, depending on how many children the worker had... Consequently, the Polish weaver had his hour for lunch and his designated hour when he ended his workday, and for the Jewish weaver, the workday never ended.

It has already been mentioned here that Belchatow lived off Lodz. It occurred for the following reasons: the Belchatow manufacturers brought the raw materials from Lodz and they were worked on then in Belchatow. Then the completed goods were taken back to Lodz to be washed, dyed and pressed (in the Belchatow-Lodz "jargon" it was called: apreturn) and actually immediately sold in Lodz. And if a Belchatow shop owner needed some goods for his shop, he, too, had to go to Lodz.

A particular type of middleman between Lodz and Belchatow were the liverantn [contractors] (this is what we called them). They did not need to possess any property, only a good guarantee and a little nerve. They took advantage of the fact that in our shtetl the workers' wages were much lower than in Lodz. They brought raw material from Lodz and had the work done by us and took the finished goods to Lodz and made a very fine living from this, a lot better than the weavers themselves.

So that the Belchatow manufacturers and contractors would be able to be competitive in relation to the Lodz manufacturers, all of the expenses for bringing raw material and returning the completed goods and also the manufacturer's transportation (which was not cheap) were placed on the accounts of the Belchatow workers. Thus against their own will, the Belchatow workers were a very considerable competitor in relation to the Lodz workers. The Belchatow weavers suffered from double competition: on one side they had to work more cheaply than the Lodzers and on the other side they had a great deal of competition in the form of the peasants around Belchatow.

All of the peasants in several dozen villages around the shtetl were weavers. Two hand looms were found in each hut. Little was woven by the peasants during the summer months because of the field work. The villages worked full steam during the winter months. And they worked almost for free, because their main earnings were not from weaving. It is not hard to imagine the situation in which the city hand weavers found themselves.

The greatest victims of this system were self-evidently the Jewish weavers. They worked for endless hours. The days were as long as the exile and Thursdays never ended because of the coming Shabbos. Most of the weavers worked an entire night on Thursdays.

* * *

The Kultur Fareyn [Culture Union] was founded on the 25th of January 1915 with 50 plus members. The "Union" was a non-party organization. But it was known to the founders that under the innocent name Kultur Fareyn one would find the Bund. An entirely new epoch began in our shtetl with this founding. How does the song go? "New bird, new songs..." And actually we began to hear notes different from those that we were accustomed to hearing until then.

There once had been a Bundist revolutionary movement here, but this had already been long forgotten. And those who had not forgotten continued to try to forget it.

This was the famed year 1905. Belchatow's sons and daughters, as well as Gerer and Aleksander Hasidim, carried red flags through the streets and publicly sang songs against the czar and also against God... It is no surprise that the "better" Jews made an effort to forget. Then came the sixth year; the largest number of revolutionaries were exiled to Siberia. A number escaped to America and it became quiet. The majority of them, who later survived their terms of hard labor, left for America. Several Akhdus Yungen [United Youth] remained. They behaved modestly; in the best situation, they prayed "privately." They were almost never seen in the open.

The Kultur Fareyn overran the shtetl by storm. We rented a large apartment with several rooms and a library of several hundred books immediately blossomed. A choir under the direction of Lev Herckowicz was founded (he is now in Israel). Later the direction of the choir was transferred to his young brother, Hercke (died in 1920). A little later a dramatic circle was also founded, whose first director was Shmuel Reich (died in 1919). Each administrative body established the appropriate managing commission and they carried out their activities very successfully.

We always searched for an appropriate candidate as librarian; he needed to advise the readers about the kind of books they should take for reading. The librarian had to know all of the readers in order to know what to give everyone.

An entire array of reading circles of various groups and categories was established in order to attract our members to read. There was even a group with which it was necessary to start with the alef-beis [a,b,c's – beginners]. Henekh Pigula led this sort of circle and he simply taught how to read a newspaper. Another group was "taught" beautiful literature. This was done in this way: the lecturer read a chapter of Sholem Aleichem, [David] Pinski, [Sholem] Asch or [Hersh Dovid] Nomberg, or took several of [Moshe Jacob Alter, known as Morris] Rosenfeld's poems, Yehoash [Solomon Blumgarten – known for his translation of the Bible into Yiddish] or A. Reisin [Abraham Reisin – writer of Yiddish poetry and short stories] and, after reading, a part of the group tried to explain their opinions of what was read. A discussion developed and the lecturer always was the final judge... Y.L. Peretz, for whom there was a special circle of listeners, was taught in the same way.

A. Twordowksi led the circle for socialist literature. He took a chapter of Kautsky's Erfurter Program[1] or a chapter of Marx's Kapital, read it over and then analyzed and explained it in simple, popular Yiddish for as long as it took to knock it into our hard heads. A. Bergman led the class in political economy.

Once, during such a lecture, our man of letters, Y. L. Goldsztajn, entered our meeting hall and although he did not belong to our circle (he stood at the head of the Zionists), he became so fascinated by the lecture that he asked to be permitted to attend the course. And for a short time, he actually was one of our best listeners.

*   *   *

We made our first public appearance in front of the shtetl on Purim in 1915. We arranged an evening with a not too large program in our own meeting hall. There were several recitations, several songs were sung by our choir for the first time. And then we danced the entire night. The impression made by our evening was colossal. And although our apartment did not hold more than 200 people in usual circumstances, this time more than 350 visitors gathered and no one felt it was crowded.

The evening did not happen as easily as it seems. Immediately at our public announcement in the neighborhood we recognized the first great conflict with the elite in the shtetl. We were then under German occupation. Several days before the evening we painted a few posters, sent a delegation to the office of the commander and after proper enlightenment, they permitted us to hold the evening, placing the official stamp on the poster. There was great turmoil when the "proper" Jews saw the posters in the street. They ran to the rabbi, held meetings and consultations and finally, after a short report, ended with the commandant withdrawing permission. And if this was not enough, meetings were simultaneously forbidden with the explanation that "five people together was considered a meeting and they would bear the consequences that the law provided for illegal meetings during the time of crisis." It should be understood that it was bitter to our souls. We were not concerned about saving the evening, but we saw a further purpose of the "proper Jews" and this did not please us very much. We did not rest and again sent a delegation to the office of the commander. After a great and difficult effort we succeeded in "convincing" them that we had nothing against the German government... We only hated the Czarist regime.

When we again had permission for the evening, we still were afraid that the Germans would again let themselves be "convinced" by the "proper Jews." We sent a delegation to the rabbi and through the rabbi offered our "visitor's card" to the "proper Jews" of the city. We gave them to understand that they should not make a mistake about us, that we were no longer youngsters and we warned them that from now on they should not mix into our matters so that we would not have to mix into their businesses...

During the entertainment we had a visit from the entire commander's office. The orchestra played several German marches. One of our comrades recited several poems by Heinrich Heine in German for them and they were "convinced" that we would not pick a quarrel with the German Kaiser.

They spent two hours with us, danced and spent a great deal of money at the buffet. The next morning a policeman went through the streets and tore off the placards on the walls saying that meetings were forbidden.

In addition to the material side, we had a great moral success. We were the theme of the day for a long time and weeks after, our first appearance was still being commented upon.

From then on we became an important force in the shtetl and they began to listen to our words. We became a group of which they began to take note.

At that time we had a political group that was not yet well known by the public but its existence was recognized. This was the Zionist organization. It did not have great political credit. Its activity was still limited then. To their praise, it should be remembered here that the first library in Belchatow was created by the Zionists. The library existed in the period before the First World War and young Belchatowers exchanged books twice a week. It should also be remembered here that the first books for that library were donated by Yankl Elbinger and Moric Frajtag. It should also be stated that a library already existed in Belchatow in 1905, but for understandable reasons, not publicly. After the revolution was suppressed, the books were moved into a private home and were read in secret.

*  *  *

We began to spread and intensify our work. We added several rooms to our apartment. Our cabinetmaker comrades (Itshe Winter, Shimeon Szmulewicz, etc.) removed several walls and made moving walls out of them. That is, if it was necessary, the walls could be "bundled up" and several rooms became one large hall which could hold several hundred people. In addition, they built a small stage out of the last room. We then had an entire theater where we held smaller shows in our own hall.

We bought books and enlarged the library. A reading room was set up that was open daily and was well visited.

From Lodz we brought Comrade Ahron Bergman who brought a great deal of life into the shtetl. A teacher by trade, a person with party seniority, he arranged the work on a secure basis. First of all, he detached the "Culture Union" from the Bundist organization and created two separate managing committees. It is true that the "Union" remained Bundist, but it was decided members of the "Union" should not belong to the Bund. On the contrary, in order to join the Bundist organization, some had to first go through a "quarantine" in the "Culture Union."

We then created a children's school. Several dozen children enrolled and they were taught in two groups. A little later, the friends Rukhl Likhtenfeld and Rukhl Szmulewicz were attracted as teachers.

I believe that it would not be an exaggeration if I say that we were the very first, if not the only one with a children's school in Poland at that time.

We also established a course for adults. Yiddish grammar, Jewish history and general cultural history, literature, geography and so much else were taught. And although all of the students knew how to read and to write and thought of themselves as very "able," they were convinced that they could not write a proper Yiddish letter. The same with Jewish history. They had been advised against other disciplines about which a large number of students had entirely no knowledge.

It should be understood that the teacher was Comrade A. Bergman. The education was not as from a teacher to students, but as from a comrade to comrades. The lectures were actually true intellectual pleasures. The lectures rarely ended with what they had begun. Almost always we were "caught" in a discussion and arrived far from the theme...

It can be said without exaggeration that thanks to Comrade Bergman, the level of cultural achievement rose significantly in our shtetl.

A little later, the Zionists brought down a teacher, Comrade Menachem (I do not remember his family name), if I am not mistaken from Krakow. A very fine young man with a great deal of culture. And a Tarbut[2] school was created, where Yiddish and mainly Hebrew was taught.

*   *   *

In a short time, we had non-party meetings on Shabbosim [Sabbaths]. Besides the Bund and Zionists, no other parties existed at that time. The party differences were not so great and no great party struggles took place. The themes were literary and not about party matters. Discussions for the sake of discussion took place, although a large number of those taking part knew that there were party objectives beneath the discussions...

We enlarged our choir and dramatic society, trained more and the results were very satisfactory. The performances were frequent and were well attended. Immediately afterward, the Zionists also organized a dramatic society.

A little later, the Zionist organization split off the proletarian part (it was a Bundist bit of work...). The larger segment of the split off Zionists built the new for us Poalei-Zion party. A smaller number joined the Bund.

A competition began: Poalei-Zion also acquired a library, also opened a consumer cooperative (we already had one), and also created a dramatic society.

We remained the only ones with a choir. It happened often that the Zionists needed a choir for its entertainment; they "borrowed" the choir from us.

Many arguments, mainly between the Bund and Poalei-Zion occurred, around the dramatic circle in general and in particular with the plays and there were also comical incidents. If one party began to rehearse a certain play, the other party immediately found the same play and began to rehearse it. If one party learned that a second party was rehearsing the same play, it went earlier to rent the only room in our shtetl, the firemen's hall ("the firemen's shed") for the first two nights of Chol ha-Moed[3] or Purim.

**Members of the Dramatic Society:**

(From right to left) Avraham Leib, Nachman Meir Goldberg,
Avraham Liberman, Avraham Nowak, Itshe Leib Goldberszt,
Velvel Weiss, Ruchl Lichtenfeld, Chaya Jakobowicz,
Avraham Lipman Nowak, Gitl Hartman, Hersh Leyzer
Goldberg, Shmuel Yosel Satt, Hinda Royze Jakobowicz,
Moshe Eisner, Yechiel Leibish Goldberg, Shlomo
Luszczanowski and Henoch Pigula.

It once happened that one party had triumphed with a play, for which it was impossible to obtain another printed copy. The only copy was stolen at night from the other's library, the play was copied over night and it was "smuggled in " at dawn and placed in the other library in the same place from which it was taken. And to the astonishment of the "triumphant " party, the play was also performed by the opposition.

In general we had few nights in the year to present a play. At that time the custom was introduced for us to mainly perform on the nights of Chol ha-Moed Sukkos and Passover and also on Purim. And in order to be sure of success, everyone sought to perform on the first night of Chol ha-Moed and particularly when two "troupes" were performing the same play at the same time...

**A group of young community workers in 1919**

From right to left: Yumke Leib, Hersh Leyzer Goldberg,
Moshe Eisner, Melech Galster, Henoch Szerman, Wewe
Piula, Avraham Leib, Ahron Bergerman, Avraham Liberman
and Josef Reich.

We created smaller undertakings in our lounge at various opportunities.

Our people became so "enthusiastic" with theater that in later years, when a professional acting troupe would come to our shtetl to perform, they performed to packed houses. In addition, they had the satisfaction that they were playing for a thoughtful spectator with a great connection to Yiddish theater. And the troupe that had only visited our shtetl once knew that for a second visit they needed to bring good actors and also good plays.

The Zionist organization also had a dramatic section with rather good amateurs, with whom we lived very peacefully. There were never any conflicts between us and them in this area. Leading and directing this troupe was Yoel Leib Goldsztajn. They had an entire series of very successful and interesting performances, which always left a fine impression.

Y. L. Goldsztajn was a very intelligent person and, in addition, the only man of letters whom our shtetl, Belchatow, produced. True, he was not a very well known person in the writing world. Even in Poland, he was little known. It was probably, more than anything, his "fault" - because of his modesty he did not aspire to popularity. If he would had only desired it – he would have surely been heard. He succeeded in publishing several books during the course of his writing career. His first book, Der Letster Mentsh [The Last Man] was published before the First World War by Gitlin's publishing house in Warsaw. In 1934, the Bikher [books] publishing house issued his two volume novel of over 1,200 pages, Tsusamenbrich oder Iberboy [Collapse or Rebuild] (a fanciful novel in four parts). In 1939, the same publishing house published a book entitled 1960. We also know his book of short stories entitled Mit Punim Tsum Shpigl [With Face Toward the Mirror]. In addition to these, he created a great deal of literary work that was never published in book form and he wrote in several literary forms: novels, songs and also dramas. He produced several of his dramas and one-act plays in Belchatow with great success.

In general, he was an original and interesting person. He was drawn to everything and knew something about everything; he could play the fiddle a little, the piano a little. He was also a good chess master. He was a Zionist politically and was the head of the Zionist organization in our shtetl for a long time.

His was employed in commerce. He had a paper shop (that is what it was called among us). He was the only one in Belchatow who provided writing materials, all kinds of textbooks, both for Jews and for the Christian residents.

His shop was always a gathering place for the town intellectuals, principally for the Jews. The latest news was always heard in his shop; the newest books were read and discussed and even the latest slander was learned...

In 1941, already under the Nazi occupation in Belchatow, Y. L. Goldsztajn died with a "luxurious death," as was said when someone died a natural death.

\* \* \*

The year 1918 was of great significance for us. In that year we revealed our political credo to the world. We were no longer totally unknown. In addition to being known for our work with the Culture Union, school, library, choir, lectures, reading room, theater performances, consumer cooperative – we also took part with representation in the existing "American Committee" (that is, a committee to divide products that were sent from America for poor people). And we had a reputation with our performances on behalf of the poor. We were witnesses to small scandals at the dividing of the products received. It took great work and struggle by us in the "American Committee" so that everything that came from America was accounted for and that everything was given to the truly needy.

Then we demonstrated our political activity to the community.

The weekly meetings had to be held on Shabbos between day and night because at that time it was a committee of the Bund, which consisted of seven comrades, three who still had one foot in the beis-hamedrash [prayer house]. This time was the most acceptable for the "beis-hamedrash young men" so that their appearance [at the meetings] would not be noticed in their homes and they would not have to explain where they had been. Once during such a meeting, we had a surprise: among others points on the agenda was also a point, "mass meeting." This was great news to us. Out of curiosity about this point, we quickly finished with all other points and came to the matter of the "mass meeting." Comrade A. Bergman reported: Poland is becoming independent. Parliamentary elections would be held. We needed to begin to appear in the street as a political power and we need to become acquainted with the future voting masses.

The mass meeting was set for tomorrow, Sunday, at night, between Minchah and Maariv [afternoon and evening prayers] in the beis-hamedrash. Sunday, at night, several hours before the mass meeting, we held a gathering of 40 chosen comrades, only men, the most responsible, and we assigned "roles." Several young men were sent into the street to call the crowd to the mass meeting. They did so in this way: they were allotted several streets, chiefly Pabianicer, Stercewer and Piotrkowsker, where a small number of poor lived and where they met a Jew, they gave him a mysterious whisper in his ear: "They are speaking in the beis-hamedrash," "A speech in the beis-hamedrash," "Important news in the beis-hamedrash," and before the Jew had a chance to ask a question, our messenger was somewhere else. A short time before Minchah and the was already overflowing. Such a crowd had not been seen in the for years. At the eastern wall, the best worshippers gaped and were amazed: what was happening? No famous preacher had been announced.

"Yudl Lekekhbeker" [cake baker] lived opposite the beis-hamedrash. He, as well as his entire family, were very fine and sympathetic people. Two of his daughters were our comrades. Our headquarters was located there and further roles were allotted: who needed to stand at the door, who at the eastern wall (in order to restrain the influential people), who among the crowd, a special "bodyguard" around the speaker. The main thing we were concerned with was that they be comrades with a great deal of tact and presence of mind.

A messenger announced that Minchah would be ending in a few minutes. The entire "headquarters" entered the and each took his place. Comrade Henekh Liberman, a little confused, stood on the reading stand. As soon as the bal-tefilah [person reciting prayers] ended Minchah, Comrade Henoch banged on the reader's desk and began:

"In the name of the Bund committee I have come to announce to you..." And he had no breath... He was one of those who still stood with a foot in the and sat on the Bund committee and, at the same time, probably imagined the dark Shabbos that awaited him at home...

Comrade A. Bergman stood on a bench, his cap tilted a little to the side and saw the situation with Comrade Henoch Liberman. He immediately began: "Comrades, friends," and in the course of an hour and a half, he spoke about the war and what kind of "profits" the workers and toilers awaited after the war, even a war that was won... A few influential Jews began to try to make a racket, but they were immediately quieted because one of our comrades appeared near each one and whispered a secret in his ear: "Reb Eli Feiwel, if this does not please you, it would be better for you to go home because things can end badly here..." Another: "It would be better to leave quietly and with honor because, if not, we will throw you out like something useless..." And thus all the influential people were silenced.

At the doors, the comrades warned the Jews entering and leaving: "Sh, sh, they are speaking..." After the first few minutes, the lecture went on in the best order and with the most attentive quiet.

After the lecture, listening to the comments from the small groups of dejected Jews, we had the feeling that we had established contact with the poor and that they felt our support.

One group of Jews standing in the street after the mass meeting commented and discussed the party in general and about which party had arranged today's mass meeting. One Jew said something very absurd. A Jew, Yissachar the Shulkleper[4] ("Sucher Krusis"), who was well known even in 1905 for receiving four years in Siberia for the Bund, pushed himself in:

"You should excuse me, Reb Yid [a polite way of addressing someone unknown], you do not know what you are talking about. You want to know who this is, I will tell you. This is still the Bund! And who is the Bund – ask me!"

Thus was the Bund introduced to the shtetl.

*　*　*

It was assumed that there was no anti-Semitism in Belchatow. Of the village population around the shtetl, it is certain that they were no anti-Semites. And it is natural because they were in constant contact with Jews and partly earned their livings from Jews from the produce from their villages that they brought to the city once a week (Monday) to sell. Their customers in very large part were Jews. And when they, the peasants, had time, beginning in the winter, they took to weaving and, again, needed to go to the Jews. In the main, at that time, no propagandists preaching anti-Semitism traveled through the villages. On the other hand, this cannot be said about the city's Christian population. It is true that almost no anti-Semitism was felt, but it is a fact that the larger part of the shtetl intelligentsia were anti-Semitic.

We must add that almost all gentiles here understood and spoke a not bad Yiddish. As a result, the greater number of the Belchatow Jewish population spoke a bad Polish.

The first steps of Poland's independence were "celebrated" with several pogroms against Jews. A question of self defense was placed before our committee of the Bund. It is true that we saw no great signs of anti-Semitism here. However, we did not want to be subjected to surprises and rely on miracles. We wanted to be prepared for every situation so that "we would not need to be." We turned to the Zionists with our self defense proposal and they immediately, without hesitation, but truly with inspiration, accepted the proposal. After joint consultations it was decided that several shtarke jungen[5] from the shtetl be drawn into the action (not to confuse them with members of the underworld – we, too, did not like them). These were wagon drivers, young butchers, who did not belong to any party, were respectable, toiling Jews, athletically built and could deliver a blow. If a non-Jew had a conflict with one of the people and it came to blows, such a non-Jew was careful not to "discuss" this more with the gang...

At the conclusion of Yom Kippur 1919, we had our first meeting. Those present were only those chosen for self defense. Discipline and conspiracy were considered first. Everyone was given the opportunity to withdraw if he was unable to subject himself to discipline and conspiratorial situations. The positions, although not easy, were all accepted without exception. No one withdrew. We determined a password, a sign that only members of the self defense group knew. We collected several hundred marks on the spot to buy weapons. It appeared that our bourgeois young people owned a score of revolvers and it was decided to buy a certain amount more. The revolvers were allotted only to the most responsible ones. Although we had a suspicion that more than one of them possessed one. Every one of them received a short, thick, round and hard wooden stick that could be held in the sleeve and not attract attention from anyone.

We paid special attention to two days of the week, Sunday and Monday. Sunday – because on this day hundreds of peasants from the surrounding villages came together in the city churches to pray and to listen to the priests' sermons. And Monday – because this was our market day during which hundreds of peasants from all around would bring their products to sell and on one street to buy the things they needed in the city in the Jewish shops and from what was displayed in Jewish stalls in the market.

On all other days of the week we had fewer guards, but on Sunday and Monday we had everyone active on their feet.

The city was divided into various sectors. A group of five people had command over each sector. One of them was the responsible commandant for each "small sector." On Sundays and Mondays, the headquarters was located at a central point in the city (at Yoel Leib Goldsztajn's). Couriers ran the entire day from sector to sector and from the sectors to the headquarters and back, bringing news to the headquarters and carrying away orders. The task of the "five sectors" was to not be provoked: If a gentile boy grabbed a packet of tobacco from "grobn Alter" ["fat Alter"] and ran away without paying, or stole something (as would happen) from a Jewish stall and several peasants would help to block it – lest it not immediately be thought of as a pogrom. Each leader of a "sector" had the right to resolve the small things in his sector. Only the headquarters itself had the right to decide the large things.

The task of the "five positions" was to follow the non-Jews with caution and watch their movements, where they were gathering in certain places, sitting at their tables in the taverns, moving closer to hear if someone in their group spoke and, mainly, watching unnoticed if there was a stranger, an agitator who had arrived unexpectedly.

On Sundays we would even enter the churches to hear the priests' sermons.

We had various comical episodes relating to self-defense: if someone wanted to convince someone else to observe the communal undercover precepts, he stopped the other one's bride [comrade] and gave the "password." He immediately was persuaded of the other's [part in the] conspiracy; one of the young fighters went to the other's comrade, gave the word and received the secret answer, and he asked, "So, comrade, when will something happen, we are waiting for days doing nothing?"

The Zionists were active in self defense – Mordekhai Safirsztajn, Moric Fajtos, Y. L. Goldsztajn, Meir and Daniel Warszawski, Chaim Meir Czeslawski, Berl Waldman, Pitowski's sons, and so on. From the Bund: Ahron Bergman, Josef Reich, Avraham and Henoch Liberman, Henoch Groszka, Henoch Pigula, Yehezkiel Burncwajg, Yechiel Leibish Goldberg, Avraham Nowak, and so on. From the "shtarker" – Dovid's son Nute Hersh, Yankl "Pachtshasz," Peretz Abraham Zelners,[6] Avraham Alter Khmal, Shimeon the cake baker, Yakov Hillel, Itshe Grunem's son Chaim-Yankl, and so on.

Besides the smaller unimportant excesses that were immediately settled with great tact, there was no great unrest here. We were all sure of and convinced of one thing, that if a pogrom broke out here, it would quickly be a pogrom on the attackers themselves...

\* \* \*

Our city came to life with the approach of the first Sejm [parliament] elections. All of the then existing parties, such as the Bund, Agudah, Zionists and Poalei-Zion, threw themselves into the work. First of all, each party wanted to benefit from it politically. Each party had already "counted" the number of votes that it would receive, winning members for the party, or at least sympathizers on whom one could rely for support. And there was a concern about bringing speaker-organizers. For a long time, speakers in Belchatow were not something new. We are not speaking about preachers and tedious orators, whom the religious Jews would always bring, and many of them who would come from time to time uninvited and would also speak about worldly matters wrapped in a talis [prayer shawl], because with the rise of the parties, speakers in the shtetl were not newcomers. All of the parties would bring them. The themes would be diverse; mostly direct party [themes], others indirect, on general literary themes.

It was very cozy in the shtetl when a report and discussion was presented. Then all "polished their tongues " to give an opinion. During the lectures, comrades sat with pencils and papers in their hands, noting every expression of the speaker. Every opponent was "pelted" with at least a dozen citations from newspaper articles, from journals and books to which the lecturer (if he was a writer) had contributed. There were more ways to "persuade" a speaker from the opposing party, namely, not permitting him to finish, interrupting or not letting him begin at all...

For a short time Belchatow was the ir-miklet [asylum city] for two Bundist comrades who, because of police matters, could not be in Warsaw and felt safer with us. These were the comrades Leizer Lewin and Hershl Bekerkunst. The first was with us for a time and then left; later the other one came. Obviously, as the comrades were party activists, speakers and also writers, we used them for our party purposes. We mainly held our gatherings in the woods because of their conspiratorial nature.

Once we permitted ourselves a luxury. Comrade M. Bekerkunst gave a lecture to our "Culture Union." We had a surprise in the middle of the speech: a police ambush. We successfully led comrade H. Bekerkunst and several other comrades (also not completely legal) out through a window and sent them to the forest. After several days of hiding out, he left Belchatow and our city was no longer an asylum city. We never learned if it was a provocation or a pure accident.

Each party tried to bring the most popular and the most famous speakers for the Sejm elections. Only the Bund was not successful in this because the central committee believed that it needed the famous speakers for the large cities. However, the Bund found itself in a better situation in relation to every other party here because the Bund always had at its disposal a speaker and also a very competent opponent that no other party had in the person of the previously mentioned Bergman.

A series of meetings began that incited the shtetl. There was only a problem with meeting halls. Belchatow had only one meeting hall, the firefighters' hall.

Immediately, the parties thought that as the Bund had once used the beis hamedrash [prayer house] for a meeting, why should it not again be done? All of the parties began to use the beis hamedrash and not only the synagogue. It reached the point that the religious Jews raised a tumult, banging the table and shouting, enough! It was blasphemy and it could not continue. And it was decided that with the agreement of all of the parties that no one would hold any more meetings in the religious premises.

One night when the campaign was almost at an end, we learned that a secret conference of all of the parties except the Bund was taking place in the anteroom of the synagogue. On the spur of the moment the Bund committee and several active members were quickly called together and a decision was made and an uninvited delegation was immediately sent to the secret conference. At the same time, the Bund committee went into a secluded session in a comrade's cellar bakery next to the synagogue in order to take a stand on the secret conference. Simultaneously, runners went back and forth – from the synagogue to the meeting and from the meeting to the synagogue – in order to bring news and, after quick consideration, carry back agreed upon decisions.

The above mentioned conference to end the election campaign proceeded with a concluding meeting that would take place in the synagogue. As no outside speakers were here, the only speaker would be the rabbi (to be truthful, although a very smart Jew, he was never a speaker. Even giving a sermon, he was not so strong...). The following characteristic dialogue took place at the conclusion of the conference:

Reb Yakob Hersh Sztatlender from the Agudah [Orthodox political party]:

– It remains that even at tomorrow's meeting only the rabbi will speak.

Comrade Yechezkel Birencwajg of the Bund:

– And Comrade Bergman.

Meir Warszawski of the Zionists:

– It was decided by general consensus that the only speaker at tomorrow's meeting is the rabbi.

Comrade Yechezkel:

– There will be another individual speaker – Comrade Bergman.

Moshe Szmulowicz of the P. Z. [Poalei-Zion], directly to the uninvited Bundist delegation:

– You heard that there is a unanimous decision; you always have a mouth full of democracy. How dare you oppose an accepted decision?

The Bundist representative:

– We are not violating a decision, only you! Who permitted speaking in the synagogue after it was already decided not to use the prayer house for meetings? Incidentally, we are not at today's session so that we would need to respect anyone's majority decision; we are here by chance and we have heard that tomorrow there will be speeches in the synagogue. We give you notice so that it will not be a surprise to you that our comrade, Bergman, will speak tomorrow.

The meeting took place. The synagogue was overflowing below and also above in the women's section. It had been made known that Comrade Bergman would speak. Only ten percent had probably come to hear the rabbi's speech.

The rabbi spoke first. There was a quiet stir, murmuring; we actually did not hear a word. After 10 minutes of speaking, he left the reader's desk and, immediately thereafter, also the synagogue. After the rabbi, our comrade, Bergman, spoke; there was a stir and not a word [of Bergman's speech] could be heard. We declared a short break and Comrade Yechezkel Birencwajg declared loudly in a very theatrical pose:

– We give you 10 minutes so that those who are not happy that comrade Bergman is speaking in the synagogue can leave the synagogue calmly and without a tumult. And we will have an indication that those who wish to remain have come to hear comrade Bergman and woe to those who would still try to disturb someone after this.

Perhaps two minyanim [a minyan consists of 10 men] of Jews left the synagogue. Comrade Bergman, in the greatest quiet and attentiveness, spoke for over an hour. Then Moshe Szmulewicz, Shmuel Chaim Kelman and Mordechai Sapirsztajn spoke. The first in the name of Poalei-Zion [Marxist Zionists] and the last two in the name of the Zionists.

In general, the meeting, with several comical incidents, passed in the best order.

First it must be acknowledged that the Belchatower youth benefited a great deal spiritually from all of the meetings, speakers, lectures and reports, with or without discussions.

\* \* \*

As in all larger and smaller cities and shtetlekh in Poland, there was no lack of Jewish thieves and, in general, Jewish members of the underworld here.

The thieves were not fastidious people; they "took" everything that they could. They "took" chickens and geese from the market stalls; they "took down" the wash from the attics and if it happened and they learned that a family was not at home, they took every important things of value from the house and "withdrew"...

The gang was mainly busy on Mondays when they could "cultivate" so many arriving peasants.

A particular category was the card player who "worked" jointly in larger groups. The same gang, from time to time, paid a visit, "touring," the neighboring shtetlekh around Belchatow during the special market days.

The gang had another "trade" – ambushes. They figured out when Jews would bring money to Belchatow. It usually occurred on Thursday night. Every Thursday the Belchatow manufacturers would bring money with them to pay the workers on Shabbos. Then the gang with masks on their faces would block the Dzialoszyn forest, stopping as many wagons as would arrive from Piotrkow and with weapons in their hands rob the passengers. Principally they robbed all of the money that everyone possessed; but they did not turn down a gold watch, a ring or other things of value...

Belchatowers even said that years ago the same band carried out a bold ambush. They stopped a train and robbed the mail and disappeared.

The Belchatow police mixed very little in these matters. Some believed that the police were simply afraid of them and others that they were silent partners in the "businesses"... It is entirely possible that both sides were correct.

With the outbreak of the war in 1914, the entire band disappeared and the "trade" declined.

Another group of "actors" "worked" at selling the "stolen" goods. Their work was very simple: finding the customer, leading him through a gate and placing a piece of goods that caught the eye. And because it was "stolen goods," they were sold very cheaply. At home, the customers realized that they had bought a nice... piece of paper.

Jews, too, and even smart men, purchased such bargains...

A very special category was the horse thief. The "business" was carried out on a very large scale. And although, the "main" robbers and receivers were Poles, the Jews played a very significant role, both among the thieves and among the receivers.

The chief Polish thieves, the Knopek brothers, were people of extraordinary daring. They were not afraid of anyone. On the contrary, they were the terror of the entire shtetl and even of the police. Anyone who started with them was not certain about their life and they kept quiet.

A legend circulated in our circle that all of the horses that were stolen in the area of Lodz – Kalisz – Czenstochow went through Belchatow hands.

In order to finish with our underworld, we must add that we did not need to order blackmailers from outside. We had our own. The Jews in the shtetl had great trouble from them. There were two of them. One, Shmuel, the son of Nekhemia Meir, was a very cunning and crafty person; his "trade" was to denounce and then "use influence" and free the denounced one for good money... And the other one was Leibush Mekhl Lande, a not-too-smart man (a Jew, a Hasid, certainly smart, once brought him into his house, carried on negotiations with him about freeing his son from military service and just at the paying of the "trade-money," a secret agent appeared – and the shtetl had a short time of peace ... until he came back from jail). However, he had a very "rich" career. Beginning as a revolutionary, he was active in the P.P.S. [Polish Socialist Party]. After the failure of the revolution he had to escape from Poland and in 1918 he returned from London and became a "foolish" merchant and ended as a martyr. On Purim, 1942, he was one of the 10 Jews who were publicly hung by the Nazis before the entire Belchatow population...

Actually not a great pedigree, but facts remain facts.

*　*　*

**The Forest**

Heinrich Heine said that the Rhine is his. It can boldly be said about the Belchatower forests that they belonged to the Jewish youth. We called it "the forest," although that is a great error because it would have had to be called "the forests." Actually, there was not one forest, but many forests. There was the low forest, the high forest, the young little forest, the Brzezinkas, the Smoliarne and still many other forests. And these are only the more well known that were near the city. In fact the entire 16 kilometers between Belchatow to the nearest shtetl, Stradzew, was almost only forest.

During the summer months we would (if we had the time) spend entire days in the forest. In general, we were very close to the forest. It was two kilometers by the highway by a straight road.

However we went through a closer road, perhaps one kilometer in total. The closer road was Pabiancer Street. Through each courtyard on the left side of the above mentioned street was a passage to the fields and meadows straight into the forest. We traveled over the road in a few minutes.

What did we not do in the forests? Meetings and gatherings were held there; readings, discussions, conversations and the rehearsals were often also held there; tennis was even played – lehavdil [Usually the word used to separate the sacred from the profane; here it is used ironically.] – the forest served for playing games of cards. In the years of 1914-1918, when there was no work because of the war, we actually lived there during the summer months. Yet there were no summer residences in the forest then. During the last year, the well-to-do population from Belchatow sensed the prized air that the forest possessed and erected their summer residences there.

**The road to the little forest**

**The small bridge shortened the way to the little forest**

On the other side of the highway, another forest was located about three kilometers on the Piotrokower highway, the Dobszelower forest. But this forest was unknown to our young people. We had no great involvement with it. There was something threatening there (many times bandit attacks and robberies came from this forest). If we would sometimes take a walk there, we had the feeling that we should do something adventurous... In Dobszelower forest, we felt as if... in a forest, while in our forest we felt better than at home.

After spending a day in the forest, we first began to make "improvements" in the meadows. We did not "labor" on difficult problems there, but with light flirtations. There we spoke of all of the gossip; there we learned who would marry whom, who would break up with whom. There our entire song repertory was sung. Many times, actually thanks to the songs, peasants with their dogs chased us from our gan-eden [Garden of Eden, or paradise].

The songs had a thousand allures and sounded like the most beautiful music to us, and the smells of the woods by day and of the fields at night – cannot be compared to the most expensive perfume.

*   *   *


**Hasidim**

It occurred then that Hasidism also contributed a great deal to the development of the shtetl. True, we carried out a constant war with them, both individually and collectively. We considered them as the serious darkness. However, just looking back to a dynasty of so many years and with a little objectivity, we see the great virtues that they possessed and how they contributed, without class consciousness, to the progress of the shtetl.

We had two categories of pious Jews: Hasidim and balebatim [businessmen] (not misnagdim – followers of the Enlightenment). The Hasidim were almost all well educated, knew the minute letters [were well versed in Jewish teachings] and even knew worldly things. And the balebatim were simple working people, hard toilers. As for piety, perhaps the balebatim were much more pious than the Hasidim, because the Hasidim, as was their style, were too "friendly" with God and skipping a Minchah [afternoon prayer] was not a very big thing for them... Therefore, it was easier to be able to debate with a Hasid than with a businessman.

The Hasidim belonged to various rabbinic dynasties. The largest in number were the Gerer Hasidim (near 600), next were the Aleksanderer, then the Nowa-Radomsker, Radziner, Wolborszer and Rospesher [Rozprza].These were very few in number. Therefore, they were great scholars. The last two, the Wolborszer and the Rospesher, were not scholars; the largest number of them were simple, common, businessmen who posed as Hasidim.

The most eminent and most lively were the Gerer; they controlled everything in the shtetl and administered the Agudah [the anti-Zionist Orthodox group, also known as Agudas Yisroel].

The Gerer, as the other Hasidim, thought little of the Wolborszer and Rospesher "Hasidim" and, like other Hasidim, did not consider them at all. The real Hasidim also did not approve of their rebbes because they were "women's rebbes" (they took payment for advice – mainly – from women).

Fights among the various sects of Hasidim were never lacking: once it was because of a shoykhet [ritual slaughterer] or a khazan [cantor]; another time because of a dayan [religious court judge], or about a rabbi or another religious functionary. Reasons for which to wage a mitzvah war [war of obligation] were never lacking. Very often arguments turned to beatings and even to denunciations. It happened many times that one Hasidic group banned the slaughtering of a shoykhet who belonged to another Hasidic side. Then they would send out a shamas [synagogue caretaker] to nail a declaration to each Jewish home that the food of all who had bought meat from this and that shoykhet is as treyf [unkosher] as pork. It happened that some, true, a few, who took this earnestly and the lunch was thrown out for the dog and they themselves ate heartache and, more, they had to kosher the dishes.

A number of those with religious functions were Gerer Hasidim. And although they, the Gerer, were the largest in number, they did not always come out as the victor in all of the quarrels. They had a particularly large failure in bringing a rabbi. The side of the middle class, who brought the Wolberszer Rabbi's son as the rabbi, was victorious after a quarrel of many Hasidim. And the rabbi, by the way, who "reigned" here for many years, was a very smart and cunning Jew.

With the appearance of the Bund and of the Zionists, the Hasidim found that a significant number of their young were being torn from them.

Immediately it seemed that with the renown of the Bundists and the Zionists, the Beis Asher [House of Asher] began to "suffer disgrace and shame," and no one remained to utter reproof because almost everyone had his own trouble in his own house... And a series of conferences began among the Hasidim, "What do we do?" How do we restrain the young so that they do not run to "them?" And with the approval of Agudah, it was, first of all, decided that they needed to give their young people something, something similar to that which they could have with "them." Poalei Emunah Yisroel [workers for the faith of the Jewish people] was then founded in Belchatow. The Hasidic young had the opportunity to imitate and to play a role in unions with managing committees, with meetings and gatherings, with speeches and all of the other good things.

A time later, the Hasidim, with Agudas Yisroel at the head, created the Beis-Yakov schools for girls, so that another youth organization was added for them.

One of the ways to win back their young was also that the Hasidim lowered their tone a great deal in relation to their children. It was no longer a scandal to wear a stiff collar or pressed pants and it was even once ignored that a young man met with a young girl.

And we must concede that the Hasidim won a great deal with this. True, they did not at that time carry on any great activities, but nevertheless, their presence was really felt and in time they became a side one had to consider. Several years later, the organized Hasidic young became a very great power.

Our Hasidim, may their virtues be exalted, very much believed in the saying, "Love labor and shun power, and do not become close to the authorities. " If a Hasid descended to a lower level and became impoverished; if a young man went off of kest [support of a son-in-law by his wife's father while he studies] and did not have something to do; if a Hasid was a failure – instead of becoming a teacher or a religious functionary, he became a barber. Some of them also became bookkeepers (they were called verk-firer [work leaders or guides] here).

I believe that there were not so many such Hasidim in Poland, Hasidim who were not only not ashamed of any craftsman, but were themselves craftsmen.

It is not an exaggeration if I say that 60 percent (we do not have any exact statistic) of all barbers in Belchatow were Gerer Hasidism. The first professional class union in Belchatow was actually the haircutters union, and to our satisfaction, it should be underlined here that the majority of the Hasidim in the union entirely supported the experiment of the class conscious proletarian. It is true that the leaders of the haircutters union were the Bundists. However, we had nothing to complain about the Hasidic membership. As a proletarian party, it happened that we had to carry out various strikes. However, we had very few strike-breakers to record among the Hasidic group. It must be added here that they, the Hasidim, always found themselves in an uncomfortable situation because at the time, the bread bakers also were Hasidim and came together in the same Hasidic shtibl and very often were from the same families.

If a strike took place in a trade, we made sure that several Hasidim would be found on the strike committee. At the negotiations with the manufacturers, for their comfort, we would arrange with them that they would speak little. It once happened that we were sitting with the manufacturers negotiating a new wage increase and, as usual, the shkutsim [plural of shaygets – non-Jewish male, often a derogatory term, but also indicating less pious Jews] were the spokesmen. A Hasidic manufacturer wanted to provoke a Hasid-proletarian and turned to him with these words: "Tell me, Shlomo (Liberman), you have nothing to say about this matter? Your job here is only as a quiet judge at khalitzah.[7] Let us hear your words!" The proletarian Hasid answered him: "We cannot all speak at the same time and, in addition, do you remember the Tractate: 'Silence is tantamount to admission.' It says that if we keep quiet it is a sign that we agree…"

One proletarian Hasid, Reb Moshe Aizyk (Bresler), paraphrased a gemara saying for us after each winning strike: "At first we really did not need to strike; because the weavers earned more? But, afterwards – go out."

1921 was a very stormy year in Belchatow. This year was specially engraved in memories and left a very marked impression. During this year there was a regrouping of forces, a transformation that warned of new competition; this was the year in which a split in the Bund took place.

A discussion had long gone on in the Bundist press. Long articles with arguments for and against were written from all sides. And there were three sides. Each group pleaded its viewpoint. One group pleaded for "16 points" for progress. A second – "19½ points" and the third – an entire "21 points." The groups were designated with the names of the points. Thus in the press, thus in the large cities and also in the small shtetl: "the 16s," "the 19½s," and "the 21s." It also reached our shtetl.

Meetings, consultations, gatherings, reports and discussions were held day and night. The reports and discussions took place with our forces and also with those from outside who came from the center. The greatest wrangling and arguments took place at the election of delegates to the preliminary conference that took place in Lodz. And, then, during the election of a delegate to the general national conference.

The frictions and rift tendencies were already clearly felt. We were sure that even if it did not come to a division on a national scale, we would not emerge from this matter with our bones intact.

The first one on the fire was the "Culture Union." The signs of division were already visible; many books, a flashlight and other trifles, were already missing from the library. And it was left for us to think about a very earnest question of what to do with the library? The library, which we so loved, that we thought of as the dearest of our possessions. We were ready to forfeit many things, but not our library. We were simply afraid that the books would be dragged to different places and the library that had been built up and protected with so much effort, love and reverence would become nothing.

After many nights of not sleeping, after many consultations and deliberations, it was decided with great heartache (many comrades cried at this) that for the safety and security of the library, we should provisionally remove the books from the Union and place them in private homes with two responsible comrades.

When it was learned in the morning that the library had been "captured," the other side that had also considered doing the same thing, but had come a little too late – began a very great uproar, warned and threatened, but like Jewish thieves, we got away with empty threats.

The library existed in this way in private homes for a long time. Books, although not as often as earlier, were exchanged. Until the time came and the books were replaced in their spot in the closet of the Union and everything became normal again.

After the split in the Bund, the split off group under the name "Kombund" became active in Belchatow. Two comrades arriving from outside had a great part in the split in Belchatow: one the well known name, Comrade Hershl Bekerkunst and the other, a Lodzer, Comrade Aleksander. Actually this was the birth, the beginning of the Jewish Communist organization in Belchatow.

Although it lost a portion of its members, the Bund was not weakened very much. The opposite, it had to take on new strength for new challenges. It received a new, an important opponent in the form of the Communist party which, in time, grew into a large movement.

The leader of the new party in Belchatow was our former comrade, Yechezkel Birencwajg.

*   *   *

In 1922 a great emigration of the Belchatow Jewish youth began. There were many reasons: in first place was the economic one. After the ending of the First World War, when everything slowly began to start and become normal, the situation for the Jewish workers hardly improved. Only a few fortunate ones succeeded in finding work in the mechanical weaving factories; the majority of Jewish workers had to continue working in slavish conditions at hand weaving. A second cause was the anti-Semitism from which they ran as if from a fire. Another cause, I will say, was "adventuristic" – the young learned a little about geography, read many travel writings, saw before them a large, beautiful, wide world. They wanted to look at the world and not shrivel up in a small shtetl. So they sought means and ways to extract themselves from the shtetl.

There had once been a large emigration of working youth from here into the world. This was after the failure of the Russian revolution of 1905. Then the emigration was mainly to the United States of North America. This time it would have gone in the same direction if not for the quota decrees. As it was not possible to go to America, the travel was to wherever possible: to the Soviet Union, to Germany, France, Belgium, Eretz-Yisroel, Argentina, Brazil and other American nations. So that today, large groups of our landsleit are found in the United States, in Israel, in the Soviet Union and in Argentina. And smaller groups – in Belgium, France and Brazil. And individuals among our landsleit are found scattered in countries all over the world.

On one side it is a joy that Belchatow Jews are found all over the world, and on the other side, very sad that in our dear shtetl, Belchatow, there is not one living Jew to be found.

* * *

I cannot end my description if I do not at least remember several interesting people and unusual types in Belchatow.

Our haimish [homey] and good Jews stand before my eyes and implore: Remember us, we accomplished something in our poor life!

**Reb Levi Matseyvah Kritzer [headstone carver] (Reich):** a Gerer Hasid, a scholar, a Jew, a know-it-all and can-do-it-all. The headstones that he carved were works of art adapted to each one's character: if the deceased was a kohen, one saw two hands giving the priestly blessing, if it was a levi, a hand with a pitcher that pours water on the hands of the kohen. For a Jew who was knowledgeable about Yiddishkeit [the Jewish essence; a Jewish way of life], a closet with religious books. If it was a deceased child – an extinguished candle; a grown child – a broken off tree. For a young woman who left several children – a lost flock of sheep without a shepherd... And so constantly. Today, the inscriptions on the headstones are actually poetry, it should be understood, matched to each one's character. What did this Jew not know? From exorcism from an evil eye to repairing complicated machines; from a page of the Zohar to painting a room with birds in the air. And if one of the few telephones possessed by the shtetl ceased to function – no one but Reb Levi was called. And if the rich man, Reb Mendl Jalowski, wanted to make a permanent sukkah in one room of his rich apartment, Reb Levi invented a machine, fastened in a crate on the wall and with a crank to open or close the roof from inside in a given minute. If this Jew had gone to school, he would have certainly been a great inventor.

**Reb Eli Sherer [barber] (Leib),** a rich man, also a scholar. He became impoverished during his middle years; he had to become an artisan. First a bookkeeper (with Reb Moshe Nechemia Teitlbaum) and then a simple worker – a barber (that is how he got the nickname). A great pedagogue: his days were calculated and divided to the minute. Although a factory worker, he always prayed with a minyan. He still had time every day for a few chapters of Psalms, a portion of the Chumash, a chapter of the Mishnah and then also a page of the Gemara. His closest friend was Reb Levi Matseyvah Kritzer. Like the other one, he knew everything. What his eyes had seen, his hands made: all kinds of carvings from wood and and from bone; taking apart and putting back together the most complicated machines. If a part was used up, he carved or poured another part, so that it was hardly noticed. He never took a watch to be repaired by the watchmaker and if Reb Levi ever had a complicated matter, the two Jews came together for a consultation and the mystery was solved. An artist was also submerged in Reb Eli Sherer.

**Moshe Eliezer Pudlowski**                **Reb Eli Leib**

**Reb Yeshayahu Shrage.** A respected Jew, a Gerer Hasid. Always wearing a long garment down to his knees (except on Shabbos). The constant bal-musaf [one who recites the supplementary – Musaf – prayers on Shabbos and holidays] in the Gerer shtibl during the Days of Awe. A Jew from generations of Hasidim.

**Reb Yehiel Itshe Elbinger.** A Radziner Hasid. A very bright Jew. A patriarchal Jew from a family with many branches. One of the greatest scholars of the shtetl, perhaps the greatest scholar.

**Reb Josef Leibush Gruszke.** A Radziner Hasid. Tall and straight as a stick. Always very earnest. It was said that he was never seen smiling, let alone laughing.

**Reb Eli Feywl Gelbard and Reb Yakob Hersh Stadtlender.** Two respected Jews, always dozores [synagogue wardens]. The mediators of the shtetl. One ran to them if a matter had to be undertaken with or requested of the regime. They did not make anything from this, did it only for the sake of heaven.

**Yakob Hersh Stadtlender**

**Reb Shlomo Shamas [Szmulewicz].** The shamas of the synagogue. Accurately, the rabbi's attendant. He was a very intelligent Jew and also a sort of mediator who never did it for his own self interest.

**Reb Yeshayahu, son of Zuske (Eksztajn).** A Gerer Hasid. His was a bel-tekiah [blower of the shofar or ram's horn] by "trade" in the Gerer shtibl [one room prayer house] his entire life. It never happened during the blowing of the shofar that a tkie [drawn out sound] was the least imperfect. When he died, his son, Reb Moshe, son of Yeshayahu son of Zuske, took his place.[8] He also carried on his "mission" with great success and his father was never shamed.

**Reb Mordechai, son of Josef: "The tall Mordechai, son of Josef" (Liberman).** A Radziner Hasid. The father of a family with many branches.

Tall, stiff and cold. "**The small Mordechai, son of Josef (Jalowski)**, a Gerer Hasid, Lively, joyful. A piece of quicksilver.

**Reb Lozer Szpigelman.** A Gerer Hasid. A Jew, a very poor man. He was always ready to die in the sanctification of God's name. He was always the first one, the leader, in the wars with the non-believers. He always came out of such a war with another tear in his already ripped frock coat.

**Reb Shmuel Yeshayahu (Szilit)** and **Reb Michalke.** Both were dayonim [religious judges]. Both were occupied with deciding religious questions [usually deciding whether something is kosher or not] for the shtetl. The first was young, genteel; the other – old, angry. The first – lenient; the other – rigorous. The majority of the women went to Reb Shmuel Yeshayahu with a question. Shmuel Yeshayahu used an opportunity to explain: He said that with a rich Jew's question he is just as strict as Reb Michalke, but if a question comes to him from a poor man, it hurts his heart and he cannot say something is unkosher with a light spirit.

### Reb Michalke

**Reb Hershl Shoychet, Reb Berl Shoychet, Reb Chaim Itshe Shoychet, the Grocholicer Shoykhet, Reb Leibl Shoykhet (the son of the Opter Khazan** [cantor], **the Soyfer** [scribe] **and the Soyfetre** [wife of the scribe]. Fine Jews, good Jews, some of the clergy of the shtetl.

**Rochl, Hershl Shoykhet's wife**          **Reb Hershl Shoykhet**

**Reb Meirl Gerer (Starawinski), Reb Josef Shaul Krakowski, Reb Alter Bornsztajn (the fat Alter), Reb Mordechai Szpigelman, Reb Chaim Tusk, Reb Josel Warszawski,** respectable Jews, Hasidim about whom it would be worthwhile to describe each separately with their virtues and, even, their faults.

**Reb Berl *Shamas* (Gelbart).** A Jew, a scholar and a Jew, a strong man and, in addition, unafraid. It was rare to find such a paradox in a Polish Jew: that learning and strength were united in one Jew. He was the father of 16 children (from one wife). In the synagogue in which he was the shamas he ran things with a strong hand. He had no greater respect for eminent, important Jews. Not even for the dozor [overseer]. He was not even afraid of the great show-offs. When he felt it was necessary, he gave them a loud slap and threw them out of the synagogue like a splinter. Everyone actually trembled before him. In order to characterize his fearlessness, a story such as this was told about him: Once, still in the Czarist times, he had to be a witness in the Piotrkower County Court on a very important matter. Before he was given the oath that he would tell the truth, he became bored with the game; he gave the judge a look of contempt, and blurted out in real soldierly Russian (he once served Fonya [Russia] for seven years): "Whoever bores me will have to spit me out..." He sat in jail for seven days for this statement.

**"The blind Eli" (Reb Eli Gelbart). A son Reb Berl *Shamas*.** A scholar, a misnagid [opponent of Hasidism]. A Jew, an influential man and a sage. However, he rarely used his influence, but always only with wisdom and with tact.

**Reb Moshe Lozer Tomaszewer (Pudlowski).** A Gerer Hasid. A great scholar. Spent more time in Ger than at home. And at home, the Gerer shtibl and the gemara interested him more than his own business.

**Reb Mendl Josef Przedborski (the *treybeczarcz* [one who removes the forbidden vein from meat]).** A clergyman, he would remove the veins from the cows, a Gerer Hasid, an irascible person. He was never satisfied, always had a complaint to someone...

**Reb Yitzhak Leibush Przedborski ("kleyn tatele" [small father]).** Brother of Mendl Josef. He was entirely the opposite of his brother. Also a Gerer Hasid, a very lively one, dancing, always cleaned up, happy, a fervent man of faith. He was sure that God would help, He must help! "Who else would He help if not His Jews?" He was a grain merchant. Once, it was in 1918, he failed in smuggling wheat and went to the Piotrkow jail for several months. It was the Days of Awe. He used his persuasion to have a Sefer-Torah [Torah scroll] and permission to pray with a minyan [10 men required for prayer]. He was actually the bal-tefilah [person who recites the prayers at the lectern], the bal-koyre [Torah reader] and also the bal-tekiah [person who blows the shofar or ram's horn]. When he came home after serving his term, he said that he knew why he had been in jail: not for smuggling, but in order to right a wrong. Because if not for him, the Jews who were in jail would not have prayed and, perhaps, not known that it was the Days of Awe and he not only had personal satisfaction from that, but he thought of it simply as a particularly rare honor.

**"Chaya the baker,"** their sister, a true woman of valor, a very smart Jewish woman and very pious, a Hasidiste [a female Hasid], went to the rabbis and presented kwitlekh [notes requesting the rabbi's intervention with God for a marriage for a child, a child for a barren woman, etc.]. Never ate without praying and the only thing lacking for her to be a man was a talis-katan [fringed undergarment worn by pious men]...

**Reb Shalom Amshinower, Reb Hershl Dzialoszyner, Moshe *Red* (Tsingler), Joske *Greger*** [rattle and noisemaker used on Purim at mention of Haman's name during the reading of the *Megillah*] **(Bornsztajn),** *Melamdim* [teachers]: **Yeshaya Baber, Yoske Greger's son,** types who each deserve at least to be remembered.

**Reb Shalom "Ox" (Grynwald), Reb Yeshaya Dovid "oil presser," Reb Yankl "winemaker." Nisele *Moshiekh* [redeemer]** – Hasidic toilers.

**Reb Avrahaml Patshner (Czarnilas).** A Jew, a great proprietor and extraordinarily pious Jew who believed with complete faith that he would live to see *Moshiach* [the redeemer].

**The Kliszczewer Rabbi, Judl the son of the *Rebbitzen* [rabbi's wife], Ahron Pinkhus Bornsztajn, Shmul Chaim Kelman,** impractical philosophers: it could never be learned what was more dominant with them – the impractical or the philosophy. The last one even made attempts to publish his own journal.

**Perec Frajtag.** The richest man in the *shtetl*, the first manufacturer on a large scale. He employed the largest number of workers and employees.

**Michal Avigdor Pilawski.** One of the Belchatow "Germans." An intelligent Jew, an aristocrat. He could tell a fine joke.

**Avraham *Feldsher*** [barber-surgeon] **(Laskowski).** He was once a bad weaver, became a *feldsher* and made a very fine living from it.

**Reb Yankl *Feldsher* (Warsawski).** He was a good, educated Jew in the full sense of the word (even in the Jewish religious sense). In addition, he had a very fine character. It occurred more than once that coming to a poor sick man, he would not only not take payment for the visit, but left a half ruble so that the poor man could pay for the prescription.

**Meir Warszawski**, Yankl *Feldsher's* oldest son, was a communal worker, intelligent and a very good person. He stood at the head of the Zionist organization.

**Rozenblum Brothers.** There were four of them and what a giant contrast from one to the other. Each – a separate world: Zelik the oldest was a cultured man, Yankl – actually a peasant, Yudl – a toiler, a tailor, a very fine person, and the youngest, the *Lobudzicer galakh* [priest] – was a bit of an exception, half underworld, three-quarters convert – actually a hero of a trashy novel.

**Itshe Leib Goldbersht.** A great "book eater." He was always the prompter at the dramatic troop of the Culture-Union until the split in the Bund.

**Henoch Liberman, Avraham Liberman,** from Hasidic (Radziner), rich parents. Dear, good, earnest and responsible friends. The first, the almost constant secretary, and the other, almost always the treasurer of the Bundist Culture Union.

From right to left:
seated: Avraham Liberman,
Henoch Liberman
standing: Yechezkiel Birenzweig,
Henoch Pigula, Henoch Grushka


**Ruchl Lichtenfeld, Ruchl Szmulewicz and her brothers, Eli Twadowski, Moshe and Shimeon Szmulewicz, the Avramczyk brothers, the Statlender**

**brothers, the Niwinski sisters and brothers, the Sztajn sister and brother, sisters, Yochowed and Gitl Eksztajn, Daniel and Leibush Warsawski, Chaim Meir Czeslowski, "the dark Berl" and Yeshayahu Langnas**, each in their way and in their circle made themselves useful in communal work.

**Henoch Pigula**, a mix of young man of the House of Study and a wagon driver. A son of a Radziner Hasid, Reb Yisroel-Dowid Pigula.

**Yissochar Przybylski**, from a good family. His father, Chaim-Ber, a Hasid, a very sincere man of the people, from the Jews, of whom it is said: For God and for the people. Yissochar, a dear, devoted comrade. His words were weighed and measured. The responsible missions with which he was entrusted were always carried out faithfully by him.

**Avraham-Ber "Poznanski" (Zylbersztajn), Yitzhak Goldminc, Yehiel Boruchowicz, Josef-Leib Gelbart**, dear and good Jews. Founders and leaders of *Mizrakhi* [Religious Zionists].

**Tsiml Jakubowicz**, from an aristocratic, Hasidic family. Her husband, Yudl, who was not a Hasid, died young. He did not leave any riches. Therefore a full house of children (nine little souls) remained, with whom his wife drudged until they grew up and could help earn money. Most of the children were "Bundists."

**Yechezkiel Birenzweig** possessed many qualities and also not a few defects. He came from the *yeshiva*, had read a great deal, was intelligent, smart, could speak before a crowd and knew what to say. He possessed a great deal of arrogance, courage and daring. And, in addition, was athletically built. With the virtues, he had enough defects: whims as if an only son of rich parents, thought a lot of himself; he considered himself an authority in discussions with the tone of a final judge... He came from simple people (his father was a wagon driver, "Makhl *Furman*" [driver]).

He was a good organizer, a leader (he liked this very much), but he did not allow himself to be led by others. He was a member of the party until the split in the Bund, but because of his individualistic character he never took any leadership positions. After the split he became the leader of the Communists, but in time, because of disciplinary reasons, he was shut out from it. He had three brothers. The one older than he, Kalman, was a rabbi in a *shtetl* somewhere in Poland and never visited Belchatow and the one younger than he, Shama – was also an intelligent and gifted young man, who was active in the Communist Party. He was later exiled because of this in Kartuz-Bereza, a Polish concentration camp.

**Feywl *Klezmer*** [musician, plural *klezmorim*] **(Jakubowicz).** Was renowned in the *shtetl*. The first fiddler and the leader of the *klezmorim* company, of whom almost all were from the same family: Zishe *Klezmer*, his father, Yude *Klezmer* – a brother and so on. They played at weddings and other celebrations. They also played at the weddings of nobles because they were the only musicians in Belchatow and the surrounding area. They were also invited to play at weddings in surrounding *shtetlekh*.

**The *Kradnikes* (Felds).** It was a large, many branched family that had nothing to do with its name. They were honest merchants, manufacturers, toilers such as: Yankl, Josef-Leib, Perec, Mendl (the latter was *dozor* [synagogue warder] for a time and a martyr in 1942 – one of the 10 who were murdered). Perhaps the nickname *Kradnikes* [thieves] was taken from the fact that they were all smart, ingenuous, cunning, great wits and also a little sly.

**The Kliczczewer Butcher (Lejzorowicz).** Was an honest businessman, had several children, of whom two were particularly distinguished: one – Hersh Mendele, a thief, a bandit, an aggressor who was feared all over, and the other – Yakov (if I am correct) was a rabbi. A rabbi in the *shtetl*, Kliczszew.

**Yankl Jakubowicz ("Yankl Fish").** An ordinary man, a tailor son of a tailor. An honest craftsman and a great tradesman. Mostly he sewed for the nobles around Belchatow. He was a strange Jew; he improvised extraordinary sayings and curses. It is a shame that they were not recorded. They were a treasury of folklore. Here, for example, are some of his curses: You should meet "*Moshe Rabeinu's* [Moses] tempest." "Let a black wind enter your intestines." "Let twisted lint enter your body." "Let your head push you to your heart." And so on. Older Jews said that his father, "Moshe Fish," had an even larger variety of curses. It is really a shame that they were not recorded.

**The Huberman Brothers.** "*Der Skorpis*" [the scorpions] or the Sons of *Skorpis* as the *shtetl* referred to them. They were three: Moshe, Mikhal-Wigder and Kalman. Wagon drivers. Very honest Jews, well-established businessmen. Unafraid Jews, sturdily built strong men, really athletes. If there was a Jew-gentile tumult, they were the first in the street and really saved Jewish honor more than once with their arms.

**Hersh Dowid *Furman*** [wagon driver] **(Szwarcberg), Grunem's son, Itshe**, wagon drivers. They also did not have to be asked when it came to administer blows.

The *shtetl* possessed a large group of young, bold strong men of whom the Christian population shook in deadly fear: **Dowid's son, Note Hersh, Shimeon *Lekekh-beker*** [cake baker]**, Avraham Alter Khmol, Yakov Hilel, Chaim Yankl, Grunen's son, Itshe, Yankl Pachczarsz, Melekh Krawicki** and others. God forbid, not members of the underworld, but simply working young men, wagon drivers, young giants, who could exchange blows and they did inflict them when it was necessary and even when it was not necessary. They were always ready to defend Jewish honor.

**Chaim Leib *Drupczik*.** One of the thieves in the *shtetl*. Really more a victim than thief, because wherever a robbery took place, he was taken first and was beaten with murderous blows, so that he paid for all robberies, even those which he did not commit.

**The Machabanskis** were a large, many branched family. The **Wengers** and the **Adlers** belonged to the same family. All of them were very fine craftsmen, weavers. There were complete little factories in their house, with three or four and more looms. It depended upon how many children and apprentices one possessed. They almost always stuck together. In the synagogue, too, where they prayed, they had a separate table (the first one towards the door) at which only they prayed. A great number of "initiatives" of buffoonery were born at this table: If a Jew at the table during the reading of the Torah was engrossed in thought, one of them awakened him – Reb Berish, you are being called up to the Torah! The Jew quickly went up to the reading desk, but another Jew had already said the blessing... Another time they saw to it that two Jews would go up to both sides of the reading desk simultaneously and both would stand to recite the blessing. And if they succeeded in tying a feather duster to the *tziztes* [fringe] of the *talis* [prayer shawl] of one of the wise men (Avraham Luks, Moshke's son, Leibush, etc.) they convinced the *gabbai* that this one had a *yahrzeit* [anniversary of a death] and that he deserved an *aliyah*...[9] At the *faln Koyrim* [kneeling in adoration] on Rosh Hashanah, when someone received a *Makhsor* [holiday prayer book] in his head, or even a boot – it was not from another corner, but from the Machabanskis.

The initiator of all of these jokes was Yeshayahu Machabanski, and his "scholar" was Moshe *Grois* [large].

**Tsine's son, Hershl (Herckowicz).** He had two trades; he was a shoemaker and a liar. He did not have food from his shoemaking. What he had from this trade was a pair of gallant, shiny boots, with high, small feminine heels. Try to imagine: A Jew with a wide, red beard, a Jewish hat with a long smock and boots with high heels.

He also did not have food from his second "trade," but in his fantasy (in which he very much believed) he swam away to such high worlds with such enthusiasm and winged stories that he forgot that he had a wife and an entire gang of hungry, crippled children and that he himself was also not so sated. When all of his exaggerated stories had been recorded it would have been a treasure for Jewish folklore. As he had once served in the Czarist Army, a large number of his exaggerations were about the Czar and his gang. Everyone in the *shtetl* knew the Hershl possessed a small gold sword, "a gift from him, from the Czar." The Czar's picture always hung on a wall in his home, "an award for heroism given by the Czarina herself." When the Germans occupied Belchatow in 1914, no plea and no warnings by his Jewish neighbors that he should take the picture off the wall helped. He had good fortune that the picture was already so dotted by flies that for a long time one could not recognize who was in the picture.

Many Jewish men and also Jewish women stand before my eyes and ask that if they are not described, then at least remember, remember them as they were.

How can we not remember such Jews as Reb Leibush Fajner and his wife, Mikhal's son, Mikhal's son, Shlomo, Reb Avraham Pakter, Reb Motele the shaky one (Gliksman), Reb Alyakim *Propan* [propane] (Zwierczinski) and his sons, Reb Josef-Leib and Reb Shlomo *Midlarcz* [honeyed]. Leibush Moszkeske, Zarah Polakewicz ("the coffee roaster"), Jakow Ajzner ("the blind Jekev"), the very many branched Wilhelm families, Henech Michalski, Yankl Ostrowski, Yankl Flakowicz, Itshe Meir Girwec, Itshe Meir *Valus* [heavy] (Naperstek), Yankl Czitnicki, Avraham "Soldier," Shmuel-Zakan Chojnacki, Josef-Ber "Paplok" (Jakubowicz), Manish Treger [porter], Moshle *Dorfsgeyer* [man who goes from village to village to either buy or sell things], Manele *Shneyder* [tailor], Groynem's son, Yekl, the old Binecki, the deaf Emanuel (Czikocki), Moshe-Lejzer *Voitel* [governor] "the tall Moshe," Yudl the cake baker and his wife, Zakan the shoemaker, Yeshayahu the baker, Yudl Grocolicer and more and more dear and good Jews, merchants and toilers who labored very hard in order to honestly earn a piece of bread. May their names at least be recorded in this book of memories for our vanished *shtetl*, Belchatow.

**Managing Committee from the Belchatow
Talmud Torah (Yeshiva)**

Standing (from the right): Moshe Vishniewsky, Yechezkiel Pabianicer, Yosef Pigula, Berish Novak, Israel Starawinsky, Hershl Zeidman, and S.M. Reinbad.
Seated (from the right): Zeinovl Boim, Friedlich (the oil maker), Meyer (the black Meyer), Eliyahu Gelbard (blind Eli), Nissan Meir Warshawsky, Moshel Mendel Krawiczky

**Participants in the Belchatower evening
courses with Aaron Bergman Brash**

**A group of schoolgirls from the Beit-Yaacov
School**
[The sign in the photo says "Beit-Yaacov School
Belchatow"]

---

**Translator's footnotes:**

1.  Karl Kautsky was an orthodox Marxist. Erfurt is a town in Germany at which the Erfurt Program was adopted by the Social Democratic Party.

2.  The Tarbut school system in Poland emphasized the study of modern Hebrew and Hebrew literature.

3.  *Chol ha-Moed* is the intermediate days during *Sukkos* – the Feast of Tabernacles – and during Passover, during which work is permitted.

4.  A *shulkleper* would go from house to house on Friday afternoons, knocking on windows, shutters or doors with the message that it was time to light the *Shabbos* candles and go to the synagogue.

5.  Literally, "strong youth" – a phrase that refers to strong, young men who would defend the Jewish population of a city or *shtetl* from any threats from the non-Jewish population. The *shtarke jungen* usually included butchers, because they were already "armed" with the knives of their trade.

6.  *Zelners* could mean he was the son of a soldier – a *zelner* is a soldier.

7.  *Khalitzah* is the release, in the presence of religious judges, from a Levirate marriage – a marriage in which a brother is required to marry the widow of his childless brother.

8.  It was customary to refer to someone as the "son of" or "daughter of" someone. Hence the repetition that his son was his son.

9.  A call to read a portion of the Torah at the reader's desk. This is an honor and often given to one who is observing a *yahrzeit*.

*[Pages 200–207]*

# Relief Activities
# During the First World War

### Translated from the Yiddish by Martin Bornstein

The (World War II) survivors of the Belchatow Jews, who now are found in the state of Israel, took along with themselves an interesting document, which was saved by accident and contains the

### Report of the Belchatow Relief and Backing Committee

### For the time between February 18th, 1915 till July 31st, 1917

This is a logbook that is handwritten and contains a precise report of the relief that was given in that period to the needy Jewish people in Belchatow. The said document without a doubt has historical significance for the history of the disappeared Jewish shtetl [small town] and we find it of importance to give here the full contents of the document. In the explanation, written on four sides, it says the following:

"Without support from the side, only with their own strength of a group of young people, was the first relief institution founded, by us in the town, which had been so strongly affected [found] by the war. [So] On the 12th of February 1915 the cheap tea hall was founded. Right away it was demonstrated that the tea hall is still not enough, while the little town that counted more than 800 Jewish families who were as a result of the war [largely without work], the majority of whom were employed in industry, and the need [among them] was indescribable. Therefor immediately thereafter, on the 1st of March 1915, the cheap kitchen was founded, which could exist, as did the tea hall, from the membership dues for the good of the institution. Due to the small membership one had to carry out limited activities, although the consumers of the kitchen had increased over time, such that the 50 mid-day eaters of the beginning were substituted over the duration of time and increased to 600 daily. Therefor we want to express thanks to Misters Israel Pitowski and Stadtlender, who in a critical time for the kitchen, [assembled)] collected a significant sum for the kitchen, also the circle commander for his administration [donations] and produce [production] for the good of the tea hall together with the kitchen.

We first received the financial support of the Alliance * * * in March 1916. Since the kitchen could exist, although with limited activities, we decided to utilize the money from the Alliance for other purposes. [So] During Passover of 1916 we took on wider support activities and [during] Passover of 1917 we significantly enlarged the activities, which consisted of dividing [passing out] produce free of charge and also financial support.

The summer of 1916 on account of certain people, because of "principle" themes, there was carried on a heated battle against the "Free Thinking" [non-observant] kitchen that burned to the point that a lot of Belchatower stopped paying their membership dues for the good of the kitchen. In the middle of June the tea hall closed down and by the end of August we were forced to close the kitchen too.

The need in the town was indescribable. Hundreds of families, both Jewish and non-Jewish, the majority of whom were weavers, were left literally without bread. At that time the United Salvation Committee was first reorganized, which had to carry out the relief work amongst Jews and non-Jews. There [on the committee] the Jews were represented by Misters P. Freitag, M. H. Stadtlender, and M. Warshawski [Warszawski].

Thanks to the revenues of the salvation committee, together with the money from the Alliance, we had the possibility to carry out a wide [range] of relief activities, which mostly consisted of alms, interest free loans and further.

In the winter of 1916/1917 we were able, thanks to the collections of reb S. Y. Shilit [Szylit] and reb H. Weiss, to distribute wood for heating to the largest portion of the families, as well as 300 pairs of (wooden) clogs were distributed for free.

In March of 1917 we first had the possibility to renew the activities of the kitchen, and due to the predominant need [among the people] it was converted to be a free one [when it was re-established]. This turned out to be an impossible thing, as the count of mid-day eaters shows, which had increased to 1,200 – 1,300 daily, of whom almost half were children. We also distributed for the whole poor portion of the population free bread and to another portion we sold bread at cheap prices.

From June on we stopped receiving the financial support of the Alliance, so that whole branches of our activities had to be discontinued. In the end of

July the kitchens in general were also discontinued, among which also was our kitchen.

Now that an entire period of our relief activities has ended, we decided to deliver [publicize] openly a judgement – accounting of the incoming [influx of] money and of our activities.

With this opportunity we want to publicly express thanks to people openly who serviced different branches of our activities, the Misters reb S. Y. Shilit [Szylit], reb H. Weiss, I. Pitowski, M. Stadtlender, B. Waldman, A. Y. Rosenzweig, Mrs. Rosenblum, Mrs. Shilit [Szylit], Miss Fela Warshawski [Warszawski], and in general to everyone who was helpful to us in the work. "

The Organizing Committee
Belchatow the end of July 1917

* Alliance – Probably the "Alliance Israelite Universelle", which was founded in Paris in 1860 and was the first modern Jewish international organization.

[Page 203]

## The Tea Hall
## 18 February 1915 – 11 June 1916

| Income | | Expenditures | |
|---|---|---|---|
| 246.64 | Membership Dues | 908.84 | 5,453 pounds of bread [2,726.5 Kg ** ] |
| 499.47 | Donations | 416.56 | 886 pounds of sugar [443 Kg] (as part of it 64 pounds that came from the circle commander) |
| 450.11 | 16,204 glasses of tea sold at 1 krone each [about 3 glasses per ruble] * | 61.39 | 10 pounds of tea [5 Kg] |
| 428.03 | 15,409 portions of bread sold at 1 krone each | 147.64 | Rent |
| 15.73 | 283 portions of bread sold at 2 krones each | 111.11 | Heating |
| 244.00 | 2 containers of sugar weighing 488 pounds [244 Kg ** ] | 26.44 | Petty expenses |
| 560.00 | 14 sacks of flour received from the Circle commander in Piotrkow | 560.00 | 3,392 pounds of bread [1,696 Kg] that was distributed for free among 848 people |
| | | 212.00 | 424 pounds of sugar that was distributed for free [212 Kg] |
| **2,443.98 Rubles** | | **2,443.98 Rubles** | |

The exchange rate for the krone was 36 kopecks [for 1 krone] [The ruble is Russian currency, and 1 ruble is divided into 100 kopecks; the krone is Austrian/German currency.]

The Tea Hall gave out during the time of its existence:

| | |
|---|---|
| 24,191 | Glasses of Tea [*] |
| 17,451 | Portions of bread with 12 pieces comprising a portion |
| 3,392 | Pounds of Bread [1696 Kg] given out free of charge |
| 224 | Pounds of sugar [212 Kg] given out free of charge |

* [Tea in Poland, Russia, and much of Eastern Europe is drunk from glasses and not cups or mugs.]

** [The "pound" in this table and all subsequent tables is the German "Pfund," which is equal to half a kilogram or 500 grams. Therefore 2 pounds = 1 kilogram. ]

———

*[Page 204]*

## Wood for the Winter [heating] 1916 – 1917

| Income | | Expenditures | |
|---|---|---|---|
| 1,494.80 | collected by Reb S.Y. Shilit [Szylit] and Reb H. Weiss | 2,344.80 | 28 fathoms of [fire] wood [a measure equal to 6 feet] |
| 250.00 | from the Salvation Committee | | |
| 600.00 | from the Alliance | | |
| **2,344.80 Rubles** | | **2,344.80 Rubles** | |

## Wooden Clogs 1916 –1917

| 1,582.30 R | from the Alliance | 1,582.30 R | to purchase and distribute 307 pairs of wooden clogs [about 5 rubles per pair] |
|---|---|---|---|

## Medicine for the Sick

| 200.00 R | from the Salvation Committee | 106.00 R | for medicine for 14 persons (free of charge) |
|---|---|---|---|
| | | 94.00 R | remaining in the treasury |
| **200.00 Rubles** | | **200.00 Rubles** | |

*[Page 205]*

## Passover 1916

| Income | | Expenditures | |
|---|---|---|---|
| 1,879.62 | income from flour money | 2,051.40 | 2,085 pounds of matzah (distributed among 287 families) |
| 208.34 | income from a Passover sugar sale | 1,831.30 | Financial Support (distributed among 92 families) |
| 200.00 | income from the Salvation Committee | 995.60 | 128 measures* of potatoes (distributed among 282 families) |
| 2,600.00 | income from the Alliance | 9.66 | assorted expenses |
| **4,887.96 Rubles** | | **4,887.96 Rubles** | |

[*the actual measure amount listed is – "kerz"]

### Passover 1917

| | | | |
|---|---|---|---|
| 2,497.00 | income from flour money | 4,617.40 | 3,360 pounds of matzah (distributed among 301 families) |
| 1,853.00 | income from [the sale of] Passover flour | 4,882.70 | financial support (distributed among 334 families) |
| 5,150.10 | income from the Alliance | | |
| **9,500.10 Rubles** | | **9,500.10 Rubles** | |

### Alms

| | | | |
|---|---|---|---|
| 381.00 | from the Salvation Committee | 2,182.40 | alms given out to 398 families |
| 1,351.40 | from the Alliance | | |
| **2,182.40 Rubles** | | **2,182.40 Rubles** | |

### Family Honor

| | | | |
|---|---|---|---|
| 3,607.50 R | from the Alliance | 3,607.50 R | alms given out to 160 families |

**Interest Free Loans**

| 681.50 R | from the Alliance | 681.50 R | money lent to 9 people |
|----------|-------------------|----------|------------------------|

---

[Page 206]

**Last Page of Handwritten Ledger**

[Translation of above document follows:]

| Balance on July 31, 1917 | | | |
|---|---|---|---|
| **Income** | | **Expenditures** | |
| 17,244.16 | Salvation Committee | 14,388.06 | Passover 1916/17 |
| 19,468.50 | Alliance | 681.50 | loans |
| 4,376.62 | flour [donated or from sale] | 5,789.90 | alms (together with honor) |
| 208.34 | from Passover sugar | 106. | medicines for the sick |
| 1,853. | from Passover flour | 1,582.30 | wooden clogs |
| 5,227.81 | donations | 2,344.80 | firewood for the winter |
| 1,464.58 | membership dues | 1,621.98 | Tea Hall |
| 893.87 | income from the Tea Hall | 19,960.79 | Kitchen (Produce) |
| 830. | from the Circle Commander | 4,011.53 | Kitchen (Expenses) |
| 127.98 | income from the Kitchen | 712. | distributed produce bread and baked goods |
| **51,694.86** | | **51,308.86** | |
| 386.00 | treasury resources [balance on hand] | 386.00 | |
| | | 51,694.86 | |

[The seal in German reads:     Belchatow the end of July
Jewish    Community    (Project) 1917
Administration Belchatow.]     The Organizing Committee:

Yakov Hirsh Stadtlender
[illegible signature –
possibly in Russian]
[signature – possibly P. Freitag]
[illegible signature]
[illegible signature – possibly B.
Piewszy]

[Based on the other tables the amounts given in this handwritten one are all
in Russian Rubles]

*[Page 207]*

**Belchatower Talmud-Torah (Yeshiva)**

**Youth committee of "Tzishoy" in Belchatow**

**FROM A RUINED GARDEN**

## The Memorial Books of Polish Jewry

Edited and Translated by
**Jack Kugelmass** and **Jonathan Bioyarin**
With Geographical Index and Bibliography by
**Zachary M. Baker**
Published in association with the
United States Holocaust Memorial Museum
Washington, D.C.
INDIANA UNIVERSITY PRESS
< http://www.indiana.edu/~iupress/ >
Bloomington and Indianapolis

————

*[Page 208]*

## The Struggle for the Right to Work

### Hersh Goldmints

("From a Ruined Garden" pp. 76-79)

In the early 1920s, with the revival of the Polish textile industry, the machines in the factories of Belkhatov were set in motion after having sat idle during the entire First World War. The youth of the shtetl, and even some adults, gaped at the machines as if they were magical. Before then the factories had been lifeless; their windows--especially those of Perets Fraytog's factory, which stood on the new road-had been targets for the stones hurled by children playing at war.

The noise of the machinery was something new for most of the young people. Before, we had only heard our parents describing what it was like before the war, when all the factories had been in operation.

The workers who sat at the mechanical looms were Poles, along with a few ethnic Germans. There were no Jewish workers, with the exception of one or two, in the mechanized factories. Jews worked in the factory administration; also, most of those who did the manual preparatory work were Jews. For members of bourgeois or Hasidic families, whose fortunes had declined; becoming a cutter was no shame. Indeed, many young Hasidim did become cutters. A young cutter stood a good chance of obtaining a fine bride with a dowry.

Just as before, Jewish weavers were employed at the hand looms, rather than the mechanical ones. On Pabyanets Street, which was inhabited almost exclusively by Jews, not one house lacked a hand loom. Children whose feet barely reached the pedals were set to work by their parents.

Beginning on Sunday morning (and often on Saturday night immediately following the end of the Sabbath) and continuing until Friday afternoon, one heard the monotonous clatter of the hand looms, accompanied by the tones of a nostalgic love song, a workers' anthem, or simply a hasidic melody, which carried through the open windows out into the street.

The hand-weavers' situation grew worse and worse. They were paid by the piece, and as the boss demanded larger and larger pieces, they had to work longer hours. Sometimes people had to work all through Thursday night in order to have enough money to buy food for the Sabbath.

The Jewish youth, who were already in the habit of frequenting the locals of various left-wing political parties and the textile workers' union, began to envy the legal benefits that the Polish workers enjoyed: eight-hour workdays, health and unemployment insurance, annual vacations, and so forth. The Jewish workers, who had to work halfway through the night, had no legal protection whatsoever, since they worked at home. Furthermore, it grew harder and harder to protest for better pay, because a new type of competition had arisen. These were the peasants of the surrounding villages, who installed looms in their homes did the work much more cheaply. For them it was an extra source of income, which they did when they weren't busy in the fields; for the Jews it was only source of income.

Beginning in 1926, on the initiative of the National Council of Jewish Professional Societies, a campaign was undertaken to struggle for the right of Jews to work. The council that started the campaign included representatives not only of the Bund (which had a decisive influence in the National Council), but also of 'the Labor Zionist parties and the "leftists." We in Belkhatov responded actively to the National Council's initiative. For a few zlotys one could start learning mechanical weaving from one of the local Polish or

German weavers. But there was still no work, even for a Jew who knew how to operate the machines. And new troubles arose: claiming that if Jews learned mechanical weaving there would be a rise in unemployment, the textile workers' union discouraged their being taught, even though Jews belonged to the union. The restriction didn't apply to Christian working-class youngsters, because children of employed weavers automatically had the right to work.

The Jewish members of the textile union began a bitter struggle against this measure, and against the transformation of the union into a guild. I took part in this action as the delegate of the cutters and I was supported by the handweavers' delegates. As the representative body of a workers' organization, the Polish majority delegation couldn't come out openly against the Jewish workers, but all sorts of chicanery were employed in order to prevent the Jews from being allowed into the factories.

Meanwhile, several Jewish workers had managed, by means of connections and bribes, to become trained at the mechanical looms. In addition, some Jews had worked the looms earlier. Yekhezkl Birntsvayg, Yisekher Feld, and others saw to it that more and more Jewish workers made the switch from hand to mechanical weaving, but since all of the jobs were occupied and no new factories were being built, most of the trainees moved to Lodz and sought work there.

A new crisis arose in the years 1927 and 1928, when the Jewish factory owners almost entirely ceased giving piecework to Jewish weavers, giving it to the peasants instead. Only a few of the older hand-weavers retained their jobs, through force of time and privilege; the rest, especially the youth, were simply thrown out of work. The situation was further exacerbated by the taxation policies of the Pilsudski government, which forced children of merchants and petty traders to look for factory work. Most of these were cutters, and those who were related to the factory owners were given jobs at the expense of the previous workers. In certain cases the expelled workers were even given severance pay.

In response to all this, attempts were made to organize the remaining Jewish hand-weavers, and to convince the peasant weavers to charge higher prices so as not to compete with the Jews. Unfortunately, the crisis in the textile industry in 1928 ruined our attempts to resolve the differences between the peasants and the Jewish weavers.

In 1930 M. Zhukhovsky built a large factory and brought about 130 mechanical looms from Pabyanets. We began to intervene in order to have Jewish workers employed as well. The manufacturer agreed, on one condition: the Jews were not to work Sabbaths or Jewish holidays, and on Friday they were to work only the morning shift. After long negotiations, the Christian workers agreed to work only the afternoon shift on Fridays and to let the Jews work the morning shift. Thus the Christian workers also benefited from the Sabbath day: the Jewish workers had no choice but to agree to all of the conditions, although they lost six hours of work every week. Finally, good relations were established between the Christian and Jewish workers.

Meanwhile new winds were blowing from Lodz. The Polish professional unions, which were dominated by the National Workers' Party, began to agitate against the employment of Jewish workers, and even went out on strike over this issue.

Good relations between Polish and Jewish workers prevailed for a long time in Belkhatov. Jewish delegates were elected alongside Poles, and we conducted economic and political actions together, because we were under the jurisdiction of the central office of the professional unions in Lodz. But bit by bit antiSemitic influences became visible in the ranks of the Polish workers, some of whom were reluctant to accept the idea that Jews were also to be employed in the factories. Anti-Semitic agitators began to appear in Belkhatov, attacking the unified socialist spirit that reigned there, and it didn't take long for them to bring about tragic results. One day the Polish majority in the union passed a resolution saying that every worker had to work the standard eight-hour day. In other words, the Polish workers were no longer required to work for the Jews on the Sabbath, even though they, received special wages for doing so. Furthermore, the Friday shifts were no longer to be switched to allow Jewish workers to work mornings only. If Jews wouldn't work on the Sabbath, the machines were to stand idle. Of course, many Jewish workers would have been willing to work on the Sabbath, but the Orthodox Jewish manufacturers would under no circumstances agree to this, nor would they, allow the machines to stop.

At the initiative of the Bundist party, committee, a meeting of all Jewish mechanical weavers was called. All of the Jewish workers' parties in Belkhatov sent representatives. After discussing the anti-Semitic actions of the executive council of the textile union, in which Jews had long been loyal and active members, it was decided to withhold union dues for the time being, to renew the effort to establish Jews in mechanical jobs, and to obtain equal rights for Jews and Christians in every respect.

These resolutions were immediately announced to the union executive and to the Jewish manufacturers, and a committee was elected to lead the campaign. The members of the committee were Yekhezkl Birntsvayg, Moshkovitsh, Yisekher Feld, M. Yakubovitsh, Gedalye Shtayn, and the writer of these lines. The situation was very tense. The main struggle was conducted in Zhukhovsky's factory, where mostly Jewish workers were employed.

Thus several suspenseful weeks passed. The anti-Semitic agitators spread propaganda saying that Jews wanted to destroy the eight-hour day; meanwhile, we began an educational campaign among the more class-conscious workers. With great effort we succeeded, and the factories remained open. On the one hand we warned the Polish workers that under no circumstances would we allow ourselves to be pushed out of the factories; on the other hand, we argued that the maintenance of the previously established conditions was in the common interest of all the workers. The conflict continued for quite some time, but seeing our determination to defend our right to work, the Polish delegates eventually announced that they would accept our demands. Thus ended in Belkhatov a chapter of the struggle for the right to work of the Jewish working class.

The Jewish workers of Belkhatov continued in the avant-garde of the struggle for better working conditions. Under their influence, the textile workers of Belkhatov took part in several demonstrations against the prevailing political terror in Poland, and even on behalf of the rights of the Jewish population. In addition, several political actions were conducted in common, including those during the Vienna events of 1932 (the workers' revolution against the Dollfuss regime), during the Pshitik affair, against the institution of separate seating for Jewish students in Polish universities, and in various other instances. True, the black shadows of anti-Semitic propaganda more than once attempted to poison the peace among the workers, but in Belkhatov, thanks to the determination of the Jewish workers, it rarely had much success.

*[Pages 218-245]*

# Once There Was a Shtetl . . .

## By Shlomo Zytnicki

## Translated from the Yiddish by

## Dr. Khane-Feygl (Anita) Turtletaub (pages 218-234)

## and Gloria Berkenstat Freund (pages 234-245)

[with footnotes at end of chapter]

## Edited by Gloria Berkenstat Freund

[with comments in brackets]

(Translation of pages 218-234 donated by **Sharon and Samuel Shattan and Shmuel Shottan**; translation of pages 234-245 made possible by **Jack and Jules Freeman**.)

Here at five o'clock in the morning, at the same time the cocks crowed, one could hear the whistling of the factory chimneys accompanied by thick black smoke.

The sound of the church bells would interrupt the serenity of the shtetl [town]. If a car horn were heard, everyone ran out of the gates to look at this strange wonder, to see what had happened, who had gotten lost and wound up here?

"Stojkele," the little gentile with the moustache, roused the town from its slumber with his noise, his reading aloud the various new "decrees" issued by the local city hall concerning the town's citizens.

Tsirl-Toybe, the butcher's wife from the old marketplace, also would disturb the peace of the town with her horrible hiccupping that echoed through the surrounding streets...

## The Old Marketplace

The center of town was the old marketplace ("stary rynek"). The bus station was located here. From here cars left for Lodz, Piotrkow and Stertzev

[Szczerców]. Groups of Jews gathered here, talked about "politics" and shared the news of the day. Yankl Mareyne's tavern was nearby. He was a young man with a broad back and a pair of wild eyes. Amazing stories were told about his strength, about how he had grabbed the strongest gentile and threw him out of the tavern. People even knew enough to say that the town police trembled before him. Everyone always wondered how this jewel became the son-in-law of such a fine Jew as Black Meyer, a Ger Chasid.

**The old marketplace**

The berze[1] was also here, the hangout of the playboys of the town, who were the owners of the buses and some wagon drivers. Yakov Hiler, an attractive, successful young man who always had a smile on his face, Dovid's son, Nute Hersz – always gloomy, the cake baker's son, Shimon Yudl (although from his appearance one would not put him in the category of "playboy"), Yankl Pachczasz, who spit whenever he said anything and accompanied that with a three-tiered curse. Itshe Grunen's son, Chaim Yankl, considered himself the hero of this "crowd." Avraham Dziadek,[2] a Jew who wore a black frockcoat, who sent his wagons laden with merchandise to Lodz, was also no slouch. He spoke quietly; one barely heard him, as if he weighed every word. Chaim Leyb Drubczyk, whose fame in town was that he had danced a kozaczok [a Russian dance], and his brother Meyer. Avraham Alter Khmal was a tall, healthy young man, whose voice could be heard over the whole marketplace when he spoke. And his language was "colorful"; for example,

"May you get gangrene. Get away from here; if not I'll slap your belly." His brother-in-law, Beryl, was on the contrary more serene. He rarely answered questions, because he was stone deaf. The clown of this group of playboys was "Meylechl Kradnik." His strength lay more in clever backtalk than in his arms. [His] every word was accompanied by clowning around. If a group of men were standing in the street arguing about world politics, Meylkhl would appear out of nowhere and cover them all [by throwing] a dirty sack over their heads, or he would push them, causing one to fall over the other and the group would break up. However, when it came to a contest of strength, his mouth was of little help to him. So it was no surprise to see him often sporting a black eye or with a bandage over his lip. This Meylech had a sweet, quiet boy, who was always reading. One of his daughters survived the present war and is now living in America. All of these playboys created a certain "caste," and looked down on everyone else and considered themselves the elite. Their differences were not straightened out by means of a court, but by the use of their own fists.... They were also among the first to be killed by the Nazis.

One of the happiest of these fellows was the blond, Avrom Mendl. He did not much like his trade of shoemaking. He was drawn to the streets. He became a porter and could go where he pleased. [He] was full of life, a simple but devoted Bundist, loved by all.

Among the most famous love affairs that were carried out in the old marketplace, we must include that of the porter and Ester Tsirl, the chatterbox. They eventually got married and lived their last years in Lodz. They, too, died during the Nazi occupation.

Reb Itshe Meyer Gewertz's "kamenitze" (brick house), one of the oldest houses in the town, stood out from all the other neighboring low houses. This is where the Talmud Torah[3] was located, which was later moved to a building of its own. The teachers were: Avraham Cukerman, a good, quiet person, who never lost his patience; Herszl Poszladek, an angry Jew, with stern eyes, who made the children tremble [with fear]; Avroml Ponczner with his glasses on his forehead, who was never stingy with beatings; small Yitzchakl, whose knowledge came from Yiddish books – all of these teachers taught their students in this building from early in the morning until late at night.

There were also a whole series of stores in this house. Mordkhe Szpiglman's large hardware store: the Pole Mientkewicz's liquor store, a brother of Burmistzh, Shmuel Leyzer Szmulewicz's booth; [this Shmuel Leyzer] in later years became a big manufacturer.

Reb Itshe Meyer was a very rich Jew, but had a reputation in town for being very miserly, someone who watched every penny he gave his wife. Everyone was looking forward to that happy moment that he would have to pay something of a dowry for his two not-very-desirable daughters, who were always seen walking together. This is how the town wanted to have its revenge for his stinginess.

Did you want to snack on a piece of halva, a few fresh sprats, a smoked herring, not to mention if you could afford the luxury of buying a "blood" orange – then you simply had to go to Meyerl's little store. There you could also get a banana; that was one of the seldom [seen] fruits in town, and not everyone could afford to buy them. Reb Meyerl, a small Jew with a bit of a beard on his chin that looked as if it were pasted on, with a foolish gaze, was not himself comfortable in his own shop. His thoughts were more with the little chasidish synagogue. He looked like a character actor from the Yiddish stage. His wife, however, was very competent. Seeing how helpless he was, she would send him home to rock the baby, and she managed everything [in the store] herself. She would greet everyone by saying: "Why are you rushing so? You do not have time?"

If you wanted to snack on some good ice-cream, you had to go the old marketplace to Yankl Sztejn. People would actually lick their fingers from his ice-cream. The milk here was never scalded as it was at Meyerl's or salty as at Malkele Asher Bide's. And what kind of customers there would be? One could run into Leybish Fajner's son from the seltzer factory with Reb Berish the watchmaker's daughter. Yankl Klug's and Borukh Starowinski's daughters came here. Such guests were served in a special room. His wife, Shifra, and their daughter, Chava, would greet everyone with a smile. And Yankl himself would meander about as a conqueror, the only one who knew "the true secret" of making ice-cream. Friday evening, when the shops were closed, Reb Yankl donned his satin frockcoat and his velvet hat and rushed off to the Gerer shtibl [small Chasidic synagogue], which was just a step away from his apartment. A little further down was Reb Meyerl Gerer's fabric shop. [He was] an angry Jew, haughty about his Gerer pedigree. Day and night he pored over his religious books. His wife, Odl, ran the business, and his youngest daughter, Sortshe, helped out. Reb Meyerl was very stingy with words, and paid no attention at all to the common people; [he] did not even respond politely when greeted. The following anecdote is told about him: On Sabbath morning, when Reb Meyerl was going to the ritual baths, he encountered Yoynele Dreksler, a person who liked to clown around. Yoynele went over to him and said: "Reb Meyerl, kiss me . . . ."

— "You scoundrel, get out of here!" Reb Meyerl answered angrily.

— That was some answer! Yoynele Dreksler laughed and never tired of telling this to everyone. The town enjoyed it: that an angry Jew had been taught a lesson.

In the marketplace, there was also a haberdashery owned by Reb Yakov Hersz Sztatlender, of the most respected Jews in town. If something was needed from the authorities, everyone knew that the appropriate candidate for this was Reb Yakov Hersz. Lame Herszl was considered the best of the custom tailors. There was even an argument: some thought that Eidl Rozenblum's tailoring was more modern, was more chic; others, however, said that Meyer and Khaml, who had made a special trip to Warsaw to learn cutting, would surpass everyone. However, no one could take away "the crown" from Lame Herszl. His two sons, Mordekhai and Ezriel, were his steadfast apprentices.

Another business was owned by Henekhl Adler and his sons, Moyshe Shia, and Mendele, who had frittered away his dowry on tailoring, and his son-in-law, Yossl Piekno, who wanted to go from dealing in second rate clothing to being a custom tailor. Mordechai Granek had a shop nearby. There was no garment that he had measured that did not fit. He always spoke in a refined manner, nicely, and thus managed to confuse people, so that one never knew where one stood with him. Wewe Piula considered himself to be the wise man among tailors, although his work was somewhat bungled.

The old marketplace also had tailors who did alterations on second-hand clothes. First place was held by the widespread Binecki family. The father was a small Jew with a few hairs in his beard. During the afternoon and evening prayers on Sundays, the shopkeepers never let him near the reading desk, because they believed that if he led the prayers, it would rain the next day, and Monday's market would be ruined...

Nakhman's son, Shimshon, who in addition to being a tailor, was also a gravedigger; the Nowak's, or as they were called in town – the "little mites"[4] also belonged to the line of second-rate tailors (ready made clothes).

There were respectable representatives in the shoe business. Herszl Gorszkowicer thought of himself as the king of this line of business. A stout Jew with red cheeks, which did not speak of hunger, would always stand before his gate with his belly sticking out, his fingers folded over his vest. From his appearance, it was obvious that he enjoyed himself and was proud of his successful sons, who were running the business. The khilketa [combative shopkeeper] also had her business, or more accurately, her little business. Sharp Manya, her talented daughter, showed her abilities here. The shoemaker from Piotrkow and his business were strong competition here. His servant, "the crazy courier" brought him a lot of publicity. When a military orchestra from Piotrkow marched around town, the "crazy courier" was always at their head conducting them with a little stick.

Beyond the shoemaker lived Dovid, the son of the tall Moyshe, who in addition to shoemaking, was employed with burying the dead.

Yankele, the barber, also had his barbershop here. The chasidic Jews always gave him the evil eye and more than once threatened to excommunicate him. They said that on the Sabbath, his shop only looks closed in front, but in the back he was "shaving" beards.

There was also no lack of food shops in the old marketplace. Moyshe Hersz had his wholesale business, Moyshe Perets's, which provided all of his children with food stores: except for his son, Shimon, who was a tailor, and his youngest daughter, Soratshe, who married a laborer. Soratshe felt restricted in her poor parents' food shop. The shop was not to her liking, so she learned how to sew clothes and was proud of her new trade, although her parents were not pleased by her proletarian work.

Soratshe read a great deal and was always studying. She was very familiar with both Yiddish and Polish literature. She was also interested in painting and would paint posters for various events. Soratshe was very active in the leftist movement. Because of her serious involvement in communal work, she was well respected by all.

During the years of the occupation, Soratshe was one of the most courageous female fighters in town. She consoled and encouraged everyone believing in the [eventual] victory over the Nazis. At the beginning of the occupation, she received travel documents – papers from Argentina, but the Germans did not permit her to leave, and deported her to a concentration camp, where she perished not very long before the end of the war.

**Soratshe**
[diminutive name for Sarah]
[Additional information provided
by Dora Szczukocka Bornstein:
Last name is Statlender.
She was married to Shlomo Zitnicki]

The [abovementioned] Moyshe Perets's tried to combine ordinariness with chasidus. He was delighted with his chasidic son-in-law, Yankl, who was married to his daughter, Dintshe.

Of the whole family, only his son, Perets, survived. (He now lives in Belgium).

The chasidim were envious of the blond-headed Yoyne, who provided room and board to his successful son-in-law while he studied. [Yoyne] was another food shop owner. His daughter, Blimele, gave birth to another child every year.

Herszl Plawner's son Shloyme and his stout wife, who was always out of breath, were also among the food store owners in the town. Reb Yosef Leybish owned another food shop that was run by his two daughters, who were not very lucky in getting married.

There were also hatmakers in the old marketplace. The first spot was occupied by Meylekh Galster, [then came] Itshe, the hat maker, and his sons, the Joabs, and also Chaim-Faywl Naparstek, the happy-go-lucky guy.

The town's feldsher [barber-surgeon] had his house here along with a small garden, which was a rarity in town. Yankl, the feldsher, was a sympathetic person with a serious face, a nicely combed beard. He commanded respect and was respected by all. After his death, his son, Avrom (a little emotionally troubled), who had for years lived in Germany, tried to take his place, but without success.

Bakeries in the old marketplace: Shie the baker, who was fined more than once for not keeping his bakery clean; Chaya, the baker lady; Shmuel Shneltsug,[5] were often cursed by the women because they either mixed up or burned their cholent [6] in their bakeries. Itsik's wife also baked large, old-fashioned, white bread, which everyone enjoyed. However, she was troubled by having a disturbed daughter – Libe, who always stood at the door with unkempt hair and created fear in everyone.

There was also no lack of butcher shops in the old marketplace. Hertske, the butcher was a respectable Jew in town, in spite of his trade as a butcher. Yitskhok Norszkewicer was one of the wealthiest butchers in town, who built himself a one-story brick house. Feyge Reyzl and her sons, Leyzer the butcher, the lame Sore, [and] Feygele of Radomsk, who spoke with a soft 'l,' all of these belonged to the abovementioned trade.

There was also a pharmacy in the old marketplace, and there was an "illegal" pharmacy as well, in the house of the Chasidish Jew, Reb Noyekhl Bekl[7] (because he was always seen with a bound up cheek). The indigent of the town would buy their prescriptions in his house, because it cost a lot less there. He would actually tremble lest he fail...

Y. L. Goldsztejn had his business in the marketplace, but his mind was more involved in reading and writing than in business. [He] was short and had a serious look. When he went for a stroll in the street, he walked slowly – as if he were measuring every step. He had a piano in his house, and that was no small matter in the town.

The dentist in the old marketplace, Michal Rezurnik, brought a son-in-law from Czestochowa. [He] set him up in a small shop, where one could also play dominos – but the book of debts grew as if with yeast. Things kept getting worse for him, even when he tried his luck at the shoe business. This gave [those in] the old marketplace something to joke about: "He had to import this kind of bargain?"

The paupers of the old marketplace were: Moyshele Bejrekh's, whose wife was always sick but was always having children: Moyshe, the dorfsgeyer [man bought products from village peasants], and his six sons: Asher fun hober [of oats], who sold horse feed: Binecki's wife, Ester, who provided the food for the home, although her husband was a tailor and many others. There were women, who had very good reputations, [for example] Beyle Ester, an old woman with a kupkele [bonnet worn by a pious woman] on her head, who would sit in the marketplace and sell fruit. When she learned of a house in which there was hunger, she would go there immediately, and never empty-handed. If a poor girl needed a dowry to get married, she was one of those who took care of it. Zelda's daughter, Perl can also be included among other women of note in the old marketplace. And why not mention the woman with five names: Leah-Heltshe-Foygl-Gitl-Manele's, whose name could only be remembered by heart by someone with the head of a [government] minister. The true woman of valor of the old marketplace was the wife of the bookseller, whose white rolls and filled pastries had people licking their fingers.

The old marketplace also produced child prodigies. The Langnas family was among the most solid citizens. [The family] had a small shop, which was mostly empty (empty boxes hid their poverty). He, Yeshaye Langnas, read a great deal, got along well with people. They had two good children: Riwtshe and Hetsush. Hetsush showed a great talent for painting. His parents, however, did not possess the means to permit him to study. Many houses had paintings Hetsush had done. He magically produced beautiful portraits from old worn-out photographs. When he found himself in a concentration camp in the current war, a Nazi learned that here was a talented painter and gave him a family photo to reproduce with an artistic outcome. This helped Hetsush to have more to eat and drink, and, and therefore, he had enough to share with his hungry friends. Hetsush hoped that this would allow him to survive the hard times, but fate decided otherwise...

Our family also resided in the old marketplace. Our parents came from Lodz to Belchatow in great poverty during the time of the First World War. Our mother, a refined and deeply religious woman, was the reciter[8] in the women's section of the synagogue. She took it very much to heart that her children were veering away from the "straight path." Once she grabbed a knife and threatened to commit suicide if we would not pray. Even while sick, she would go to the village, Koldeniw, to buy poultry, butter, cheese, eggs and later sell these things to the rich homemakers in Belchatow, and in this way help our father provide a livelihood.

Our father was a maker of boxes by trade, but he did not have much of this work to do in Belchatow, so he became a wedding jester and "played" the bass in the municipal band, pulling the bow up and down. He was always in a good mood, and despite his poverty never lost his sense of humor.

Our family lived in a small room in which the shoemaker's workshop of my step-brother, Yossl Rozental, was located. During the day, he patched shoes and at night he strummed tunelessly on his mandolin. During the winter, cotton hung around the room to dry, later to be wound by two spinning wheels, which were also located in the same room. There were only two beds, and everyone else slept on the ground.

Nevertheless, it was one of the happiest homes in the old marketplace. Groups of people would often stand under our windows and listen to my father's melodies and the playing of the instrument, which carried out to the street.

My brother, Moyshele, came from this house.

Moyshe made himself a fiddle of "dikt" [plywood] and taught himself to play. He was accepted into the municipal band. Everyone at home was very surprised, when Moyshele brought a new horn into the house. Everyone stood around astonished: [they wanted to know] "Where did you get the money for this?" He smiled: "I saved it up" he said, "penny by penny, carried a suitcase, churned ice-cream, and that's how I managed." He stood himself in the middle of the room and played a lively tune on the horn. Our mother cried with joy. Moyshele now played his new saxophone in the band.

A child from this same impoverished family was one of the prize winners in a contest for the best young person's autobiography held in 1934 by "YIVO" of Vilna in which 300 young people from many different counties took part.

"Magicians" also often came to the old marketplace to showcase their talents. They pulled ribbons from their mouths, swallowed fire, did summersaults in the air, and the children of town accompanied them with [shouts of] "Hurrah!"

In the old marketplace, one could see a "Jew" walking around on the Sabbath, smoking a cigarette, something that the biggest heretic would seldom dare to do. Once, the policeman from Wojtashek was looking for a thief, and he decided to disguise himself as a Jew; he forgot that it was the Jewish Sabbath and smoked a cigarette. That was a happy time, because we were able to make fun of the police, whom we disliked.

During the day, the old marketplace had a certain appearance, but once night came and the small lamps were lit on the few poles, which threw a dull light, the marketplace took on the appearance of a cemetery, through which it seemed strange to walk.

**Pabianicer Street**

Actually, this street had two names: Pabianicer and Belchatowke. The paupers knew that they lived on Belchatowke, as if the name were suited to their poverty. The wealthy, on the other hand, considered themselves to be residents of Pabianicer Street. The street was paved with large stones. The relay wagons loaded with goods and with passengers sitting on top, created such a din as they rode through that the women of the street would shout that they were being deafened. After a struggle of many years, the street received its own pump, whose only activity was giving water. In the winter, when it was slippery, one had to be an acrobat to get to it. Therefore, those who lived on Belchatowke were proud when they saw that the citizens of the old marketplace had to make an effort to get to their pump, because that pump would often "play tricks" and go on "strike." [How different] the pumping of today! More than one Jewish woman could barely catch her breath after such work.

Here one could count the "businesses" on one's fingers: Issachar Piaskosz and his food shop; the tall woman with the long chin, who sold mirrors, who was always complaining about the [other] women as to why they were fingering her shmalts herring; the bakeries owned by Makhl Kornaser, Stobiecki, and Chane Riwe, whose bread was renowned in town. Moyshe Gute's had a butcher store, and Hersz Eidl Szpigelman had a tavern, which was later transformed into an inn. If a stranger happened into town and needed a place to spend the night, he was taken to Hersz Eidl's.

The population of this street was diverse. The first spot was occupied by the weavers. It was rare to find a courtyard, in which the beating of the handlooms accompanied by song was not heard from dawn until late at night.

**Pabianicer Street**

The Jewish horse traders lived here, such as: Grunem's son, Itshe, Avraham Czuremure's, Moyshe Grocholicer and his pretty daughters, Tshotsh Meyer with the sick eyes, who spent more time in jail than he did out of jail. Here lived Jews who studied [Torah] day and night, such as: Reb Yidele, the rabbi's son; Reb Mikhalke's son-in-law; Shloyme Mendl Gowinski; Reb Yekheskl Lajbish; Shmuel Zanwel Boganski; Eliezer Szpigelman; Reb Mikhal's son, Shloyme; Reb Chaim-Ishe, the shoykhet [ritual slaughterer], about whom everyone in the area would gossip that he does not get along too well with his workers, Avrom Faktor and others. The fishermen also lived on this street: Levi's son, Yume, who hit the women's hands, yelled and cursed; Hiler, the rope maker, who in addition to fishing also braided ropes. He mumbled nasally, so that one never [quite] knew what he was saying....

Here were the tanneries and the dyeing factories that gave the town a not so "impressive" aroma. [Among these were] Zakan Garber[2] and his sons, Perets, Sheya, and Dovid; Moyshe Zalman Puldupek, who was dissatisfied because his lovely daughter, Chava, had taken up with Welwel, the tailor's apprentice. The lame Menashele, with his horse and small carriage, was always arguing with the mare when she lay down exhausted and didn't move. . . . One time, when the horse was not joking and never again got up, he took it so to heart that he too died soon thereafter.

Koifman, the shoemaker, and his wife, Shprintse, who spoke with a thick tongue, also lived here. The "politicians" from Pabianicer Street gathered in that small shop that was both a workshop and a residence. Their ten-year-old daughter ran to the library and asked someone to read her Marx's "Kapital."

Another shoemaker occupied a similar dwelling: Gershon, his wife Golda and their 5 children. This is where they ate, they worked and they slept, and more than once held political meetings there. This shoemaker, half illiterate, in time became a member of the City Council. Such a thing could happen on Pabianicer Street. There was also no lack of wagon drivers on Pabianicer Street. Mikhal Wigder Skorpis, [was] a tall, broad-shouldered Jew. He was tremendously proud of his son, Moyshe, in whom he saw a copy of himself. He did not have much confidence in his second son, Gabriel Gape – to be able to turn over the "reins" to him, and that is why he made him a tailor.

Moyshe Skorpis with the red neck bristled with good health. His sons, Yisroel-Yitzhok, Noyekh and Shmuel-Leyb carried on their father's work. Meyer-Ber was not overly delighted with his trade. He turned his children into artisans.

Who in town did not know Tsiml of Pabianicer Street, the mother of 5 daughters and 4 sons? Her son, Issachar, always wore his hair with a shiny part and considered himself to be the best dancer in town, even though younger Leybke tried to outdo him. Shmuel Kishke and Dovid's son, Rakhmiel Hersz, competed for the heart of her daughter, Manye. The other daughter, Chane, was one of the liveliest and, at the same time, prettiest girl in town. Chaye-Dine was one of the best known women in town. Her name was pronounced Khadine; she toiled from dawn until late at night. She was always traveling to Piotrkow with bundles for her children, Zalman and Perets, the "world upheavers," who were more in jail than out of it. Makhl the wagon driver lived here in a low hut; he was a Jew with two red eyes which spoke of many sleepless nights. Wonders were told about his two sons, Yecheskel and Shame – that they had "great minds" and that they would move worlds.

In addition to the following used clothes dealers: Issachar Paplok, Dovid Pieknis, Mordekhai Morgensztern and others, Pabianicer Street also had tailors of good pedigree. Manela was not just anyone. He sewed for noblemen. He never trusted anyone else to iron the belt of a pair of pants. His greatest pleasure was grabbing hold of the water-carrier, setting him on the table, taking a full mouth of water and spraying him from head to toe – then throwing him out. If he needed something while he was sewing, he used to point a finger in the air: "Give me this!" without indicating what it was. Someone could hand him a scissor, chalk, thread, buttons, and when what he wanted was finally guessed and he was handed the measuring tape, he was very pleased and called out: "Now you please me!" This spectacle would constantly be repeated. He was completely different on the street. There he was approachable, eager to chat and had a weakness for talking about the Torah, in which he was not very well versed.

Deaf Luzer also lived here in great poverty – a Jew who went out into the villages, bent over from always carrying his sack over his shoulders. He never bothered a fly on the wall. Once when a Polish hooligan caught him, he gave him such a smack that the hooligan ran away in great shame.

Zanwel, the cigarette seller, rolled his own cigarettes and then sold them. Wawe, the oil presser, prepared oil for cooking and the enjoyment came principally from frying latkes [potato pancakes].

Herszl Tzine's [Herszl, the son of Tzine] was considered the "most popular" resident of Pabianicer Street, an old Jew with a white beard, the only Jewish strazak (fireman) in the shtetl. Early on Sunday when the firemen paraded through the streets with music, the children felt proud that there was also a Jew among them. Tzine's Herszl, in his uniform and fireman's hat, walked straight as a string. He was one of the first at a fire. He was a shoemaker by trade. He did not have to be begged for long to tell about his "service" with Russia where he made a pair of golden slippers for the Czarina. He was asked by a group of jokesters, "And how had he taken her measurements?" Herszl was waiting for the question. "Why do you not understand, imbeciles," he answered them. "She placed her foot in the snow and that was how I took her measurements..."

Manish, with the large, red nose, was a porter. It was said that the redness came from drinking a great deal of aquavit, which he did gladly. His wife went around cursing him. "Whatever he earns, " she said, "goes right into his bodnye (stomach), with overeating and guzzling..."

"Bright" Mashawas the letter writer for the shtetl. She always knew how to write to the children in the Americas, so that their pockets would open and they would remember their remaining poor relatives in the old home. Not much had to be said. Her letters would always begin in this style: "Dear children, we are healthy, may God grant that we always and forever hear the same from you."

Yisroel Lenkower was a glazier. He lived in one room with seven children (five sons and two daughters); the children worked on hand-weaving in the same room.

Although not appropriate for Pabianicer Street, the manufacturers, Mendl Shmuel's [Shmuel's son Mendl], the Felds (Kradnikes), Beryl Rubinsztajn, among others, lived there. The contrast between their living space and the life of the weavers was too sharp, as it was, for example, for the deaf Emanuel or Shlomo Szelps. Of course, if someone rushed to greet them with an expansive "gut morgen [good morning], he had another wish in his heart. The wealthiest man in the shtetl, about whose wealth legends were woven, also lived here. This was Yankl Flakowicz. It was known that he employed no servants so no one would see how much he owned. Half of the town belonged to him, along with many factories and houses that he owned in other cities. He, himself, was a modest person, but his wife would always emphasize that they were assured of an income for their entire life. Only one son survived out of the entire family and he is now in Israel.

You could also meet Poles here who spoke Yiddish: Gotwald, Gaszewski – the shoemaker's son, who even threw in Hebrew verses from sacred books.

The Germans of Pabianicer Street – Walberg, Milbrandt, and so on – also spoke Yiddish well. At every opportunity, they stressed their "friendly" relations with Jews.

A rebbe also lived here on Pabianicer Street. A Jew with an old, wide hat and a worn out kapote [long, black coat worn by religious men] came and stated that he was descended from a line of great rabbis. He had his own shtibl in which he lived. His Chasidim were the simple Jews from the town. His name rapidly became famous and many stories were told of his miracles. One Shabbos, while praying, he approached a Jew and gave him a loud slap. Nu, if the rabbi slaps someone, he likely knows why? Later the Jews made an effort and asked: "Rebbe, what did your slap mean?" After long consideration, the Rebbe said, "Do you remember that you told me that your child was dangerously ill? They know that the slap redeemed the child." The prestige of the rebbe grew greater from then on.

There was a kino [movie theater] on Pabianicer Street that showed movies twice a week, Shabbos and Sunday. Concerts and speeches would also occur in the movie hall. Here, our dear B. Ejsurowicz entranced the crowd with his stories about India.

However, Pabanicer Street was not important because of its residents, but because of the spiritual homes that were found there:

In the secular Jewish school – the Mizrachi's Yavne[10] school with its many children – the female teacher, Rozenband, was surrounded by small children who thought of her as a mother and would not move from her. Almost all the libraries in the town were like universities for the young. Here were the premises of various parties, such as the Bund, Mizrachi, Right Poalei-Zion [Workers of Zion, a Marxist Zionist party], and Poalei Emunei Yisroel [orthodox group – Faithful Workers of Israel]. Here was the location of the needle workers union. Here was the textile union of the Jewish and Polish workers that gave instructions for the large strike that lasted six months and was the theme for many articles in the proletarian national press. At that time, Josef Khmurner[the pen name of Josef Lestchinsky] wrote, "Belchatow should be recorded in the golden book of the history."

The socialist artisans had their home here. Here a siyum-hasefer[11] was held that was transformed into a holiday for the shtetl. Here secret meetings were held that often ended with the participants put in chains and led to the Piotrokow jail. At night choirboys formed a workers' chorus here and deafened the street with their song. Here young male and female workers prepared their gymnastic performances with which they called forth delight in the shtetl.

Children in their blue blouses and red ties marched in song from Pabianicer Street into the woods to their outings.

Here flying demonstrations took place where the police felt helpless. Here the May 1st demonstrations formed; here ordinary people received their first lessons in reading and writing. Frequent talks about the education of children, and also about communal questions, were held for women in the school premises. The women were organized and some, even though they were very religious, (wearing sheitlen [wigs] on their heads), carried red flags in the demonstrations on the First of May.

The Radziner and the Aleksanderer shtibl were also located here. For a large part of the population the above mentioned institutions were their first home, where they devoted their free time to make life interesting in the Jewish shtetl.

When a proposal to name a street after Y. L. Peretz [Yiddish writer of poems, plays and stories] was made at a city council meeting, it was clear to all that the most appropriate place to be considered was Pabianicer Street.

At this point, it is worth noting something interesting: when the Bundist City Council faction made the mentioned proposal, it naturally caused a storm among the reactionary circles. The Polish councilman Helwak (Helwik) demanded to have a say during the discussion and began his speech as follows:

— "It is true that Mr. Peretz is a good person; he is my neighbor. I have nothing against him. Just the opposite, I even play cards with him. However, what is his patriotic worth that we should name a street after him – this I do not know. I might not demand to speak, he added. I only wonder why such a proposal should come from socialists..."

The curiosity consists of the fact that Helwak confused this with the name of his neighbor, who was also named Peretz – and this was the rich manufacturer, Peretz Frajtag.

**Our Theater**

The shtetl had a strange weakness for the theater. One of the main entertainments with children was acting. A group of children was brought together and a "troupe" was created, tickets were sold and then in a poor house a curtain or sheet was drawn across creating a sort of stage. The girls were dressed in motherly, long clothing, shoes with high heels. The boys pasted on beards, put on long kapotes [coats worn by pious men], or just turned their own jackets around and in this manner the young people performed. It should be understood that there was no shortage of homegrown "directors" who prepared the spectacles. Everything was in imitation of the great actors in which the shtetl was so rich.

Our homegrown actors were:

Moshe Eizner, a housepainter, who considered himself the lead dramatic actor. He wore glasses with golden frames. This gave him more dignity among the town's "intelligentsia." Someone said that he had earlier looked him over, as it is said, "Do you know to whom you are speaking?" And it seemed that he was even acting on the street.

Natan Goldberg had everyone in his pocket [Translator's note: Everyone enjoyed his performances]. Later, he was also a great success in Lodz. But he was not from Belchatow; he came from Zdunska Wola. Therefore, he was unable to take the title of lead actor from Eizner.

**Members of the Dramatic Circle with Natan Goldberg as Director**

In addition there was Yeheil Leibish Goldberg, Moshe Abramczyk, Maks Jakubowicz, Avraham Novak (Milbl [little moth or mite]), Henekh Pigula, Moshe Szmulewicz. The comedians of the troupe were Avraham Lipme "Podlotz" (Novak) – now in Sao Paulo, and Yudl Feld. Women's roles were played by Ruchl Likhtenfeld, who had a claim on acting the role of mothers, Sheyndl Leah Drezner, Ester Czikacki. Rokhama Blat and Chana Jakubowicz were in the roles of the prima-donna. Acting with the others were Freyde Naparstek, Chaya and Hinda Royze Jakubowicz. Yumke Leib always played the role of children with great success. The prompter was the lame Itshe Lieb, who felt as if he was in his own home when he was in the prompter's box. There was long preparation for the performance. Posters (done by homegrown "artists") would announce coming presentations. Every presentation was awaited with impatience by the town. Later, every presentation would be the theme of conversations for weeks. People became "street critics," praising or tearing down. Many actors received the title "clumsy." The home of the actors was at the Szwartzer [dark] Ruchl's. Here they would grab something to eat and also played cards. The repertoire was in great part an old one, principally theater pieces by Jakov Gordon.

**A scene from a performance presented by the Dramatic Circle**

The "straszhatske shope" [firehouse] was located on the market. The firefighters had their tools on the ground floor, and above was a room with a stage and gallery [theater seating]. Plays were presented here. On one side the windows looked out onto the street and on the other side onto the orchard of the Polish priest. On both sides of the stage, spaces were divided and served as wardrobe rooms for the actors. An experienced eye could see from the street how the actors were changing their clothes. Raising the curtain was not an easy thing. The curtain often stopped in the middle of its rise and the ensemble remained standing as if lost. The scenery was always the same, only it was turned around each time to the other side. The performance of Sh. Anski's Dybbuk, directed by Y. L. Goldsztejn, was a surprise in the shtetl. It was such a success that it had to be repeated and this in itself was unusual.

Some "actors" traveled across the world. Several married and the troupe broke up. New strength from the adult young people created a dramatic circle at the Jewish secular school.

**The corner where the fireman's hall is found**

This was: Emanuel Joab, Shlomo Zalman Krizman, Zanwel Luszczanowski, Ezriel Lipinski (all perished in the recent war), Moshe Leib Frajman, Hersz Avigdor Zilbersztajn and the writer of these lines (the last three are in Argentina). Women: Sura Rywka Szitnicki, Fradl Nowak, Chava Krizman (all three perished), Frimet Lajb and Ester Eksztajn (now in Argentina). Z. Libin's Gebrokhene Hertser [Broken Hearts] and Der Batlen [The Idle Person], etc. were performed. A new chapter began when Rywka Konska, the teacher from Vilna, arrived. Young, she had just graduated from the Teacher's

Seminar and was also a gifted revue actress. She did not wait long when asked and took over the leadership of the circle, preparing the first performance with a repertoire taken from the Lodz revue theater, "Ararat." She also took part. After each song, the hall thundered. This Konska was picture-gorgeous with a pair of dark, burning eyes and a beautiful figure. She appeared in man's clothing and singing Dos Ganefl [The Little Thief], the audience literally rose from their seats and would not let her leave the stage.

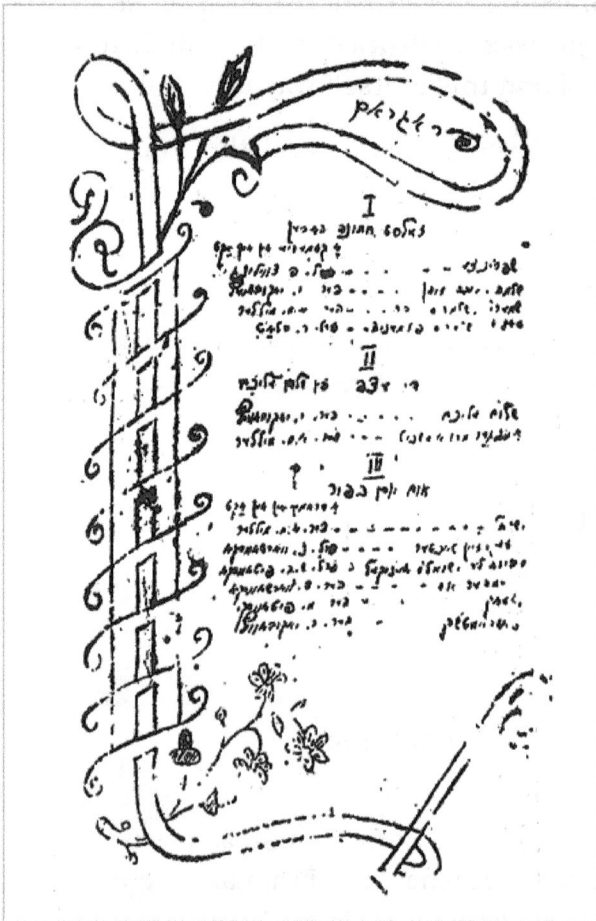

**Programs of Belchatower Amateur Presentations**

This was such a hit that she had to repeat it during each performance. Each revue performance was played in a fully packed hall. The songs were city hits. This dramatic circle would also appear in the surrounding towns such as Stradzew and Zelow and had success everywhere. In addition to the city orchestra, which would accompany all of the songs, the young violinist, Binem Gelbard, also took part. Troupes would also come from Lodz and Zelow to perform. However, when "stars" with names in the bigger cities began to appear, the dramatic circle had to retreat to the shadows.

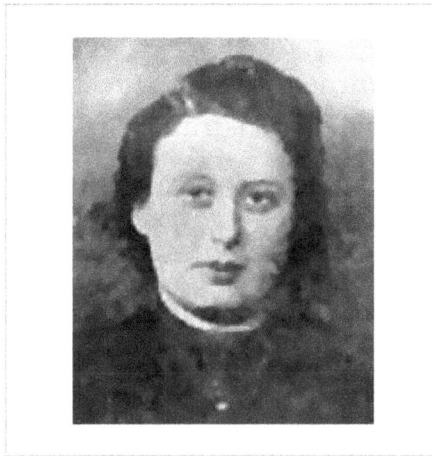

**Rivka Konska**
[Additional information provided
by Dora Szczukocka Bornstein:
She was a teacher in the Yiddish School
originally from Vilna.
She was married to Peretz Freitag]

Lydia Ptocka came to town several times with a good ensemble. Y. Turkow and Diana Blumenfeld often came. They were always satisfied with the hearty reception and promised to come again soon. Ida Kaminska, Klara Segalowicz and Klajnlerer acted here with a simple theme, Mir Froyen [We Women] in an overflowing hall. Jakob Weislitz with some of the Vilner Troupe had a success with Kidush-haShem [In the Sanctification of God's Name – usually said when speaking of death as a martyr]. The same for Y. Kamen and a troupe that performed Tog un Nakht [Day and Night], Der Zinger fun Zein Troyer [The

Singer of his Sorrow by Osip Dimov] and others. [Ayzik] Samberg had great success here. A. Wolfsztat and Y. Weislitz were frequent guests here with an evening of recitations. Lola Polman also gave concerts of songs here. The Lodzer Ararat left the shtetl very unsatisfied. In the middle of performing, a whistling was heard; several people who had seen the program in Lodz yelled that they were taking the shtetl for granted; there was no scenery, a part of the ensemble was missing.

Ukrainian [in other words, non-Jewish] troupes would come here to play for 10 or 12 uninterrupted days, and principally for a Jewish audience. Each theater troupe was warmly welcomed. When Jewish actors appeared in the street, everyone's gaze was turned in their direction. Their departure for the shtetl was always turned into a demonstration.

Yiddish theater was so beloved in the shtetl that even the religious Poalei Emunei Yisroel could not resist the temptation and "sinned a little" with it. They performed Mekhires Yosef [Sale of Joseph]. The women's roles were played by men disguised as women and this brought a great deal of cheerfulness to the shtetl.

* * *

The old market was burned.

Pabianicer Street, with its surrounding alleys, is destroyed and empty.

The Jewish actors, who brought so much joy and life to the shtetl, shared the fate of the entire Jewish population.

Only the surrounding field and mountains remained untouched and look on the small town emptiness.

If the mountains and fields could speak, they would be able to describe a great deal about Belchatower Jewish life, with which they were tied and bound.

Yes, once there was a shtetl …

**The New Market**

**The mikvah [ritual bathhouse]**

**The Belchatower synagogue;**
in the background, the Talmud Torah
[elementary religious Hebrew school]

————

**Translator's footnotes:**

1. Berze usually means "the stock market" in Yiddish, but here it is used
   metaphorically to mean a gathering place. [K-FT]

2. This could be his last name or it could be a nickname, since the word means "grandfather." [K-FT]

3. Hebrew elementary school. [K-FT]

4. Milblekh: This might also be translated as "little moths." [K-FT]

5. Shneltsug means "fast train." Sometimes it is difficult to know whether an appellation is a nickname or a valid family name, which derived from a long-ago nickname. [K-FT]

6. Traditional Sabbath stew that had to cook for 24 hours and was, therefore, placed on top of the baker's oven by the wives before the Sabbath and retrieved for the mid-day meal on the Sabbath. [K-FT]

7. Bekl means "cheek." [K-FT]

8. Since not all the women could read, one who read well said the prayers out loud for the others. [K-FT]

9. Garber in Yiddish is a tanner. His last name reflects his profession. [K-FT]

10. Mizrachi was the religious Zionist movement. The Yavne school system stressed the importance of both a secular and religious education. [GBF]

11. Celebration at the conclusion of writing a Torah scroll. [GBF]

*[Page 246]*

# Y. L. [Yoel Lajb] Goldsztejn - A writer who wanted to solve the most difficult problems of man and Jew

## By Jakob Botoshanski

**Translated from the Yiddish by Jerome Silverbush**
**Edited by Katie Eisenstadt and Jerry Liebowitz**

[with comments in brackets]

(A paper about his two works, "Collapse or Rebuild" and "1960")

### An apologetic beginning

In Zalman Reyzen's lexicon there is no information given about the life of the writer Y. L. [Yoel Lajb] Goldsztejn, the author of three published books ("Collapse or Rebuild" – a fantastic novel, "1960" – a utopia, and "With Face to the Mirror" – Three Stories). One knows roughly that he was born in the eighties of the past century, was physically weak and had a "guten kop" [literally "a good head"] and he studied a lot. He was self taught. He lived almost his entire life in Belchatow, and was a teacher and a book dealer there. Ideologically, he was a Tzeirei Zion, and during the Second Aliyah he immigrated to Eretz Israel, from where he returned considerably disappointed (which also is reflected in his works). However, he didn't fully lose his belief in Eretz Israel, and he believed he could find the right way to solve not only the "Jewish problem," but the entire "world question." And with his work he really intended to solve the main problems of mankind in general and the Jewish people in particular. It is thought that Y. L. Goldsztejn died in 1940.

Of the three works that Y. L. Goldsztejn left in book form, we are only personally familiar with two: "Collapse or Rebuild" and "1960." I have never seen "With Face to the Mirror," and I don't know what kind of a character the Three Stories of this book have and when the book was published. My work was therefore reduced to two papers about the two works by the Belchatow Jewish author that were known to me. I must remark that I once wrote a treatise about "Collapse or Rebuild," in which I used a lot of sharper words than I use today. And one should not find a contradiction in the two. Then I wrote about a living man with whom I could argue, while today I write about a man who is dead and whom one must rescue from being completely forgotten.

**Y. L. Goldsztejn**

**Collapse or Rebuild**

"A fantastic novel" (in four parts) is what the author called this book. It was published in 1934 by the publishing house "Books" in Warsaw. The author says in his preface to this novel that he wrote the book under difficult, impossible conditions, and he does not consider it as a complete work, only as a sketch for a book which must be written. He says that we live in such a time, in which anyone who has the smallest possibility must speak out and not wait for some famous people because the storm breaks the ordinary trees before it breaks the poplars and cedars. And many signs show that the storm is near.

According to what was just said, the author did not intend to create a work, but to give his views. And he really asks the reader that, when he finishes reading the book, he should extend his hand and help make a reality (he doesn't say what to make a reality, but we understand he means the ideals which he preaches in Rebuild). This work occupies two large volumes, one with 565 pages and the other with 657 pages. And although there is a lot of discussion in both books, the essential idea is barely brought out in a few dozen pages, and the bulk of the over 1200 pages is dedicated to the treatment

Belchatow Yizkor Book

205

and description of the heroes. If the chief goal of writing was his ideas, he could have been brief with the fictional part and written at length the idealistic part. One must realize that although Y. L. Goldsztejn set up ideological goals with his writing, he was really a fiction writer.

It must be said at the outset, that in the treatment of the story the novel is not fantastic, but thoroughly realistic. Only at the very end of the work is something described which never occurred in life and which the author saw in his fantasy, namely: when the people were called for the Second World War, they did not want to go and they followed the call of peace. The author wrote the above-mentioned five years before the war broke out, and that was his utopia (or fantasy) which unfortunately did not become reality.

Really, only the conclusion is fantastic, but the entire story is like a fairy tale, which gives the impression that the essential concept was taken from an old book or a folktale.

It takes place in the Shtetl Stawek. A Jewish shopkeeper borrows money from a Christian peasant, and, because he finds himself in a difficult financial situation, he partially denies his debt. The farmer complains to the "ksiadz" [priest (Polish)], and the Christian pastor goes to discuss the problem with the [religious] leader of the Jewish community. Both leaders are unusual men. The Christian priest [galech (Yiddish)], Leo Janson, is an educated tolerant man and he even has inclinations to heresy [apikorsut]. The rabbi, Tanchum Zemach, is a great scholar, and he speaks fluent Polish, is a do-gooder [mazeg tov], and is clever and has all good qualities.

The rabbi is already an old man and he has a twenty year old daughter, for whom he had prayed to G-d for eight years until he got his prayers answered. The daughter, who is called Brochele, is pretty and clever and also has no fewer good qualities than her father. And the priest is also young and, in addition to all his other aforementioned qualities, is handsome. And a love flickers between these two young people which brings much misfortune and almost destroys all of Stawek.

At first, he [the Rabbi] does not pay much attention to what is happening, and he maintains the best friendship with the priest, and the forbidden love flickers stronger and stronger. Sparks turn into flames. Violin and piano (the priest plays both), the moon and stars, and Polish poetry and world poetry accompany the love which in the end will stop bringing joy and good fortune and will only bring sadness and misfortune.

Brochele is already in the matchmaking process [shiduchim]; at first she found means to reject all the candidates, giving various excuses – those who were fools and those whom she flat out didn't like. One time it was embarrassing, when the father and the future bridegroom were to come and it [the shiduch] was set aside.

In the end, nothing helps, and the rabbi's daughter must become a bride. And they arrange an engagement. She disappears from the celebration and struggles within herself, and [then she] comes back and, only after [this struggle], runs away with her lover.

The priest and the rabbi's daughter travel to America through Romania. They find themselves in the port city Constantza, where they both live the punishment of the wicked after death [khibut hakever]. She knew that her running away from her father's house means bringing in the Angle of Death, because there ruled the very "dry law without compromise, without logic and without flexibility." She once went away from [her] home for three days, and, coming home [to her father's house], she met another father, a greyer one, a frightened one. He looked at her with such eyes, as one who stands by a fire and sees that everything of his is destroyed. The father had rushed with the marriage of the daughter because he wanted in that way to rescue her from the priest's hand and he hastened her running away. And also the young priest suffered, because what he had done caused much pain for his friend, the rabbi. They [Brochele and the priest] felt like two criminals who have committed a murder and whose conscience does not stop tormenting them. They wanted to console themselves by talking themselves into the idea that they gave to the two victims – her father and mother – the great idea of freedom and love for all mankind. They decided to fight capitalism and false faiths, and they thought that this would be easy to achieve. They did not understand why this had not been accomplished until now. If not for the belief in the realization of their new religion, they would have collapsed under the load of their suffering. They tried to create a movement for their beliefs, and they knew that they must write a fundamental work about it. But they decided in the meanwhile to write down a "sketch" and give it to a literary authority and at the same time to continue with the verbal propaganda. They should have given their work the name "Out of Hell," but they decided to give it the name from her father's book, "The Eternal Shabbat."

The work on the book gave them consolation. They were eager like little children to finish their treatise, but the work dragged out because of a variety of reasons and also because of the arrival of a child. The child brought them comfort of another kind. Before the child came, he used to fear leaving her alone in the room; he continually thought that she would commit suicide. Now he did not have that fear anymore. And she really changed. Although she was sick and broken, occasionally she would smile. The child had become for them in great measure, "The Eternal Shabbat."

In publishing their work, they ran into problems. The publisher to whom they gave it said that he would not publish anything that was illegal. Their ideas were ridiculed, and they were warned to be careful not to land in a Romanian jail. They decided to publish the book at their own expense, and the government confiscated it. When it was in print, it was neither easy nor cheap to keep them from being arrested.

And then Brochele began talking about returning to Poland. She was certain that they had changed so much that no one would recognize them. She is called Mariana and he Constantine Binke, and they have papers with these names, and there isn't any danger. He believed that in Poland it would be easier for them to publish their book and to realize their idea. But he did not want her to be close to Stawek. Because of the book, they had to travel. Because of the child, they could not travel. Her heart was terrified by what had happened in her home. He also thought that he had carried out a "bloody piece of work."

And they were not mistaken. Her mother was soon paralyzed, and she died, as the father said, with a twisted [crooked] mouth. The father, alone, fell into melancholy and went into a stormy confused mourning that bordered on madness. The old rabbi saw all sorts of hallucinations. He sang songs together with the Gilgalim [transmigrated souls], and he saw how his wife, the mother of the sinful daughter, struggled in the claws of the demons and [how] the devil [samech mem] rules over her. He cries out:

"You doors of hell – open up, your fires will never go out."

The only remedy would be if the daughter would die. He saw such pictures that he talked in a faltering way, and, in the shtetl, the people knew that the rabbi was deranged. All the students and friends who came and consoled the rabbi and the committee which had attempted to guard him and to feed him, got weary. The rabbi was abandoned by everyone except for his only faithful student, the shining Aryeh Meir Jakubowski. When he would burst into tears, the rabbi would eat something.

And the daughter and the son-in-law had come back to Poland and settled down in Lodz. Leo traveled alone to Stawek. Brochele was not strong enough to make the trip. And the former priest saw that the mother was dead and the rabbi was out of his mind, and he came back to his wife and admitted to her that there was no one to travel to. He did not tell her that her father was deranged. He told her that both of her parents were no more.

They had already made a plan to travel back to Romania, but because of the work, they remained a few more weeks. Brochele had once seen in Lodz her father's trusted friend, Jakubowski, and she started to go to him and fainted. She thought that he had not seen her. She was not even certain if she had really seen him. However, he did see her, and he reported it to the rabbi.

And when Leo and Brochele published the book, Leo was the first to travel, and Brochele was supposed to follow him. One time, he thought that Jakubowski told the rabbi that his daughter was in Lodz, and therefore he was frightened and turned around. But, after he convinced himself that nothing happened, he continued his trip. On the way, he was arrested. He was sent back, was confused, and he did not know where he was in the world. He felt guilty toward his wife and child, and he told the doctor in the hospital, "Madam, the child is also dead." And they assumed that he had really killed his wife and child, and they put him in jail.

And the old rabbi traveled to Lodz and went to his daughter and spoke harshly to her of Jewish law and punishment. The meeting between the two was a nightmare. They hardly recognized each other, since both were so aged and changed. And the daughter fainted and died. Earlier he had yelled at the daughter that she was worthy of death; now he wanted to resurrect her from death. Crying over the death of the daughter, the rabbi's glance fell on the child, and he had the crazy thought of killing it. But he gained control of himself and felt that "one must not destroy the sinner but the sin." And he felt a stormy urge to rescue the child and circumcise him and make him into a Jew; and he took him and left and carried out a conspiratorial piece of work with rare impetuousness, and he gave the child to his trusted friend, Jakubowski, together with the dowry that he had prepared for the daughter. When he comes back to himself, he sees the fearful hallucinations, and when he recovers a little he says to the daughter, "My child, in the world I have evened up the account; now I am coming there to help you."

In his house, he again loses his thoughts, and when a janitor comes to get information from him, he can't find out anything from him, and in the city they assume that the priest had really killed his wife and the child. And the old rabbi with the confused thoughts wanted to be together with his daughter, and the only way for him to achieve this was to commit suicide, but according to Jewish law a suicide would lose a place in heaven and would be sent to hell, and he began to throw his holy books on the ground. Also, he threw down his work "Day of Eternal Shabbat," and he poured kerosene on the whole pile of books. And together with the Torah scrolls and with the lamp from the table which he extinguished and from which he took off the glass, throws himself on the "martyr's pyre," and he does not stop saying, "so acts a father, a simple man." It is dark in the room and he sees before him his daughter like a dead solemn dove. He finds a light, ignites it, wants to stand it up between the books, but it does not want to stand, so he puts it on the kerosene soaked books. A few drops fall down, it takes a long time, and the pile does not ignite. The flame licks the kerosene and jumps away [not igniting]. He questions himself; perhaps he is doing a bad thing. Perhaps he should get off the books and remove the flame. He thought about confessing his sins, but after long deliberation the whole pile went up in flames. A terrible burning engulfed his hand, and he let down the Torah scroll and lifted his hand. His back started to burn, and so he died in the flames. All that remained of him was a black mass, not at all like the form of a man. All the books were burned. The surrounding houses caught on fire. A two-year-old twin was burned and the mother lost her senses. The synagogue, the church, the entire market, and most of the streets burned. Stawek was gone with the smoke.

And such a fire was caused by the love between the priest and the rabbi's daughter. The priest was cynically interrogated in the court, and, being certain that he had murdered his wife and child, he was condemned to eternal imprisonment.

With that ended the first volume with the two parts. The second volume describes the life of the son of forbidden love, who was called Tanchum, after his grandfather, and Meyrantz, after the name of the Jew who adopted him. Tanchum the second was described as a child with extraordinary capabilities and with crazy inclinations. He gets along well also with the non-Jewish children and is inclined to the mystic. Until he was four years old, he was in the house of a Jew called Baruch Meyrantz, and afterwards Jakubowski took him in and raised him together with his little boy Gabriel, who was older than the rabbi's grandchild by a few months, and with his daughter Chavetche, who was one year and six months old.

Jakubowski's wife controlled herself with all her strength not to have a bad relationship with the "bastard," and she imagined her Gabriel like an orphan, but her antipathy slipped out. And that probably had an effect on the character of the boy, who made friends with Gabriel and whom he made a partner to his bizarre activities. Tanchum did not want to eat any meat, and then Gabriel also did not want to eat it. And when Tanchum carried away the chicken that was to be slaughtered and put it in the forest, Gabriel took responsibility for it and was punished.

Tanchum had extraordinary capabilities, and he became a scholar and a Kabbalist. Gabriel was often jealous of him and wanted to keep pace with him. Gabriel became sick, and they spent on him everything that was in the house. And Jakubowski decided to ask permission from Tanchum to take his money to save Gabriel, but from where he had the money and where he took it, he did not tell him. Tanchum was so angry that they were asking for his money that he decided that when Gabriel became healthy he would leave the house. But Gabriel did not get well. Earlier, one of his feet was amputated and then, later, the other one. Rolling on the ground, Gabriel told his friend that he did not believe in G-d. And, as a non-believer, he died in great agony.

The First World War had already broken out. Tanchum's sacred structure, his belief, had started to waver. He could not forget the words that Gabriel told him. "You, a mortal, sacrificed yourself for me. And G-d, the compassionate and gracious one, tortures [me]" .... And the war had reached Stawek, and our hero found himself between the opposing armies, who turned the road into a bloody slaughter-house, and a voice called to him: "Go, go don't permit any more slaughter, go, go, they must stop the slaughter." And there at that time, when the old Jakubowski felt that he would be killed, he told Tanchum where he came from. He was afraid that he would marry his daughter Chavetche, and he demanded from him an agreement that he would not marry her, and for that reason he told him about his lineage. According to the agreement that he had with the rabbi, he was supposed to have told him when he was Bar-Mitzvah, but he did not have the courage to do it then. After the agreement with Tanchum, Jakubowski feels remorseful and pardons him and asks him to marry his daughter.

Then Tanchum gets extraordinary strength and, with a wild outburst of courage, rescues Jakubowski and his wife and Chavetche. He convinces a German officer that he should let him guide his unit to a place where there was Russian military, and the officer lets himself be persuaded and he arrives at the right time and rescues them.

After the war, Tanchum becomes a Zionist and ultimately travels to Eretz Israel. Chavetche, who always believed that he would become her husband, does not go with him, but she writes to him. In Israel, many disappointments await him, and he grapples with them. Chiefly, he was afraid that the Jews had to arrive in a land, awakening the hatred of the Arabs. (This was the chief reason for his disappointment and the basis for his book, "1960.") He was so shocked by the hatred that, during a discussion in a colony that was located near Mount Tabor, he says that we must stop immigration into the land. Everyone jumps up and he asks for quiet. He says, "The Jewish blood is still not dry in Ukrainian fields. The Arabs also want to do that [kill us]. They are millions and we are thousands." He spoke his thoughts out and also before an English officer, who silently agreed with him. And he preached in Israel for a sort of order that would have three solutions: "amor, libre, stziyo (love, liberty, knowledge)." Actually, those were the same ideas that his father had advocated. He stated his ideas in a brochure that was called "Collapse or Rebuild." And he demanded first reconstructing the psychology of mankind.

In Israel, Tanchum made friends with a Jew with the name Ezra Kosmola, who was the very opposite of him. One was very pious, the other – very cynical. One mild, harmonious, and warm – the other a giant, a wild one, a brutal one. When Kosmola advocated his cynicism and disbelief and people reacted angrily, Tanchum defended him with words and calmed the crowd, and they remained friends. Idealogically, they wanted to destroy each other, but personally, they helped each other.

Tanchum went back to Poland preaching his ideas. Kosmola also came back on a later ship, and he continuously tried to convince him that outside of vile things [nemeinkeit], man possesses nothing. And, in spite of his own will, Kosmola brought together his pious friend with his [the friend's] father, the former priest, Leo Janson from Stawek.

The former priest was in prison for 20 years, and, when he found out a million dollar inheritance awaited him in America, a lawyer won his release. The millionaire Aba Tzemach died in America and left his entire fortune to the Polish priest Leo Janson. The former priest came out of prison bitter at many things and mainly Jewish fanaticism, and he could not forgive himself for not seeing what was going to happen. He should have understood how far Jewish fanaticism would go. But he had not lost his belief to be able to change mankind and educate them against capitalism and false faiths and he had also not lost his hope to find his son.

He traveled to America, where in Chicago he got the great inheritance, and there he found out that Aba Tzemach, who had given him the inheritance, was the brother of the Staweker rabbi, and he had fallen from the path and he was his father. He had raised him as Johnson and as a Christian, because he did not want him to suffer as a Jew. In the sealed envelope which he opened, he read:

"Leon Janson, you are my son, my only son, whom I have never forgotten in my sad life. You are a Jew born from a Jewish father and a Jewish mother. I had to bring you up as a Christian."

Leo travelled back to Poland, but on the way back he stopped in Eretz Israel. And there he met with Kosmola and they traveled back to Poland on the same ship. The Jewish cynic was strangely surprised to see how this Pole advocates the same ideas as Tanchum and he draw upon several earnest people [to support] his ideas. He wanted to bring Tanchum together with him, but he reconsidered and thought it would strengthen their work, so he did not do it.

But the father and the son did meet each other. Kosmola brought them together. Tanchum had given a talk, and Leo heard him. He looked exactly like his mother. And when Tanchum told him that he was the grandchild of a rabbi and the son of a priest, he fell on him and said that he was his father. Kosmola wanted to shoot them both, and he wrestled with himself for a long time and finally committed suicide. He did not have the courage to shoot them, and he could not make up his mind to go with them, so he removed himself and left the way free for them.

And the Movement grew bigger. Only a few thousand copies of Tanchum's brochure, "Collapse or Rebuild," were distributed, but when the father came to help with his capital, the organization was able to put out a weekly publication which quickly became a daily paper and soon, in another European land, a daily paper of similar characteristics appeared and a well organized apparatus was formed. Then the fantastic part started, which told how the ideas from "Rebuild" had conquered and millions joined the Organization. Governments took over the re-building of their lands in compliance with the principals of the organization, borders were wiped away, and people hugged each other with love. And when a conflict arose between two governments and it came to an ultimatum and there was talk of cannons and gas clouds, the world trembled for joy. Tanchum, the president of the great organization, gave a command that a million men should march out to the threatened border and make a living "wall of peace" with white flags. And so it was done. And orchestras played and cordial kisses and hearty handshakes were the order of the day. And a plan was proposed to which all governments agreed, that the first land which the new movement rebuilds should receive all ammunition and chemicals, and the people should remain disarmed and, with that, war should be ended.

When Tanchum came back from Eretz Israel, Chavetche had a fiancé, a communist. And although he still loved her, he made a sacrifice and left her behind and alone went away to his work for love, freedom and knowledge. He grew with his work and the Organization grew larger and stronger. Chavetche came to him, a broken woman. She had helped her fiancé kill a young man who was also in love with her, because he suspected him of being a spy. Afterwards, her fiancé convinced himself that the young man was innocent, and he committed suicide. Tanchum allowed his former fiancée to become a member of his organization and she had displayed great heroism and self-sacrifice. Friends published a brochure for her called, "Chavetche Jakubowski." She had lain sick in a hospital and she wanted to see him. He went to her with the brochure and she called to him, "President." She told him that she was dying. Tanchum said to call him by his name, and said to her that the time had come when she could laugh again and that she would not die. And two professors were brought to her and rendered a diagnosis which was neither happy nor hopeless. And she was saved.

One, however, whom Moloch [the Angel of Death] did not release from his claws, was Tanchum's father. The president of the great organization was overwhelmed by Chavetche's return to health. Then he enthusiastically told her about resurrection from the dead, and he pointed out to her how many million people left their graves (among them were, really, Nero and Torquemada and Johan the horrible, but there also were good ones, Moshe, Isaiah, and — Jesus), and all said that thousands of deaths cannot weaken the happiness of one minute of life. Then, his father had to die. He said to him:

– My son, so is the fatal destiny of mankind. When I wanted to die, I was forced to live ... and when the new land beckons, life slips away from me.

And the old one saw Brochele, heard her singing Mitskevitch's "Dream," and he died.

The book ended with the words: "Moloch had triumphed again."

The evil of mankind father and son defeated, but the evil of the cosmos, Death, they were not able to defeat.

So there you have the contents of the over-1200-pages-thick book that the author considered a "sketch." And the idea of a rebuilt world is only developed in a sketchy way. Both in the places of father and son's work and in their talk, there was agitation against fanaticism, false creeds, against capitalism, dictatorship, against war, for a world with love, freedom and knowledge. How that is all to be achieved is not stated. The capital that Leo inherited helped to achieve the rebuilding and rescued the world from destruction, when the Second World War had threatened.

## 1960

The same publishing house, "Books," that in 1934 published "Collapse or Rebuild," in 1939 published "1960," which had no more than 74 pages.

Just from the title one can see that here a utopia is dealt with. The author wants to imagine what it will be like in the year 1960, 21 years after he wrote his book. The essence is here again an idea, but he expresses it through a story. A Jew wanted to commit suicide and cut his throat, lay rescued in the hospital, and, when he comes back to consciousness, the doctor asks him why he picked this particular moment, exactly one year after the catastrophe, to commit suicide and why he did not seek to take along into the grave a few enemies. The catastrophe was that hooligans broke into his house and murdered his two sons and shot him, but not to death. The daughter threw herself on one of the murderers with an iron bar. He saw how they dragged his daughter to a stream, and when he later came to consciousness, there were no more sons and no more daughter.

And the rescued one does not answer directly. He tells about his thoughts which pained him. He had not stopped thinking about his people, who consist of less than 17 million individuals, dispersed over the world, who do not have their own land and who were blamed for every unhappiness. He went back to the Middle Ages. He heard how the new German Chancellor said, "One must suppress the Jews." It became clear to him that the "Führer" wanted to found a new religion and to destroy the Christian religion. He had to humiliate and degrade the race that Jesus originated from. And the Jewish people did not stir themselves. Apparently Bialik was right when he says: [quoted first in Bialik's original Hebrew] ("He will not rise up unless the devil stands him up, and he will not wake up unless the whip wakes him up.") He thought about Palestine. These words alone had robbed him of more than one night's sleep. And he brought much clarity and sharpness out of this thought that he started to express in "Collapse or Rebuild." "Palestine," he said, "is a small land, a poor and mountainous land without natural riches. In almost all colonized lands, the colonist receives free land and even free livestock and equipment. And in Palestine, the colonist is forced to buy a small piece of inferior land (a dunam), for the highest value (pounds). After what the Jews put into the land, a sum of 20 million pounds, ninety-five percent of the land is in Arab hands. Eretz Israel has 70% Arabs, and when the land has one million Jews, there will be around two million Arabs. In a span of 14 years, 250 thousand Arabs have settled in Eretz Israel and none have left. Ben Gurion said that the 300 thousand Jews who were brought into the land made it possible for the same number of Arabs to enter. And if two million Jews should be brought in, in a short period to create a Jewish majority, the land will have 1.5 million Arabs, and they will always be underprivileged and will wish to establish the approximate hundred million Muslims from Egypt, Iraq, Turkey, Tunis.... The Arabs are in total 23 times as numerous as the Jews. The land is surrounded on three sides by Muslims, and the little state will find itself constantly crowded by neighbors and be threatened from within. For Jews in Palestine, he thought, really the body and the soul, but the Jewish people who were for hundreds of years killed and humiliated by the Christians may not fight against an enemy of one half billion people (he calculates a thousand million equals one billion, J.B.). He thought that then, before his accident had occurred. And he had quickly seen into another world. He had lost the memory, and he found himself in the hospital of the new Jewish Republic, and he had a conversation with the nurse in which she assured him that he was recovering and he would become healthy. He thought that it was 22 years since then (that is, 22 years since 1938) and Jews have their own land which is called New Eretz Israel. And now, he finds himself in a hospital in that land. He read newspapers and a friend brought him a brochure that the 15 year old student, Chaim ben Naftali Yeri, had written, and he demanded that he should read it quickly. And he read in the brochure the story of Eretz Israel.

It is a story about how the hardware store owner, Daniel Barzel from Diselberg, witnessed in Tevet [4th month of the Jewish calendar] 1939 the persecution and murder of Jews in his land, and he sent a letter to the president of the United States, Oliver Franklin, in which he asks for a piece of land for the Jewish people because there is no lack of land in the United States, Australia, or somewhere else. He wrote to the president that in one part of the world a prophet had arisen, a prophet of hate and falsehood and that in another part of the world, a prophet of mercy and justice must appear, and he, the great president, must be that messiah ...

And Daniel Barzel sent the letter in Yiddish to the president who had someone read it to him, and the president wired the writer of the letter that he should come. And the Diselberg store owner came to the president, who received him in the presence of his friend, the great Zionist Rabbi Silver. And he had a deep and significant discussion with the Zionist leader about Eretz Israel and he convinced him that at the moment when millions of Jews want to be in a Jewish land, the Arabs want to stop fighting the Jews in Palestine, and the enmity between the two peoples will disappear. The discussion lasted for twenty days and Rabbi Silver did not call his opponent "traitor" one time. And that one did not get flustered. He could not stop thinking that before the noose is thrown around Jewish necks all Jews must disappear from the eyes of the people and live by themselves. And he defeated the obstinacy of Rabbi

Silver, and Silver convinced other Zionist leaders, and a questionnaire was distributed to all Jews and 80% said that a Jewish state should be created, not necessarily in Palestine. The Jewish people saw the sword which hung over their heads and they realized the danger, and they started a great movement to settle in their own new land which consisted of an area of one hundred thousand square kilometer in Canada. And the Jews could not forgive themselves that they did not do this a thousand years ago; they would have avoided the Spanish Inquisition, the Ukrainian mass graves, the German slaughter. And women took off their jewelry, and hundreds of thousands of young men and women joined the Pioneers. At no time since they were dispersed, said the author, was there ever such unity as then (also before they were dispersed there was no unity, J. B.). The Franklin Declaration, and being freed from troubles and need, had welded them together into one people.

And in that brochure was described how anti-Semitism disappeared from the entire world press and how unemployment disappeared in all of Canada. And in the new Eretz Israel, the Arabs are the shop keepers because the Jews do not want to be shop keepers and they bought Arab land in Eretz Israel for farms in all Eretz Israel.

And the dream continued. He became healthy and went out and freely saw the great joy that rules in the Jewish land and the great celebrations that were held. And when he awoke he read in a newspaper that in Gliwice the Nazis set fire to a synagogue and three Jews were burned to death. In Vienna, three synagogues were burnt down and mass arrests took place and Jews committed suicide. He did not know if he was in a "Nazi museum," or if he saw the reality and that which he saw earlier was a dream. And then it was horribly painful to him and he lost all desires and wanted to quickly commit suicide, and he grabbed a knife and cut his throat. This story ends with the words which the hero said to the doctor:

"Listen, dear doctor, it will be hard for me to live now, after what I have seen in that beautiful free world, although it was only a dream. Go to the Jews and tell them: We the grey men call to them: Jewish people, it was only a dream, but it will not remain a dream if you yourself do not want to disappear like a dream.

**He possessed genuine ardor**

It is not necessary to point out that life turned out differently than Y. L. Goldsztejn had anticipated. The Second World War came, and the masses did not follow the call of the pacifists, and tens of millions of people died and almost all of Europe and great pieces of Asia were destroyed. And now one talks of a third world war, and it is unlikely that the masses will try and stop it, and the false creeds with the dictators rule with more strength. The main problem of humanity today is not death that nature brings, only the mass death which man alone brings upon himself. And also, Jews did not follow Goldsztejn and they did not build another land; instead they built purposely Eretz Israel, where today there are over one million Jews and less than 150 thousand Arabs. And although the Arabs remain stubborn and do not recognize the Jewish land, their obstinacy is substantially broken by reality.

And so, the thoughts which Goldsztejn expressed are not uninteresting and they will remain as a document of the thoughts of a Jew, an intelligent man, at the start of the Hitler era at the beginning of 1939. The territorialistic leader Ben Adir also wrote similarly in Yiddish. And the European Jewish people were really wiped out. It would have been better if Goldsztejn had been a real prophet. We will remember him as an upright Jew who had the courage to speak out his thoughts and who thought that reason was enough to solve the most difficult problems. However, man lives not by reason, but by instinct, which sometimes leads to life and sometimes to death. Although life turned out differently than Y. L. Goldsztejn had demanded, he was not incorrect – and woe to the correctness.

It is not the aim of this work to assess the artistic worth of the two books that I have reviewed. Their goal is not artistic, and one must not judge their value on the basis of their "artistic" qualities. The author was not interested in "how" but in "what." He wrote in a straightforward and clear manner and with temperament and passion. In his way of story telling he is comparable to Dinezon and even with Shamir. His language was more modern, comparable to that used by the current Jewish pamphleteers. It appears to me that linguistically his writing is closest to that of Hillel Zeitliner, and it can also be said, idealogically he was not far from him. One can also find in him ideological influences from Peretz and from Zhitlowsky and even from the aforementioned Ben Adir. He had the temperament of an artist. When the treatment had to have fire, he gave it fire! The scenes in "Collapse or Rebuild" that describe how the half crazed rabbi goes to the daughter when she is a broken soul with her gentile child in Lodz and precipitates her death and how he rescues the child and how he burns himself together with his books are able to kindle the imagination. While he was writing, the writer was burning [with passion]. And it appears to me that this is the strongest compliment that one can give Y. L. Goldsztejn the writer:

He possessed a genuine ardor which burned in him alone.

*[Page 268]*

# "Hands"

## Moshe Yanovsky (Janowsky) [*]

### Translated from the Yiddish by Martin S. Bornstein

(from the cycle "Small World")

United Hands - In Two Tablets
And Ten Fingers - The Ten Commandments
Opposite the Face - They are being held
Begin: I am – I am G-d.

Taken Hands - G-d Assigned
Swords, Spears the Fingers Become
With Sharp Nails, in order to stab
A Small World to Upset (disturb)

For What Purpose (were they) Created
Branch Hands, Such Clearness
Perhaps the same (purpose) as thorns?
To Stab and throw out fear?

Your Hands should not be lifted to lynch
It is the Hangman's, the Wildest, Ruins,
Your hand human being, is only to pray,
A Cohen you are, a Cohen.

(Lift up your hands to "Dochenen"[**]
With your face standing to the Masses,
They should search without looking
Head, moist tears, of pale anguish...)

————

* The author of this poem, Moshe Janowsky, who perished for (kiddush hashem) the holy name of G-d, in the death camp Chelmno, was the chairman of the Tzareh Agudat Israel in Belchatow. This poem was written on the eve of the outbreak of the Second World War.

** Dochenen = The priestly benediction of the Cohens.

*[Page 271]*

# III.

# Political movements

## Belchatow and Zionism

### by Moshe Efrati (Freitag)

### Translated from the Yiddish by Martin Bornstein

After a passage of time of 50 years it is difficult to depict for our generation, what a strain and considerable work was achieved through a small bunch of Belchatower youth in the struggle against the aggression of clericalism and Hasidism. They (the Hasidim) had in that time reigned in Belchatow against Jews or small groups (this coming) from the cursed (cholera –d) Hasidim: Ger(er) (Gur(er)), Alexander(er), Walborsz(er), and Ruspsz(er). In their hands was the rule over the Jewish community and its institutions, and they were against culture, knowledge, progress, and freedom for Jews – woe was to anyone who did not follow in their path.

Belchatower from the older generation certainly remember those times, when the economic situation of the Belchatow Jews was not looked upon as a shining one (most being weavers, village wanderers (peddlers), and small peddlers). They always waged a holy war of hegemony above the holy instrument, above (over) the community. Hatred reigned, as well as controversy, fights and Jewish arguments transpired among the Hasidim. This would take place between one rabbi and with the Hasidim of another rabbi. In one thing they were united, in the fight against knowledge, against a newspaper or book, against striving to learn, against culture and schooling, and against the revolutionary youth who wanted to work, study, gain knowledge and fight for a free life. The war between the parents and children began, it took on all types of middles, almost to block (foil), to hold back or be harmful to the new stream (movement). Those who were on the side of said "holy war", even used reports that denounced others to the Czarist rulers.

One must however notice, that from the beginning of the nineteenth century, newspapers began to arrive to the Jews of Belchatow, and among them also "Ha Tzefirah" ("The Herald"), which was hidden and even willingly read by Hasidim. It was quietly being sold – shekels (money) from the world zionist organization. In the years 1905 – 1906 the Poalei Tzion party was organized in Belchatow, and its' delegate participated in the world congress of Poalei Tzion in Cracow in the year 1908.

Through the influence of several friends of the Lodz Tzareh Tzion, who from time to time came to Belchatow, a Tzareh Tzion group of Belchatow youth was established. Almost so that they should not be arrested and sent off to Siberia, on account of Tzareh Tzion being illegal in Russia, a lot of the friends of Tzareh Tzion registered themselves as members of the "Odessa Committee" (the Hovevi Tzion). The Hovevi Tzion (Lovers of Zion) being a group whose activity was permitted under Czarist rule in Russia and who had as an aim the creation and running of bath houses in Israel.

A legal group was established for (the creation of) a library and reading room, that stood under the influence of Tzareh Tzion. Several hundred books were collected and a library and reading room were opened on the spot. Evening courses were organized, lectures and evenings were arranged, they were called assemblies, that dealt with all Jewish matters and (where) one learned the geography of the land of Israel.

About 50 subscribers were generated for "The Jewish People", a zionist weekly, that was published in Warsaw, under the editor Yitzchak Greenbaum.

When a world war broke out in 1914, the activities of the Tzareh Tzion in Belchatow were strengthened.

A). By organizing a Jewish self defense against Polish ruffians (pogroms).

B). By organizing constructive and social help for the needy.

C). By opening a union of the Tzareh Tzion organization in the surrounding towns and organizing a collection for Keren Kayemit L'Yisrael and for transferring it to Vienna (the zionist congress).

D). By cultural activities among the youth, the opening of a school for children and evening courses for adults.

E). Speakers were invited from the larger towns/cities to gatherings of national celebration.

F). At every opportunity evenings of a cultural character (nature) were arranged.

G). A union was established with the name "Redemption of the Land" ("Geh-ulot Ha-aretz"), for (the purpose of) creating baths (bathhouses) and for sewer systems.

The Belchatower young men and women worked energetically and industriously during the times of the world war from 1914 – 1918, and for whom it was loose (easy), for (the sake of) their townspeople and for their people. Immediately after the first World War 10 score young men and women were among the first that left for the land of Israel as pioneers, workers, and constructors. The mass (majority) of them participated in agriculture, industry, and trade (professions). They also maintained a live contact with their town, (and) as a result you can find now several hundred Belchatower in our land – in Israel, where they are active activists in the upbuilding – work of the Jewish state.

———

*[Page 275]*

# The Zionist Groups in Belchatow

## By Elimelech Pudlowski

## Translated from the Yiddish by Jerome Silverbush

## Edited by Roni and Jerry Liebowitz

[with comments in brackets]

It is difficult to create a concept of the social and cultural life in the little shtetls of pre-war Poland, if one does not first of all become familiar with the activities of the various political and religious groups, because the whole social life of the little shtetls in Poland was concentrated around the parties.

**First Zionist Activists**
(Tseirei Zion): Meir Warszawski, Berl Waldman,
Yechiel Meir Krawiczki [Kravitzky],
Meir Jakubowicz, Yishayah Langnas,
and David Lusczanowski [Lustshanovski]

One can assert with full certainty that 95% of the youth of Belchatow were organized in parties. Also the older generation was for the most part organized in parties or religious groups.

I will attempt here to give a picture of the activity of the Zionist groups in Belchatow, whose activity is well known to me.

## Mizrachi

The Religious Zionist party "Mizrachi" was founded in Belchatow in 1917, during the Austrian occupation. At that time in Belchatow, Zionist movements already existed, like "Poalei Zion" and "Tseirei Zion," in which there also were found religiously oriented comrades. But, not able to exist in a non-religious environment, the group of religious Zionists, under the leadership of Yechiel Borochowicz, founded the "Mizrachi," which – in the years between the two world wars – became the strongest Zionist group in Belchatow.

The founders and first party workers of "Mizrachi" were Yechiel Borochowicz, Yosef Lejb Gelbard, Avraham Ber Zilbersztejn, and Yitzhak Goldminc. It is worthwhile, in a few lines, to give a few biographical details about just the first four Mizrachi elders in Belchatow.

**Yechiel Borochowicz** – a Chasidic young man with a small amount of secular education, he gave himself over with Chasidic ecstasy to the Zionist activity in the religious circles. He created a meeting hall, founded a prayer house [bet tefilah] and held fiery lectures, intertwined with the Words of our Sages [in the Talmud], about colonization of Eretz Israel. He literally gave away his life for the Belchatow Jewish population. In 1919, during the typhus epidemic that had raged in the shtetl, he created a provisional hospital for typhus victims (in the building of the former Czarist Peace Court).

While working in the hospital as a volunteer nurse, he caught the disease from a typhus patient and died. The Belchatow Jewish population mourned for him for a long time. Incidentally, the Mizrachi library in Belchatow carried the name of Yechiel Borochowicz.

**Mizrachi Youth Organization in Belchatow**
Among the leaders are found Kalman Gelbard and Mendel Lipman

**A group of Mizrachi pioneers**
[the sign in Hebrew says "Kibbutz Yechiel of the

Mizrachi pioneers Belchatow"]

**Yosef Lejb Gelbard** – a traditional adherent of the Haskalah [the secular Jewish Enlightenment movement], he was at the same time a Gerer Chasid. In his private library, which was incidentally the biggest in the city, he collected Shas [the    Talmud]   and poskim [post-Talmudic   commentaries], together with Professor Gretz and I. L. Peretz. Next to the Zohar [the holiest mystical book of the Kabbala], were found the works of Mitzkevitch, Shiller, Tolstoy, and others, in the original. Only selected individuals had access to his library. Only rarely would he lend secular intellectual [maskilishe] books to someone. He did not want unexpectedly to be a promoter of the Haskalah.

**Reb Yosef Lejb Gelbard**

He made a living from a little grocery shop [speiz-kremel], in which his wife was employed, and from teaching. In the czarist period he taught Yiddish, Hebrew, Russian, and German; after the independence of Poland – Yiddish, Hebrew, and Polish. He also supplemented his income by writing requests to the court and to other government offices. He also gave legal advice, using the legal codes which were found in his library.

Yosef Lejb Gelbard was one of the founders of "Mizrachi" back when he prayed in a Gerer stibl [small Chasidic house of prayer]. Until the outbreak of the Second World War, he was among the most active of the party workers of "Mizrachi". He was a delegate from "Mizrachi" to various institutions: chairman of the Jewish community, councilman in the city council, etc. Because of his honesty and decency, he was loved by the Jewish and also the Christian population.

**Abraham Ber Zilbersztejn** – Among the Belchatow Jewish population, his name was not well known, although he was among the most active of the party workers of "Mizrachi," where he held the most responsible offices. He was a very modest, unassuming man, who never pushed himself ahead and hated every koyfets berosh [someone who is the first to jump out and the first to speak]. Abraham Ber did his work in the party without noise and clamor, but constantly energetically and successfully.

**Abraham Behr Zilbersztejn and Yacob Ehrlich**
[right to left]

Abraham Ber Zilbersztejn was the founder and leader of the Yavneh school in Belchatow, where a whole generation was educated in the spirit of Eretz Israel and became skilled readers of Hebrew in the Sephardic dialect. He had categorically declined the director's office [minahel amt] in the school, although he found himself at that time in extremely bad financial condition. He displayed a very earnest interest in working for the good of society. He always came to the meetings of Keren Kayemet [JNF – the Jewish National Fund], Keren Hayesod [the Palestine Foundation Fund], etc., five minutes before the designated time, although he knew that the meeting would first start an hour or even two later. Eventually he brought it about, furthermore, that all the others started coming punctually to meetings.

Even on his death bed, he did not give up his party work. The entire shtetl came to his funeral. But a strange thing happened there. At the funeral of Abraham Ber Zilbersztejn, who all his life managed to get along avoiding every conflict, an extremely big feud occurred. The Burial Society, which was ruled by the "Agudah" [a non-Zionist religious party], wanted to take revenge on the deceased person for his sharp anti-Agudah position. Because of that, they allotted him a plot in the cemetery which did not do honor to someone learned in the Torah [ben Torah], an Alexander Chasid, and a strongly pious Jew. If only the deceased's Chasidic party and friends had carried out the burial in another distinguished place.

**Yitzhak Goldminc** – came from a worker family. Only a weaver, he was a knower and a lover of books. He spent every free hour with a book. A man with a hot temperament, he reacted to every injustice. Because of that, he had many opponents, even in his own Mizrachi circles. He was the last Mizrachi chairman in Belchatow. He was also on the managing committee of the kehila [the Jewish community] in the years 1935-1939, when the kehila was dominated by the Agudah on the basis of the notorious paragraph 20 [which allowed them to strike from the voting list every Jew who was – according to their understanding – not religious enough]. Belchatow Jews would go to the meetings of the kehila administration just to hear Yitzhak's angry attacks on the Agudah.

Also during the years of the Nazi occupation, when distinguished Mizrachi party workers took leading positions in the Judenrat [Jewish Council] (Yankel Ehrlich, Mendel Feld, Sholem Feder, Mendel Lipman and Meir Szukowski), Yitzhak Goldminc always criticized them publicly and categorically spoke out against all who worked with the Nazis.

Mizrachi was the strongest Zionist group in Belchatow and had a strong influence on the whole community life in the shtetl. It always had a majority in the Folksbank [People's Bank] (which was directed by Yankel Ehrlich) and – in the span of several years – also in the kehila (with Yosef Leyb Gelbard as chairman). In those years, the kehila had started to subsidize the Jewish library and sport clubs. The kehila budget had at that time also foreseen subsidies for Keren Hayesod [Palestine Foundation Fund] and KK"L [Jewish

National Fund], but the allotment was repeatedly annulled by the city-governor after intervention by the Agudah.

There existed also in "Mizrachi" a Yavneh school [Zionist religious school sponsored by Mizrachi], in which in which a large part of the youth of Belchatow received a national [Zionist] education. The language of study was Hebrew. The teachers had certificates from the Mizrachi teacher seminar.

In the last years before World War II, a large group of young Mizrachi elders settled in Belchatow. The most important among them were Mendel Lipman and Kalman Gelbard.

**Mendel Lipman**

**Mendel Lipman**, a son of [the] Zdunska Wola dayan [morah horah = a rabbinical judge], a learned man, well versed in the Bible, spoke a beautiful Hebrew, and was gifted with a fine talent for public speaking. During his lectures, the school was always filled to capacity. He built his speeches on the Words of our Sages [in the Talmud], midrashim [Talmudic commentaries], and verses from the Bible. Mendel Lipman had a great influence on the internal life of Mizrachi. He was a member of the party council of the "Mizrachi" in Poland. In Belchatow, for a period of many years, he held the post of party secretary.

During the Nazi occupation, Mendel Lipman was a member of the Judenrat. Although no concrete complaint can be made against him, the office brought him no honor. It should also be mentioned that, when a relief committee for people from Belchatow was formed in the Lodz ghetto, he worked in it actively.

**Kalman Gelbard**, a son of observant, comfortable [balebatishe] parents, [he was] educated in cheder [Jewish religious elementary school] and later in the bet hamidrash [religious school of higher learning]. He distinguished himself everywhere with his quick intellect. He would understand the most difficult Talmud topic on the first reading. He solved the most complicated mathematical problems literally in seconds. He read a lot, had worldly knowledge, knew Yiddish and world history, learned bookkeeping, and finally also earned a diploma in teaching.

In the years 1922-1923, he was active in "Tseirei Agudat Israel" [the youth division of the non-Zionist Agudah] and was co-founder of their library. But when he came to the conclusion that the work of the Agudat Israel for Eretz Israel was not serious – together with a group of his comrades he came over to "Mizrachi," where he quickly became very active and later became the de-facto leader of "Mizrachi".

Kalman tried to avoid all publicity and honors. He seldom appeared in public, but if he did, people listened carefully to his words.

He was also the leader and mentor for the Mizrachi youth. During the occupation, he was – in contrast to other party members – strongly opposed working with the Judenrat. In 1941 Kalman Gelbard was in the first transport that the Germans sent from Belchatow to the infamous Poznan camps. Thanks to his knowledge of the German language, he got work in the camp office, where he was much favored and was appointed second-in-command of the camp [unter-lager-fuhrer], i.e., ruler over life and death for all the camp inmates.

But even in that office, Kalman set an example as a mensch [human being] and a Jew. He used all his influence on behalf of the camp population. He tried with all means to improve the food supply (in this regard, he came across the infamous Rosensztok brothers, the young sons of Reb Yosef, the scribe).

He obtained permission that, of the food packages that had arrived from Belchatow, twenty percent should be taken out for the poor [literally, not well-to-do] Belchatowers who did not receive any packages. He cheered up the camp residents, urged them to maintain hygienic conditions, smoothed over for the S.S. camp commander the "sins" of the inmates, and thereby put his own life in danger. In the end, he was exposed for concealing offences, and he was removed from his office. In his place was put the Belchatower Tamir Wisniewski, and soon the tragic significance of the change was seen. Already in the first days of Wisniewski's "rule," the Belchatower Jew Moshe Yosef Feld was hung for leaving the camp and seeking bread from the local farmers. Moshe Yosef had previously left the camp, but Kalman used to conceal this. Wisniewski, however, did not want to place himself in danger and sent Moshe Yosef to the gallows.

My words should serve as a gravestone for my friend Kalman Gelbard, who was killed in the camps.

The Mizrachi party worker Ben-tzion Berkowicz should also be mentioned. He totally devoted himself to the KK"L [JNF]. That for him was a holy work, and to that work, he gave his time, energy and effort.

### General Zionist Organization

Until 1930, the General Zionists in Belchatow were not organized, although – as individuals – they took part in all the Zionist activities like Keren Hayesod, Keren Kayemet L'Yisroel, etc. In 1930, at the initiative of Shlomo Hersh Topolewicz, Faiwel Regirer, and Leybish Zuchowski, the Zionist organization was founded. The first officers were: Shlomo Hersh Topolewicz (chairman), Melech Pudlowski (secretary), Faiwel Regirer, Leybish Zuchowski, and Chaim Natan Zendel.

The General Zionist movement did not play a big role in the public social life of Belchatow. The entire work for the Fund for Eretz Israel was done by none other than the Organization.

There existed within the General Zionist Organization, a "Pioneer Craftsman" [Halutz Bal Meloche] [group] made up of artisans with a Zionist viewpoint who were preparing themselves to emigrate to Eretz Israel. They were directed by Eliezer Wengliszewski.

Already, the first administration of the General Zionist Organization created the Hanoar Hatzioni – a Zionist youth group, which with time occupied a thoroughly respectable place in the Belchatow youth movement.

The last administration of the General Zionist Organization consisted of: Pinchas Szeslawski (chairman), Leybish Zuchowski, Hannah Haft, Baruch Rozencwejg, and Melech Pudlowski. In the People's Court – Yehiel Meir Ferszter, Feige Pudlowska-Ajzen, and Eliezr Wengliszewski. In the Audit Committee – Aharon Feiner and Meir Jakubowicz.

**The first bazaar of Keren Kayemet L'Yisrael [JNF]**

## Hanoar Hatzioni

The Hanoar Hatzioni was founded in Belchatow in 1931 at the initiative of Mr. Faiwel Regirer (today a lawyer in London) with the help of a friend from the management of Lodz – Janek Dzsewiencki.

The first management of "Hanoar Hatzioni" consisted of attorney F. Regirer (rosh haken [head of the youth branch]), Hannah Haft, Yidel Altman, Bronke Drezner, and Ruchel Lejb.

In "Hanoar Hatzioni" comrades from all strata of the Jewish population in Belchatow came together. The majority got their education in the public schools and had no Jewish knowledge whatsoever. A small percentage came from "Hashomer Hadas" ["Religious Guardian"] and "B'not Agudat Israel" ["Sons of Agudat Israel"] and already had received a national-religious education.

Almost every day in "Hanoar Hatzioni," "Circles" took place where information was given to the comrades about Jewish literature and history, Eretz Israel, etc. Also, from time to time, social themes were dealt with. The circles were led by Faiwel Regirer, S.H. Topolewicz, Zalman Feiner, Melech Pudlowski, and, from the youth themselves Meir Borochowicz and Aryeh Shatan.

The top management of Warsaw also would send instructors. Evening courses run by Aharon Pinchas Borensztejn were given in reading Hebrew.

Before the Second World War "Hanoar Hatzioni" in Belchatow was one of the largest youth groups, with almost one hundred members, their own library, football [soccer] team, and the best ping pong group. When, in the winter of 1938-1939, there was a ping-pong competition in Belchatow among all the local ping-pong clubs (Jewish, Polish, and German), "Hanoar Hatzioni" won the championship (thanks to the comrades Yankel Zilbergold and Aryeh Shatan).

The last management of "Hanoar Hatzioni" of Belchatow consisted of: Zalman Feiner (rosh haken), Bronke Drezner, Meir Borochowicz, Aryeh Shatan, Sime Wieszbitski, and Shmuel Nachtigal. When an underground movement was organized in the Lodz ghetto with the name, "Chazit" ["Front"], led by Aharon Jakobson, the Belchatower comrades took an active part in it.

**The Revisionist Organization**

**The Committee from Betar in Belchatow**
On the picture: [right to left] Henech Szukowski, Leibel Feder,
Moshe Klub [sic], and Yossel Nus

There also existed in Belchatow a Revisionist Organization with all its branches, like "Betar," "Brit HaChayal" and others. The Revisionist Organization did not play an important role in Belchatow Jewish communal life. An exception was the Sports Movement, in which Betar was well established.

Among the most active Revisionist leaders in Belchatow were: Gedalia Sztatlender, Moshe Klug, Abraham Nowak, and Henech Szukowski.

## Rightist Poalei Zion

**Shmuel Chaim Kelman**

Also the Poalei Zion (Right) had a well organized movement with a leadership which existed on a high cultural plane, like: Aharon Pinchas Borenshteyn, Shmuel Chaim Kelman, Chaitshe Zigmuntowicz, Abraham Minc, Mosheh Binem Farber (now in Israel), Abraham Litzanowski, and Yidell Lejb.

The Rightist Poalei Zion had the largest library in the city.

[Page 291]

# The Leftist "Poalei Zion"

## [Zionist Workers' Party]

## by Fishel Szmulewicz

## Translated from the Yiddish by Jerome Silverbush

## Edited by Roni Seibel Liebowitz

The Poalei Zion movement in Belchatow was created in a very unusual way: It grew from the ranks of [the] Belchatow "Bund."

So that, in order to understand the curious thing we are talking about, I have to turn to a chapter in our history, to that period in our shtetl, when the young men in the Beit Midrash, while studying our Talmud or other religious books, obtained books of worldly literature and read them in secret. One borrowed these books secretly for three kopeks a week from Yakob Elbinger, who was called "Yankel Shpiliter"[1] in the Shtetl. Later, when we were discovered and we had already left the Beit Midrash, we became official members of the library, and one part joined the Zionistic movement, and the other part joined the Bund. We reorganized our library into the Zionist Club, which at that time existed upstairs in Yankel Ostrowski's house, the only two story house in Belchatow at that time.

A large part of the members of the Zionist Club originated from the poorer strata of workers, craftsmen and small businessmen who ideologically tried to solve the Jewish national problem through Eretz Israel, but intellectually, the environment of the Zionist club was strange because they tried to get the children of rich people and even several factory owners to join. In Bund circles the initiative then originated to divide the unsatisfied worker youth from the Zionist party and create the Poalei Zion Party in order to have a worker majority at the next general meeting of the library to determine the future fate of the library, which had about 900 books. It is clear that because of the Bundist's feat, Poalei Zion had become a self sufficient party and two branches of activity developed in the shtetl. The first leaders of the Belchatow Poalei Zion were Ruchel Lichtenfeld and Moshe Szmulewicz, two capable and intelligent young people who had been very valuable for the Bund.

That was in 1917, when the Bund took over the library from the Zionists. On a Shabbat afternoon we were called for an urgent meeting, which took place in the home of the teacher at 29 Pabianiczer Street. There Moshe Szmulewicz gave a program talk, and soon an organization committee was created on the spot made up of Shlomo Goldsztejn, the son of Avraham Yaakov Goldsztejn, who died in 1919 in Hungary, Avraham Warshawski, Yeshayahu Abramczyk, Yisrael Gelbard, Ruchel Szmulewicz, Ruchel Lichtenfeld, and the writer of this essay. The second Shabbat afternoon was the founding meeting to which a large number of people came, and immediately about 30 people joined the new party. An administration was elected in which were: Moshe Szmulewicz, Ruchel Lichtenfeld, Max Jakubowicz, Avram Szmulewicz, Fishel Szmulewicz, Yeshayahu Abramczyk, Miriam Buszikowski , Shlomo Goldsztejn and Moshe Pigel. In the Revision Committee were: Yisrael Gelbard, A. Warszawski, and Shlomo Pelcman.

Our first task was to recruit members and that went very well for us. From the Zionist organization we obtained a large number of members and, after some more discussion, the general meeting of the library was called. The Zionist organization had already found a place, on the second floor at Malja the baker, there where the post office used to be. The Chairman of the meeting was the leader of the Belchatow Zionists, the writer Yoel Leyb Goldsztejn.

**The Party Committee of the Leftist Poalei Zion Party in 1923**

Seeing that they no longer had a majority in the library, the representatives of the Zionist organization caused a tumult and broke up the meeting. Later all the organizers of the Poalei Zion party received a letter from the Zionist organization, stating that since the library was located in the Zionist meeting hall, it is declared as the Zionist library. If we didn't agree with that, we should meet them with a delegation from the Bund to discuss it. We, the Poalei Zion, had already about half the members of the library, and there had already been a split between us and the Bund because of the following reasons:

The Bund thought it would succeed in influencing our party, but one saw that this opinion was an error. Right from the beginning, we took the initiative to independently lead all the workers, and we didn't want to be subject to any outside influences; only alone would we be an effective factor in local Jewish life. Between the Bund and Poalei Zion negotiations were started concerning working together in cultural areas, with a complete autonomy for each party to lead its political activity. The cultural organization was then located in Rozner's house on Piotrkower Street and belonged to the Bund. We had to help keep the school open, which already existed in the culture organization, and all members in good standing belonged to the organization. In the organization we needed proportional voting for the administration. The agreement between the Bund and Poalei Zion was close in principal, and we started as an active political and cultural activity. From the two organizers of our party, Ruchel Lichtenfeld was quickly back in the Bund, in contrast, Moshe Szmulewicz remained in Poalei Zion, although not in a leading position. Intellectuals from among our young members had started to take over the leading offices. One of them, Shlomo Goldsztejn, a dynamic young man who came from the Yeshiva, became the party secretary. We also started to invite speakers, and one of our first guests was Comrade Krol from Lodz. The second guest speaker was Comrade Rapaport, also from Lodz, who gave a lecture called, "Bund and the National Question." When he called the Bund members "Bundistlekh" [little Bund members], a disturbance started in the hall which turned into a fist fight and the meeting was broken up.

A short time later the general meeting of the Culture Association took place and the Bundist majority accepted a resolution: Poalei Zion members could individually belong to the Association, but not as an organized group. With that, our demand for proportional voting was thrown out; it was decided That only the candidate list which received a majority would administer the Culture

Association. Then Poalei Zion closed the meeting and decided to create the "Worker's Home." So, the library remained under the authority of the Zionist organization, and the Culture Association went totally to the authority of the Bundist majority. We had a consultation and decided to raid the Zionist library and seize the books. The Zionist library opened at 5 in the afternoon every Sunday, Tuesday and Thursday, and on Shabbat the library was open the entire afternoon. Since very few people come into the library on Sunday afternoons, we decided to make our raid on Sunday afternoon as soon as the library was opened and there still weren't any people in it. We elected a group of strong young men who were to carry out the raid. We put men at the entrance to prevent anyone from entering the library, and one group under my leadership went in the library with sacks which we filled with books, and a second group under the leadership of Avraham Warszawski had to be on the outside of the fence and take the sack with books to a certain place where we had already dug a hole to hold the books until the storm caused by the attack had passed. Among the attackers of the library were also Moshe Abramczyk, Toybe Szmulewicz, Miriam Borszikowski, Ruchel Szmulewicz, Moshe Pigel, Pinye Naparstek, Yosef Morgensztern, and others.

**A group of activists from the Leftist Poalei Zion**
A. Novak, K. M, Przedborski, S. Przedborski, A. Szmulewicz ,
S. Abramczyk, L. Safran, S. Yoab, David Altman, Feldman,
Yankel Grinszteyn, Abraham Gelbard, P. Szmulewicz,

David Szmulewicz, Y. Novak, Y. Morgensztern, M. Szmulewicz,
Yidel Feld, M. Abramczyk, and others.

When we went in the library at the designated time, we met there the
librarian, Moshe Rajbenbach [Reybenbach], his assistant Moshe Ostrowski,
and a girl who came to exchange a book. The whole plan for the raid was
successful. We 19 took about 600 books. At night, the leaders of the library
came with the police and pointed to us, all the perpetrators of the "heist." But
the police commandant, seeing that it was a political affair between Zionist
groups, freed us immediately and didn't start a process.

After the storm caused by our skillful piece of work died down, we set up
our library first at Moshe Przedborski's (Moshe [the] Grocholicer) on
Pabianiczer Street and later, in a larger location, at Moshe Bohm's on
Piotrokower Street, and we started to run our cultural activity. We had created
a choir under the direction of Max Jakubowicz (today in Buenos Aires) and at
the yahrzeit [anniversary of death] for Ber Borochowen (founder of Poalei Zion
in Russia) we arranged for a mourning service at which our choir did almost
the entire program and performed very strongly. Under the leadership of the
same Max Jakubowicz, we also created a dramatic circle. A youth circle was
created that developed very well, and since our work was developing in two
directions, we rented for the "worker home" a nice apartment with several
rooms from Ozer Szikowski, leaving the earlier smaller location for the youth.

The Zionist Organization, however, couldn't forget our raid on the library
and decided to take revenge.

While we together with the Bund put on a theater performance in the hall
of the fire house, playing "God, Man and Devil" by Yaakov Gordin, the
members of the Zionist organization came into our meeting hall and took
approximately 400 books. The next day with the help of the police we found
the books. They were, however sent to the court and the judge divided the
books in two parts, one for each library and with that, the incident was
forgotten. We also created our own school with about 100 children. The
teachers were: Ruchel Szmulewicz, who died at the age of 23 years, Chia Blime
Rubin, who taught Polish and Moshe Szmulewicz. We had 200 members in the
Workers Home, but we couldn't afford to keep the hall with the school open
and we then created a cooperative in order to cover the deficit from the school.

**A group of Leftist Poalei Zion**

[Additional information provided by Dora Szczukocka Bornstein, daughter of Mendel Szczukocky:
Seated front row, far right is Mendel Szczukocky's sister Sarah Szczukocka.
Third row back (next to last row) third from left is Mendel Szczukocky's twin sister,
Esther Galster (Szczukocka), wife of Meilech Galster.]

Between the guest speakers who we invited from Warsaw and Lodz were to be found the following: Zorobabel Natan Buchsboym, Aharon Wald, Yosef Rozen, Yisrael Stolarski and others.

We also carried out a cycle of lectures with our own speakers and so Moshe Szmulewicz lectured on Jewish history and about cultural history, Mr. Astler a student lectured on political economy and the history of socialism and the like. The cooperative had a very important place in our activities. We made the capital by selling shares to our members, sympathizers, and various consumers and even borrowed money for interest. Moshe Szmulewicz was elected administrator of the cooperative, Avraham Gelbard became secretary and Yaakov Flakowicz, the salesman. That was the most glorious time in the activity of our party in Belchatow because later amid the collapse of the cooperative also came the decline of the party itself. It became apparent that the leaders of the cooperative had no experience in that area, and also the Bund had its own cooperative and there was a strong competition between the two cooperatives. Many friends, who put their last penny into the stocks, lost the money and could hardly creep out from under the debt which they had accumulated by borrowing the money at interest. There was confusion in the shtetl and the prestige of the party suffered badly. We also had to close our school and make the location of the Worker Home smaller which we moved into the house of Chana Lipes. The activity was made more difficult because of the persecution of the worker organization by the police.

With these difficult conditions, however, we continued our activities, and among the more active members in the later years were: Yocheved Ekcztajn, who went on the fourth aliah to Eretz Israel but was forced to come back because of her health (she died in 1932), Yeshayahu Abramczyk, and Moshe Pelcman (both went later to Soviet Russia), Toybe Szmulewicz, Miriam Boszikowski, Avraham Warszawski, Yisrael Gelbard, Kalman Mendel Przedborski, who came to our movement from Labor Israel, Mendel Feld and Shlomo Szmulewicz (both were among the 10 Jews hung on Purim of 1942), Moshe Pigula, Avraham Gelbard, Yaakov Szeslawski (today in Israel), Pinya Naparstek, Yaakov Naparstek (today in North America).

In the years 1922 – 1923 a large emigration started from Belchatow. People went to North America, to Argentina, Brazil, Eretz Israel, Soviet Russia, and our party was not very active. The most active at that time were: Kalman Mendel Przedborski, Yisrael Jakubowicz, Zorach Feld, Avraham Ruszitski, Moshe Ali Niewinski, and the writer of this essay. We rented an attic room on Pabianiczer Street, and from time to time we bought a speaker from Lodz, but not in the former quantity. We still had, however, a good youth group among whom we can mention Itche Abramczyk, Melech Zilbersztejn, Avraham Hartman and others. Along with the death of the Polish Jews, the Belchatow Jews died along with their best men and heroic fighters.

---

1.  A purchase agent or transporter of merchandise [editor]

*[Page 300]*

# The Orthodox Movement in Belchatow

## By Leib Pudlowski

## Translated from the Yiddish by Jerome Silverbush

## Edited by Gloria Berkenstat Freund

[with comments in brackets]

At the end of the 19th century, a group of young men, most of them weavers, including Shmuel Zanwel and Zaken Altman at the head, existed in Belchatow who would study the Mishnah or the "Ein-Yakov" ["Jakob's Well" – 16th century book of rabbinical Talmudic literature] every day at dusk in the beis hamedresh [house of study and prayer]. To preserve the sanctity of Kabbalat Shabbat [the Friday evening service welcoming the Sabbath] they would take everything out of their pockets. (At that time there was no Shabbos eruv [an area marked off by a string, beyond which you could not walk or carry anything on the Sabbath] in Belchatow). They had a room in Ezriel Graber's house where they would daven [pray] with their own minyan [quorum of ten males necessary to hold a Jewish prayer service] and even presented their own Torah.

At the beginning of the present century [20th], there already existed a yeshiva in Belchatow with 400 students from every corner of Poland. The yeshiva was located in the beis hamedresh, and its director was the Belchatower Rabbi Braun, later Lukower Rebbe [Chasidic rabbi], who was famous throughout Poland as the Lukower Gaon [genius or brilliant man]. The students in the yeshiva ate and slept in the homes of the property owners of the shtetl.

Belchatow had a masonry shul [synagogue], a large beis hamedresh, and many small Chasidic shtiblech [small prayer houses]. The ordinary people prayed in the shul and in the beis hamedresh. The Chasidim rarely prayed there, although they did purchase "shtet" [seats]. On the Shabbosim [Sabbaths] before Yom Kippur and Passover, the Belchatower Rabbi Zemach Tornheim would give his sermons in the shul, and on the remaining Shabbosim of the year he preached in the beis hamedresh. The meetings about all important city legal matters used to take place in the ante-room of the shul. During the time of the Tsar, the dozores [members of communal council] used to have their meetings in the ante-room. Before the First World War, the Belchatower dozores were: Mordekhai Szpigelman, Alter Borensztajn, Hershl Plawner, Yakov and Hersh Szotlender, among others.

In Belchatow before the First World War, Jewish life, in general, was mainly concentrated in shul or in the beis hamedresh. In 1905, during the weavers' struggle against the factory owners, the weavers once entered the shul while the property owners were saying slichos [a prayer said during the days preceding Rosh Hashanah] and beat them with murderous blows. On the birthday of Nicholas the Second and at other official "galuvkes" [the birthday or anniversary of the death of the tsar or members of his family] the occasion was marked with solemn prayers in the shul. Yoske, the teacher of the youngest children, used to bring his students to the shul where they would receive sweets. Yoske's cheder [religious school for young boys] was the only legalized cheder in Belchatow. On the wall in his cheder hung a picture of Nicholas the Second with his family. The other cheders (Sholom Amshinower), Leyzer Malamed's, Mendel Grocholicer's, and others, were "secret," and they would actually disperse the students when the Tsar's school inspector came into the city.

**The Belchatow Synagogue,
in background the Talmud Torah**

During the years 1909-1910 vigorous struggles took place in Belchatow over the introduction of new ritual slaughterers. Three sides were formed: the Gerer Chasidim, the Aleksander, and the property owners with their rabbi.

The entire struggle was carried out in the ante-room of the synagogue. Each side had its supporters and its "starke" ["strong ones"]. Alter Borensztajn of the Gerer would come to the meetings, surrounded by "starke" in order to protect himself from blows. The dispute lasted two years and finally they accepted three new ritual slaughterers, one for each side. The property owners brought in Leibl Muszkat from Piotrkow, the son of the Piotrkow cantor. He was the ritual slaughterer in Belchatow for 30 years.

The Belchatower Jews spent their time mainly in the beis hamedresh. Even when the yeshiva had permanently shut down, the young men would sit there the entire day and study. The Gerer and the Aleksander would each sit at their own tables. They liked to talk about business and politics in the beis hamedresh. The Rabbi would ban the rebellious. Khalitse [release of a man from the obligation to marry his brother's childless widow] was also granted there.

Around 1911 a secret group of Maskilim [adherents of the Enlightenment] was created in the beis hamedresh, and in 1912 it reached the point that the title pages of prayer books were torn out and Gemaras were thrown in the toilets. Suspicion fell on the group of Maskilim, and a trial was organized for them. The rabbi took out a Torah scroll and called upon the Maskilim to atone. One of the Maskilim, Chaim Dzialowski, went to the Torah and kissed it and promised to be good and pious before the entire congregation.

On the Shabbos, the scholars of the city would study the Pirkei Avot [Ethics of the Fathers, one of the 63 tractates of the Mishnah], the Mishnah, the Chumash [Five Books of Moses], and Rashi with the property owners. The Belchatower rabbi led a rabbinic table at which they sang Jewish nignunim [melodies] by the Wolborzer Rebbe.

The Gerer Chasidim were the most numerous. They had two shtiblech [small prayer houses] in Belchatow, and they also had the greatest influence on the city. They made the decision whether to accept a rabbi or ritual slaughterer. They were followed by a part of the middleclass element and, often, even non-organized weavers, who obtained weaving work from the Gerer, wagon drivers, and so on. The Aleksander Chasidim held second place after the Gerer, and there was always a struggle between the two for power over the religious Jews in Belchatow. The hatred between them was so great that they would not even arrange marriages among their families.

The ordinary people would travel to the Radoszycer Rebbe. Every Shabbos at night, the wagon drivers would hitch the horses to several wagons, fill them with men and women, and drive to Radoszyce, which was right next to Belchatow. On the way back, the women used to tell each other about the miracles of the Rebbe, Reb Ber.

It is necessary to remember the Khevra Kadishe [burial society] from those times that consisted of truly pious Jews and great scholars, such as Josef Gutman, the city's bookbinder, who would awake every night at midnight to study and recite prayers in commemoration of the Temple in Jerusalem; Alter Bresler, the Bel Musaf [man who recites additional prayers on Shabbos and holidays] from the Gerer prayer house, and others. The burial society also would spend the night with the sick, give charity, and hold celebrations. That is how religious life looked in Belchatow until the end of the First World War.

* * *

At the end of the First World War, a severe change occurred in Jewish life in Belchatow. Jewish communal life grew rapidly. The Po'alei Zion [Workers of Zion], the Bund [the Jewish Labor Organization of Poland], and others started public activities. The young started to flow into the parties. The religious Jews were also pulled along with the current. In 1918, the first religious groups were formed, under the name "Tiferes Bukherim" [magnificent young men], which consisted of members from the houses of study and prayer and members from the property owners class. Similar organizations already existed in a series of cities in Poland, but there was no organized contact among them. The organizations were not involved with political problems. Their only task was to give the religious youth the possibility to live a spiritual life. The youth from Chasidic and Misnagdish [orthodox opponents of Chasidus] circles were grouped ideologically in the Tiferes groups. They used to conduct celebrations, dancing and singing, as the Chasidim did, and they also studied The Ethics of the Fathers, the Five Books of Moses, and Rashi. The young from various strata lived together in a friendly manner, from Chasidic young men to butcher boys and porters. The majority of the members consisted of workers and craftsmen from various trades: weavers, barbers, tailors, porters, butchers, wagon drivers, and young Chasidic men from poor homes. There was rarely one from a rich home.

The "Tiferes Bukherim" had its own self-help fund. In an emergency, one was obliged to help the other. On Shabbos, the members would spend the entire day at the organization and would only go home at the Shabbos meal time. Friday nights they would study Chumash and Rashi, Shabbos morning they would all pray in their own prayer house. After noon they would study the Pirkei Avot and Mishnah. At shalosh-sudos [the late afternoon meal on the Sabbath], they would celebrate with a barrel of beer, dancing and singing. Right at the beginning of its existence, the Tiferes had over one hundred members. Among the most important workers and founders of the organization were:

**Jakob Machabanski** - the chairman of the organization, a son of simple people, weavers and hand workers and he himself was a weaver who could study a little Chumash and Rashi. He had organizational talent and was very influential with his straight-forwardness. He later became the chairman of the Tseirei Emunei Israel [young, faithful followers of Israel] and Agudas - councilman in the first Belchatower city council.

The second important activist was **Moshe Przybylski**. He was called "Moshe God," because he was always gazing absent-mindedly at the heavens. He was the actual leader of "Tiferes Bukherim" in Belchatow. He would mainly dedicate himself to the education of the young men. Later, he was the leader of Agudas Israel in Pabianice.

Mention should also be made of Moshe Eksztajn, Zajnwel Muszkat, Ishaye-Yudl Rzeslawski (Kiperniak), who later became chairman of the first Belchatower Kehilla [internal governing board of the Jewish community] in independent Poland.

The "Tiferes" also had a dramatic circle. On Purim 1919, they put on a performance of "Ahasueros" [King of Persia from Purim story]. They gave the performance in their own meeting hall without scenery, with a temporary stage of boards and benches. A large audience came in honor of Purim. Women were also allowed to see the performance.

In time, a group was created in "Tiferes Bukherim" that demanded that the organization modernize its work, create a newspaper, join the religious cultural organization "Tevunah," etc. The most outstanding member of the group was Shlomo Muszkat, the son of Belchatow's ritual slaughterer. He was very well versed in spiritual subjects as well as in secular subjects, possessed a quick mind and a significant speaking talent. He later became active in both "Tseirei Emunei Israel" and in "Po'alei Agudas Israel," and was the representative of the Agudas in the Kehilla and in the City Council.

In 1919, the "Tiferes" in Belchatow was dissolved and was reformed into a "Tevunah" organization. The activity of the new organization was not much different from that of the old Tiferes. Zajnwel Muszkat (the Belachtower ritual slaughter) and Moshe Przysbylski studied with the young men in Tiferes. The leaders remained the same, but in time, the membership became exclusively members of the middleclass element.

Also, the activities of the "Tevunah" did not find favor with its members. An internal fight started around the question of Eretz Yisroel [the Land of Israel]. At the time of the Balfour Declaration, one group demanded more Zionist work; a second group was not satisfied that "Tevunah" concerned itself only with religious education. The bitter end came as "Tevunah" fell apart. The Zionist-oriented element joined Mizrachi [an Orthodox Zionist movement founded in Vilna in 1902], while the majority, together with the leadership, joined the then-forming "Tseirei Emunei Israel" [a non-Zionist Orthodox movement].

* * *

"Tseirei Emunei Israel" was founded in 1920. Its membership consisted mainly of former members of "Tiferes Bukherim" and "Tevunah". It was also joined by groups of Chasidic young men from the Gerer, Radziner, and other prayer houses. The group carried out a series of changes in the new organization. The most noteworthy members of the group were: Yitzhak Pigula, Elimelekh Pudlowski, and Zalman-Peretz Gelbart. In the later years, they played an important role in various Belchatower parties.

The following members were the first provisional administrators: Jakob Machabanski, Moshe Ecksztajn, Zajnwel Muszkat, Shlomo Muszkat, and Ishaye Yudl Przybylski – all former active members of "Tiferes" and "Tevunah." Among the administrators were also the Pyuro brothers. One of the brothers, Mayer, had quickly risen to the top of the Belchatower "Tseirei Emunei Israel." He was an expert on orthodox literature, a capable educator, a good speaker, and he also was capable of interpreting the bible clearly. Israel Frenkl and Moshe Chaim Grynblat were also members of the initial administration. Both were representatives of "Shlomei Emunei Israel," which supervised the youth.

They were later among the most respected activists in the "Agudah" and the founders of the Beis Yakov [religious schools for young girls] movement in Belchatow. During the first two years of activity of the administration (Machabanski – chairman, and Mayer Pyuro – secretary), no important changes took place in the life of the organization. The leadership sharply opposed every attempt at reform by the "young" ["Yunge"] members. Angry struggles occurred during the entire time among the younger members who demanded political activity, a library, a reading room, vigorous activity for Eretz Yisroel, etc. There were stormy meetings and, although the youth succeeded in attracting a large group of the "Tseiri-Emuneikes" to their cause, their efforts did not have any success with the leadership. The only innovations were the studying of the "Horeb," the "13 Letters" [sic 山] by Dr. Shimson Rafael Hirsch, and "God's People" by Dr. Nusen Birnbaum. Most popular were the lessons from "Guide for the Perplexed" and "Duties of the Heart," taught by Dovid Shoykhet. The Belchatower rabbis [morah horahs, or religious judges], Shmuel Yehoshua Szilim and Moshe Eliezer Pudlowski, also gave Talmudic lectures.

**Yitzhak Pigula**

**[no caption]**

The Tseireim would distribute the orthodox organ, "Der Yid" ["The Jew"]. Students would come from Warsaw, Lodz, Piotrkow, etc.

Many Hasidic parents did not want to send their children to the Tseirim. They were afraid that their children would get infected with the spirit of the "yunge" [young people], and it also was not fitting that their children mix with the common young people who were members of Tseirim.

The finale of the struggle between the "alte" [old] and the "yunge" [young] played itself out at the general conference at the beginning of 1922. Both sides mobilized all of their supporters. Almost 120 youths came to the meeting and the youth who had the majority in the new administration won.

The new administration opened a library and a reading room (the new librarian was Elimelekh Pudlowski). Later, there was a vigorous fight about the character of the library. A decision was even made that non-religious books would not be allowed in the library. But the majority of the library committee consisted of the "Yunge," and they actually smuggled in books from worldly authors. However, Peretz, Mendele, Sholom Aleichem, Asch, Opatoshu, etc., were not allowed in the library.

**Three Belchatower young men who received rabbinical diplomas**

[from right to left:] Kadzial, Borzykowski, and the dyer's son

**A group of Chassidic young men in Belchatow.**

[Additional information provided by Dora Szczukocka Bornstein: Second from left is Benczkowski]

The library principally relied on translations of foreign works from which any pages with sexual content were cut out. At the end of 1923, the library had 500 books.

In the organization, there also existed an Eretz Yisroel committee (with Zalman Peretz Gelbart as secretary), which raised money for Keren Hayeshuv [fund for the Jewish homeland].

In 1923, one of the most important efforts of "Tseirei Emunei Israel" was the dedication of a new Torah. The collection action for the purpose was started by the "Tiferes Bucherim," but the work finished only with the end of the existence of the Tseirim.

The dedication celebration lasted an entire month. Every night Jews would come in and write a letter [in the Torah]. Feywel's klezmer band played joyfully. On the day of the dedication, Abraham Keynisls and Leibush Pelcman came on white horses with disguised faces to relay the news to all corners of the city. At dusk all the religious Jews came to the meeting hall of the Tseirim, from where the new Torah was carried under a wedding canopy to the synagogue. Jews danced and sang along the entire way. Leibl Shoyket sang chapters of Psalms with a choir in the synagogue. The celebration ended with a great feast during which sermons were given.

**Agudasher Kibbutz-Hachsharah in Belchatow**
[members of the Agudas training kibbutz, a preparatory agricultural community for prospective agricultural immigrants to Eretz Yisroel]

**Leave-taking evening of the Belchatower Tseirei Agudas Israel
in honor of the secretary Yitzhak Alfiszer
for his making aliyah to Eretz Yisroel. (1937)**

After the dedication, the fight in "Tseirei Emunei Israel" about the Eretz Yisroel question became more intense. A large group of members, including Zalman Perec Gelbart, Sucher Jutkewicz, and Yitzhak Yosef Flam, had demanded more activities for Israel and closer cooperation with the Zionist Movement. When the leadership did not satisfy their demands, the entire group left the Tseireim and joined "Mizrachi."

The most respected activists from the group were the Gelbart brothers. The older Zalman Perec, who suffered from lung disease, was the soul of the movement. Even on his death bed he continued the party work. The younger brother Kalman was also an activist in "Mizrachi." It was known everywhere that his opinion and position was right and just. He later perished in the Poznan concentration camp.

In the second half of 1923, again another group formed in the organization, which requested that "Tseirei Emunei Israel" be transformed into a religious workers party. This suggestion found a deep resonance with the majority of the members, which consisted of weavers, shearers, and other related trades in the textile industry. At the end of 1923 it was decided at a general meeting to give the organization the name "Poalei Emunei Israel." After the decision, a small number of members – children of Chasidic factory owners – did leave the organization. Those who left even created a new managing committee for "Tseiri Emunei," but the organization did not carry on any tangible activities. "Tseiri Emunei" first regained its strength in the 1930's. In 1935, the Belchatower "Tseirei Emunei" had 50 members. At that time the important activists were: Moshe Janowsky* (chairman), Yitzhak Alfiszer, Borzykowski, and Fakentreger.

The Belchatower "Poalei Emunei Israel" was compatible with the "Poalei Agudas Israel" in Poland. This was actually the first religious worker party in Poland. The second was an organization with the same name in Piotrokow.

[The banner in the photograph identifies the group
as the "Managing Committee of the Youth Group".]

[Page 312]

The Belchatower Poalei Emunei was one of the few religious organizations that had a worker element (weavers, tailors, shearers, those who worked at home, artisans, etc.). "Tseirei Emunei" were not willingly in the same organization as the children of the manufacturers, against whom they were carrying out a strike. The main principle of "Poalei Emunei" was that only in religious matters were they bound to the Agudah; the organization was independent in all other areas.

It the first leadership were: Shamai and Sholom Borukh Feld, weavers; Jakov Szmulewicz a teacher, Yehuda Leib Kaplan, a weaver and Yitzhak Pigula, a shearer. The ideologue of the organization was Yitzhak Pigula, who also belonged to the executive committee of the first central committee of Poalei Agudas Israel in Poland. He was very beloved and respected by everyone. He was very modest and he did not even sign his frequent articles which appeared in the Agudah press unsigned. He was convinced that the Poalei Agudas Israel had a great mission to carry out in Jewish life, which had to be carried out according to the social laws of the Torah. During the Nazi occupation he continually intervened in the Judenrat against the injustices against the Belchatower Jews.

Until then, the organization carried on varied activities. There were circles in which social problems were discussed, that carried out press reviews, read the works of Dr. Nusan Birnboym and which held lectures about natural science and philosophy. Three times a week, every member had to attend Tanakh [Bible] courses. Most of the work was done by Yitzhak Pigula with the help of Itshe Meir Wolfowicz, Moshe Eliezer Pudlowski, Shmuel Yehoshua Szilit, Dovid Shoyket and Moshe Josef Litmanowicz..

The Poalei Agudas Israel was one of the strongest organizations in Belchatow. From almost 100 members during its rise, it reached 250 members at the outbreak of World War II (100 older members and 150 in the youth section). The youth section had its own managing committee. The most important activists were: Sender Sendik, Shmuel Kalman, Shlomo Pigula, the Lewkowicz brothers and Avraham Szerman. The youth section dedicated itself mostly to education work.

In 1924, the organization made an attempt to organize a kibbutz with the Piotrkow Poalei Agudah. 25 young men traveled to the noble estate of Niechcic which belonged to the Jewish landowner, Moshe Fefer (the former Jewish representative in the War Council during the First World War). He placed the condition that the young men would have the same hours as his Polish farmhands. The kibbutz had to be dissolved, however, because the Polish workers thought that the kibbutzniks had come to take their bread.

The attempt was repeated in 1931. The kibbutz consisted of 30 young men who did various "unskilled" labor: chopping wood, turning yarns for the dyers, house work for Yiddish families, etc. They were not allowed in the factories because of resistance by the organized workers.

The organization's library possessed over 1,000 books. In the reading room, one could read all the Jewish newspapers from Poland and abroad. The "Volks-Zeitung" ["Peoples' Newspaper"] was removed from the reading room when it started to appear on Shabbos. Later, the Bund's organ was brought back, but the Shabbos issue was still banned.

The organization also had a choir directed by Yitzhak Muszkat and a drama club, which from time to time gave public performances, sometimes in their own hall and sometimes in the city auditorium and evening courses for the youth and adults.

In 1929 the Belchatower "Poalei Zion" founded a school for girls from 9 to 16 years old. The school, under the name "Khorev," had four divisions with 150 students. The language of instruction was Yiddish. The school was authorized by the state, and Yiddish, Hebrew, Jewish and general history, religious law, the Jewish bible, and various religious subjects were taught. The teachers were Josef Szmulewicz, Yitzhak Pigula, and Khantsha Fajwicz.

The professional field also occupied a respected place in the activities of the organizations, which even had a majority in the shearers' trade, because Hasidic parents often would teach their children this trade, which was considered as more respectable than all other trades. In the trade committee of the shearers were: Aaron Przybylski, Sucher Litmanowicz, Moshe Liberman, and Yitzhak Pigula.

# ולא תביא תועבה אל ביתך!

## כי חרם הוא!

**יודען!** קויפט נישט קיין צייטונג וועלכע ווערט געדרוקט אין שבת און יום כיפור!

היינט קומט מאר א פרעסע מאן פון דעם בונדישען אָרגאן די „פֿאָלקס־צייטונג" און יעדער רעליגיעזער יוד וועט זיכער באצוכט ווערן דורך די בונדישע יונגלען און מיידלעך, האו זיי וועלן פרובען איהם פארקויפען צו צייטונג.

מיר ווענדן זיך דעריבער צו אלע יודען, וואָס עס איז זיי טייער די תורה און טראדיציע, צו אלע יודען, וואָס ווילען נישט, אז די נשמות פון זייערע קינדער זאלען פאר'סמ'ם ווערן פון'ם מארקסיסטישען גיסט – צו זיי אלע ווענדן מיר זיך מיט אן'אפעל;

**יודען!** די חוצפה פון די בונדישע כופרים וועלכע טרעטן אלעס וואָס עס צו אונו הייליג און טייער איז, וועלכע פארשפרייטען מינות און אפיקורסות דוקא דורך די צייטונג, מיט וועלכע זיי קומען היינט צו דיר רעליגיעזער יוד, דיר איינצודען זי צו קויפען – שטימט איבער יעדע גרעניץ.

**רעליגיעזער יוד!** צו וועסטו אריינלאָזען אין דיין שטוב א צייטונג, וואָס איז אין שׁול מים כפירה און מינות ??

צו וועסטו אריינלאָזען אין דיין שטוב א צייטונג, וואָס טרעט אנ־אויפהער מיט גאלינגער שנאה אלעס וואָס האט טו טון מיט דער יודישער אמונה אין אז מאדם, וואָס מען טרעפט נישט אפילו ביי נישט יחדישע סאציאליסטן

צו וועסטו קויפען א צייטונג וואָס פערליימקענט דעם יודישען אפשטאם און ווילען אז דעם יודישע פאלק זאל אויפ:הערן ח'ו צו עקסיסטירען ??!

רעליגיעזער יוד! צו וועסטו נעמטן אין דיין האנד א צייטונג וואָס איז נעדרוקט אין שבת, וואָס איז ע'פ' דין אסור בהנאה ??!

צו וועסטו אונטערשטיצען א צייטונג, וואָס פרעהט זיך ווען יודיש בלוט גיסט זיך אין אונזער היילינ ארץ־ישראל ??!

ניין !!! פארזאגנם מאל'ניין !!! דו טארסט עס נישט און וועסט עס זיכער נישט טון.

די מוח פערשטעהן אז מיט'ן קויפען א „פֿאָלקס־צייטונג" העלפטסטו צו די בו:דישע משחיתים זייער אינקוויזיטארישע ארבייט;

קויפסטו א „פֿאָלקס־צייטונג" דאן בעשמוצטו דיין כבוד און דעם

כבוד פון יודישען דת !!!

די גרעסטע חרפה וואָלט עס געווען פאר דיר!

דעריבער רעליגיעזער יוד, ווען מאן וועט צו קומען צו דיר, פערקויפען א „פֿאָלקס־צייטונג" זאלסטו זוכטיג אין שארפל ענטפערן : טראגט אייך אב איהר פערברעכער, מיר וועלצן ביי צייך אזא צייטונג וואָס בעקעמפט יודען און יודעטשום, נישט קויפען.

קיין איין רעליגיעזער יוד טאר נישט אריינלאָזען צו זיך אין שטוב די מיסטאנעריש „פֿאָלקס־צייטונג" אויב האסטו שוין אויסנעקומען א קויפן, דאן צורייס און צושליק זי אין די אורגאן פון די מסיתים און מדיחים.

זיי מקיים דעם ובערת הרעה מקרבך !!!

## דער פעראיי'ניקטער קאמיטעט

## צו באקעמפען די פרייע פרעסע.

Druk. Żarkowski.      Wydawca: „Agudas Israel" w Bełchatowie.

[Poster of the Agudah's United Committee to fight the Free Press, urging Jews not to purchase the "Volks-Zeitung"]

[Translation of above poster follows:]

## Do not bring an abomination into your house!
## There is a religious ban!

**Jews!** Do not buy any newspaper that is printed on Shabbos and Yom Kippur!

Today is the press day of the Bundist organ the "Volks-Zeitung" [People's Newspaper] and it is certain that every religious Jew will be visited by the Bundist boys and girls who will try to sell him a newspaper.

Therefore, we turn to all Jews to whom the Torah and tradition are dear, to all Jews who do not want the souls of their children poisoned by Marxist venom. To them we turn with an appeal:

Jews! The nerve of the Bundist non-believers who step on all that is holy and dear to us, who spread heresy through the newspaper with which they come today to you religious Jews, to convince you to buy – advance across every boundary!

Religious Jews! Will you allow a newspaper into your house that is full of denial and heresy?!

Do you want to let in your house a newspaper that constantly tramples with bitter hatred all that has to do with the Jewish faith, in such a form that one does not find even among non-Jewish Socialists?!

Do you want to buy a newspaper that denies Jewish origins and wants the Jewish people, God forbid, to cease to exist?!

Religious Jews! Will you take a newspaper in your hand that is printed on the Sabbath, that one is forbidden to enjoy, according to Jewish law?!

Do you want to support a newspaper that is happy when Jewish blood is spilled in our holy Eretz Yisroel?

No!!! A thousand times no!!! You must not do it and certainly will not do it.

You must understand that by buying a "Volks-Zeitung" you assist the Bundist apostates with their inquisitorial work.

If you buy a "Volks-Zeitung," then you soil your honor and the honor of the Jewish religion.

This would be the greatest shame for you!

Therefore, religious Jews, when someone comes to sell a "Volks-Zeitung" to you, you should courageously and proudly answer: Take it back to its owner, you traitor, we will not buy a newspaper that combats Jews and Judaism.

Not one religious Jew should let in his house the missionary "Volks-Zeitung" or if you have already bought a coupon, then rip it apart and tear it up in front of the seducer.

Carry out the destruction of evil amongst you!!!

**The United Committee to Fight the Free Press**

Printing company Zarkowski. Wydawca: Agudas Israel Belchatow

The Poalei Agudahnikes would actively participate in all the strikes. They would often send men to knock down strike breakers and break panes of glass of Agudishe factory owners.

There were very heated discussions within the groups in connection with membership in the professional organizations. Some (with Abraham Zigmuntowich at the head) demanded that members of the organization should not be permitted to belong to unions that fight Eretz Yisroel.

The Belchatower "Poalei Agudah" acted independently in all the local election activities. Only during the election for the first Kehilla [Jewish self-governing body] did it work together with the "Agudah". In 1924 the "Poalei

Agudah" took part in the election for the office for health insurance. In the election, it received barely 65 votes and did not win a single mandate. In the election only one Jewish representative was elected, and that was Zalman Pudlowski from the Bund. In the first and second City Council elections the "Poalei Agudah" elected two councilmen: Sholom Borukh Feld and Jakov Ishaye Szmulewicz. (In the second City Council election, Shlomoh Muszkat was elected to Szmulewicz's seat).

**A group of Hasidic young men,
among whom stands Moshe Lewi,
who was condemned to be
hanged as a partisan.**

During the last Seim [Polish Parliament] election in Poland, when the entire Jewish community boycotted the election, and merely the Agudah went along with the Ozon [Camp of National Unity] (the party of the Sanacja government [created by Pilsudski]), the Belchatower Poalei Agudahniks did not participate in the election.

A separate chapter in the Belchatower "Poalei Agudah" was the constant internal factional struggle about belonging to the Professional trade union. The Belchatower organization was one of the most leftist oriented of the Poalei Agudah in Poland. There was a group with Shmuel Kalman at the head that wanted to sever itself completely from Agudah because of its antisocial politics and its rapprochement with the Pilsudski government. A second group, with Sender Sendik at the head, went still further: They demanded full cooperation with the "Bund" and even with the Communists, but the majority, along with Yitzhak Pigula at the head, believed that the "Poalei Agudah" did not need to formulate a new program and had to merely continue with the social laws that were contained in Mosaic Law. It is exclusively to the credit of Yitzhak Pigula, who always managed to resolve the frequent crises, that the organization did not come to a split.

In the last years "Poalei Agudah" exhibited strength with those such as: Abraham Mordechai Szilit, Yona Rozenberg, and Sokher Litmanowicz.

* * *

The Belchatower "Agudah" originated in 1918. Until the Vienna congress of the Anshei Knessia Hagedolah [the Great Congress, a meeting of rabbis that led to the establishment of the Agudas Israel political party], the Belchatower organization called itself "Shlomei Emunei Israel". The Belchatower Agudah did not carry on any stable activity. Only from time to time, it would mobilize its members for selected activities. The party center was located in the Gerer shtibl [a small Chasidic houses of prayer]. A letter from the Gerer rabbi was read for every action, an appeal to support the action. The Radomsker and the Radziner Chasidim also belonged to the Agudah. The Agudah also had an influence on some of the property owners who prayed in the house of prayer and, in various elections, they often would place the names of property owners who had an influence on the ordinary people on their voting lists. The most important of the property owners were: Kalman Wiwiecki, Yehuda Rozenthal, Moshe Huberman, and Hillel Zajdman.

Among the first and most important Belchatower Agudah activists were: Jakov Hersh Szotlender, Moshe Leib, Avraham Jakov Goldsztajn, Meir Eliezer Szatan, Mikhal Starowinski, and the Belchatower rabbi, Shmuel Yehoshua Szilit. Jakov Hersh Szotlender was a respected elder from Tsarist times. He helped build the new masonry synagogue; during the Austrian occupation he was one of the founders of the communal kitchen.

In 1919 the Belchatow "Agudah" founded the Talmud Torah [tuition free elementary school for poor children]. During the first years, the Talmud Torah was a cheder [school where boys typically learned Hebrew and studied the Torah] where only the Chumash [first five books of the Bible] and Rashi's commentaries were taught. In the thirties, they started to teach secular subjects using Polish teachers. In 1925, the Belchatower Talmud Torah moved to its new building, which was built by Yitzhak Yakov Warszawski, a Belchatower Jew in America. The most important Talmud Torah activists were: Meir Yoskowicz (the "black" Meir) and Hillel Zajdman.

The Belchatower "Agudah" helped to found the "Tseirei Agudah" in Belchatow. It delegated its members, Yisroel Frenkel and Moshe Chaim Grynblat, for the work. The Belchatower Agudah sent Rabbi Shmuel Yehoshua Szilit to the Knessia Hagedolah [the Great Congress] in Vienna in 1921.

Already an organized party, the Belchatower Agudah took part in the elections for the first Seim [Polish parliament]. It supported Rabbi Perlmuter, who was presented in the Piotrokow election district by the Agudah. The Agudah did most of its "campaigning" in the Chasidic prayer houses. Campaigning in the synagogue and in the house of prayer met strong resistance from Zionistic and Marxist oriented elements, which had a great influence on people like the Agudah members. It also had to endure a fight on the part of "Mizrachi" and the Aleksander Chasidim. Only in the City Council election did the Agudah work together with the Mizrachi. Both sides acted in this way in order not to splinter the middle class vote and in order to oppose the influence of the Belchatower "Bund" and of the Jewish Communists.

Agudah lost the first elective competition with its opponents during the first Kehilla election in Belchatow. The block of Mizrachi and the artisans was victorious and Ishaye Yudl Szeslawski, an artisan activist, was elected as chairman of the Kehilla.

The fight about the question of the shochets [ritual slaughterers], which arose at that time, occupied the seat of honor in the first Belchatower Kehilla in independent Poland. After the death of Leibl Muszkat, the cantor-shochet, the Kehilla majority decided to bring Mlot, the Dzialoszyner shochet, here. The Agudah brought a shochet from Podembic [Poddenbice] and simultaneously forbade the slaughtering by the opposing side. The quarrel lasted for years until, in the end, both shochets remained in Belchatow, each side not eating [what was slaughtered] by the other side.

The Agudah received a majority in the second Kehilla election. This occurred only thanks to the famous "paragraph 20," which provided it with the possibility to reject a number of its opponents [who were not in their opinion religious enough]. The chairman of the second kehilla was Mikhal Starawinski, a Gerer Chassid.

In 1938, during this kehilla's term in office, a heated battle about the election of the rabbi took place. After the death of Rabbi Zemach Tornhaim, Belchatow was without a rabbi for several years, because both sides – the Agudah and the "Mizrachi" – did not have a certain majority, and therefore they suspended [discussion of] the matter. When the Agudah received a majority in the kehilla, it felt more confident and began the struggle.

Every Shabbos the Agudah brought the most respected rabbis from Ger to Belchatow in order to support the candidacy of the Pabiancer Rabbi Horowicz, a son-in-law of Mendel Alters. The "Mizrachi" candidate was the Dobrer rabbi [from Dobra, Poland]. The "Aguda" candidate was victorious, and they were principally indebted to the Kehilla apparatus, which they controlled, for the victory.

The Belchatower Agudah also had its own bank, which was run by Leibl Kon and Moshe Chaim Grynblat.

* * *

The religious women's organization "Bnos Agudas Israel" ["Daughters of Agudas Israel"] and the Beis Yaakov School were founded in 1924 by Sura Szenirer of Krakow. Maltsha Borensztajn (chairwoman), Golda Landsztajn, Rywka Frenkel, Beyla Lakhman, among others, were elected to the first managing committee. The actual activity of "Bnos Agudas Israel" started three years later in 1927. At that time, new activists appeared: Malka Koszol – a young woman who was well versed in the Tanach [Bible] and in the Orthodox literature, she worked at the treadle all day, and at night she worked in the Beis Yaakov School; Toba Szatan (the secretary); and Glika Joskowich, a young woman with great capabilities from a poor home, and others. In 1927, the "Bnos Agudas Israel" had 30 members. There would be gatherings four times a week, during which they learned the religious laws from the Shulchan Aruch [the collection of laws and prescriptions governing the life of an Orthodox Jew], Jewish history, and other subjects. The teachers were: Malka Koszol, the female teacher Nowomiast, Itshe Meir Wolfowicz, Moshe Chaim Grynblat, and Israel Frenkel.

**A group from Beis Yaakov**

The Beis Yaakov School was also founded in 1924, and at that time 24 children studied there. But at the beginning of the 1930's, the number of students had climbed to 250. The school had four divisions and its own dramatic circle. In 1928, the school performed three presentations in the Belchatower firemen's auditorium: "Shulamit," "Bar-Kokhba," and "Yehudit" [plays by Abraham Goldfaden, who is considered the founder of Yiddish theater]. Only women were permitted to attend the performances.

The "Bnos Agudas Israel" had its own library, which at first consisted only of Polish belles-lettres ["elegant literature" of value for its aesthetics rather than its human interest or moral content]. In the 1930's Jewish books published by the Agudah publishing house in Poland were also brought in. Here were all of the works of Dr. Leman and Rotsztajn, Meshulem Kaminer's Jewish history, and others.

The library was directed by Rywa Przemyslawski. Right before the last war, the Belchatower "Bnos Agudas Israel" put in place a new group of activists, among whom the most important were: Sura Wiwiecki , Chava Starowinski, and Ethel Szerman.

**The administrators of Bnos Agudas Israel in 1929**

**A group of activists from Bnos Agudas Israel in 1936**

[Additional information provided by Dora Szczukocka Bornstein:
back row, fifth from right is Ms. Dresner]

**Managing committee of the Belchatower Tseirei Agudah Israel
in 1936 with a guest from Warsaw, Dr. Hershel Klepfisz.**

————

\* See an interesting song written by Moshe Janowsky on page 268.

1. [The book's title is actually "19 Letters", ed.]

*[Page 323]*

# From the *Bundist* Movement in Belchatow

## by M. Gliksman

## Translated by Pamela Russ

**Note**: [ ] contains translator's comments; ( ) contain original textual comments

When the Jewish Labor Movement began in Poland, Lithuania, and Russia, when the Jewish worker began to understand that he could no longer rely on the kindness of the baalebos [boss, person in charge, superior] – the rise of the "Bund" flowed into the very dark Jewish life of the time. While everything was still in the hands of religious leaders, the call for a new, just order, such as those who are working should benefit from their work, was also heard in our far–flung proletariat weaving town. The mission of the pioneers of the Jewish Labor Movement was not a simple one. An enormous darkness ruled over Jewish life. It was first the "Bund" that filled the historic mission of creating a social strength that had a double mission: to raise the spirit of Jewish life, and also to create out of the backward [primitive] laborer, a conscientious fighter for a new world.

Our town, even though it was not from the large provincial cities in Poland – was still among the first that began social activity. Even before the First World War, many Belchatower were among the revolutionaries that Czarist Russia sent to Siberia. Incidentally, the proletariat character of our town also participated in the development of a multi–faceted social life.

*[Page 324]*

With the establishment of the "Bund," a new life flow streamed into the city. The first Bundist activists were several young people, such as: Avrohom Yeshaya's, Khaim Shlomo, Michoel Yosef's, Fishel Meyer, Perel the Bosterin's [?], Moishe Kaizer, and others. With them was a weaver from Lodz, Berel Bines. Quietly, they began an agitation for change in the economic life in general, and in Jewish life in particular.

At that time, it was boiling and broiling in the ranks of the Jewish laborer. It was several years after the founding of the "Bund." There was great excitement across the cities and towns. In Lodz and in Pietrokow there was strong revolutionary work happening. Belchatow, which was in close contact with the aforementioned cities, was also broken by these voices.

The existence of this Bund organization was not accepted by the leaders of Jewish life in Belchatow. They felt a danger to their leadership and they took up an opposition. The first opponent was the Rav [religious leader] who was very revered in the town. He led a large yeshiva [religious studies seminary, school for men], and his influence there was great. His speeches against the "Bund" (he called them "union–niks") became more enraged, and went so far that the Lodz weavers Berel Bines and Khaim Shloime had to leave Belchatow.

Another disturbance, a serious one, was the foremen. They used their power, other than for work, for beatings. Provoked by the factory owners, for whom they transported merchandise to Lodz, they frequently attacked Bundist activists, beating them almost to death. These beatings were stopped by the Lodzer Bundists.

In the Lodzer "Bund" organization, there was an active military man [policeman]. This militia warned the Belchatow foremen not to mix into the Bundist activities of Belchatow. One of the chief militia, the one who put forth this warning was Yissochor Abramowycz (today he is in the United States and is a busy professional activist in the Pressers Union Local 35 in the "International" in New York).

*[Page 325]*

This strict warning gave good results and made its impact.

The authorities of the "Bund" went so far that instead of going to the general courts or religious courts, people began turning to the "Bund." For the most part, the organization declined to get involved in these types of issues.

The influence of the Gerer [chassidic] court was very strongly apparent in Belchatow. The Gerer chassidim held boundless reign, even when the Haskalah movement ["Enlightenment"] moved into the middle of the settlement. A typical event one can describe is with a Jew named Avner. He came to town and opened a cheder [religious school for young children] that was run not according to the Gerer custom. This "sinner of Israel" had to pack his bags quickly and then he left town.

In the whole town, there came one figure "Hatzefira" ["The Siren" Hebrew language newspaper] and one figure "Freint" ["The Friend" Yiddish newspaper].

There were several young people in town who were fired up with a new spirit. They kept themselves discreetly as Maskilim ["Enlightened"]. These were two brothers Yoel Leyb and Velvel Goldstajn, Shia Langnas, Yekhiel Meyer Jakubowycz, Dovid Luszczonowski, Yekhiel Meyer Krawicki, and others.

There was a second group of Maskilim among the Beis Medrash ["Study Hall"] young men. In this group were: Eli Twardowski, Aron Pinkhas Borenstajn, Moishe Shmulewycz, and Zalman Pudlowski. They read newspapers and Jewish literature in secret. They also had discussions among themselves about all kinds of issues. They debated very strongly, for example, about the question of whether it was true or not that Hillel Ceitlin could possibly have eaten non–kosher food? ...

The group grew. New people joined: Avrohom and Henekh Lieberman, Henekh Pigola, Henekh Gruszke, and Shimon Shmulewycz.

*[Page 326]*

The majority of the abovementioned group later became activists of the "Bund" in Belchatow.

The opening of the Society "Kultur" ["Culture" youth workers' organization] made a huge impression on the Belchatower youth. Almost the entire group of Maskilim from the Beis Medrash ["Study Hall"] young men joined up with the Society. In the first administration were these Maskilim: Avrohom and Henekh Liberman, Eli Twordowski, Moishe Shmulewycz, Zalman Pudlowski, Yosef Reikh, and Avrohom Leyb. A library soon opened in the Society, run by Gershon Perkol. Aron Bergman was brought from Lodz as a teacher who did the job in an exemplary manner. Evening courses for adults were organized. Long boards placed on trestles decorated the tables around which the students sat. They studied: reading and writing Yiddish, Jewish history, literature, and other topics. In a short time, the location became too small to hold everyone who wanted to study.

There was also political work being done. There were circles, meetings, and lectures about all kinds of political and literary themes.

There also opened a Jewish secular school where there were over 100 students. Other than Bergman, there were others who assisted in the school: Frajtag's daughter and Ita Zilberszac from Lodz, R. Shmulewycz, and R. Likhtenfeld. But the work would not have been so successful if not for the exceptional loyalty of Khaver [friend] Bergman.

## The Founding of the Bundist Organization

In the summer of 1915, followers of the "Bund," and members of the "Kultur" Society, expressed their desire that a Bund organization be established in town. The group of Bundists, with Bergman at the head, sent a representative to Lodz (to the committee there) and the Lodzer organization delegated Khaver Yeshaye Zak [to the task].

[Page 327]

The founding meeting had a festive atmosphere. The hall was beautifully decorated and filled with people. Khaver Zak gave a report about goals and tasks of the "Bund" and totally electrified the audience.

The activities of the "Bund" before World War One left deep roots for the renewal of a Bundist movement after the war.

**Members of the Bundist Party Organization with Azriel Lipinski, Yissokhor Przibilski, Peretz Frajtag, Zalman**

### Pudlowski, Gedaliah Stajn, Shloime Zhitnicki, Avrohom Mordekhai Niwinski, Rivka Konska, Esther Nekha Sztotlander, and others

Many types of other Zionist groups also began activity, and later there was also a communist party with which the Bund had a strong ideological dispute.

There was rarely a party in Jewish life that did not exist for us, and each of them, on its own level, bore the many colors of local Jewish life.

*[Page 328]*

The disputes between the parties very often took on a very sharp edge, but even this was a window into Jewish life.

Among the many colors of our town, the "Bund" still had great influence. It was the strength that awoke our town from its lethargic sleep and it was a given, in fact, that it became one of the strongest parties. The "Bund," that was rooted in the depths of the Jewish masses, found its real ground in Belchatow. The "Bund" was active in all areas of Jewish life and made great efforts to raise the Jewish generation in a revolutionary–socialist spirit.

For the Bundist country–conference, that took place in the beginnings of independent Poland – in Warsaw – Khaver Aron Bergman went as delegate of the "Bund" in Belchatow. At the first assembly of the "Bund" in Poland (that was in the year 1920) the delegate was Yosef Reikh.

Because of the economic difficulties in the country during the Austrian occupation, many Jewish workers were forced to leave their homes and look for work in unfamiliar places. Their roads took them to Germany, Austria, and Hungary, where there was a shortage of workhands.

The young Bundist Yitzkhok Przibilski was killed in the Hungarian revolution.

In Belchatow, until the end of World War One, there was no visible social movement among the Poles. Since 1905, when Belchatower Polish nationalist organizations held a large street demonstration, where there were many arrests and exiles to Siberia – since then Belchatow did not hear of activity of a Polish organization.

Soon after the war, young Poles appeared with guns on their backs, and their first task was to "revise" [interrogate] the "Kultur" society, with the intention of searching for ammunition...

*[Page 329]*

At the first election campaign in independent Poland, the "Agudah" [religious party] emerged in Belchatow as a political power. The chassidim shtiebelech [chassidic small synagogues] and schools became places for election meetings and excitement. Also, the "Bund" used the school for election meetings. The Bundist election campaign was very lively, and Aron Bergman, during the election campaign, became even more beloved among the people.

As a result of the elections, the Agudah took first place and the "Bund" took second place.

In Pietrokow, a county sick fund was established, where Belchatow was given an honorary place and representation.

**The Belchatow Bund Committee in the year 1937**

Seated from right: **Y. Przibilski, Peretz Frajtag, Zalman Pudlowsk**
Standing: **E. Lipinski, Leybel Goldmintz, Shloime**

### Zhitnicki, and V. Berkowycz

In Belchatow, a division of the Pietrokower Sick Fund was established. This was done in the early years after the War.

In the year 1928, at the city council elections of the Pietrokower Sick Fund, Khaver Zalman Pudlowski was elected, who was very beloved by the Jewish and Polish workers' population.

*[Page 330]*

In Belchatow, a youth organization began to form in the first years of independent Poland. It was at that time that the Bundist organization did not have a place, and the Bundist activity was held in the home of Zalman Pudlowski. Here, for all the years, there was also the Bundist library, and here the committee meetings were held, assemblies, celebrations, and so on. The home of Khaver Z. Pudlowski, one can say, was for years a location for the Bundist party. His wife – the warm Khaverte [female friend] Rokhel, welcomed everyone warmly and together with her husband, was beloved in the movement.

The first activists and founders of the Belchatower "Tzukunft" ["Future" youth organization] were: Yakov Paula, Yisroelke Berkowycz, Yakov Yoav, Shimshon Zimberknop, Yitzkhok Przibilski, Gedaliah Stajn, Fradel Khana Saad, and a group of young girls.

The youth Bund "Tzukunft," was one of our finest youth organizations, both because of their goals and because of their social tasks. Our youth organization raised a new type of youth. It was a pleasure to see how yesterday's cheder [religious] boys, simple and young, became ripe, educated, and proud fighters.

In the later years, we already find a large part of the youth were important activists in the Bundist movement.

Our youth organization had about 100 members, divided into "circles," that carried the names of famous Bundist leaders Vladimir Medem, Bronislaw Groser, and Y. Likhtenstajn. In these circles all the actual social and political problems were addressed.

During the summer, the youth would take its work into the forest and into the field. Our youths' trips into the forest around the town would attract everyone's attention with their song of revolution and folksongs.

*[Page 331]*

Our youth was dynamic and participated in almost all events that the party held. The youth's participation added a particular glow to the May First celebrations and demonstrations.

**Medem Circle**

The youth also participated in the election events of the party to the Sejm [Polish parliament] and City Council by distributing propaganda literature and giving details to the people.

In the press, our youth held a prominent place. There was not one project, lecture, or meeting of the party where the youth was not avant–garde.

The youth Bund " Tzukunft" led multi–faceted culture activities. Among the youth workers, the " Yugend Weker" ["Youth Awakener"] (an organ of the

Central Committee of Y.B. " Tzukunft" in Poland) was spread very far, and from time to time distributed their own posters, organized question–answer evenings, meetings, and open lectures, where there were speakers sent from the Central Committee of the "Tzukunft," such as the dear Khaver Leybel Olszanecki, Refoel Riba (today's well known Bundist activist in France), Rena Hister, Sergei Nutkewyc, Berenstajn, Leybel Friedman, and others.

[Page 332]

**The Lichtenstein Circle of the Bundist Youth
Organization**

At the same time, the youth organization ran an extensive promotion for the Jewish book, and almost all the youth were readers in the library. When the Jewish secular schools were established – the "Zukunft" made sure that there would be evening courses for the working youth.

At the gatherings, which the district committee of the "Zukunft" used to organize, our youth always participated. Also, the Belchatow youth organization did not miss the first countrywide gathering in Warsaw of all the "Zukunft" organizations, arranged by Tz.K. and Y.B. "Zukunft."

From time to time, our youth organized general meetings with the Pietrokower youth khaveirim [friends].

*[Page 333]*

Alongside the multifaceted activities in the political areas, our youth organization took care of the physical culture of the youth, and founded the sports club "Morgenstern" ["Morningstar"].

**Gathering of Pietrokower and
Belchatower Zukunft activists**

The older khaveirim actively participated in the work of the youth. People from the youth itself began to participate and take on work:

Yitzkhok Przibilski – a weaver laborer, he was – thanks to his older brother who later became known as the Bundist leader Sukher – was pulled in very early on into the youth organization. Yitzkhok possessed a tremendous determination and loyalty. Until 1930, when he left Poland, he served in our organization like a soldier.

Similar to Yitzkhok, there was Yankel Pizlo who worked actively as well. He came from a poor tailor family. Always sickly, he nonetheless gave of himself completely to the youth movement.

*[Page 334]*

Moishe Yakubowycz – son of the well–known Bundist family Czimbal, came forward and became one of the leading individuals in the youth movement. By nature, Moishe was very energetic, and this often expressed itself in his work. Very often, he would attend the "circles," and "meetings." His bass voice left the impression that he was angry, but in truth, in real life, he was a good–natured and devoted friend. Today, he is in Argentina.

Gedaliah Stajn [Stein] – As a young man, he was already attracted to the work, thanks to his sister Perel Laya, who at that time, already belonged to the Bundist organization. By nature, he was a chassid [pious follower]. He possessed an unusual preciseness, was always dissatisfied, but gave a lot of time for working with the youth. He was a member of the Youth Committee. For many years – also a member of the Party Committee. Because of his precision, he was the regular treasurer of the organization. Tragically, Gedaliah died during the Nazi occupation.

**Peretz Frajtag**

Peretz Frajtag, Dovid Frajtag's son. As a young student, he was attracted to the workers' youth and he joined the youth society of the "Zukunft." Thanks to his intelligence and sharp intuition, he moved into the front ranks of our youth. He went to France for further studies. When he returned, he began again to take the honored positions in the Bundist movement. He became the chairman of the committee of the "Bund," came on as speaker in the "circles," "gatherings," and meetings. He becomes a correspondent for the PPS [Polish Socialist Party] "Robotnik." One can sense that he was becoming an important social activist not only in our movement, but also in the whole city. Had the World War not cut off his young life, he would have achieved great successes in his social activity.

*[Page 335]*

Naftali Huberman – came from a simple working family. He joined the movement as a very young man. He read an enormous amount, and worked on himself without end. He became a respected activist. Today he is in Argentina.

Menakhem Huberman – Naftali's younger brother, under whose influence he came to our organization. As someone who was thirsty, he drank in the books from our library. He possessed a strong urge to be educated, read a lot, and was blessed with an incredible memory. Very quickly, Menakhem became the intellectual leader of the youth. He was a very kind type, but had very little practicality in everyday life. If Menakhem would have had the opportunity to study – he would certainly have held an important position. In 1930, he left for Russia. With his intellectual refinement, Menakhem brought a higher level into the work of the youth.

Heshke Goldmintz – came from a completely different environment. His father Yitzkhok, contrary to all the other parents, was already himself a social activist. He was a progressive individual, secretary of the "Mizrachi" [religious Zionist] organization in our town. By the time he came to our youth, Heshke was already a mature person. He went right through the town's youth organization. Here, in our youth, he quickly became a devoted activist, attended the "circles," open projects, meetings. He possessed, in great capacity, the skill to relate facts and events in a clear manner. Very quickly, Heshke became a respected activist in the party. He was also elected to the committee and worked diligently in the professional textile guild. During the next great strike of 1932, that lasted a complete five months, Heshke was elected to the strike committee. He became one of the most active leaders of the strike – naturally – and then he was chased by the police.

The Sanacja [trans: "Sanation" movement was a coalition of rightists, leftists, and centrists whose main focus was the elimination of corruption and the reduction of inflation] newspaper in Lodz featured him as an agent sent especially to lead the strikes.

*[Page 336]*

Shloime Zhitnicki – a child from a proletariat home. While still very young, he came to join the Bundist youth. His entire family was Bundist. His older brothers, Alter and Yosef, were already active Bundists then. While still in the folkshule [Jewish People's School], the young Shloime had the capacity to attract children around him. In our youth movement, because of that, he got his true tikkun [reward]. While still young, he became an activist and one of the young leading friends in the Medem circle. Thanks to his activity, the Medem [trans: Vladimir Medem, one of the Bund's first ideologues] circle became an important component of our youth organization. Shloime also had an inherent capacity for music, theater, sport, and other interests. In our youth organization, he had the opportunity to apply his talents. When the mandolin orchestra was created in the "Zukunft," he became one of the best students. When a drama circle was created, he took on one of the most important positions. With time, he himself became a stage manager for some things. When the "Morgenstern" was created, once again great opportunities opened for him, in order for him to use his talents. He himself was an exceptional sportsman, and with time, after passing some instructional courses, he became the main instructor of "Morgenstern." At the same time, he took up the position of speaker in the circles, meetings, and May First celebrations. He was one of our best youth speakers. For a long time, he was chairman of the "Zukunft." Until he left Argentina in 1938, he was always elected to the party committee. He was secretary of the needle union. When he left Argentina, the organization experienced a palpable loss. Today he lives in Buenos Aires.

*[Page 337]*

Unfortunately, it is impossible to account for all the youth who grew up during our younger years and later became significant activists in the Bundist movement. We will limit ourselves by mentioning only a few names of our friends who played a significant role in the youth work: Yakov–Yekhiel Kusher, Ezriel Lepinksi, Leyb and Avigdor Makhalski, Tuvia and Dovid

Przebilski, Yankel Rotstajn, Zalman Levkowycz, Esther–Rokhel Makhabanska, Shmuel Gelbart, Tzirel and Emanuel Yoav, Netta Goldmintz, Itzik Goldberg. And a group of "SKIFists" ["Sotsyalistisher Kinder Farband" (Polish, "Socialist Children's Union")] who were sent over in their youth and quickly became activists: Yekhezkel Przeborski, Yerakhmiel Goldberg, Manya Stajn, Soroh Gliksman, Hertzke Frajtag, Rivka and Faige Brajtberg, Yekhiel and Simkha Hertzkowycz, Dina Wiener, Leybel Goldmintz, Avrohom Stajn, and Rivka Pudlowski.

## "SKIF"

Our Bundist organization also took care of the young generation that was growing up. When – in Warsaw, in the year 1927 – a group of teachers and "Zukunft" activists gathered together, and they created the socialist children's union "SKIF" – a short time later, this children's organization was also created by us. Shloime Zhitinski, Peretz Frajtag, and the author of these lines assumed the responsibility of this project. At the first meeting there already was a group of school children and cheder [religious school] of young boys, and also 11– 12–year–old children who at that time were already working with textiles, tailoring, and shoe making. The news that we wanted to create a children's organization for them that would give them back some children's fun and raise them to become educated people, was accepted with great excitement by the children. Among those in the first group were those later to become activists in the SKIF: Khatzkel Przedborski, Yerakhmiel Goldberg, Simkha Hertzkowycz, and others.

The organization began to grow and it became apparent that founding the SKIF was in fact a necessity. As a children's organization of the Bund, the SKIF became the largest in our city. There were about 100 children, divided into a few groups. The SKIF there was a multi–branched educational project.

*[Page 338]*

Frequent outings were organized into the surrounding forests and fields, in order to familiarize the children with the beauties of nature. And it was a pleasure to see how the so–recently uneducated worker–children were so attracted to the beautiful and open nature. With their song and liveliness, they attracted everyone's attention.

With great impatience, the children would wait all week for the Shabbath day, when the outings would take place. During these outings, the children were taught songs, and all kinds of games. There were also discussions. From a largely uneducated group of children, the SKIF raised a healthy, knowledgeable element.

When the Jewish secular school organized evening courses, our children were of the first students there.

Each year, the SKIF would hold an anniversary celebration that always became a great holiday for the entire Bundist movement. The children would fill the program, and no efforts were held back to make these celebrations very impressive. At these celebrations, representatives of the central SKIF were in attendance, such as friend Sergei Nutkevitch, Artur Lermer, and so on. At one of these events, there was the well–known PPS ["Polska Partia Socjalistyczna" "Polish Socialist Party"] leader and Sejm [Polish parliament] deputy, Zygmunt Zaremba.

To the annual celebration, almost always some groups from the SKIF were sent to the "Zukunft." In that way, the SKIF provided the reserve for the party.

Other than the regular outings, SKIF organized camps during vacation time, where the SKIFists spent several weeks in the fresh air and lived in a real children's republic, run by children and assistants. In one camp in Dombrowa [Dabrowa] not far from Tomaszow, Leybel Kirsz and the SKIF activist from Lodz, Zhimalkowska, joined into the work. Shloime Zhitinski did his share of work as well.

*[Page 339]*

Very often, outings to brother organizations were arranged, to Pietrokow and Zdunska–Wola. For a very long time, the children would remember the warm gatherings with the brother organizations.

**Administration of the SKIF**

But the most beautiful moments of our "SKIF" was definitely the regional assembly, which hundreds of SKIFists from the surrounding cities and towns would attend, towns such as: Pietrokow, Tomaszow, Zdunska–Wola, Sulejow, and Lodz.

The entire summer camp that came from Lodz, came under the leadership of friend Sergei, and the instructor from "Morgenstern" Jakubowyc. The gatherings turned into a powerful expression of the entire Bundist movement. The street marches with torches at night were unforgettable. Hundreds of children aroused the proletariat city with their song. At the end of the torch march, a large number of children gathered on the plaza in front of the theater hall. Friend Sergei spoke from the gallery to those assembled. It is impossible to describe the feelings that reigned over the large assembled crowd when they heard Sergei's thunderous voice against the capitalist order. Those moments will remain forever etched in our memories.

*[Page 340]*

**Summer camp of the "SKIF"**

The "SKIF" brightened all the Bundist events. In particular, the May First demonstrations, when more than 100 SKIFists in blue shirts and red ties would open the Bundist May marches. It was the greatest joy to see how yesterday's students, young cheder boys and working children, were marching, proud and with song, in the May demonstrations.

*[Page 341]*

The "SKIFists" would present gymnastic performances, play football, and so on.

At the SKIF assembly in Warsaw, 1936, an assistant from the Belchatow SKIF was elected to the central SKIF.[a]

The SKIF educated a conscious youth element and produced important activists for the whole Bundist movement. Some of them w already we already mentioned in their connection with the "Zukunft." We will mention a few of these names here:

Shmuel Glogowski, Hinde Liberman, Mordekhai and Leybel Pietrokowski, Rivka, Faige, Hershel Meyer and Mordekhai Brajtberg, Manya Frajtag, Perl Gliksman, Avrohom Stein, Khana Roiza Gliksman, Mendel and Rivtche

Pudlowski (these last ones were active in the illegal movement during the Nazi occupation – both were children of friend Zalman), Faige Dobra Hartman. The teacher R. Konska was very active in the later times.

Sadly, almost all these children died during the German occupation. Only a very small percent survived.

## Sport

Under the name "Sturm" ["Storm"], football group was founded, that was exclusively for football. Among the founders of this group were: Yerakhmiel Szwarzberg, Leybke Jakubowyc, Shmuel Grinberg, Peretz Frajtag, and so on. The "Sturm" frequently held competitions with local clubs [teams] and also with those of other cities. A short while later, in the place of "Sturm" the "Morgenstern" ["Morningstar"] was established, which made gymnastics events its main focus, and also was busy with football. There were all kinds of sections of gymnastics for boys and girls. After great exertions and efforts, the "Morgenstern" was hardly able to acquire the necessary sport equipment. There was no support from the government or municipality for the "Morgenstern," during a time when sport organizations were often funded. The "Morgenstern" had great difficulties with their location. For almost all the time of their existence, they were located in the Bundist place. But the greatest difficulty was in the struggle for instructors for the gymnastic exercises. In the beginning there was no other way than to use soldiers who were in service. But it seemed that their exercises were not appropriate for our youth. Only when Shloime Zhitinski conducted an instructor's course in Lodz, did it became possible to do the work in an appropriate manner.

*[Page 342]*

**A group of sportsmen from "Sturm" with the instructor Moishe Yoel Jezhi**

*[Page 343]*

Very soon, they planned a great opening gymnastics event. For this event, the instructor from the Lodzer "Morgenstern," friend Hiller, came to Belchatow. The featured gymnastics event made such an exceptional impression that the crowd demanded an encore. From that point on, a tradition was established for an annual gymnastics event. In the summer months the exercises were held in the open field. Some of the youths became instructors. One of these was the devoted activist from the "Zukunft" Yerakhmiel Goldberg. For a short time, the "Morgenstern" was united with the sports section of the leftists in our town. Thanks to the dedicated work of friend Shloime Zhitinski, Zalman Lefkowycz, Avrohom Mendel Goldberg, Noteh Goldmintz, Leizer Huberman, Sh. Sztotlender, Hillel Belchatowski, and others, "Morgenstern" became one of the best sports organizations not only on the Jewish street, but also among the country's distinguished. The sports festivals that "Morgenstern" organized, would always draw a large crowd of people.

**Sports celebration of the "Morgenstern" with instructor Hiller (from Lodz)**

*[Page 344]*

**Notice for gymnastics event (Polish)**

*[Page 345]*

It is important to add that the city–president also occasionally came to us with the request for us to participate in a military ceremony. For obvious reasons, we declined.

**Professional Movement:**

The "Bund" held a very prominent position in the professional movement. In the textile guild, that had a few thousand workers, our friend Zalman Pudlowski was the vice–president and for many years one of the busiest activists. The Jewish and Polish workers well knew that in Zalman there was a loyal, honest fighter for their rightful demands. There was not one action or strike when our friends were not in the actual front lines. In Belchatow, the city council had friend Zalman Pudlowski as its chairman. When in 1932, the famous five–month long strike took place, about which the entire Polish press reported – our friends Zalman Pudlowski, Heshke Goldmintz and others, were the main leaders. When the work inspector from Pietrokow held a large open gathering of the textile workers in order to persuade them not to take any action against the factories – he did not want to open the meeting until friend Zalman Pudlowski left the hall. When, upon the inspector's demands the police forced friend Zalman to leave – all the Jewish workers and some Polish workers left the gathering with the song of the "Red Flag" and the "Internationale." In this guild, the friends Gedalia Stein, Sukhar Przibilski, Levi Goldberg, Alter Rozental, Moishe Jakubowyc, and others, were also very active.

Our friends were also very active in the needle guild, and friend Shloime Zhitinski, almost without interruption, took the office of secretary. Among the busy activists of the administration there were Nuteh Goldmintz, Zalman Lefkowycz, and Sh. Zhitinski.

*[Page 346]*

**First of May Celebrations:**

The Belchatow workers annually held May First celebrations and street demonstrations in which many workers from the surrounding areas and villages always participated. The majority were hand weavers. The demonstrations were almost always conjoint: the PPS [Polish Socialist Party], the Bund, and the Professional Union. For weeks before May 1, the workers would prepare for the holiday. On May 1, all the factories would stop their work. With particular excitement, our organization would prepare for May First. Weeks before, our choir would echo through Pobjanyc Street, where the Bund was located, with all kinds of fighting songs. All kinds of meetings would take place, and the invocations of the Central Committee would spread to all the Jewish workers' homes. The ones who opened the procession were always from the youngest branch of our movement – the "SKIF." The close to one hundred children, wearing blue shirts and red ties, added a special charm to the marches. Also, the "Zukunft," in the same uniforms as the "SKIF," would proudly and energetically march, and always toss out all kinds of slogans. The choir, directed by Emmanuel Yoav, added all kinds of liveliness to the procession. The camp of older Bundists closed the procession.

**Bundist May First demonstrations**

*[Page 347]*

In the year 1938, in the Bundist procession, the flag of "JOF" [Organization of Jewish Women Workers] was carried, and behind that – were rows of Jewish worker women. This was a new branch of the Bundist family. In this abovementioned organization, the following were active: Rivka Konska, who was the speaker, Esther Nakhe Sztotlender, Brajndel Pojla, and others.

**In the City Council**

In 1925, when Belchatow received rights from the municipal authorities and an elected city council, our organization began directing extensive education work about the significance of this self–governing body for the good of the interest of the people. Closed meetings were held in party locations and open meetings in City Hall with the participation of the representatives of the Central Committee, such as: friends Hershel Himelfarb, Gershon Ziebart, Milman, Efraim Luzer Zelmanowyc, Artur Zigelboim, Moishe Levin, Yitzkhok Samsonowyc, and others. We also shared in appeals, and gave out a special number for the "Head of the Katowa [Katowice] Wakers" and conducted intensive house–to–house propaganda work. To the first City Council, friends Zalman Pudlowski and Henekh Liberman were elected. The devoted work of the Bundist practical efforts in the City Council evoked great recognition for the Jewish workers' population.

Their reports on the City Council tribunal took up most of the meetings. They became the representative speakers of the Jewish and Polish poor, and that's how they earned great respect and acknowledgment in town.

*[Page 348]*

It is worthwhile to relay the following facts:

Pobianycer Street was heavily populated by a poor Jewish population and had no water. After long–time demands by the Bundist faction, the magistrate was forced to create a water–well which the town called "Zalman's well."

The same street, after a stormy conflict with the Bundist faction, had its name changed to Y.L. Peretz [Yiddish writer].

The Bundist faction fought in stormy meetings, with great obstructions from the gallery – and it was quickly implemented – regarding the issue of subsidies for the Jewish secular schools.

At the second City Council elections, in the year 1927, the following were elected from the Bund: Zalman Pudlowski and Shia Zharski.

It came about that the Bundist faction fought against the "Bechatower Berl Kutchme [fur hat]" – which was Shmuel Jakubowyc (alderman), who abused his official position in many ways. As a response to this conflict, he enacted all kinds of gangster–type incidents onto the Bundist councilmen. Understandably, this did not go without backlash from the Bundists.

This resulted in seven Bundists spending three months in a Pietrokow prison.

The influence of the "Bund" increased. In the additional election in the year 1933, friend Shia Zharski was elected as alderman.

The elections to the third City Council were run with a new election ordinance. The number of councilmen was decreased from 24 to 16. Of the elected seven Jewish councilmen, there were four Bundists. The four councilmen were Henekh Liberman, Gershon Brajtberg, Rokhel and Zalman Pudlowski.

*[Page 349]*

At the beginning of 1933, there was a political action in the country against the new election ordinance. The Bund, along with the PPS [Polish Socialist Party] also in Belchatow, participated in the abovementioned campaign. On March 5 of that same year, there was a General Meeting in the fire department hall. At the meeting, there were representatives from the PPS – Dr. B. Kahn from Tomaszow Maz. [Mazowiecki], and the Bundist Heszke Goldmintz. On January 6, 1934, the class–guild of the Belchatower textile workers organized a large meeting against worsening the social laws. In attendance were the Sejm [Polish parliament] deputy Z. Zaremba, the representatives of the professional class–guilds in the Pietrokow province of Kolodej. The meeting was run by friend Z. Pudlowski.

In connection with the Dollfuss event[1] in February 1934 in Austria, under the Bundist initiative, a protest strike was proclaimed for February 19. During the strike, the entire Belchatower proletariat joined, and that was on a Monday – a market day in town, when the peasants from the surrounding areas were already present during the demonstrations. Our friend, Peretz Frajtag, empowered the many thousands of masses of people with his Polish speech during the street gathering in the new market.

At the same time, just as in the rest of the country, there was a socialist handworkers' union division created in Belchatow as well. The creators of this newly–established handworkers' union were: Mendel Gliksman, Henekh Liberman, Rokhel Pudlowski, Peretz Frajtag, Emanuel Yoav, and others.

The socialist handworkers' union, along with the Bundist City Council faction helped organize handworkers' cards, which actually addressed a life issue for the poor workers in connection to the anti–Semitic guild laws. In the year 1937, the jubilee celebration of 40 years of the Bund, took place in

Warsaw. There was a large delegation from Belchatow attending this gathering. These were: Peretz Frajtag, Rivka Konska, Shloime Zhitinski, Yissokhor Przibilski, Esther Nekhe Sztotlander, and Z. Pudlowski. Friend Zalman was decorated by the Bund director Henryk Erlikh, with a medal as main shock–worker while selling "the People's Newspaper" during the press days. In order to emphasize the point, during the press days 600 copies of the "People's Newspaper" were distributed – a record number for Belchatow.

*[Page 350]*

## Culture–Activities of the "Bund"

The Bundist organization did not limit itself with internal cultural activities. In spite of the exceptionally difficult material circumstances in which the Jewish workers were living, they managed to create a secular Jewish school. The Polish government, understandably, provided no help. So, with love and devotion, the Jewish people enveloped the school. The teachers often went hungry, but the faith that in this school a new type of person and Jew was being formed encouraged and strengthened them. A cadre of devoted school activists was formed. These were: Henekh Liberman, Melekh Galster, Gershon Brajtberg, Zalman Pudlowski, and others. Evening courses for young and older workers were formed. The location was too small for the large number of children, young and older students.

We also had a local drama circle, which from time to time would present dramatic and review performances under the direction of the teacher of the secular Jewish school, friend Rivka Konska. These were exceptional in the drama circle: friend Emanuel Yoav, Moishe Leyb Fridman,Shloime Zhitinski, Soroh Rivka Zhitinski, Hersh Avigdor Zilberstajn, and others.

The library, the largest in town, had its work done peacefully and modestly. It was the university from which the youth gleaned its knowledge and from which all the above–mentioned activists were created. The quiet and modest librarian, Avrohom Mordekhai Nowinski, contributed greatly to the development of the library.

Thanks to the activity of the Bundist organization, our town was raised to a higher cultural level.

*[Page 351]*

### The Belchatow Veker ["Awakener"]

The Bundist organization would periodically distribute the Belchatow Veker ["Awakener"]. For every city council election, the "Veker" would inform the Jewish population about the multi–faceted work of our representative in the City Council, in the magistrate, and in the professional unions. Reb Zalman would do a lot of work for the "Veker." Also, friend Levin, well–known Bundist activist in Pietrokow, had a large share in the "Veker."

### Press Days

From time to time, the Central Committee of the Bund proclaimed "Press Day" for the "People's Newspaper." For this event, our committee would mobilize the entire organization. On that designated day, the Belchatower streets were filled with young and old merchants. Our friends always held a prominent place among the exceptional people on the Central Committee for the press event. Once, in fact, our organization was given a large Medem bust, that for many years enhanced the Bund location until the Nazi bandits destroyed it along with the Jewish population.

### Political Reports

Reports with actual political themes that the Bundist organizations would present, were renowned in our town. Belchatow, which was not one of the large, provincial cities, merited to hear the best Bundist presentations and lectures. There were: the beloved Bund director friend H. Erlikh, B. Szepner, Yakov Pat, Artur Zigelboim, Likhtenstajn, Isser Goldberg, Abrashe Blum, Majzler, Milman, Zelmanowycz, and others. There presentations were really a well of spiritual voice for the population, and the town would wait impatiently for these presentations.

*[Page 352]*

### Resistance – The Reaction at Home

Our town had a great revolutionary tradition. Pogrom incitements never really had a great following with us. The long–time collaborative work between the Jewish and Polish workers gave the expected results. While Pietrokow, Stercow [Strzyżów], and other surrounding areas often suffered from anti–Semitic episodes, our town hardly tasted this. That does not mean that there were no reactionary anti–Semitic elements who wanted to provoke incidents.

But they contained themselves because they knew that the Belchatower Jewish and Polish workers would not permit any anti–Semitic provocations.

Not having the opportunity to accomplish anything in the actual city itself, the Polish reactionists began to organize the surrounding village, uneducated elements, and there, the familiar anti–Semitic arguments (your poverty is the Jews' fault, and so on), acquired an easy following. Serious information was passed on, that a band of pogromists were preparing an attack on the Jewish people on a market day. The Bund committee quickly summoned an urgent meeting where it was decided to turn to the PPS [Polska Partia Socjalistyczna, left–wing Polish political party], and also to the leftists, and to the textile union about a general armed resistance. Our request was received positively, and groups were immediately assigned with the goal to create an armed resistance to the NDK [Polish National Democratic Party] and the Sanacja [Sanation (non–partisan bloc) Party] hooligans. Bund representatives went into the Batei Midrashim [Study Halls in synagogues] and called the Jewish population to resistance. The NKD and Sanation "heroes" found out about the preparations, and with great trepidation they called off their planned attack.

This is what happened several times. The Bund always stood ready when Jewish honor was at stake.

*[Page 353]*

**Arrests**

The activities of our movement were always a thorn in the eyes of the city reactionists. With irritation, the Sanacja [Sanation] vice–president of the magistrate, Miller, was discussing the Bund. Naturally, his words had great impact on the police, and that's how the first arrest of two busy Bund activists took place: Esther Ekstajn, and Moishe Jakubowycz. Since the Bund at that time was still legal – they created false accusations against some friends, and after they were in prison for a few months in the Pietrokow prison – the courts had to release them. Some time later, the author of these lines was arrested, and also friend Meyer Krizman, but, several months after the arrest, the courts had to release them as well. The wild rage of the city reactionists was particularly focused on friend Reb Zalman Pudlowski. They tried to find all kinds of cunning reasons to be able to send him for a "cure." Our organization undertook a strong tactic and with the help of the Pietrokow friends Yakov

Berliner and Avrohom Weishof (both died in Treblinka) friend Zalman evaded the concentration camp.

The local reactionists believed that with the arrests of the Bundist activists, they would be able to destroy our movement. But they accomplished the opposite.

## The Activist

It is worthwhile to mention a list of friends who played an important role in the Belchatower Bundist movement between the two World Wars.

*[Page 354]*

Friend Zalman Pudlowski – the son of the well–known religious Jew Moishe Luzer Tomaszower. He was raised in a strictly religious environment. For many years, he learned in Beis Medrash [Study Hall] which was also the yeshiva in town. It did not even occur to his parents that their son who sat day and night in front of the Gemara [Talmud], would secretly be reading revolutionary literature. It did not take long, and Zalman became enticed into the revolutionary flow, left the Beis Medrash, and threw himself with all his might and passion into the Bundist work. Along with Yosef Reikh, Eli Twardowski, Avrohom and Henekh Liberman, and others, he established the culture society in Belchatow, which grouped together almost all the youth of our town. Zalman became one of the most important people in the society. The First World War broke out, and the social work was stopped. Zalman was sent into forced labor. As the war ended, and life began to normalize – once again you saw Zalman doing the social work. Along with a group of Bundists, such as Avrohom Leyb, Liberman, Alter Rozental, Berl Leyb, Yissokhor Przibilski, and others, he once again brought life into the Bundist organization. He devoted himself entirely to the movement. He was the speaker in the circles, meetings, and gatherings; he was correspondent for the "People's Newspaper," secretary of the Bund in Belchatow. He was strongly involved with the intellectual and practical work of the movement. He found time for everything. He was a leader and accomplisher.

For many years, Zalman was vice–president of the textile guild and was loved by the Jewish and Polish textile workers, just as he was hated by the reactionists. He was one of the founders of the Jewish secular school in Belchatow. He was always elected into the City Council, where, along with the other Bundist councilmen, he conducted a bitter struggle for the good of the Jewish population. He was also a councilman in the Sick Fund. You had to be in his house to know what Zalman was for the poor Jewish population. He found time for everyone, for everyone – a good word. Because of all his work for society, he neglected his own health. He did not belong to those who give orders to others and themselves do things differently.

**Zalman Pudlowski**

*[Page 355]*

Zalman himself was also a member of the Party Council in Poland and was a delegate to almost all the assemblies of the Bund in the years between the two World Wars.

During the time of the great devastation [Holocaust], Zalman was cast into North America, and even in his new home, he did not stop his aid work for anyone who came to him for help. Even today, eight years after his arrival in America, he writes: "This large New York is a tragedy for me, for me Belchatow was perfect." One can say confidently that Zalman's life story is the story of the entire Bundist movement in Belchatow.

Henekh Liberman – also came from a religious family. He followed Zalman's road from the Beis Medrash to socialism. He was part of each stage of the Bundist movement in our town. In personality, he was the opposite of Zalman. He was cold, always withdrawn, and also bitter in his convictions.

With this demeanor, he evoked a serious respect for himself. He was a long-time member of the Party Committee and of other existing blocs. For all the time, without interruption, he was elected onto the City Council. During the Nazi occupation he was in the Lodz ghetto and there was actively involved in the Bund's underground movement. He breathed his final breath in the ghetto.

While the City Council existed, other than the two people mentioned earlier, friend Rokhel Pudlowski (Zalman's wife) was also elected as a member. She came from Pietrokow, became active in the Bundist movement at a very young age, and later – in the Belchatower organization. She died during the Nazi occupation.

*[Page 356]*

Yehoshua Zharski – from Lodz. He was a devoted activist in the Belchatow Bund organization. He was an alderman in the magistrate for a while. He served the working population in town with heart and soul. He also died during the Nazi occupation.

**Yissokhor Przibilski**

Yissokhor Przibilski – He joined the movement as a young man, but he soon became exceptional, and took an important place in the work. He headed circles, took part in meetings, and for a long time was a member of the Party Committee, and a candidate on the City Council elections. Later, friend

Yissokhor settled in Lodz, and became an activist in the local Bund organization. During the German occupation, he was part of the local underground of the Bund. According to the report of friend Yakov Nirenberg of Lodz – Yissokhor Przibilski died in Treblinka.

Gershon Brajtbarg: An old, devoted Bundist, a shoemaker. For many years, he was on the Party Committee, and on the administration of the Jewish secular school. Always sick, still there was no work too difficult for him. An exemplary organizer, Reb Gershon was exceptional during the elections to the Sejm [Polish parliament] or to the City Council. In his poor shoe store on Powianyc Street, in Yankel Plakowycz's house, where he lived in one room which was separated with a curtain from the shoemaker's workshop, there were always Bundists present. With the noise of the shoemaker's hammer they would spend warm times with him and his wife Golda. We would call Golda "the mother of the Bund." Friend Gershon and his wife and their two daughters died. The three sons are in Belgium today, and are active there in the Bund's work.

*[Page 357]*

Leybel Pudlowski – a younger brother of Zalman. He came to the Bund in his later years. He acquired the skills quickly and sharply to address issues and problems. He was very active in the movement, ran the circles and led public projects. During the war, he went to Russia, but some time later came back to Poland where he was very active in the partisan movement. After the war, once again he helped re–establish the Bund movement, and was a member of the Central Committee of the Bund. He also belonged to the leadership of the former partisans. Later, he left Poland.

Esther Eksztajn – comes from a very religious and chassidic family. She was very active both with the youth and in the party, and belonged to the leadership of both organizations. Today, she is in Argentina.

We should also mention: Alter Rozental, Berl Leyb, Levi Gerbart, Avrohom and Faivel Naparstek, Yankel Rotstajn, Khamel Dzhialowski, Moishe Yoel Jezhi, Eliye Klug, Berkowycz, Sh. Gelbart, and others.

It is impossible to list all the friends [male and female] who were active in the Bundist movement in Belchatow. Almost all of them were killed. Only a few orphans were miraculously saved. And those who remained, spread all over the world, and remember their hometown with love.

---

**Footnote**

a.  This was the author of the work of M. Gliksman – (editor).

**Translator's Footnote**

1.  Engelbert Dollfuss (4 October 1892 – 25 July 1934) was an Austrian Christian Social and Patriotic Front statesman. Having served as Minister for Forests and Agriculture, he ascended to Federal Chancellor in 1932 in the midst of a crisis for the conservative government. In early 1933, he shut down parliament, banned the Austrian Nazi party and assumed dictatorial powers. Suppressing the Socialist movement in February 1934, he cemented the rule of "austrofascism" through the authoritarian First of May Constitution. Dollfuss was assassinated as part of a failed coup attempt by Nazi agents in 1934. Wikipedia.

[Page 358]

# The Story of the Leftist Workers' Party

# [Labor Party]

### by Zainwel Przedborski

### Translated from the Yiddish by Jerome Silverbush

### Edited by Roni Seibel Liebowitz

### with the assistance of Gloria Berkenstat Freund

[with comments in brackets]

The workers' movement in Belchatow dates back to 1895. The organization of Polish and Jewish workers started then. In his book, "History of the Worker Movement in Poland," the well known worker activist and writer Lucjan Rudnitsky tells the story of the heroic fighter and political arrestee, M. Goldfish from Belchatow. Belchatow is also one of the shtetls which distinguish themselves with their activity in the revolutionary uprising in 1905. Then great arrests took place and many workers were sent to Siberia, like Spiegelman, Kanatski, and others. The work, which was then interrupted for a little time, came back to life because of comrade Gottlieb (who lives today in Argentina), who came to Belchatow to organize more fighting groups, which can be confirmed by a photograph taken of a meeting held at that time.

Because of the outbreak of the First World War, the factories closed and the political work was effectively stopped. There remained the cultural societies, which led cultural work, and the help committees were organized.

In 1919, in the entire country, discussion of the "21 points" started, and the Bund split in two groups. Also in Belchatow, a "21 Points" group was created, which enrolled a great number of Jewish workers. Because of legal requirements, the group had to leave the cultural society, which remained in the hands of the Bund. The leader of the leftist movement was Yehezkel Birencwajg, a dynamic man who was much loved by the Belchatow workers. Under his influence and with the help of other activists who came at that time to Belchatow, like Herszl Bekerkuntz, who carried through a large recruiting campaign, the majority of Belchatow workers joined "Combund."[1]

When the war broke out between Poland and Russia in 1920, the leftist movement directed intensive agitation not to go in the military. Then there were massive attacks by the Polish gendarmerie, and the best activists were arrested. Others were forced to enter the military.

After a short time more, Bekerkuntz came again and called a meeting, which was raided. Bekerkuntz succeeded in escaping through a window, and the meeting hall was closed. No arrests were made, but the leftist movement was forced to go over to illegal work.

At the same time, in Lodz, the leftist Nodl ["needle" ] Organization was attacked. An important group came to hide in Belchatow. They helped organize the work on the basis of party cells, and a party committee was organized, led by Yehezkel Birencwajg, and a youth committee led by Shamai Birencwajg and Chaim Yosef Yaab.

Ten cells were organized with approximately 60 members. The political and cultural work was directed by Ruchel Lichtenfeld, Birencwajg, H. Finkel and Lozer Abramczyk. There was a lively activity and the movement called itself P.P.K. (Polish Communist Party). The main work consisted of intensifying the fight against the miserable conditions that the workers were subject to. We started with the Jewish workers and then immediately included the Polish workers. The first textile strike was organized, in which we won all our demands. But we were far from enjoying victory, because a fall in the value of Polish currency caused new conflicts with the factory owners.

When a general professional union for textile workers was created in Belchatow, P.P.K. organized within it a craftsman section, which mainly had Jewish workers. The section was directed by Yidel Meir Kochmanski, Szlama Lejb Moskowicz, Yosef Gliksman, and others. Both Polish and Jewish workers were in the administration of the textile union.

P.P.K. started to work with the Polish workers, and a group joined the party, through which the Communists won a large influence in the union. But that didn't last long because the Party sent functionaries to Belchatow to do everything to change the union into a section of the P.P.S. (Polish Socialist Party).

In 1925, there was a textile convention in which the delegation of Birencwajg and Koczmarek represented Belchatow. In the same year, two activists came to Belchatow as employees of the health insurance, Huzar and Schmidt, who the Central definitely wanted to become functionaries of the textile union. Big fights started between the leftists and the P.P.S. Huzar used an unsuccessful resignation of the leftist chairman Yidel Meir Kochmanski, concerning the taking down of a holy picture that hung in union hall, so that the Communists could stir up the unaware Polish workers. The situation was cooled off thanks to Yehezkel Birencwajg, who came as a guest to a meeting and helped create a successful protocol. He suggested that they should send a delegation to Lodz in order to get information and to see if they had holy pictures in the union hall. The picture was finally taken down, and the Communists got rid of the functionary used for their anti-Semitic agitation. The leftists succeed in starting to work with the Polish workers again.

That period of work was the most glorious for the party in Belchatow. A Nodl Union was created, led by Yosef Luft, Peretz Sztatlender and Chaim Yosef Yaab. Well known speakers were brought to lectures that were organized by the Nodl Union. Aharon Wali Gutman (Mikhlin) came. The Nodl Union, however, shared the same fate as the textile union – the Bundist Central disbanded it and organized a new union run by the Bundists.

In earlier times, the party was strengthened by a new group, a group which had split off from the Leftist Poalei Zion, whose best activists had joined the Communist party. Their leaders, Moshe Szmulowicz and Kalman Mendel Przedborski, came with the larger part of the Leftist Poalei Zion Party. Moshe Szmulowicz immediately took over the leadership of the Textile Union. In the same year he was arrested during the great textile strike.

During the discussions in the party after the May upheaval (1927), Belchatow took an active part. Then Eiger, Zak and Mrs. Grosser came to Belchatow. The party in Belchatow went with the majority group (Warski-Kostshev), while the youth joined the minority.

In 1928, City Council elections took place in Belchatow, for which the Communist Party put up lists that were called "Worker Unity." The first candidate was Yehezkel Birencwajg. The authorities had no grounds to invalidate the Left. They did, however, think of a device and disqualified the first candidate, Birencwajg. This caused the Party embarrassment, because the remaining candidates were satisfied merely with a weak political arrangement. It was decided therefore to send a party member to every session of the City Council, who was to orient the four elected Communist council members. The reactionary parties used that to discredit the Communist councilmen in the eyes of the population.

The work with the peasants represented a special chapter in the activity of the Communists. Cells were established in a large number of villages and a division of the leftist peasants called "Samopomoc Chlopska" [peasant self-aid cooperatives] was created with branches in many villages. The Communists put two peasant activists on their slate for the elections. Those were Makovka from Drubice and Soltis from the neighboring Village Wadlew. The slate was called "Workers and Peasants Unity." The Peasants' representative often visited the surrounding villages. The representatives Sipula and Bitner often came to Belchatow on market days to talk to the peasants. The Communist list attracted a large number of peasant voices.

After the election, a new series of repressions started against the Party. A large number of activists were arrested, which seriously hurt the party. Also, the Jewish workers, who were almost all craftsmen, suffered because of an economic crisis. There came a need for longer hours in the mechanical factories, and then it was necessary to withstand attacks from all sides. The Polish workers were being told by agitators that the Jewish workers were competing with them; and when there was success in getting a certain number of Jewish workers in the factory, there came a problem from the Jewish factory owner, who didn't let the Jewish workers work on Saturday. That meant they could represent the Polish workers and work 12 hours, which is against the law concerning the length of the working day.

In the years 1929-1930, the leftist P.P.S. was created in Belchatow, which gave the Lefists a certain strength to organize the Polish workers. Dolinski (from Piotrikow) came to hold conferences. But more mass arrests were made. At a regional conference where Belchatow was represented by Stefan Bush, he was arrested, and the Leftist P.P.S. party was dissolved in the entire land. In the same year, a meeting of the party committee in Belchatow was called off. Moshe Geldbart, Gotsche Hofman, Zalman Salomonowicz, Wojczek Rozga (now living in Lublin), and the Party functionaries were arrested. They all received long sentences, from two to eight years. Also arrested was the functionary of the Peasant Youth, Aleksander Szelinski.

After all these events, it was difficult for the Party to carry on its work. Terror reigned in the land. The best men, like Shamai Birencwajg, were sent away to Bereza Kartuska[2]. Many of the older members quit. The work fell totally on the youth. That was used by the other parties, like P.P. S. and the Bund, and they dominated the whole professional movement.

Yehezkel Birencwajg was in Lodz in that year, where he, together with Hele Weintrot from Warsaw, directed the Party work. He directed the election in Lodz in the name of the TS. K. After the election, he came back to Belchatow, where he ran a series of conferences in the sports club to which he invited the other parties for discussions. Great numbers of Belchatow Jewish workers attended the conferences. It should also be noted that there was a large participation by the middle class. Even the middle class youth took part in the discussions. The following comrades were also involved in these lectures and cultural activities: Shamai Birencwajg, Moshe Grushka, Kalman Mendel Przedborski, Itche Lejb Goldberszt, Henrek Pigula.

**Moshe Grushka**

Then came 1930. The entire capitalistic world was engulfed by a dreadful economic crisis. As usual, the workers were the victims.

The businesses which normally competed with each other got together to cut the hours, although, in reality, the workers under the best conditions could hardly make a living. In 1932, the Belchatow textile factory owners agreed to cut the wages 40%. The weavers, who couldn't tolerate such a large reduction, declared a strike. It wasn't a favorable time to call a strike. The bitter fight was waged courageously. The strike lasted six months, and it had strong reverberations in the entire land. Even abroad, comments were made about the events in the Lodz region.

The progressive movement committed its best activists to lead the fight to organize help for the starving workers and their families. Great demonstrations took place in the shtetls. The result was that the police carried out mass arrests, and the leftist movement lost its best activists, who were sent to jail.

It should be remarked that during the great strike a crisis occurred in the life of the active party member Yehezkel Birencwajg . His actions in his factory as a party delegate had forced the party to eject him from the movement.

Because of this and a number of other factors, and not being able to continue the fight, the great strike, perhaps the greatest in the history of Belchatow, was lost.

Committees were organized and meetings were held, at which Mendel Szimkewicz from the Leftists and Perec Frajtag from the Bund appeared. Work was conducted in cooperation with other movements in the Jewish school.

The leading bodies of the progressive movements came often to Belchatow, which was one of the most advanced shtetls in Poland. There was almost never a week when our shtetl wasn't visited by a chairman from the Central. When the unrest broke out in Krakow, the Leftists were the first to prod the P.P.S. workers to shut down the factories as a sign of protest. During the sit-down strike in that year, many progressive peasants from the surrounding villages, under the influence of the Communist party, brought help for the striking workers. In the last years before the outbreak of the Second World War, the Leftists achieved great influence, even in middle class circles. The Party did all that was possible in order to use the help of the intelligentsia in a substantial way in the Movement. Many of them directed the culture work. For example, "Agro-Yid" was directed in Belchatow by Simcha Gelbard, Naftali Huberman, Chaim Ber Markowicz and Dr. Tenenbaum.

Belchatow wasn't totally dependent on the Central for propaganda material. A secret printing press operated in the shtetl, which from time to time published illegal literature and also material adapted to the actual conditions in the land.

There also existed a many-branched organization to help the political arrestees which was patronized by the Party. The Movement had embraced hundreds and hundreds of workers and ordinary people. The work stoppage was led by: Bronek Eichner, Herszel Richter and Alek Levensztejn (from Czestochowa).

At that time the P.P.S. split, and, with help from the government, the party "Frakes" was created. The Piotrokower Warubeilski, who was known to all as "Frak" ["dresscoat" or "tails" ], came to Belchatow and called a meeting of all textile workers, at which he sought at any price to tear down the prestige of comrade Zalman Pudlowski, a Bundist and devoted fighter for workers, and demanded that he leave the meeting. Warubeilski "rode on an anti-Semitic horse." At the same time, he tried to win the Jewish workers with a demagogic speech about the Jewish Polish patriot Berek Yoselowicz. Here, Yehezkel Birencwajg, a political opponent, turned to the P.P.S. activists and said that they should condemn the activities of the anti-Semitic inspector. The P.P.S. members, however, did not have enough courage to do that, because they themselves had an anti-Semitic attitude. Then, at the urging of Birencwajg, the Jewish workers and a small number of leftist-leaning Polish workers left the meeting. Some time later, Wolczek and Milman came to Belchatow from Lodz and built a truce between the Bund and the P.P.S.

Considering all the facts, we give a partial historical illumination of the important role that it had played in pre-war Poland. The Proletarian avantgarde, in the battle against reactionary fascist Poland, determined the honorable part which Belchatow had in the above mentioned fight. We only want to add here that, in Belchatow, the party produced good social activists and capable people in all areas. We just want to mention several of them: Shimon Szmulewicz from the Bund often stepped forward as an opponent at hostile meetings and worked well with the masses. Itche Lejb Goldberszt was a simple worker who lacked one foot and he always had to work hard. He was well versed in classical literature and his lectures drew a large audience. Shamai Birencwajg was the young genius of the shtetl. He was a good teacher, skilled in politics and culture, always involved in political, economic, and scientific socialism circles. He died in the Lodz ghetto, where even the sadly-famous Rumkowski had to acknowledge him. Last should be mentioned Kalman Mendel Przedborski, who was one of those who gave up all his free time for society until the day of his death. He was not only the leader of the leftist faction in the professional association during the absence of Yehezkel Birencwajg, but he was also the leader of the entire cultural program. With others, he organized the library in a room at comrade Goldberszt's, where he spent a lot of his free time.

**A group of left wing women activists**

The liveliest moments of the work were the inter-party discussions that were held in the sports club and were watched by large crowds who had come to hear the interesting lectures by Shamai and Yehezkel Birencwajg about the international situation. The lectures mentioned, and the discussions, were the expression of political activists with a wide outlook in contrast to the members of the other parties.

The political activities of the Communist party had a great effect on the masses and, chiefly, among the youth, of whom today there are several who occupy responsible posts in the new Polish nation, like Gotsche Hofman and Kaufman, among others.

[Page 369]

# The Leftist Workers' Movement
# Between the two World Wars

### by Jakob Tsingler

### Translated from the Yiddish by Jerome Silverbush

### Edited by Jerry Liebowitz

[with comments in brackets]

In contrast to the neighboring Jewish Shtetls, where the great part of the Jewish population lived from "air businesses" [*luft-gesheftn*], at the end of the First World War Belchatow already had a large Jewish work force, and that had a great effect on the social and political life of our shtetl. At that time, already, two Jewish workers parties existed in our shtetl: the "Poale Zion" ["Workers of Zion" – a Zionist labor movement] and the "Bund" [a Jewish socialist party]. The second of these two parties was the stronger and was more recognized among the Jewish population.

The political events after the First World War, in particular the reverberations from the Russian Revolution, had a clear influence on the subsequent development of political life in Belchatow.

Already in 1922, there occurred in the shtetl – just like in the rest of Poland – a split in the earlier arrangement of two workers' parties, and the Leftist Workers' Movement was organized.

In the period when in all of Poland the Leftist Movement grew up in the bosom of the Social Democratic Party of Russia, Poland, and Lithuania, which had taken over the best revolutionary traditions from the old time "Proletariat" [the name given to socialist groupings in the Congress Kingdom of Poland] and from the left wing of the P.P.S. [Polish Socialist Party], in Belchatow, however, the Leftist Movement from the beginning was absolutely Jewish.

The first task of the new party was to change itself into a mass-movement of Belchatow labor [*arbetershaft*]. Therefore we started immediately to organize the class trade-unions [*klasn-faraynen* "class" denoting their distinctly

Marxist-socialist orientation ] of the weavers. There was a possibility for the workers of both nationalities to find a common language to defend their common interests. In 1924, the first combined strike broke out. The battle was a long and very bitter one. After four months, we succeeded in breaking the obstinacy of the owners and in winning the strike. In the course of the battle, our comrades were found in the very front lines. Our activity among the Polish workers was particularly difficult. In Belchatow, then, the Black Reactionary Catholic Worker Parties, "Cha-De" [chadecja – Christian Democrats] and "N.P.R." [Narodowa Partia Robotnicza – National Workers' Party], still had influence among the Polish workers, and their chief task, moreover, was to sharpen the antagonism between the Polish and Jewish workers. Even the leaders of the Polish Socialist Party, Huzar and Schmidt, educated their party members in the spirit of ultra-patriotism and nationalism.

Therefore, it was difficult for Jewish party men to go to Polish workers poisoned with anti-Semitic ideas and to say to them that they had common interests with Jewish workers.

The organizers of the Communist party understood that if they wanted to have a substantial influence on Polish society, they would have to proceed building their party among the Polish workers. That succeeded completely with the continuous strikes, when the party inculcated a marked influence among the Polish workers.

Leading the workers on the Polish street, the party did not neglect its activity among the Jewish workers. In class trade-unions, meetings were often held in the Yiddish language, where one handled, besides economic matters, also ongoing political issues. In the framework of the legal possibilities, public meetings were organized and numerous publications were given out by the party. The legal party paper, "The Week," was the most widely distributed among the Belchatow Jewish workers.

Every political activity found its echo in our party activity in the shtetl. A Jewish library was organized, and great importance was put on the development of its members, both political and cultural. Because of the continually growing reprisals and arrests of leftist activists, in Belchatow, just like in the entire land, the Red Relief Campaign [hilfs-aktsiye] was organized.

Our party came to the workers and showed them the way to fight for better living conditions. At our call and under our leadership, a whole series of strikes then broke out. Thanks to the good leadership most of the strikes were won. That elevated the prestige and popularity of our party among the Belchatow workers.

When in 1926 the leftist faction of the P.P.S. (*Levitse* P.P.S.) originated, we got the opportunity to be published in public semi-legally. At the next City Council election, we received the largest number of worker votes, and our faction was the strongest in the City Council. We also got the greatest influence in the professional movement, and the Belchatow class trade-union found itself for a certain period under the leadership of the Communist party, particularly during the great textile strike in 1928. Regardless of the success from our strike actions, the Communist party was unable to put down deep roots among the masses of Polish workers. There were, in my opinion, three main reasons for that: 1) The Belchatow Polish workers did not have any proletarian revolutionary tradition; 2) The initiative to organize in the Communist party came from the Jewish worker circles, and, for Polish workers with little awareness, any initiative that came from the Jews was a motive for resistance; 3) The fact that the Communist party was illegal.

Parallel with the enlightenment work on the Polish street, a widespread task among the Jewish workers was developed. The "Sport Society," which played a powerful important role in developing our organization, was founded. Besides the physical training, great stress was also placed on the intellectual development of the Jewish worker youth. Lectures were given on literature and politics. Groups were organized for theoretical education. By this means, the "Sports Society" prepared cadres of activists for the party organization.

In the same year, 1927, the first arrests of party activists took place. Yehezkel Birencwajg and Esther Szmulewicz were arrested then.

In the years of heavy fighting for the right to work for the masses of Jewish workers, the Leftist Movement consistently led the action and defended the rights of Jewish workers. At the same time, we did not neglect our enlightenment work among the Polish workers, warning them that the anti-Semitism and the antagonism between the Polish and Jewish workers exclusively served the goals and interests of the Reactionaries. We also made great efforts to organize the village workers in a class trade-union. We did not have any great success in this attempt, and that was because of two primary reasons: first, the leaders of the trade-union held a negative position toward the problem, holding that with farmers one cannot do anything; and, second, because we had to send Jewish workers as organizers, since we did not have any Polish workers for the purpose.

We also suffered from the constant arrests among our leaders, which moreover caused a sharp reduction in our activities. It should be mentioned that among the arrested were: Shmuel Gershon Morgenstern, who later perished in a battle in Spain, Jacob Dovozshinski, who later was killed on the Ukraine front in battle with the "Hitlerites," and Moshe Gelbard, who later was killed in a German prison camp.

**Left wing activists as
soldiers in the Polish Military**
[right to left] Z. Przedborski,
Shmuel Pudlovsky, and T. Przybilsky

Of tremendous importance was our action in the conflict of 1932. Feeling responsible for the fighting workers, we stormed the Central Committee of our party, demanding substantial and effective help for the striking workers. In response to our demand, a party conference was held in Lodz, which was attended by a representative from the Secretariat. At the conference, we demanded the proclamation of a general strike by all textile workers in Poland. The Lodz comrades assured us that within a few days they would proclaim the strike. Our comrades indeed fulfilled their promise, but the strike did not have any effect, because the P.P.S. did not support it. Struggling Belchatow did not get support and remained alone in its fight.

Our organization also carried through a mass campaign among the village workers about material and moral support for the striking workers. We also tried to spread the strike to the village workers, which even succeeded partially. But it did not have any decisive influence on the outcome of the fight.

**Left wing activists**
[right to left] Yishayah Kreizman,
Pzedborsky, and Moshe Chayt

During the period of time of the strike our party received the strongest blow because of the arrest of our party activists. The [party's] influence on the strike therefore greatly fell apart. The strike went into a phase of demoralization, and after upwards of five months, the strike was lost. That was a great defeat for the Belchatow worker-class and, together with that, also for our party. One had to start rebuilding the party from the very beginning.

In fall of the same year we opened the Peretz Club [named for the famous Yiddish author, I.L. Peretz] which led to a divided culture effort. Our library was also located there. Groups for political and literary discussions were again established. Especially active were the comrades Simcha Gelbard (perished in Belchatow in 1942) and Naftali Huberman. The Peretz Club helped considerably in doing the party work. We also organized the defense of comrades who had been arrested in the course of the strike. But a short time later, at the end of winter, the police closed the Peretz Club.

Hitler's coming to power in Germany in 1933 brought essential changes in the strategy and tactics of the proletarian movement. The change to a unified front, and later to a "people's front" [*folks-front*], found a positive reverberation also among the Belchatow workers [*arbiter-reyen*]. At every opportunity we displayed our good will to realize the united front, and in 1934 we finally came to an understanding to arrange a joint May Day demonstration. This demonstration attracted the majority of the Belchatow workers and made a tremendously strong impression. Unfortunately, however, it did not succeed in creating a continuous unified front of the Belchatow workers, and all the discussions on the topic did not have any positive results at all.

The anti-Semites in the land – and consequently, also those in our shtetl – consistently grew in number, and we experienced the organization of anti-Semitic "excursions" ["*oysflugn*"] in our shtetl. Together with other groups of Jews and with some Polish workers, we completely destroyed all the anti-Semitic plans.

During the Spanish Civil War, when the Polish worker-class organized the relief campaign [*hilfs-aktsiye*], our organization in Belchatow also did not lag behind the other centers, and. although we led the action independently, it produced good results. As already mentioned earlier, our comrade, Shmuel Gershon Morgenstern was an active fighter in the "Dombrowski" Battalion and died on the battlefield.

In the difficult fight against the Polish reactionaries and anti-Semitism, we were successful, not only in working with the leftist inclined Polish workers, but we were also successful in coming to an understanding with the Bund and partially with the P.P.S.

Our party also played an important role in the sad times of the pogrom in Przytyk [in March 1936]. We organized a protest strike with participation of all the workers [*arbetershaft*] in Belchatow. Even the Polish workers, who were poisoned by anti-Semitism, were afraid to go against the strike and took part in it. At the same time we carried out a widespread educational activity among the Belchatow population against anti-Semitism. Also at the same time, we successfully carried out a money collection for the victims of the pogrom.

However, our work was made very difficult by the constant arrests of our best activists, and we consequently had to concern ourselves also with the arrested comrades, organize their defense, and be worried about sending them packages of food and clothing. Within the limited range of our possibilities, we also cared for the parents and the relatives of the arrested ones.

In the period that we worked together with the Bund, we combined both our sports organizations, which, thanks to the merger, earned high esteem in the Lodz region. Unfortunately, the union did not last long.

Also, in that period, both Jewish worker libraries were combined. When the Nazis marched into Belchatow, together with Comrade Hertske Frajtag (a futurist), we succeeded in saving the combined library from the Nazi hand and departed for the Soviet Union, where I walled then into an oven for baking matzo. Later, the library shared the same fate as those who had read the books.

We also organized and legalized with the authorities the organization, "Agro-Yid", which formally had the task to spread agricultural knowledge among the Jewish masses. Actually, the society inherited the closed-up "Gezerd"[3] and popularized the idea of the Jewish Autonomous Region in Birobidzhan[4] [the far eastern province of the Soviet Union]. Because of the frequent police searches, one had to work strictly within the limited framework of the legal statutes. But, the activity of "Agro-Yid" was also used for party work, and, at the same time, an extensive cultural work was carried out. "Agro-Yid" existed for about two years until the police closed the society.

When the Polish Fascists had started to destroy the Polish professional movement and organize their own syndicate, the pestilence didn't omit Belchatow, where it immediately found careerists who tried to make a career in the new workers movement. The old professional organizations were persecuted by the authorities and often were forced to operate illegally. When the new leaders wanted to personally spread their wings over the factories, we were the first to categorically oppose this – especially in electing factory delegates and other important actions. In spite of observing the P.P.S. activist's guilt in the rise of Fascism, and the breaking of the Professional Organization, we supported the P.P.S. representative in the factories in order to maintain the opposition against the Fascist regime and protect our common position in the class trade-unions.

In 1938, regardless of the fact that the "Comintern" [acronym for Communist International – name given to Third International, founded in 1919] had dissolved our party, we continued our work and expressed our protest against the Polish conquest of Czechoslovakian territory which happened as a result of the Munich agreement.

When at the end of 1938 Hitler carried through the expulsion of Polish Jews and the relief campaign was organized, Belchatow was one of the first to react, and, together with the Bund, we organized the relief campaign, sent money, clothing, and books for the Jews who were driven out, who found themselves in no man's land – in Zbonshin [Zbaszyn, a Polish border town to which Hitler deported many German Jews].

In 1939, after the outbreak of the war, it turned out that we were to lead the last election-battle [*val-kamf*] in Poland. The reactionary government used the war mood in the land to increase the terror against the workers, prohibit the May Day celebration, arrest worker leaders, and the like. In the same atmosphere, the elections for City Council were held in Belchatow, and, although we proposed that the remaining worker parties create a combined worker front, our proposal was not accepted, and the elections were held with an internally splintered worker front, which merely strengthened the victory of the Polish Fascists.

But, the new City Council was not destined to hold its office for long. A short time later, the first of September, when Hitler invaded Poland, a new chapter started in our fight for liberation....

———

**Editor's Footnotes:**

1. **Combund** – Communist Bund and the so-called Combundists, who agreed with all the twenty-one points and who also demanded to get rid of all right-wing leaders. After weeks and months of heated discussions, the Bund split up and a Combund was established.

2. **Bereza Kartusk** – a concentration camp in the marshes of eastern Poland (present-day Belarus). This was, along with Dachau, one of the first camps for the politically "undesirable" established in Europe outside the Soviet Union.

3. **"GEZERD"** is a Yiddish acronym equivalent of the Russian OZET (Association for Rural Placement of Jewish Toilers), a Jewish Communist group founded in the mid-1920's, whose purpose was to raise money for and carry out a Jewish socialist agricultural settlement in the USSR. Unlike the Zionists, they wanted a Jewish socialist settlement project in the Soviet Union in which Jews would have cultural autonomy.

4. In 1934 the Soviet government established the **"Jewish Autonomous Region" (JAR)** in Birobidzhan, a remote and sparsely populated region of the Soviet Far East. This was part of the Communist Party's effort to set up a territorial enclave with a secular Jewish culture, rooted in both Yiddish and socialist principles, which could serve as an alternative to Palestine.

[Page 379]

# Portraits of Progressive Activists

## by Y.M. Pukacz

### Translated from the Yiddish by Jerome Silverbush

### Edited by Roni and Jerry Liebowitz

[with comments in brackets]

*Shamai Birencwajg*: Somewhat shorter than average height, back bent a bit, almost always looking at the ground, carelessly dressed, Chassidic movements – that is the outer appearance of Shamai Birencwajg.

Looking at him, no one could imagine that he was the leader of a revolutionary movement. Just the opposite, he gave the impression of a man who has no interest in anything.

A man who could excel in the rules of conspiracy and who likewise excelled in looking into taking a position for any political situation. For years he was at the head of the Progressive Movement in Belchatow and put his stamp on the work. Ever weary with worries about making a living, he nevertheless found time to read and to teach himself and others.

At meetings, he remained a long time and listened carefully to what others had to say. Then came his few calm and measured words which contributed clarity and simplicity, even in the most heated discussions.

In 1938, he was arrested and banished to Kartoz-Bereze [Bereza Kartusk – a concentration camp in the marshes of eastern Poland (present-day Belarus)]. He bore the suffering and torment there with the same patience with which he had led the Movement for years. Then came the tragic year, 1939. After the liquidation of the Belchatow Jews, Shamai turned up in the Lodz ghetto. Also there, he was socially very active. Also there, he quickly became popular and loved.

In the end, the capable activist shared the same fate as millions of Polish Jews: Majdanek and ashes in the wind!

**Kalman M. Przedborski**


_Kalman Mendel Przedborski_: A long and thin face. Expressive clever eyes. Always ready to do a good turn.

A child of poor parents, poverty had bound him from childhood on in the yoke of hard work, but the bitterness of his personal fate never had any influence on his character and his relationship to humanity.

If it is at all possible for goodness to have an embodiment, it would be found in his person. From his earliest youth on, he was occupied with social and political activities. And wherever he was active, he gained prestige. Even political opponents respected him greatly.

Brought up in the Borochowistisher [named after the founder of Poalei Zion in Russia, Ber Borochowen] Leftist Poalei Zion Party, he later found himself in the forward ranks of the Progressive Movement.

One seldom saw him alone. [He was] always surrounded by comrades and friends, who listened to him like Chasidim listen to a Rebbe. One knew that he was always ready to do a favor and give a piece of advice. He wanted to help everyone and take care of everyone, but he constantly forgot to do one thing – to think about his own welfare.

Already at the beginning of the Hitler occupation, he was arrested and sent to Chelmno, where he was murdered together with the majority of the Belchatow Jews.

*Shmuel Gershon Morgenstern*: Young and tall, with a pale and boney face, with a pair of black fiery eyes and constantly with a smile on his lips. Anyone who has contact with him must like him. He speaks softly with a ringing tone, but he speaks little, because he has a shy nature. He preferred to listen rather than to talk himself. However, he possessed a temperamental and partly also a stormy nature. He hated to wait and put aside until tomorrow what should be done today, because he was always afraid that he would be a little late.

From time to time he would cough and spit, and with every cough a bit of blood would come out of his mouth from his diseased lungs. Just as he was from childhood on used to hunger and want, likewise it made no big impression on him when his lung disease threatened his life more and more. He just didn't want to talk about it...

In 1936, when the Spanish Civil War broke out, Shmuel Gershon could not remain indifferent, and, ignoring his poor health, he traveled to Spain and enlisted in the famous Dombrowski Brigade. Enthusiastic letters from him arrived in the town. He was happy that he had an opportunity to fight against Fascism. At the beginning of 1938, every trace of our heroic friend and comrade Shmuel Gershon Morgenstern was lost.

His friends will never forget him.

*Jakob Lejzer Dobszynski*: A young man of abut twenty years of age, Jakob Lejzer Dobszynski was already an old party activist. He loved to constantly have discussions with everyone to convince them of the correctness of his ideas. He gesticulated wildly when he spoke, and everyone loved him because of his simplicity and honesty

Although in the last few years he was busy with a very important office in the Movement, he constantly avoided being conspicuous. He did his work quietly but precisely.

After the outbreak of the war, he escaped to the Soviet Union, and after Hitler attacked Soviet Russia, he voluntarily enlisted in the Russian army and fought on the Ukrainian front, where he died heroically in a bloody battle with the Nazis.

_Itche Lejb Goldberszt_: A pauper in seven coat tails [idiomatic expression, meaning "a king of the poor"], he was never downhearted. [He was] always happy, joyful, and ready to tell a joke or a story.

A thin one, skin and bones, and on top of that a physical invalid, one would constantly meet him, satisfied, shakily supported on his wooden crutch. His physical shortcomings had stopped him from earning a decent livelihood, and because of that he suffered great need.

Because the Progressive Movement did not have a meeting place, for years his poor room held the I. L Peretz Library.

A passionate reader, he was well versed in both Jewish and universal literature. From time to time, he would give a lecture on literature. His ringing voice and poetic manner of speaking captured and held his listeners.

In 1936, because of a provocation, he was arrested and sent to prison for a year. But when he came out, he was as joyful and lively as always.

After the Nazi occupation of Belchatow, he was part of the first group that was murdered. During a selection, he was sent to a mass death along with all the sick, weak and aged.

Finding himself on the truck about to be driven away, he screamed to the gathered crowd: – Jews, they are sending us to death. Take revenge for us!

## Mendel Szymkewicz

*Mendel Szymkewicz*: An energetic and genial comrade, he was one of the most enthusiastic activists in the Progressive Movement in Belchatow. At meetings and rallies, he was the eternal opponent and heckler, always putting in his "two cents." Often, he tended to stammer a little, but that did not stop him from bringing down the house with his argument.

Mendel Szymkewicz was in prison for years, but that did not break him, and he was always cheerful and ready for a fight. He loved to take on difficult jobs, which he always completed on time. He never let any opportunity whatsoever pass by to lead an active party agitation. That was his favorite work.

Like the majority of Belchatow children, he came to the Movement harassed and plagued by hunger and need. His trade was carpenter, but he strived to achieve something higher and more beautiful.

When the Nazis occupied Poland, Mendel left for the Soviet Union, and, after the founding of the Polish Peoples' Army, he immediately joined as a volunteer and was involved in a series of battles against the Nazi army. In the famous battle of Lenino [the author may mean Leningrad, since Lenino was the site of a Nazi massacre, not a battle], he was killed by a Nazi bullet.

*Gotsche Hofman*: She came to the Movement from a middle class home, where she received a traditional Jewish upbringing and threw herself into the Revolutionary Movement with complete youthful fervor. She sat for years in Polish jails, but she was always ready for new accomplishments. She had a middle school education, and she was active doing education work with the workers and farmers.

After the outbreak of the Second World War, she emigrated to the Soviet Union, and today she is actually the only Belchatower who lived to see the liberation of Poland, to which she immediately returned and where she continued to be active in the complete fulfillment of her ideals.

## The children's group "Pioneer"

Even though the Leftist Movement in pre-war Poland had very limited possibilities for mass work, it had, like every mass-movement, paid much attention to the education of the youth.

Soon after the creation of "Combund" [Communist Bund], the Leftist Movement had struck deep roots among the youth. It is characteristic to underscore that, thanks to the specific conditions in the Party, whether because of what happened after the great arrests or because of the divergence of views in the Movement (after the year 1925), often the entire job fell on the youth. And one must admit that the Belchatow workers and children of the people [Volks-Kinder] always carried out with full comprehension all [the tasks] entrusted to them.

It is quite understandable that one ran into many difficulties trying to recruit members for the children's group "Pioneer." These difficulties were caused first of all by the illegality of the Leftist Movement conducting its activities, and, following from that, the lack of a location in which the youth would be able to spend time and interact socially. The Progressive Movement was not able to give the child all that the other legal parties had the possibility to give. However, because of that, the Leftist Movement stood higher, because it planted in the child a clearer look at life.

The candidates for the Pioneers were recruited mainly from the children of the Belchatow poor: children of 11, 12 and 13 years of age. Because of special conditions, every Pioneer only knew the members of his group.

First of all, every candidate had to take a precise course in which he was instructed on the basic responsibilities of everyone involved in the Movement, like discipline and conspiracy [secrecy]. The work of teaching the fundamental principles was taken on by several older comrades, who at the same time were the link between the Pioneers and the youth. In 1932, the following people carried out this task: Hiller Belchatowski, Shabtai-Yechiel Moszkowicz, Mordechai Huberman, and Chayah-Tzviah Farber.

Besides the tasks mentioned above, our older comrades also paid much attention to the political education of the child, discussing current events with him and also teaching the history of the Workers' Movement.

The Leftist Movement understood completely that every "Pioneer" must be well prepared, both politically and intellectually, so that he will be able to courageously defend his position and, when it is necessary, not to waver and to be prepared to make sacrifices. This work was not easy to accomplish, because one had to consider that the Pioneers had to be very careful that at home they did not suspect that the child was involved with political activities. Many children came from Hasidic homes, where the least suspicion could lead to literally tragic consequences for the parents and the children themselves.

Another problem was arranging the meetings since – as mentioned – the Progressive Movement did not have its own meeting place. One could not even get a room where the children could gather. It finally came to conducting the work mostly in the summer months, in the forest and in the fields, and even in winter, in the great frosts and snows, we had to meet from time to time in the forest. Very often we had to hold consultations walking in the street.

In 1933, the children's organization "Pioneer" was highly respected by all the other children's groups in Belchatow. At that time, a whole series of activists joined the Movement, both boys and girls, among whom, one should especially mention: Pesse Kaufman, Hinde Szmulewicz, Mendel Kaufman, Meir Borochowicz, Ziske Eksztajn, Mendel Pigula, Moshe Machabanski, Sholem Machabanski, Frejdl Belchatowski, Ephrim Lozer Machhabanski, and others.

The task of "Pioneer" was not merely to educate future political activists, but also to its work belonged the stimulation of reading of our classical books and works of Jewish and world literature, which were later discussed and commented on during the meetings. For that purpose, the Movement had put at the disposal of the children, the so-called "Pioneer Library," which really did a lot for the education of the worker-child as a politically responsible activist as well as an educated Jew and human being.

At various opportunities, older comrades came to chat, give lectures, and have discussions with the Pioneers about actual political problems. I am especially reminded of comrades Jakob Tzingler and Jakob-Lejzer Dobszynski.

What were the tasks of "Pioneer"?

It must be noted that in pre-war Poland there was almost no youth that was not under the influence of a political movement and was almost always having discussions and taking positions on local and general political problems. Every Pioneer was obliged to bring out in such cases the viewpoint of the Party. Also, the Pioneers took part in various social gatherings, lectures, and meetings. As an illustration, it is worth while remembering the great action that was carried out in Poland in 1936 against the introduction of the "numerus clauzus" law [a law limiting the number of Jewish children] in the Polish high schools. When it happened, except for those explicitly forbidden by the police, there were protest meetings and manifestations of every political stripe on the Jewish street, and also in Belchatow the protest movement played a large part. A day before the protest action, the "Pioneer" together with "Skif" ["*Sotzialistisher Kinder Farband*" – the Bund youth movement] called together almost all Jewish school children and explained to them the meaning of "numerus clauzus" and the position that one must take. The children were gathered in the courtyard of Meir Ber Szwartzberg. Speeches were given by a chairman of "Pioneer" and a chairman of "Skif". Also present was Jakob Lejzer Dobszynski as chairman from the Leftist Party and Mendel Lajb Gliksman as chairman from the "Bund". The second day, pickets were placed at the schools, and none of the children were admitted into the Aryan schools. At that time, I stood together with Lejbl Goldminc of "Skif" and Mendel Kaufman of "Pioneer". That was one of the nicest actions in which the Belchatow youth were actively represented, showing the growing will to fight anti-Semitism and [rightist] reaction [reaktsia], which was then rampant in Poland.

It should also be mentioned that when Poland was still engulfed by the crisis year of 1930 with waves of strikes, the then famous "occupation strikes" in the factories were carried out, and our children also took an active part in the fight. The Pioneers were used to throw packages of food into the occupied factories, for the striking workers, who were stuck in the factories, surrounded by police. Not one of the children avoided being hit by the police, but that did not stop them from carrying out their task.

The children from "Pioneer" also had the task of convincing their school comrades to skip school on May 1, and although the director had threatened them with sanctions, every May 1 a significant number of children were absent from school.

* * *

That which I described earlier was no more than several images and episodes of what the "Pioneer" in Belchatow actually was – a work that was always connected with the readiness to sacrifice oneself and which was opposed by Polish reactionary power. But even then, the children of the working class without any fear opposed the danger from Polish Fascism.

The Pioneers have consciously drawn the thread of a magnificent continuum, the continuum that stretched from Hersz Lekert and Naftali Botwein.

*[Page 389]*

# IV.

# The Destruction of Belchatow

*[Page 391]*

## Under the Nazi Occupation

### by Leib Podlowski (Layb Podlovsky)

### Translated from the Yiddish by Martin Bornstein (pp. 391-395, 432-438)

### and by Dr. Khane-Feygl (Anita) Turtletaub (pp. 395-432, 438-455)

(Latter translation donated by Sharon and Samuel Shattan and Shmuel Shottan)

### Edited by Roni and Jerry Liebowitz

[with comments by editors and translators in brackets]

The martyrology of the Jews of Belchatow began immediately, starting with the first day of the outbreak of the war. Belchatow, which finds itself 50 kilometers from the pre-war German border, had directly by itself sensed all of the horrors of the Second World War. Already on the second day of the war, Saturday morning, there began to arrive refugees, naked and barefoot, from Wielow and from other small towns from the border pass. They were running away from their burning homes, which had been bombed by the German airplanes and artillery. The refugees settled into the synagogues and the Beit Hamidrash [house of prayer and study], by people they knew, and whoever did not have anyone, they stayed in the meadows and the fields. The entire Sabbath day the Jews of Belchatow were occupied with providing food for the refugees and making arrangements for them. On the same day, in the evening, the Jews of Belchatow, along with the refugees that had come to them from Wielow, Widawa, Szczercow, and other settlements, had to leave their homes. They had to leave behind and abandon their work and effort [what they had toiled for], because it became apparent, that the Germans had broken through the Polish defense line by the Warta and Widawa [rivers]. Everything was running in the direction of Lodz. Old and young people alike ran, Jew and Pole alike. The peasants took everything that they owned and put it onto wagons; they took along their cows and other cattle. The Jews wore packs on their shoulders, a lot transported their possessions and goods on children's carriages. On the way a lot of things were thrown away, since they didn't have the strength to carry on themselves all the packs, because of the great heat that occurred while running by foot to Lodz. The entire highway from Belchatow to Pabianice was packed full with people and returning Polish troops. From the skies, the Germans pelted the people running away with bombs. There began a riot, one person lost the other on the road.

A lot of people perished from the bomb splinters. Such a splinter from a bomb found its way into Chaim Zendel, Welwel Ferster's son in law. When the Belchatow Jews dragged themselves on the fourth day to Lodz, they first found the same scene that they had experienced a few days earlier by themselves while at home. Lodz also began to evacuate itself. Here too all roads that led farther, towards Warsaw, were clogged up with people. The large majority of the Belchatow Jews did not have any more strength to drag themselves farther to Warsaw. Only a small number, about 50 young people, pushed their way through to Warsaw and participated in the brave defense of the capital city. At the defense of Warsaw, Yankel Altman perished, and several Belchatowers were wounded. About 500 Belchatowers broke out and ran away to the Soviet side.

————

On the sixth day of the war the German army took Belchatow.

While marching in, they lit fire to a portion of the town, especially the Jewish part. They did this exclusively in order to find the Jewish population – there weren't any strategic reasons here, because in Belchatow there wasn't any focal point of fighting, nor was there any Polish military presence.

Where the few Jewish people, that is those who had then remained in Belchatow when the Germans came in, which was on the fifth day of the outbreak of the war, were turned over, the German baker's son, Ertek Lechelt, [was] lying in the meadow that goes to Szczercower Road, and from there was giving signals to the German military. Immediately, as he was doing this, the Germans began to throw firebombs on the Jewish part of town, and it was later said that this was especially organized by the local Germans [Folk Germans – German people that were living in Poland before the war]. Incidentally, it is in comparison with what they did later, that this said little piece of work was child's play. The shrapnel fell so calculatedly that all the Jewish houses in Old Market [Stare Rynek] and on Pabianicka Street, that bordered Wallenberg's house, were burned down, and only Wallenberg's house remained intact. Almost the entire Old Market [district] was burned, from Ferster's Factory up to the firehouse. This went from one side, from Factor's house, and from the other side this continued until Wallenberg's house on Pabianicka Street. Only a few houses survived, on the side of the Gurer shtibl [prayer house of the Gur Chasidim]. In the German documents one finds a list of 123 Jewish families[1]), whose homes and fortunes [worldly goods] were burned on the first day of the outbreak of the war.

————

Several days later many Belchatower Jews, who were not far away, returned to their hometown.

On the way home they were exposed to many troubles from the German army that was marching through: they stripped off their best clothing, they shaved off their beards, and thereby dreadfully scarred their faces. They were pulled away to the most difficult work. They had to bury the people and horses, which were lying on the road slain. They didn't spare [giving out] any blows. On the way home, the Germans tormented Meyer Franis. Only when at home, did the ones who returned first find their burned houses, and where they weren't burned, the dwellings had been robbed. The robbing of the Jewish homes was carried out by the local Germans [that had been living in Belchatow] unashamedly in the open. They did not even have the patience to wait until the implanted Hitlerites would make this possible for them. One stole everything that one could: furniture, manufactured cloth, hand as well as powered weaving looms [used for home manufacturing of cloth], new machinery, and things of household use. They removed the combined threads [ketn – thicker yarns formed by combining threads, used to weave cloth] from the factories.

In a German document, from the first days of the German occupation, one finds a characteristic exchange of letters, between the mayor and the commissioner, concerning the fortune of Zalman Markowicz, which is found in the factory locale of Epstein. In the document the conflict between the German bodies becomes clearly expressed, concerning who has more right to grab the Jewish fortune.

The fact presents itself thus: a known Belchatow Folk German, by the name Hermel, took the combined threads [ketn] that belonged to Markowicz. The commissioner from the Markowicz firm protested against it, as he considered himself to be the seated natural inheritor of Zalman Markowicz's fortune. The interesting part about the exchange of letters is this – what the mayor answers concerning why they sold the yarn so quickly. It was explained that because it might have been possible that the local Poles could become aware of this, which according to their thinking they would have also had a desire for the goods, and according to what he writes, he didn't want to permit this. The yarn was sold for 9 Marks [German currency] per kilogram, and the town management confiscated the money.

In the course of only one day, all of the Belchatow Jews were transformed into a camp of beggars.

———

During the several war months, until 1940, the Jews of Belchatow came to suffer all sorts of torments and troubles on the part of different German military formations. Every German sergeant considered it his duty for his soldiers to put forth the Jews as guilty of everything, as war criminals, and the soldiers already on their own knew what to do; they were already well used to it. As soon as the Germans came in, the soldiers were allowed to pursue the Jews. They grabbed Zerach Cymberknopf and tortured him for so long, until he was brought home half dead. They cut off the beard of the gray haired shochet [butcher – ritual slaughterer]. They grabbed Jews on the street and cut out swastikas on their head [cut away hair to leave a swastika]. The Jews were forced to pick up with their hands the manure from the horses, on the grounds where the German military had passed by; with old Jews they had them do different gymnastic exercises. They already from the beginning were doing everything to break the Jews physically and spiritually. The Germans took Yankl Ostrowsky and sat him on a chamber pot [taptshan]. A group of Jews had to carry the pot on their shoulders. A second group of Jews had to follow in procession and beat and clap on platters and on a basin and to shout: that "we Jews are the ones at fault in the war and that 'Moses' should come to help us"... So one had to carry on throughout the whole town, and afterwards, after the procession had filed through all the streets, the German who had arranged this spectacle ordered that we should dump the victim off from the pot. Such sights repeated themselves a few times a day. They had, for example, carried out such a play: on Yom Kippur (concerning the Yom Kippur days there will be more to say later) they carried out Shlomo Jakubowicz and sat him on a ladder dressed in tallis [prayer shawl and tefillen [phylacteries]. Jews had to carry the ladder. Everyone that had to carry the ladder also had to be wearing tallis and tefillen, they had to pray and at the same time make various gestures, singing in a loud voice. The Germans had these scenes photographed and sent home to the "Reich" to show what a wild people the Jews are. When the Jews were good and tired of carrying the ladder, the Germans decreed that the Jew should be thrown from the ladder. Such victims, after the "spectacle," remained crippled.

*[Page 395]*

The Jews of Belchatow lived in constant fear. They had no peace, not by day nor by night. By day, they were caught and forced into labor. By day they were persecuted, and by night they were robbed. The murderous gangs were constantly changing:

When the S. S. left Belchatow at the end of September, the Gestapo, who were even worse, immediately took their place. They surrounded the whole city, [and searched] every single Jewish house ostensibly looking for weapons. In truth, however, it was just another reason to loot. They loaded everything they could get their hands on onto wagons, from kitchen crockery to children's things. They took laundry, plates, any kind of clothing. As soon as they came, there started new episodes of more subtle persecutions of Jews. I will mention only a few of these horribly bestial acts here. They took Mordachai Josef's little son-in-law, Moshe Levi, and tied him to a pole with his own prayer-belt and beat him mercilessly. He was not even allowed to bat an eye, because another German stood over him holding a bayonet to his belly. The Germans left only when they thought he was dead. They were barely able to revive him later. The baker, Moshe Stabiecki, was forced to jump off a roof while singing the "Hatikva." They threw Yankel Krawicki into the river and threatened to shoot him if he tried to get out.

The local Germans took a great part in these sadistic actions. Especially prominent were the Belchatower Germans, Willer and Bretkreitz, and Dolke from Zelow. Willer had been a skilled workman in Szmulewicz's factory. [Now] he walked around all day with a whip in his hand and violently beat anyone he could get his hands on: women, children, old people, anyone was a potential victim. He kept a special eye on Chaim Yankel Szymkewicz. Every time he beat him, he asked him if he still considered himself to be "a strongman." "The Germans will see to it that you are no longer a strongman." It was the same with Yankel Mareyni and others. The Germans considered it their patriotic duty to every day to find Jews whom they could "honor" with beatings.

The persecutions that were carried out on the Jews of Belchatow during the High Holidays comprise an especially tragic chapter. In spite of the fact that the punishment for gathering together and praying was death, the Jews of Belchatow, nevertheless, got together in [small] groups during these days and prayed sincerely.

They were forced to watch as the Germans defiled their synagogue and transformed it into a prison for Jews. The Belchatower Jews risked their lives to remove the Torah scrolls from the synagogue, from the Beit Hamidrash [house of prayer and study], and from the small Chassidic synagogues, and hide them in various places. We know that on Rosh Hashanah 1939 the Germans caught a group of Jews praying at Zalman Krizman's home. They were lead out into the street and violently beaten. All of the persecutions of Jews during the High Holidays were carried out in conjunction with the local Germans and the gendarmes. A special division of Hitler youth, which had arrived a few days earlier, raided the Jewish houses, taking everyone into forced labor. Then they required all the Jews to bring that which they held most dear, their religious books, and bring them to New Market [Square] and burn them in a bonfire. With their own hands, the Jews had to burn their sacred objects. The pyres of Jewish books blazed until after Yom Kippur. The Germans were specially looking forward to Yom Kippur. On that day they broke every preceding record of persecuting and torturing the Jews.

Early in the morning, the Jews were driven out of their homes and forced to do the most difficult and demeaning tasks. Horrible scenes took place in the Jewish quarters. The bonfire was already burning in New Market Square, and groups of Jews, who were continually bringing Torah scrolls and holy books, were forced to throw them into the fire while singing and reciting prayers. And anyone who wanted to [could] beat the Jews; 10-11 year old little German boys, tugged at elderly Jews and beat them. Moshe Szarkowski was placed on a mattress and was carried around by a group of Jews. He held a Torah scroll in his hands, and when he was brought to the bonfire, he had to toss the Torah into the fire himself. Yona Szwaiger and Mendel Sztajer were driven through Pabianicer [Pabianicka] Street, carrying Torah scrolls in their hands and dressed in their prayer shawls and kittels [solemn white linen robes worn on the High Holidays]. They had been caught praying. They were forced to scream, "Our Patriarch Abraham has abandoned us." Chassidic Jews were lead from somewhere else: Yankel Ber Lieberman, Luzer Szpigelman, and Moshe Stabiecki, the owner of a sawmill, also carrying Torah scrolls. Young German hooligans threw stones at them and pulled their beards. Szaja-Feival Jaskowicz was forced to rake the fire with his bare hands. After he had fainted, he was carried home with serious burns on his hands. Such scenes were played out until nightfall.

On the 15th of September 1939, Pastor Gerhardt was appointed mayor by the German military government and Otto Fray as his representative. The latter was also the police commissioner. The first ruling that they issued was that Jews could not walk on the sidewalks. On the 5th of November 1939, these same newly-appointed officials ruled that every Jew over the age of ten had to wear a white insignia on his sleeve; in addition, Jews could not walk in the streets. They could visit each other between 11 and 12 but even then not via the streets, the back way, through the fields. Jews couldn't buy anything in the market. Jews were forbidden to eat eggs, butter, or meat. They had to make do with what was provided for them by the Judenrat [Jewish Council]. After they wore the white armbands for 3 weeks, the ordinance was issued that they had to wear yellow patches. In November, the ruling also came out forbidding Jews to wear beards, [and] Jews were not allowed to pray in public places. The year 1939 ended with a law about forced labor. In the official German document dated the 20th of December, the Division Head of Piotrkow, who was also the Mayor of Belchatow (Belchatow was not yet considered part of the Reich) was ordered to institute forced labor in his city and to notify the Judenrat that they would be held responsible for any infractions of this law, and every failure to carry out this law was to be reported to the Division Head by the Mayor, in a special report. What this "special report" meant was not difficult to imagine.

On the 1st of January 1940, a law was issued by the Head of the S. S. Police of the General Gouvernement of the occupied Polish territories, Colonel Krieger, that the Jews of Belchatow were not permitted to move and that from 9 o'clock at night until 5 o'clock in the morning they were forbidden to leave their homes.

This is the sad tightrope that the Belchatow Jews had to walk during the first four months of the war.

———

The number of Jews in Belchatow during the time of the German occupation kept on changing. In general, during the first few months of the war until the ghettos were established, the Jews were constantly changing their residences, moving from one place to another. Later on, in Belchatow there were special local events that helped to strengthen the wandering process, namely that Belchatow was located on the border of the so-called

"General Gouvernement" [the German administrative district during the occupation of Poland east of Lodz, which did not become part of the German Reich,] and the "Warte-Land" [Warthegau, the German administrative district in which Lodz was situated], which was part of the German Reich. In the first 3 months of the war, the indigenous Jewish population decreased a thousand percent. Some of them, especially the young people, escaped to the Soviet Union; some escaped to other directions. Some ran to Piotrkow, some to Lodz and other cities, although things were not much better there. Some had to leave, because the German police were looking for them due to their political activities before the war. The local Germans had, even before the war, prepared a list of those people whom they thought should be arrested. Zalman Pudlowski's wife, Ruchel, and their daughter, Rivka, were horribly beaten by the German gendarmes. Ruchel's hair was torn out, so that she would reveal the location of her husband, the head of the "Bund" in Belchatow.

By the end of 1939, the Jewish population of Belchatow was beginning to increase. Jews from Lodz were coming to Belchatow. Hunger drove them from there. They thought that it would be easier to survive the war in a smaller location. Jews were coming to their relatives. Jews from Pabianice and Zelow were arriving. Approximately the same number came as had previously left. Once the ghettos were established in Lodz and in Pabianice, the moving from one place to another stopped. In March of 1940, the moving process started again for Belchatow Jews. This is explained by the fact that, in March of 1940, Belchatow became part of the German Reich. Belchatow became part of the so-called Warte-Land [Warthegau].

Previously, Belchatow had become part of the so-called General Gouvernement, but the Belchatow Germans worked very hard to ensure that the city would become part of the Reich. They weren't satisfied to belong to the General Gouvernement, which represented the Polish state to a certain extent. Their efforts were crowned with success: Belchatow did indeed become part of the Reich.

In reality, the situation of the Jews in the General Gouvernement wasn't any better than in the Reich, but there was a notable difference in that even the Poles' lives weren't much better. Many Jews were under the illusion that their situation would improve there. It is not possible to say with any accuracy how many Jews left, because no statistical material exists from that time. But according to the opinion of the surviving Belchatow Jews, the number was between 800 and 1,000. People escaped to Piotrkow, because that was the closest town to Belchatow. Jews risked their lives by stealing across the border between the "Reich" and the General Gouvernement, but they did it anyway. When the number of Jews and Poles decreased in Belchatow, the number of Germans, who took their place, increased. According to statistics published by the Germans, there were 1,039 Germans in Belchatow in 1938, and in May of 1941 there were already 1,380, and three months later, in August 1941, that number had grown to 1,450. They came from the destroyed towns of the Reich, which had been bombed by the Allies; they came from the area around Wolyn as well as from the Baltic lands. They were given the nicest residences. The best Jewish businesses were confiscated and given to the Belchatower Germans.

According to official German statistics, there were 5,560 Jews in Belchatow on the first of January 1940, but half a year later, there were 5,050. This is because Jews were beginning to be sent to the Poznan Camps, and from that time on the number of Jews in Belchatow constantly decreased. The numbers did not even increase when the Jews from Kleszczow, Grocholice, Lenkawa, Dobrzelow, and other towns arrived. That was in 1941. Of course, there wasn't the natural population increase either.

This is what the Jewish population of Belchatow looked like in 1941.

———

The hygienic and living conditions of the Belchatow Jews were difficult, even though there was no official ghetto in Belchatow. There was a Jewish Quarter in which 90% of the Jews in Belchatow lived. The following streets were in the Jewish Quarter: Pabianicer [Pabianicka], Old Market [Stare Rynek], Ewangelicka, Piotrkower [Piotrkowska], and all of the houses which were located behind the synagogue. Although there were some Jews who lived on other streets, communication between them was limited. The reason the Germans did not establish a ghetto in Belchatow was because, technically, the Germans could not push 6,000 Jews into one place and enclose them there, because all the streets in Belchatow were thoroughfares, which connected the various towns. It was not possible to cut off a main road. The Jewish Quarter was extremely crowded. It shouldn't be forgotten that most of the Jewish houses had been burned down at the beginning of the war, and afterwards, when other people began to arrive, the population was increased by a thousand people. The Germans themselves had to admit that the crowding in the Jewish Quarter was horrendous. As proof we have the following German documents:

On the 24th of November 1941, the State councilor of Lask asked Mayor Trahner of Belchatow to make room in Belchatow for 2,000 Jews, who were going to be deported from Pabianice. The mayor responded that it was impossible to absorb any more Jews; as it was there was the threat of a typhus epidemic due to overcrowding. He suggested three alternatives: 1) that part of New Market Square be added to the Jewish Quarter, which would permit 1,500 more Jews to be absorbed, but the negative side of this plan was that some to the nicest houses in the city would become part of the Jewish Quarter; 2) that it was also possible that Szczercower Street be annexed to the Jewish Quarter via the fields, but the danger here was that the Jews would then be too connected to the outside world. The third alternative was to build barracks for the new arrivals inside the Jewish Quarter.

In addition to the already difficult conditions in the Jewish Quarter, the Germans continued to confiscate the nicest houses for newly arrived Germans. Then the [displaced] Jews had to leave everything that was in the house. The Judenrat was supposed to provide those Jews who had to leave their houses with other living quarters.

In a German document dated the 4th of April 1940, Belchatower Mayor Trahner gave the following Jews, David Szmulewicz and Shimon Eliezer Wolfowicz, who lived on Pabianicer Street, three days to leave their homes, which were needed for German officials. In another document, dated the 10th of December 1940, the Judenrat was notified that Motl Gelbart, who lived in one room and a kitchen at 27 Pabianicer Street, was to immediately make his residence available to the German Waldemar Gutknecht. It is clear that the hygienic conditions in such crowded circumstances were not of the best. Nevertheless, even under these conditions, Jews tried to keep their homes and even the streets clean in the Jewish Quarter.

The Jewish population in Belchatow, which had suffered so much right from the early days of the war, did not lose hope, did not lose its courage. The majority of the inhabitants, especially the proletariat, did everything they could to avoid emotional collapse, something which the Germans were especially interested in seeing happen.

The [former] vibrant social life was not as visible; [but it didn't disappear,] it went underground. In the underground, there existed almost all of the social groups that had existed before the war. The first job of those Jews who had returned from their "journeys" right after the outbreak of the war was to see that the over 300 families whose houses had burned down had a roof over their

heads and clothes to wear. An assistance committee was immediately created, which included people who had had social-work experience before the war. On this committee were: Henech Pigula (who later died in Chelmno), Issachar Przybylski, Lajzer Lewkowicz (Woytls's son), and the lame Goldberszt (all of them later died in Chelmno). In praise of the Jews of Belchatow, it must be said that they responded warmly to the requests of the assistance committee. People shared whatever they had, and all of those who had suffered due to fire were provided with living quarters and all their necessities. In addition, the Jews of Belchatow, ignoring the horrible conditions in which they themselves lived, took food out of their own mouths and even managed to send aid to their relatives in Lodz, who at that time were practically dying of hunger. Thousands of people were dying of hunger in Lodz every month. Typical is the following letter from the Mayor of Belchatow to the State Councilor [Landrat] of Lask. From this letter we can how the Jews of Belchatow made an effort to help their suffering relatives in Lodz. Here is the complete text of the document dated the 17th of May:

Belchatow, the 17th of May 1940

**The Mayor**
Nr 40/2303

To
The State Councilor [*Landrat*]
Of the Lask Region
**In Pabianice**

**Concerning:** The collection of a large number of Jewish packages at the local post office.

The head of the Belchatower Post Office told me today that in the last few days, there is an ever-increasing number of Jewish packages being sent, addressed for the most part, to Litzmannstadt [Lodz].

It is strongly suspected that in these packages to Litzmannstadt, the Jews are sending necessities of life. We (the postal gendarme and I) are not able to check these packages which are delivered to the post office. The post office only permits checking [of packages] when there is an ordinance from the secret municipal police.

I request, please, if the State Councilor feels that such checking is required, that he contact the secret municipal police about this matter.

I further bring to your attention that the Jews are providing large sums of copper coins (*groschens*). The value of *groschen* today is the same as a pfennig. In this transaction – groschen equal to pfennig, the Jew sees [a bit of] good business and is therefore exchanging the copper coins, which he has thus far hidden.

If the State Councilor should receive instructions from the secret municipal police that checking is possible, I ask that he let me know.

At this time, I permit myself to call attention to the fact that there is a lot of counterfeit money of 2 and 5 marks around. In many cases they have been confiscated.

Perhaps a notice concerning the circulation of counterfeit money would be useful.

> The Mayor
> and Department Commissioner [*Amtskommissar*]
> **Trahner**

> The circular seal:
> **The Mayor of the city of Belchatow**

From the letters that the Jews of Belchatow received from their relatives in Lodz it appears that the Germans confiscated all of the packages anyway. At the beginning of 1942, the post office of Belchatow received official permission from the Mail Minister to detain all the Jewish packages, until the Mail Minister could make a determination concerning this question.

There were also various political party groups active in Belchatow. There was a Bund group, a Communist group, and Poalei Emunei-Yisrael [a religious Zionist Socialist party]. There was stable cooperation between the Bundist and Communist groups. From time to time there would be cooperative meetings with the Bundist, the Communist, and the Poalei Emunei-Yisrael groups. At these meetings, the Bundists were represented by Issachar Przybylski, Gedalia Sztajn (who died in Chelmno), Avraham Binem Sztajn (now in America), [and] Herzkowicz. The Communists were represented by Henech Pigula, Shimon Szmulewicz (who died in Auschwitz), [and] Chaim David Kaufman (who died in the Poznan Camp).

At these meetings, questions of how to help themselves were considered, [such as] the institution of a soup kitchen for the poor. The question of how to set up the illegal schools was discussed. Also discussed were cases of abuse and occurrences of stealing at the Judenrat, since it appeared that some of the money, which had been paid into the treasury of the Jews-Council by Jews buying their way out of forced labor, had disappeared. The Poalei Emunei-Yisrael group was represented by Yitzhak Pigula, a leading member since before the war. A Beis-Yakov group existed, led by Hinde Jakubowicz and Miss Joskowicz.

In the summer of 1941 a demonstration was organized by the Bundists, the Communists and the Poalei Emunei groups against the machinations of the Judenrat. Several hundred people took part in this demonstration.

In 1940, three illegal schools existed in Belchatow; one was organized by the Communist group. Surcze [Surche, diminutive for Sara/Sura] Sztatlender taught there. In 1942, during the resettlements, she was sent to Lodz. From the Lodz Ghetto she was sent away to Czestochowa in "HASAG" [Hugo Schneider Aktiengesellschaft, a privately owned German armaments company that used camp inmates as forced labor], and she died there. Zalmen Bilz also taught there. Ruchel Pudlowski and Dina Winer taught in the Bundist school. Both schools taught Yiddish, Polish, and Jewish History. The children were taught the works of Jewish writers. Poalei Emunei Yisrael also offered courses, but it difficult now to be certain who the teachers there were. And there was also a cheder [Jewish religious school]. There were also secret libraries. Right at the beginning of the war, Mendel Kaufman, risking his life, carried out the books from the Bundist library and hid them. Itche Lejb Goldberszt had a secret library in his house. The place in the Jewish Quarter where Jews used to gather was behind the synagogue, where Yankel Warszawski's houses were. There painful questions were discussed. The front was discussed. Some cheered up those who were there with letters they had received from Russia, saying that soon "Aunt Ruzha" would arrive. That's where they took anything that they had to sell. From time to time, the police showed up and crippled anyone who didn't manage to escape in time. Especially sadistic was the gendarme Rempl. Whatever social life there was completely withered in 1941, when the German-Soviet War began. The terror increased even more. People were afraid to get together. The deportations began. At first only the men were deported. The barely extant social life that had been there died completely. The schools were closed, because the parents were afraid to send their children to the schools.

———

As was already mentioned above, all sources of livelihood had been taken from the Jews. The factories and the businesses had been confiscated. The tradesmen were not allowed to work in their workshops; their machines were taken away. The Jews couldn't enter the textile factories that the Germans had taken from the Jews. Jews were caught and sent to do forced labor and paid in beatings. Due to the severity of their lives, the problem was – how does one survive? The 30 deca [10 grams] of bread, which were doled out by the Judenrat, without any fat or any other food, were not enough to live on and not little enough to kill. The Jews were left no choice other than to do such jobs at which they risked their lives. And this did indeed cost many human lives. During the dark of night, Jews stole into the village to get some potatoes. If someone was caught doing this, he was either shot, or – in the best scenario – so severely whipped that he would remember it for a long time. But nevertheless, the smuggling continued. Smuggling and illegal dealings grew, because between Belchatow and Piotrkow was the border between the German Reich and the General Gouvernement. Textiles were smuggled out of Belchatow, and leather and other articles were brought in. The persons engaged in this knew that their lives were in danger, but they had no other choice. Starvation forced them into it. The majority of their earning they had to give to the bribed gendarmes. They were dealing with all kinds of extortionists and blackmailers. They too had to be cut in. The Jewish police, Shmuel Jakubowicz's gang, also had to be bribed. Then a battle started between the richer and the poorer smugglers. The wealthier smugglers, who had the greater wherewithal with which to bribe the gendarmes, helped to liquidate the poorer ones. The smuggling took place only at night after police hours. They took a sack or a backpack on their shoulders and, with careful steps, slipped through the fields and meadows to the border. Others would be waiting to get the merchandise from them, Jews or Christians from Piotrkow and surrounding areas. Also waiting for them were German border guards with bloodhounds.

In June 1941, the Commandant of the Security Police announced to the mayor that, on Zelower Road, he had intercepted a wagon with merchandise and had arrested the Jews Avraham Berkowicz and Shmuel Goldberg. In the majority of cases, such an arrest meant certain death. This was certainly the case in the situation mentioned above, when the gendarme was unable to take the goods for himself, which was certainly noted from the sidelines and but couldn't be reported. Moshe Stabiecki, the baker, was chased 5 kilometers by two security policemen. He had contraband goods. They chased him until he jumped into a river. They left him there, having convinced themselves that he had drowned. He, however, succeed in saving himself. The gendarmes tortured [Lajbish] Melot, the butcher, to death. They poured a liter of denaturat [denatured alcohol not for consumption] down his throat. Avraham Nafelyan was also tortured to death. He had been caught with smuggled goods on the road to Szczercow. The following were shot: Yankel Rosental, Lozer Szpigelman's son, the butcher Machabanski, and his son. Another report by the Security Police describes a serious crime committed by Jews: 100 kilo potatoes were found in possession of Jews who were in forced-labor near the road. The police confiscated the potatoes and sold them to the Germans for 2 marks a kilo.

The Jews sold all of their possessions to be able to buy a piece of bread. If ever a peasant had put himself at risk to obtain a piece of bread for a Jew, he asked to be well compensated. There were also, however, known cases where peasants brought their Jewish acquaintances food and did not want to accept any payment.

The Jews in Belchatow tried different ways, tricks, and methods to keep themselves alive. Their instincts led them to various means of finding a bit of sustenance for themselves, their wives, and children.

———

In Belchatow as in other cities, the Germans set up factories and workshops where Jewish workers had to work. They labored in these workshops from sun-up to sundown, expending their last ounce of energy with nothing in their bellies. Anyone who refused to toil in these workshops was subject to another fate – deportation to the camps. The largest factory using Jewish labor was the tailors' workshop, which had been established in Dzialowski's factory. The Germans had taken out the looms and replaced them with sewing machines, which were owned by Jewish tailors or had been found in Jewish homes. Six hundred and fifty Jewish workers were employed in the tailors' workshop. Szlama Jakubowicz was named technical overseer. The real manager appointed by the Germans was Alfred August, a sociopath and a sadist. He would beat someone half to death for the slightest infraction. The reason which made it possible for him to occupy such a position was that he had divorced his Polish wife, and during Polish times the Poles broke his hands when they suspected him of spying for the Germans. When the Germans entered Poland, they appointed him mayor of Grocholice. It was there that he earned a reputation for his sadistic acts. His [constant] scoffing at the civilian population went so far that the Germans themselves were forced to remove him from this position. And it was this thug that the Jews got as head of the tailors' workshop. There was also a shoemakers' workshop with 50 workers. The shoemaker's shop was located in Hersh David Szwarcberg's house. A carpenters' workshop was already in existence, run by Itche Winter. In addition, there was a factory which produced things made of straw. The number of Jews officially employed in all of these workshops is estimated to be more than 1,000. These workers were the worst off economically, since they had no time to earn anything on the side. The only food that the workers received consisted of 30 decas [10 grams] of bread in a soup, which was doled out to them from the kitchen in the Judenrat. After this, the Judenrat established 2-3 kitchens, which served 1, 200 lunches. The people didn't receive any fuel, so they sat with their wives and children in the unheated rooms. For water, they had to go from Pabianicer Street to Old Market Square [Stare Rynek]. "Zalman Pudlowski's pump" broke down. Because of a lack of fuel, the bath house was not used, and if someone became ill, he had to wait several days for medicine, because people were allowed to go to the pharmacy only one hour during the day. There was no hospital. There were practically no doctors either. Dr. Jakubowicz went to Piotrkow and played a shameful role there. He collaborated with the Gestapo. He sent hundreds of people to the crematoriums, among them many Belchatowers. In 1939, Dr. Payewski was taken into the Polish Army and never returned. He probably died in a German prisoner of war camp. The non-Jewish doctors were not allowed to treat Jews. There were Jewish doctors in Belchatow: [one of them was] Dr. Basier, one of Josef Lejb's sons-in-law. He later died in Chelmno. There was another Jewish doctor from Warsaw, whose name was Tifenberg. One of them had been appointed to treat Jews as early as 1942, when the typhus epidemic broke out in Belchatow. At that time, the Mayor requested permission of the Land Council for a Jewish physician, Dr. Hart of Wlodzimierzow, to come to Belchatow. He said that his request was motivated by his not wanting non-Jewish doctors to examine Jewish typhus patients, because they might infect non-Jews with the disease. At the beginning of 1942, even Jewish doctors were forbidden to practice. Their instruments were confiscated and given to Germans. And under such conditions, the Germans demanded that all hygienic measures be taken, after having done everything to make it impossible to do so. Of course, the Jewish population's health deteriorated greatly, due to hard work and unsanitary conditions. People began to die in droves. Many suffered from lung disease. Many of the older people died of exhaustion. The small number of children who were born at that time had rickets. Of course, the first to suffer were the Jewish poor and, along with them, those who toiled in the workshops and in the factories.

———

The role that the Judenrat played in Belchatow during the German occupation was the same in all the cities of Poland: they obediently fulfilled all the German commands and even, in certain cases, collaborated. Often, they voluntarily told the German officials and the Gestapo what was going on among the Jews. The majority of those in the Judenrat and the Jewish police were people with no integrity, who sought a way to make a living by selling out the impoverished masses.

For the bone that the Germans threw them, they did the dirtiest jobs, helping to liquidate even their own families. It is true that among them there were some who would not have been in the Judenrat if they had not been forced to do so. But there were also those who didn't care what kind of mission they carried out. In Belchatow's social life, such people as Shmuel Jakubowicz and his ilk would never have attained any prominence. Any efforts they may have made before the war to attain social positions in Belchatow did not meet with any success. The culturally developed Jewish population of Belchatow always decimated their power. Only under Nazi occupation were they able to get a leg to stand on. It is not by chance that when Ehrlich later went to the gallows, he tried to find merit in the eyes of the Germans by reminding them that even during the First World War, he had made money for the German occupying powers.

Immediately after the Germans marched into Belchatow, a Jewish "delegation," not empowered by anyone, approached the German military commandant to request permission to bake bread for the Jews. This "delegation" consisted of M. Jakubowicz, Shmuel Jakubowicz and Yankel Ehrlich. Their main motivation was not to help the Jewish population but to ingratiate themselves with the Germans and to receive from them permission to dominate the Jews. Their later actions entirely confirmed these intentions. They received from the commandant a mandate to form the Judenrat and to provide the necessary personnel for the work in the Judenrat, according to their own vision. They conscripted people from all over for the Judenrat in order to make the impression that all of Jewish society was represented there. Those whom they approached to be on the Judenrat found themselves in a difficult situation: refusing might carry with it serious consequences. So they had to agree. his is how the following came to belong to the first Judenrat that had already been formed in September 1939: Michal Jakubowicz as Chairman, Shmuel Jakubowicz as Vice-Chairman, Yankel Ehrlich as Secretary, and Aron Liberman, Issachar Przybylski, Binem Hendeles, [and] Melech Galster as members of the managerial board.

The real power lay only in the hands of the first three. The Judenrat did not have any special activities. It was thoroughly corroded by corruption and abuse. It was hated by the Jewish population. They feared the members of the Judenrat. With their actions, they created a net of intrigue around the Judenrat.

There were those who conspired to depose the Judenrat leaders. They were the ones who were upset that they hadn't been selected. The Mizrachi activists, Sholom Feder and Mendel Lipman turned against the Judenrat using both legal and illegal means. If Shmuel Jakubowicz and his clique had on their side the police and the Gestapo, with whom they made mutual deals, Sholom Feder's and Mendel Lipman's group had the Mayor on their side. These activists, known as communal workers from before the war, now got involved in such an ugly thing; they explained, first of all, that they were enraged that their group was not represented in the Judenrat. It is, however, also possible that they sought to eliminate the thievery and the corruption in the Judenrat, but the means that they used toward this end were, unfortunately, not entirely respectable. Let the facts speak for themselves.

On the 18th of October, the Mayor announced that Michal Jakubowicz, Shmuel Jakubowicz, and Yankel Ehrlich must be removed from the Judenrat and replaced by Sholom Feder and Mendel Lipman, Shamai Grinberg, Melech Galster, and Issachar Przybylski. The two last mentioned were from the old Judenrat and remained. They had not taken part in any of the disputes of the clique. That Sholom Feder and his people did not use completely straight means is evidenced by the fact that a month after Shmuel Jakubowicz was removed from the Judenrat, he was arrested. The police did this at the behest of the Mayor. They accused Jakubowicz of being in cahoots with the smuggling gangs, of having also been in jail for six months before the war, and of forging artisans' cards. Of course, the Mayor could not have found out all of this by himself. This was a piece of work done by those who had taken Shmuel Jakubowicz's place on the Judenrat. Shmuel Jakubowicz also did not take this lying down. On the 20th of October 1940, two days after the new Judenrat took over, the Mayor gave Shmuel Jakubowicz notice that if he didn't stop slandering the new Judenrat, he would incur dire consequences.

Here is the actual text of that document:

### "To the Jew Shmuel Jakubowicz, barber in Belchatow:

I am letting you know that the strongest means will be used against you and against other former members of the Judenrat, if you will not stop [spreading] your lies and agitating against the work of the newly formed Judenrat, for which you want to create difficulties. Rest assured that this can have the direst consequences."

**(---) Trahner**

20<sup>th</sup> October 1940

On the 21<sup>st</sup> of October the head of the Judenrat, Sholom Feder, was arrested along with Mendel Lipman and Yechiel Marczak. All three were sent to Lodz. There the Gestapo accused them of belonging to the illegal Zionist organization. They were accused of giving anti-Hitler speeches. They were even told the title of the given speech. It was supposedly called: "Thoughts about Hitlerism".

The Jewish population had no idea that any of this was happening. All of this happened in the offices of the Gestapo and the Mayor. In the Gestapo in Lodz, it seems that they were convinced that these accusations were groundless. It could be that they asked the Mayor of Belchatow. The fact is that all three were once again freed. The lawyer, [Yitzkak] Bogdanski, Avraham Laskowski's son-in-law, who came from Piotrkow, was confirmed in the place of Sholom Feder as Chairman of the Belchatower Judenrat. He was the Chairman of the Judenrat until the 21<sup>st</sup> of July 1941. His term in office was, perhaps, the quietest time that the Belchatow Jews had under the German occupation. We don't know a lot of details about that time. It is only known that, in Bogdanski's time, the kitchens were set up. He also tried to improve the hygienic conditions for the Jewish population. Whatever reasons arose for removing Bogdanski from office were not real. We can only imagine that it was a bit of underhanded work, because the already familiar Yankel Ehrlich was confirmed in his place as Chairman. Peretz Altman and Itche Winter were confirmed for the Judenrat along with Yankel Ehrlich. All three were not very popular figures among the Jews of Belchatow. In the Mayor's announcement the function of each member of the Judenrat was precisely indicated.

According to a document that was found, the offices were apportioned in this way: president – Yankel Ehrlich, his two assistants: Peretz Altman and Itche Winter. For the other members of the Judenrat, he suggests the following work divisions: employment: Szlama-Hersh Topolewicz; social services: Binem Hendeles; bread allotting: Mendel Lipman; food distribution: David Pakertreger; milk allotting: Moshe Pakertreger; treasurer: Beryl Zuchowski.

The Judenrat aided the German government in a series of actions against the Belchatower Jews. This was in the effort to deport Jews to the camps in

Poznan in August 1941, as well as creating a list of very sick people, who were also deported.

It could be that one of the things that led to changes in the Judenrat was the fact that the Mayor wanted to have as many of his own people there as possible. It is, perhaps, also not by chance that Issachar Przybylski and others left the Judenrat. Peretz Altman started a business, taking 500 marks from someone not to send him to the camps. Of course, this discriminated against the poor, because those who couldn't pay were sent out [to the camps]. On the 24th of September, the make up of the Judenrat changed again. The star of President Yankel Ehrlich was extinguished. In his place, the lawyer Bogdanski was once again installed.

The Judenrat consisted of 9 people. In addition, 12 officers were appointed to various positions, and [there were] 8 errand boys. The following is a list of the positions of the Judenrat at that time and those who held them:

Chairman: **Itzik Bogdanski**, his two co-chairmen: **Itche Winter** and **Peretz Altman;** workshop department: **Moshe Klug**; finance department: **Meyer Feder**; food distribution: **Avraham Weintraub**; social welfare: **Yankel Machabanski**; employment department: **Mendel Sapirsztajn**; person responsible for the sewing factory: **Szlama Szmulewicz**. The offices were: technical secretary: **Josef Lejb Gelbard**; evidence: **Regina Galster**; in the workshop department: **Moshe Wolf Starowinski**; social management: **Ziskind Klug**; means of life apportionement: **Szaja Zertzl** and **Hertz Lejb**; treasurer: **Avraham Szmulewicz**; work department: **Moshe Buchman**; mail department: **Szlama Gnatik**; bread apportionment: **Aharon Lieberman**; in the kitchens: **Ezra Stabiecki** and **Chana Rozenberg**; the messenger boys were: **Daniel Gerst, Avraham Alter Goldberg, Itzik Sztern, Meyer Szymkowicz, Moshe Baum, Motel Gelbard, Berish Piula, Itzik Handelsman.**

In the new Judenrat, exactly as in the previous one, the first three had all the power. The others were no more than figureheads.

In April of 1942, at the time of the "barricade," when the whole city was surrounded by the Gestapo and the Jews of Belchatow thought that their end had come, the president if the Judenrat tried to escape to Piotrkow. He had an agreement with a German driver, who, for a large sum of money, was supposed to drive him to Piotrkow. But instead of Piotrkow, he drove him and his whole family to the police. From the police station, they were taken to the prison with the worst reputation, Radogoszcz Prison, where they were all killed. Those killed were: Avraham Laskowski, his wife and all of their children, his son-in-law, [and] the president of the Judenrat, Itzik Bogdanski.

In Bogdanski's place as president of the Judenrat, Szlama Hersh Topolowicz was confirmed.

On the eve of the liquidation, Topolowicz was shot upon order of the mayor, who was taking revenge on him.

The other members of the Judenrat, who remained until the end, assisted the Germans in the liquidation of the Jews of Belchatow.

————

The role of the Jewish Police in Belchatow was absolutely no different than the role of the police in other occupied cities. The Jewish police obediently fulfilled all the German decrees.

The Jewish Police in Belchatow was created and confirmed by the German government on the 15th of October 1940. A young criminal element found its way into the Jewish police, which blackmailed the smugglers, and squeezed sums of money out of the Jews by beatings, persecution, and the like. Also to be found in the Jewish police were young citizens, who had the money to bribe the individual members of the Jewish police. From [others'] misfortunes, they made an easy living for themselves and wangled their way out of forced labor camps. These were people with weak moral resistance and who, of course, did everything precisely as the German government told them to. Among the Jewish policemen, there were almost no proletarian elements, except for someone like Note Szpigelman, who, even before the war, had been thrown out of the proletarian ranks for embezzlement. The Jewish police in Belchatow consisted of 33 persons. These are their names: Yisroel Baum; Avraham Bogdanski; Hershl Bram; Yakov Galetski; Yechiel Fishl Dichtwald; Leybish Zuchowski; Szame Grinberg (who for a certain time was also on the Judenrat); Avraham Meyer Goldberg (khmal [?]); Moshe Goldblum; Shimon; Josef Goldberg; Hershel Jakubowicz; Moshe Klug (who was also a member in the Judenrat); Yankel Lipszyc; Moshe Mendel Lipman; Fishl Levi; Kive Lipmanowicz; Yakov-Mendel Lejb; Tuvia Machabanski; Yitzhak Miller; Wolf Przemyslawski; Lejb Rozencwajg; Itzik Sztrauch; Note Szpigelman; Moshe

Wielniwicz; Itik Wishniewski; Henoch Zuchowski; Ber Markowicz; Melech Galster (also a member of the Judenrat); and Berish Grinberg. The latter was the wagon worker in the Poznan Camp and distinguished himself by beating the Jews and taking their food away from them. In addition there were: Jakob Sztern, Mendel Dzialowski, and Berish Piula. The latter, along with his brother, played a shameful part in the Poznan Camps. He was a camp "kapo" and beat [the Jews] black and blue. Many Jews became crippled because of him. He was responsible for the deaths of many people, who were sent to the crematoria because of him. The Belchatower police distinguished itself by assisting the Germans in the rounding up of Jews in the aktsion [action] of April, 1942. Together with the Germans, they went down into the cellars and up into the attics to search for hidden Jews. At that time, they succeeded in dragging another 400 Jews out of their hiding places. These Jews were sent out to be liquidated.

The Judenrat also helped in this evacuation.

But it didn't help the scoundrels themselves, because they also could not escape their fate, [the same fate] that awaited the Jews of Belchatow.

---

In the beginning, when the Germans first arrived in Belchatow, all the positions were filled with Folk-Germans, [Volks-Deutschen, ethnic Germans living outside of Germany], the majority of the local population. They filled the positions in the city administration, in the police force, and as commissars over Jewish fortunes. In time, however, Reich-Germans [Reichs-Deutschen] took their places.

In March 1940, the Germans replaced the local mayor, Pastor Gerhardt, with the Reich-German Trahner, an old member of the National-Socialist Party. He was the real liquidator of the Belchatow Jews. He strictly obeyed all the anti-Jewish ordinances, and not only those that were ordered by his superior, but he himself added many things that helped make it so that a large part of the Jewish fortunes should wind up in his own possession. Soon after Pastor Gerhardt was removed from his position as Mayor, he was accused of "sympathizing" with the Jews. The German government accused him of protecting Jews. As proof they showed the State Councilor [that] the Pastor asked the commissar of the tailor's factory, August, about hiring the Jews, Idel Lejb and Lipman Waloszczowski.

Here are a few sample documents concerning this matter:

To
**Herr Commissioner August**

If it is possible, employ Chil Walosczowski and Litman [sic] Walosczowski.

7/12, 1940
Heil Hitler
**Gerhardt**

To Herr Commissioner
**August**

Here

If it is possible? . . . as a worker Yudel Lejb?. . . who will surely do his work for the future for his superiors.

Belchatow, the 4th / 1/ 1941
Gerhardt

——0——

Belchatow, the 5th January 1941

**To Herr**
**Pastor Gerhardt**
**Belchatow**

The manager of the Jewish tailor's workshop has received several notes from you in which you recommend or ask that Jews be hired in the Jewish tailor shop.

I must, therefore, make you aware that you, via these recommendations, are in danger of being considered as a friend of the Jews. It might perhaps be necessary to advise you as someone in a prominent position and as a German to show more restraint.

**The Mayor**
**And Department Commissioner**
Trahner

It is difficult to determine whether Pastor Gerhardt was indeed that friendly to Jews as it appears in these documents. The fact is that Pastor Gerhardt was the founder of the National-Socialist Party in Belchatow and the founder of the German Choral Society as well as the German Sports Club before the war, both of which were Nazi nests. The fact is also that the Germans appointed him Mayor as soon as they entered the city; and the most convincing fact is that during his term of office, he never reacted to the terrible anti-Semitic acts that the Folk-Germans committed.

The case against Pastor Gerhardt shows the various mini-intrigues among the Germans – one German pitted against another.

It is worthwhile here to mention a case in which a German was victimized because his father was sympathetic to Jews; they were the German weaver Pyetrik and his wife.

Both of them belonged to the Baptist sect. They helped both Jews and Christians in any way they could. Quietly, they carried food to the houses of the poor. They conveyed news from the fronts; they agitated against Hitlerism; they openly said that the anti-Christ, Hitler, must be defeated. That is why in 1944 they were sent to the concentration camp Dara [?]. [And] the possessions of the Pyetriks were confiscated.

––––––––––

From the very first day he took office, the new mayor showed that he was capable of doing the job. He immediately threw the Jews out of the best residences and watched over not only his own city but neighboring cities as well. In one of his letters to the mayor of Zelow, he asks if it is true that the two Breitsztajn brothers were part of the football [soccer] team of the German sports club in Zelow.

He was interested in every triviality. He was doing his utmost to please his superiors, and one way to please was to persecute Jews even more. And nevertheless, even against him infractions vis a vis Jews were found, that is, leniencies, insufficient brutality. On the 20th of November 1940, the Commissar of Lodz came to the mayor of Belchatow, Trahner, and demanded that he explain several things about the relationship of the Germans to the Jews of Belchatow. Here is the complete text of the "crimes" that the Jews of Belchatow were committing against the German Reich:

"I found out from a confidential source about the following situation, which exists in Belchatow: one Jew was given the responsibility to buy poultry from a Folk-German who had the poultry concession. Some of the poultry were slaughtered and sold to Jews.

Until today there are one or two Jews who have their own wagons.

In your security police there are employed Jewish women, and they are permitted, after the security police [do so], to bathe in the same bathtubs in which Germans bathe.

I ask that you confirm if these things are correct and to report back to me as soon as possible."

According to the Mayor's answer we can see that only one of the above-mentioned "crimes" is correct. It seems that the Jewish woman, Langnas, had indeed bathed in the same bathtub as the Germans, but she had already been fired.

Regarding the wagon, that is, the horse and wagon, which belonged to a Jew, it turned out that according to the announcement of the Mayor of Belchatow, that the Jew with the horse and wagon was carrying the wood of the disassembled synagogue, and it was immediately confirmed that as soon as the Jew was finished with this job, the horse would be given to a Folk-German, but no one wanted to take it, because the horse was not worth the feed. It was an old and sick horse ...

As soon as Trahner took over the office of Mayor, there began, in Belchatow, the legal, official plundering of Jewish property. The Jews were made to furnish the residences of the arriving German officers. There are documents, official requests to the Judenrat. In a document dated the 20th of January 1941, from the Head Commissar of the city of Belchatow, the following is said:

**"To the Elders of the Jewish Community in Belchatow:**

The Gendarme of Belchatow, Gen. Litzman-Gas, needs various kitchen tools for his kitchen. You must be in contact with the head of his kitchen in order to take care of this.

Mayor and Department Commissioner
**Trahner ["]**

Or another document dated the 25th of January 1941:

**To the Belchatow Judenrat:**

Please deliver to the police department, [which is] under the leadership of Commandant Fisher, mattresses for sleeping.

Mayor: **Trahner**

There are also documents, which speak of delivering [Jewish] possessions via the Germans which were demanded by the police.

It says in a document dated the 12th of February 1941 that the peasant, Rudolph Kiel, must deliver to the magistrate the velvet blankets that he took from the Jew Jakubowicz. Among the documents of the same month, there is also a letter from the Police Commandant to the Mayor:

"This past month I delivered a full list of the thinin my possession. I behaved in the way that you, Herr Mayor, desired of me. I gathered all of these things, which were almost lost to private ownership that various people had taken for themselves. In so doing, I myself suffered a great loss: I was ordered to sell my own things, which were at my mother's house in Pabianice, and sent her others. Some of my things I gave to my acquaintances. Two sets of beds, with your knowledge, I exchanged with Jews. Is it possible to buy these things? You ask for my advice as to what to do now so that as an officer I should not suffer any losses because of the Poles and the Jews, who hate me. In addition, I would like to let you know that various people still have certain things, things that were taken from the Jews illegally. I beg of you not to believe everything that you will hear about me. There are a lot of people, who hate me. I stand before them with a clear conscience. The truth can be brought out into the light. I am someone, who has done everything for you and am ready to continue to do everything. I ask that you not deny my request; otherwise, I might think that I am being treated worse than the enemies of the German Reich."

In a document dated the 2ⁿᵈ of January 1941, there is an order from the Mayor that Jews should deliver a closet for the leader of the Hitler youth, Jansen. On the 20ᵗʰ of November 1941, the Mayor gives the Police Commandant Bloch permission to confiscate a clothing closet and a mirror from the Jew, Hershel Granek. Worse were the decrees by the Mayor, which made the Jews' lives more difficult. He completely forbade communication among the Jews. This detail made the conditions of the Jews of Belchatow worse than those of the Jews in the ghetto. The latter could at least move freely within the bounds of the ghetto. Here [in Belchatow] the desire to visit another Jew, to walk from one house to another meant risking one's life. If on the way, one happened to meet a German or a policeman, it could even cost one his life. In the best case, one could escape with only a bad beating or by bribing them with large sums of money.

Until the 18ᵗʰ of February, the Jewish policemen could still move about the streets freely. After that date, it was forbidden for even Jewish policemen to move about in the so-called "curfew hours." The German police were ordered to watch carefully, and any Jew who was caught in the street during the "curfew hours" was to be severely punished. The "curfew hours" were all day. Jews were permitted to walk in the street for only one hour a day. And even this hour was fraught with difficulty. One had to be careful not to go out a minute earlier or stay out a minute later.

Pursuant to a decree by the Mayor, on the 10ᵗʰ of June 1941, all Jewish religious books and religious articles were to be gathered for the German Eastern-Institute for research into the Jewish question.

On the 10ᵗʰ of June 1941, the Mayor of Belchatow announced to the Land Office of the Lask District in Pabianice that he had finished the collection.

With this collection, the first period of persecution of the Belchatow Jews ended. Then the second period starts, the worst one: the Liquidation.

———

With the outbreak of the German-Soviet War, the German administration received an order to intensify the course of action they were taking regarding the Jews. Raids and requisitions start once again. The Jews of Belchatow felt that something was hanging over their heads. They became even more frightened of meeting one another. Victims were killed arbitrarily. All movement stopped in the Jewish quarter. Cultural work ended completely; the illegal schools closed down, because the parents were afraid to let a child out on the street. Suddenly the Germans began to tamper with the political rectitude of a whole slew of people, both Jews and Poles. On the 1st of August 1941, the Land Office in Pabianice sent a circular to Belchatow concerning the "feeding" of the old and infirm Jews.[2])

———

This German document is the height of cynicism and perfidy, because it didn't take long to be convinced that the abovementioned category of persons [represented] the first victims of the Nazi extermination plan. Soon a second order arrived, which was that it was forbidden to send very sick Jews to the hospital in Lodz. It was decreed that a whole house should be cleared of its Jewish inhabitants and isolated for patients with infectious diseases. The Germans wouldn't tolerate a house with infectious patients in their city unless they knew that this was just a gathering point for a short time; that the people of this house would soon be transported [elsewhere].

94

Der Amtskommiſſar
der Stadt Belchatow
Kreis Lask – Wartheland

Belchatow, den 10. Juni 1941

An den

Herrn L a n d r a t des Kreises L a s k
in F a b i a n i c e .

Tgb.Nr. 2021/41

Betr.: Sammlung jüdischen Schrifttums.

Vorgang: T/X. von 31.V.41

Die Sammlung jüdischen Schrifttums wurde durchgeführt.
Es kommen zur Ablieferung:

1)    Talmud – jüdische Bibel
2)    Hammerle – Gebetsbuch für Sabbat
3)    Simmerle – Gebetsbuch für tägliche Gebete
4)    Schriftrollen auf Schweinsleder
5)    1 Säckchen mit Gebetsklötzen
6)    1 Schultertuch – das jeder betende Jude beim Gebet

trägt. Die aufgezählten Gegenstände werden der Kreisleitung
zugeführt.

Der Amtskommissar:

---

Der Amtskommissar
der Stadt Belchatow

Kreis Lask
(Wartheland)
—

BELCHATOW, den  7. August 1941

An den

Herrn L a n d r a t des Kreises L a s k
in F a b i a n i c e .

Tgb.Nr. 3586/41

Betr.: Unterbringung gebrechlicher und kranker Juden.

Abt. Nr. St./XX.

In Erledigung der Anfrage vom 1.VIII.1941 über ge-
brechliche und kranke Juden melde ich für die Stadt Belchatow
nachfolgend aufgeführte Namen:

1)    Schwarzberg Tojvia, Hindenburgplatz 3
2)    Wojdyslawski Chuma, Evangelischestr. 4
3)    Landau Sara, Litzmannstädterstr. 18
4)    Goldstein Icek, Freiheitsplatz 13
5)    Goldberg Schymon, Breslauerstr...7
6)    Freimann Icek, Evangelischestr. 4
7)    Kraspicka Sura Rojza, Evangelischestr. 13
8)    Steppnicka Sura Rachla, Horst Wesselstr.24
9)    Kalmann Majnysch, Horst Wesselstr. 31
10)   Warschawski Schlama D. Adolf Hitlerstr. 7
11)   Spiegelmann Israel, Litzmannstädterstr. 11
12)   Berekowicz Ryven, Litzmannstädterstr. 8
13)   Piaskowski Mecha, Horst Wesselstr. 25
14)   Przybylski Israel Gerszon, Freiheitsplatz 9
15)   Bahn Chaskiel, Horst Wesselstr. 20
16)   Samelwicz Estera Rachla, Litzmannstädterstr.43
17)   Swarzbard Rafael, Evangelischestr. 4
18)   Xing Benjamin, Evangelischestr. 7

Der Amtskommissar:

As early as the 7th of August, the Commissar of the Land Office in Pabianice announced a whole list of infirm and crippled, which had been sent to him by the Belchatow Judenrat.

This document is as follows:

**"In connection with the request of the 1st of August 1941 concerning the infirm and crippled Jews residing in Belchatow, I send you the following list:**

1. Szwarcberg Tovah, Hindenberg Place 5
2. Wojdyslawski Chana, Evangelishe [Ewangelicka] Street 4
3. Landau Sura, Litzmannstadt Street 18
4. Goldsztejn Yitzhak, Freiheit Street 15
5. Goldberg Shimon, Breslauer Street 7
6. Frajman Yitskhok, Evangelishe [Ewangelicka] Street
7. Krzhepicka Sura Feyge, Evangelishe [Ewangelicka] Street 13
8. Sztepnitska Sura Ruchel, Horst Wessel Street 24
9. Kalman Bejnish, Horst Wessel Street 31
10. Warszawski Szlama, Adolf Hitler Street 2
11. Szpigelman Yisroel, Litzmannstadt Street 11
12. Berkowicz Reuben, Litzmannstadt Street 9
13. Piaskowska Nache, Horst Wessel Street 25
14. Przybylski Yisroel Gershon, Freiheits Place 9

15. Baum Yechezkal, Horst Wessel Street 20

16. Szmulewicz Ester Ruchel, Litzmannstadt Street 43

17. Szwarcbard Rafael, Evangelishe [Ewangelicka] Street 4

18. Klug Benjamin, Evangelishe [Ewangelicka] Street 7. ["]

On August 1941, they began to transport the Jews of Belchatow out and the strictures against the Jews become ever stronger. It is forbidden to employ Jews for any kind of work. In a special decree of the Land Office (this is a function of the former governor of the province) [it is mentioned] once again that special attention should be paid, and the local administration should take good care to see, that the Jews should not leave their residences... And so one harsh decree follows another against the Jews of Belchatow. One decree doesn't even have time to take effect before another is issued. On the 19th of August 1941, the Land Office sends a map to the Commissar showing the number of streets and residences in which the Jews should be concentrated. The Jews of Belchatow are further concentrated in order to make place for the Jews of smaller towns, who are being brought to Belchatow. The Jews of the surrounding area had only one week in which to vacate their living quarters and move to Belchatow.

The Germans used the same means here as everywhere else: concentrating the Jews from the smaller places into the larger [town], so that it would be easier for them to be liquidated all at one time.

The decree sent from the State Councilor [*Landrat*] to the Department Commissioner [*Amtskommissar*] contains the following contents:

"You should discuss with the Mayor of Belchatow the transporting of the 7 Jews from the Village of Przyrownica to Belchatow. Their move must be accomplished quickly in order not to give the Jews time to orient themselves and escape. The Jews are permitted to take their household items with them, [and] prepared food products. They are also permitted to take with them coals, wood, peat. The county must provide wagon drivers for this purpose. Please let me know if the relocation was carried out according to the above instructions."

No one would believe that the same State Councilor, who had already carried out a whole series of actions in his region, would suddenly begin to worry about the 7 Jews of Przyrownica. All of this was done with one goal: to fool the vigilant Jews, so that the victims should not catch on to what was going to be done with them and not escape in time.

On the 16th of September 1941, the Jews of Kleszczow received an order to move to Belchatow. On the 30th of September, the police announced that they had transferred the 8 Jews of Dobrzelow to Belchatow. Those 8 Jews were: Yankel Winer, Ella Winer, Moshe Winer, Sura Winer and Rivka Winer. The second family consisted of: Chaim Gliksman, Rivka Gliksman, and Avraham Gliksman. To Belchatow were sent the Jews from Grocholice, Belchatowek, Lenkowe and elsewhere. How else but as preparation for the liquidation of the Jews can the following request from the Land Office to the Mayor of Belchatow be explained. It is dated the 13th of October and concerns a specific list of Jews, which he must have for the secret police. This is how the text of this order sounds:

**"To the Mayor of Belchatow:**

For the secret police I must have a specific list of how many Jews live in Belchatow. It must state exactly how many men and how many women. Special attention must be given to the children under 6 years, who are not required to wear the Jewish insignia."

It is clear that by this they meant that when the moment comes to liquidate the Jews of Belchatow, the children should not be hidden. On the 22nd of October, the Judenrat received instructions about this from the mayor. This is its text:

**"To the Elders of the Judenrat in the Jewish District in Belchatow:**

**I order that in the next three days a true list of all the Jewish inhabitants in Belchatow according to sex be delivered to me. Special attention should be paid to children under 6. These lists must be delivered to me by October 26th at the latest."**

The Judenrat sent the list of the Jewish inhabitants of Belchatow to the mayor on the 25th of October. There were 2,067 men, 2,519 women and 536 children under 6. The document of January 8th 1942 is even clearer and more explicit concerning the plans to exterminate the Jews. The Belchatow

Department Commissioner sent this to the Land office. Because of the importance of this document, I reproduce it exactly.

Der Amtskommissar
der Stadt Belchatow
– Kreis Lask –
Nr. 4998/42

151

Belchatow, den 8. Januar 1942

An den
Herrn L a n d r a t des Kreises L a s k
– Abt. Kreissyndikus –
in P a b i a n i c e .–

Mit: Judenliste.

Laut anliegender Liste ergibt die Aufstellung der kranken und unbeschäftigten Juden eine Gesamtzahl von 3.425.

Ich wiederhole die genaue Aufstellung um Unklarheiten zu vermeiden:

a) die mit blau gekennzeichneten Juden sind Handwerker und in Handwerksbetrieben Beschäftigte.

b) die rot angezeichneten sind ohne Beschäftigung, einschließlich der Alten Männer und Frauen.

c) jene Juden ohne Kennzeichen sind die Kranken insgesamt 1597, die sofort wegtransportiert werden können.

Die Kinder unter 8 Jahren konnten nicht gekennzeichnet werden, denn ich hätte mich in die Gefahr begeben, den Juden mehr zu verraten als notwendig ist.

Der Amtskommissar:

—0—

Belchatow, the 8th of January 1942

**The Department Commissioner
of the city of Belchatow**

– Lask District –
No. 4998/42

**To the State Councilor
of the District of Lask**

**— Department of Syndicate-District [Kreissyndikus]
142/02**

In Pabianice

**Concerning:** The List of Jews

According to the enclosed list the whole sum of sick and unemployed Jews [is] 3,425.

I repeat in order to avoid being unclear:

The Jews indicated in blue are artisans and employed in handwork.

Those indicated in red are unemployed, including old men and women.

Those Jews without any mark are ill [and number] 1,597 souls, who can be quickly transported away.

The children under 8 can not be indicated by any mark lest I run the danger of telling the Jews more than is necessary.

**The Department Commissioner:**
**Trahner**

The document does not require any commentary. It not only shows that the Gestapo was, even at the beginning of 1942, ready to destroy the Jews of Belchatow. It also shows something else: that all minor German officials were informed of this—that they were getting ready to annihilate the Jews, and they did everything in their power to assist in this [matter].

*[Page 432]*

In the beginning of 1942 the terror against the Jewish people became stronger. It was a prelude to the overall liquidation. In February 1942 the German gendarmes carried out arrests among the Jewish and Polish population, most of them people known before the war because of their political activities. A portion of those arrested was killed on the spot. A portion was sent to extermination camps. It was at that time that Aaron Pinchas Bornstein was killed, an activist from the right wing Poalei Tzion from before the war. It was thrown up to him, that he was a teacher and educator of Jewish children in an illegal school. He was shot to death in the synagogue courtyard. That is where the Nazis arranged the prison for the Jews. Aaron Pinchas Bornstein was one of the nicest figures in pre-war Jewish Belchatow. This was a very modest man. According to his intelligence he could have reached a much higher esteem [importance] and better position in life. He however did not like to "push" himself. He was a Hebrew teacher. He, along with his family, always lived almost in need, even though he did not give up even for a single moment his work as a teacher, and thereby also was busy with communal work. However, with such community work, which always brought positive benefit, one did not see it [a profit]. His image and intelligence held himself up in the most difficult service. His father was a melamed [teacher in cheder] in Belchatow. Until he was 14 years old, he was a belfer [assistant teacher] for his father in the cheder [traditional Jewish primary school]. At night, when everyone was sleeping, he used to drag his books out from hiding, and by a little candle in a can studied until day-break. He was never separated from a book. One always saw him with some sort of book under his arm, both in the times of the Beit Hamidrash [house of prayer and study], when he was condemned by the fanatics of the environment of those times, and in the times of the occupation, when a book for a Jew was life threatening.

A large portion of the Belchatow youth had him to thank for their knowledge. He was also a good lecturer, well read on literary themes. He was a councilman from the Belchatow town council. Even his idealistic opponents were drawn to him with the greatest respect because of his spiritual and moral exaltedness. He remained faithful to his world view ane with his way of thinking, that a person can become better through non-verbal [unspoken] education, and from that came his life's calling, as a teacher and educator. And that is also how he perished – at the post of teacher and educator.

In the beginning of March 1942 the Germans arrested 16 Belchatow Jews, as so-called "plotters". Ten of them were hanged; the remaining six were let out, while their families had their entire fortune carried off by the Department Commissioner and the gendarmes.

The six saved ones were: Shlomo Szmulewicz, Meyer Zuchowski, Berl Rubenstein, Szmuel Jakubowicz, Yankl Flakowicz, and Moshe Klug. It was because of that, that a large [heavy] contribution was imposed upon the Jewish people. They had to provide 2 kilos [kilograms] of gold, 10 kilos of silver, and a large sum of money in cash. It is easy to imagine how it came about that all of this was put together after the Jews had already earlier been robbed. On the 13th of March the Belchatow Department Commissioner reported to the State Councilor:

> "Today the Criminal High-Secretary Walden, with an official of the gestapo, [came] to me, and it was relayed to me, that on Wednesday, the 18th of March 1942, before noon, at 11 o'clock, 10 Jews must be hung in Belchatow."

Those that observed the said terrible execution have told that on the 18th of March, in the morning, all the Jews were driven from their rooms to the synagogue courtyard. From there they were taken (driven) 5 in a row, to a place that had belonged to Yankl Ber Lieberman, where there was already standing prepared a gallows. At about 10 o'clock the Jewish Police, in the accompaniment of the gendarmes, brought the 10 Jews who had been designated to be hung. They all were with bound hands.

The 10 Jews were:

| | |
|---|---|
| Yankl Erlich, | יאַנקל ערליך, |
| Moshe Wolfowicz, | משה װאָלפאָװיטש |
| Laybish Feldman, | לייביש פעלדמאַן |
| Mendel Feld, | מענדל פעלד, |
| Yaakov Hersh Statlender's grandson, | יעקב הערש שטאַטלענדערס אַן אייניקל, |
| Moshe Aaron Taube, | משה אהרן טויבע, |
| Yechezkiel Szpiro, | יחזקאל שפירא, |
| Yerachmiel Baum, | ירחמיאל בוים, |
| Eliezer Rawicz (a Jew from Lodz) | אליעזר ראַװיטש אַ לאָדזשער ייִד, |
| and Laybish Michal Landau | און לייביש מיכל לאַנדאַ. |

A strong impression was made upon all the indicated Jews by the stance of Moshe Wolfowicz: With a steady step and a head held high, he was the first one to go up to the gallows. He himself put the noose around his neck and shouted to the Jews that they should not lose their courage, that to the Germans will come a bleak defeat, and that one should take revenge for all the crimes that the Germans commit. To the remaining condemned, [he said that] he was depending on their not having any fear and that they should hold themselves straight. The remaining people went after him. For 20 minutes they were standing with the nooses lying around their necks, until the president of the Judenrat, Topolewicz, read the "Accusation Act," which the mayor Trahner had handed him. In the "Accusation Act" he said: that in the name of German justice these 10 Jews are being punished for speculation, sabotage, and diverse things against the German war economy, for conducting illegal dealing and smuggling, and for raising the prices of products necessary for life. After Topolewicz read the "Accusation Act," the leader of the Lodz Gestapo, Richter, ordered the platform upon which the condemned were standing to be removed. The platform was pulled from under their feet by Abraham Alter Goldberg (khmal[?]).

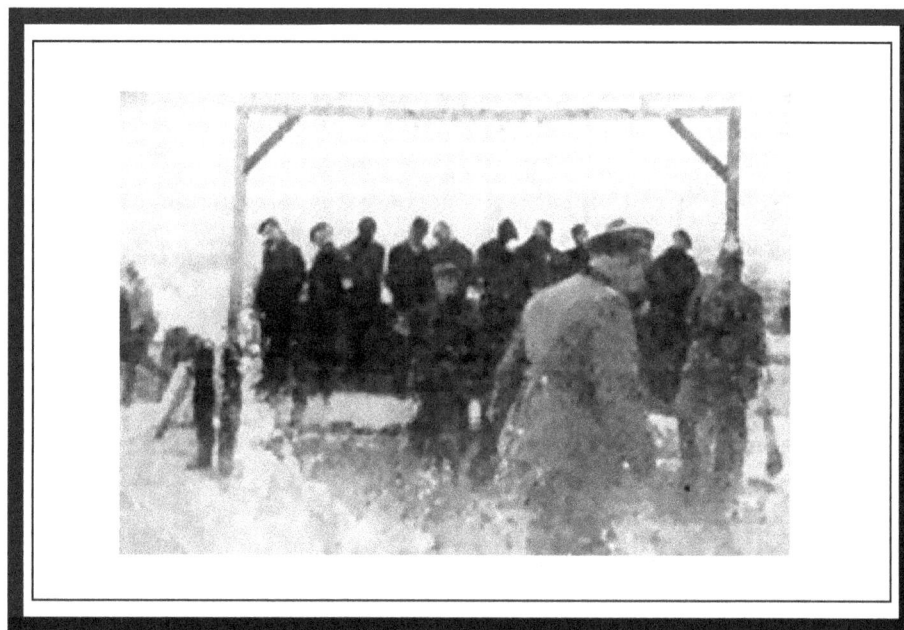

**The ten people hung in Belchatow on the 19th of March 1942**

The Jews around stood frozen, they were afraid to make any movement, because the Germans, who were standing around the community of Jews, with machine guns stretched out, had an order that with the slightest movement in the rows of Jews, to fire into the crowd. Until 5 o'clock in the evening the 10 Jews were [left] hanging on the gallows. The Belchatow Jews returned to their homes with a heavy mood, after that which they had lived through, not being sure what tomorrow will bring.

The 19th of March 1942 the Belchatow Department Commissioner reported to the Town Commander of Lask:

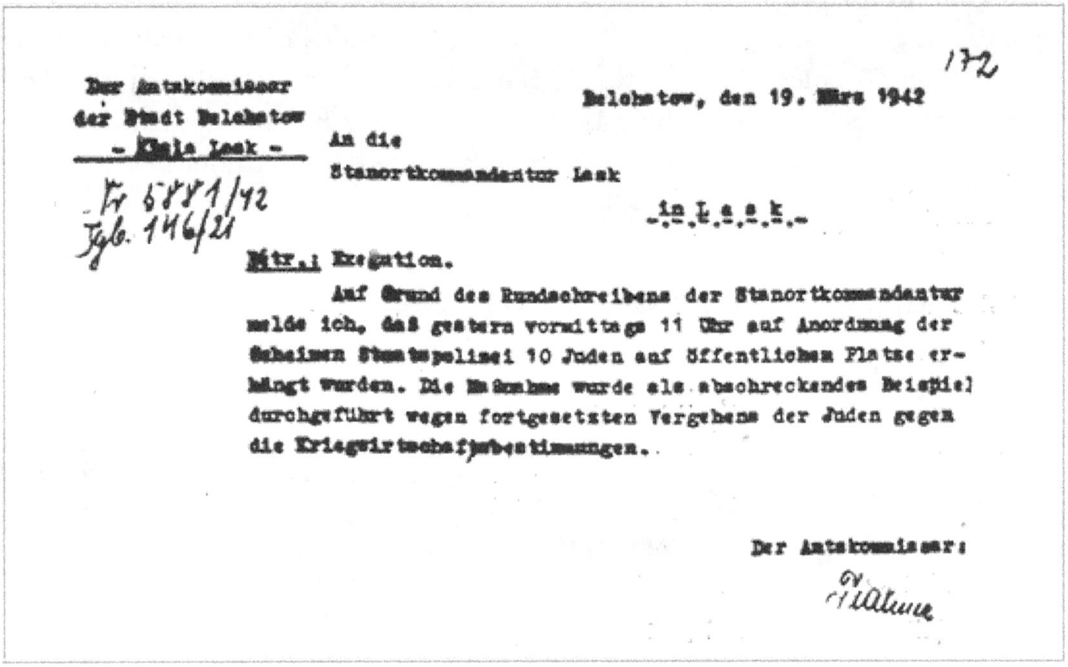

Der Amtskommissar
der Stadt Belchatow
- Kreis Lask -

Fr 6881/42
Tgb. 146/21

Belchatow, den 19. März 1942

An die
Stanortkommandantur Lask

in L a s k.-

Betr.: Exekution.

Auf Grund des Rundschreibens der Stanortkommandantur melde ich, daß gestern vormittags 11 Uhr auf Anordnung der Geheimen Staatspolizei 10 Juden auf öffentlichem Platze erhängt wurden. Die Maßnahme wurde als abschreckendes Beispiel durchgeführt wegen fortgesetzten Vergehens der Juden gegen die Kriegswirtschaftsbestimmungen.

Der Amtskommissar:

Belchatow, March 19, 1942

The Department Commissioner
of the town of Belchatow
– Lask District –
Nr. 5881/42
Daybook 146/21
To the
Town Commander [of] Lask                    In Lask
**Topic:** Execution
On the basis of the circular from the town commander, I report that yesterday before noon, 11 o'clock, upon the orders of the secret state police [*staatpolizei*], 10 Jews were hung in an open place. This measure was carried out, as a terrifying example concerning constant crimes on the part of the Jews in relation to the regulations of the war economy.

The Department Commissioner
**Trahner**

The Belchatow Germans boasted that the hanging of the 10 Jews, right in the Purim days, should serve to remind them that this is paying them back for Haman's 10 sons. [Translator's note: Haman's 10 sons were hung, in relation to the story that is the basis of Purim, in place of Jews that Haman planned to hang on those same gallows.]

From then on, there again began a period of "*sperres*" ["curfews"], house searches, and other troubles. They whipped, tortured, and killed. They whipped women, whose husbands were hidden, so as not to be sent out to forced labor. I give forth to you a document, which shows what measures the Germans were capable of.

Belchatow the 27th of June 1942

"To the State Councilor [Landrat] Dr. Stiller, service information:

I report, Mr. State Councilor, the following facts concerning that which was provided me by the chief of the workers division. Party Comrade Zander and his co-worker Party Comrade Kimpfmann. You should not have any doubt about the correctness of the facts, as I questioned each one separately, and both of them told the same [story]. According to the descriptions it goes like this: The workers division needed to put Jews to work. They were driven out at night from the rooms. It appeared that a lot of Jews ran away during this operation, or they hid themselves. Then we took in the wives and daughters, of the Jews who had run away, into the workers division, until they would be searched for by their husbands and fathers. The men did not come forward, and the question posed itself for us, what to do with the women and girls. The party comrades Zander and Kimpfmann put themselves down [on the side of] releasing the women and girls. The government councilor Stram ordered then, that the women should be given the earned punishment, and that should happen in the following form: The women and girls, who numbered 20, had to undress themselves naked and be beaten with whips and sticks, as long as they don't want to tell where their husbands and fathers can be found. The government councilor Stram not only gave the said order, but he also carried out the punishment on his own, with the help of the party comrade Zander, who was beating with a stick, while the government councilor Stram was beating with a whip. Among the Jewish women and girls was also found a pregnant woman by the name Klug. It showed by her stance [that she was pregnant], and nevertheless she received her judgment from the government councilor Stram. Concerning this, it was given over to the Judenrat and to the municipal police. Right after that searches were carried out in all Jewish homes. The searches were carried out by the secret police, and the party comrades Zander and Kimpfmann in this way received the assignment once again to control whether one still recognizes the traces of the whippings received on the bodies of the Jewish women and girls.

Mayor: **Trahner**

Such similar facts continuously repeated themselves until the day of the complete liquidation.

———

*[Page 438]*

We are coming to the tragic chapter, which marks the end of Jewish life in Belchatow, a chapter which concludes 150 years of vibrant Jewish life in one of the towns, which with its building and creativity in various fields exhibits the true face of creative Polish Jewry. It is the chapter of the liquidation of the

Jews in Belchatow. The first "relocation" took place on the 20th of August 1941.

On the 19th of August, the Head Commissar Trahner sent the following order to the Judenrat:

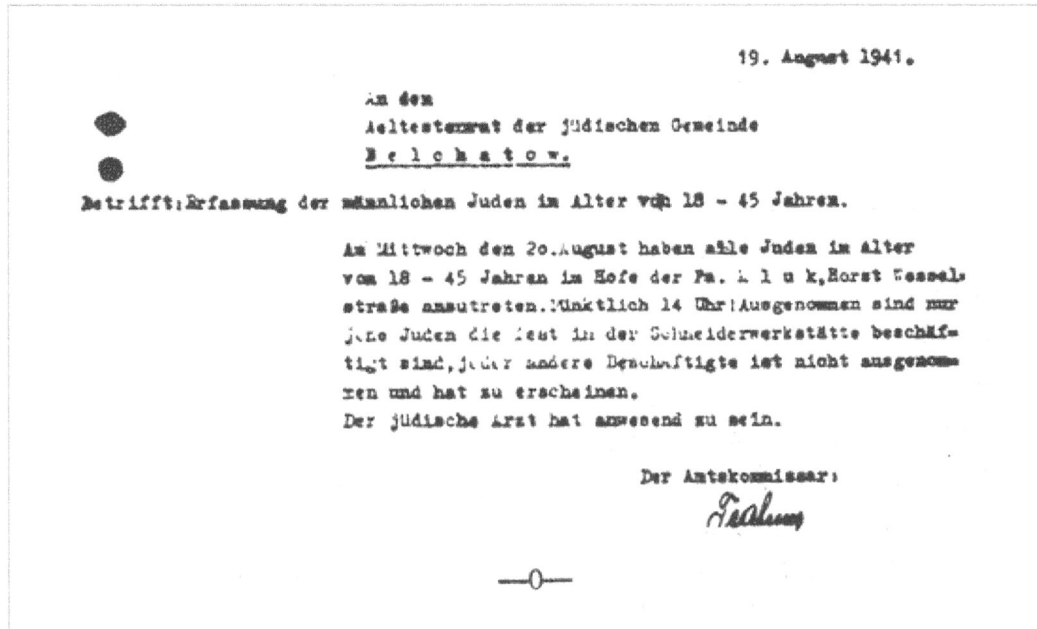

19. August 1941.

An den
Aeltestenrat der jüdischen Gemeinde
Belchatow.

Betrifft: Erfassung der männlichen Juden im Alter von 18 - 45 Jahren.

Am Mittwoch den 20.August haben alle Juden im Alter von 18 - 45 Jahren im Hofe der Fa. K l u k, Horst Wessel strasse anzutreten. Pünktlich 14 Uhr! Ausgenommen sind nur jene Juden die zeit in der Schneiderwerkstätte beschäftigt sind, jeder andere Beschäftigte ist nicht ausgenommen und hat zu erscheinen.
Der jüdische Arzt hat anwesend zu sein.

Der Amtskommissar:

—0—

[The letter is translated into Yiddish:]

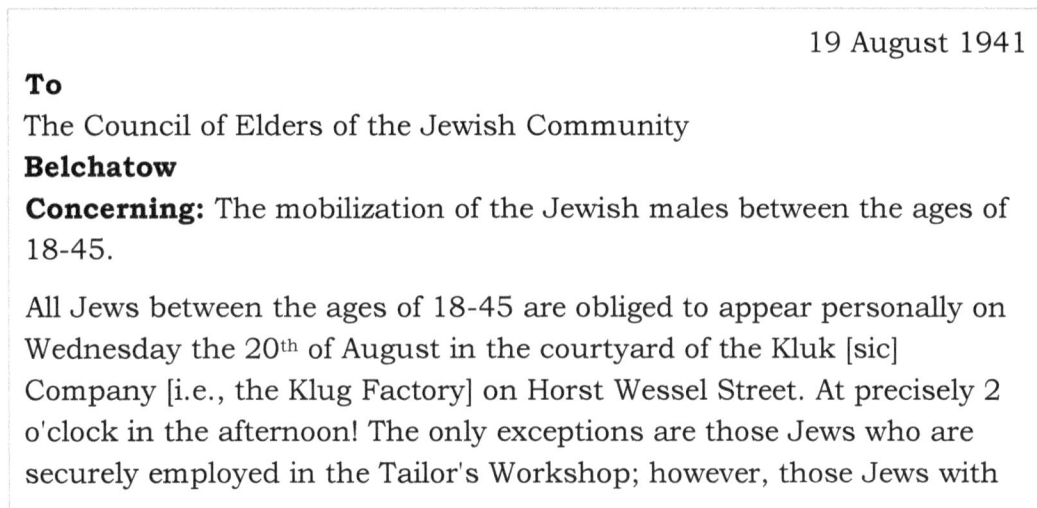

19 August 1941

**To**
The Council of Elders of the Jewish Community
**Belchatow**
**Concerning:** The mobilization of the Jewish males between the ages of 18-45.

All Jews between the ages of 18-45 are obliged to appear personally on Wednesday the 20th of August in the courtyard of the Kluk [sic] Company [i.e., the Klug Factory] on Horst Wessel Street. At precisely 2 o'clock in the afternoon! The only exceptions are those Jews who are securely employed in the Tailor's Workshop; however, those Jews with other occupations are not excluded and must appear.

The Jewish doctors must be in attendance.

The Head Commissar,
**Trahner**

At that time about 500 young men were taken away. It is true that they were not sent directly to the crematoria, but they suffered so much until their deaths that they perhaps envied those who had been sent directly to their deaths. These [young men] were first sent to the camps in the Poznan area. There they were tortured with the most difficult labor in building roads and laying railroad tracks. More than one fell under the heavy loads that they had to pull. They had to work 12-14 hours a day. They were not even allowed to catch their breaths. At the slightest attempt to rest from their work, the trained German gangsters beat them violently with sticks and the butts of their rifles.

These Jewish slaves were kept in barracks in very bad conditions. It was crowded and dirty. They got 24 decas of bread with a soup of rotten rape [a leafy green vegetable, similar to kale, generally grown for animal fodder] for lunch and a cup of black coffee for their evening meal. This was the official portion. In fact, even this was lacking, because half was stolen by the Germans by way of the overseers, the cooks, and the kapos, so that by the time it got to the inmate, there was very little left. If someone got sick or weak at work, they were immediately sent to Auschwitz to be incinerated. That is why, even with a temperature of 40 [°C], they went to work, just not to be considered sick. They never reported to a doctor. They dragged themselves around with their last bit of strength and waited for a miracle. In the years 1941 and 1942, no miracles could happen. It was in those times, when the starved Jewish slave was even afraid to leave his work to get his bit of soup for lunch, because he might be beaten over the head with a piece of iron instead of receiving his bowl of soup.

The Jews of Belchatow were scattered throughout the camps: Nekla, Poznan-Dempsen, Poznan- Wronczyn, Gutenbuk, and so on.

In the Nekla camp, the people [prisoners] slept under the open sky. Out of starvation, they ate worms. Every day, fewer and fewer left for work from Nekla camp. Each night several people died from exhaustion and starvation. In a short time, fewer than half of the 400 Belchatowers remained. Actually, the very youngest died off first. There was a German there, who didn't sit down to breakfast until he had killed a Jew. Another German's method was to hit a Jew over the head with a hammer. After being hit with a hammer in this way, it was rare that anyone remained alive. A few months after the first expulsion, it was relatively quiet in Belchatow, but in the beginning of 1942 it started again. New contingents of workers were required from the Poznan camps, because the greatest part of the former [workers] had already died off. There were "sperres" [curfews] and abductions in the middle of March and April. At the beginning of June 1942, Jews were once again required to gather in the courtyard of Klug's factory. Having learned from the previous "resettlements," the Jews were not as quick to report. They hid in cellars, in attics, in the woods. The Germans wreaked havoc: they shot a woman named Gliksman; they shot Lewkowicz, Zerach Cymberknap, all to no avail. The Jews did not come out of hiding. If it hadn't been for the Jewish police, who were assisting the gendarmerie [German police] in their search and pointing out the hiding places, the Germans would not have accomplished much on their own. At that time, the Germans succeeded in dragging 400 Belchatow Jews to the Poznan camps. It was seldom that anyone taken away ever returned home. In the rare case that someone did succeed in escaping and returning [home], Jewish informants collaborating with the Gestapo turned him in.

On the 17th of February 1942, the Commandant of the German police gave the Mayor the following report:

Schutzpolizei-Dienstabteilung          Belchatow, dem  17. 2. 1942.
B e l c h a t o w.

Tgb.N. 7/n.                                    Der Bürgermeister
                                               Bn : am
                                               Tag  L FC3
                                               N. 5518/42
                M e l d u n g.
                                               N.. 120/03

Betrifft.: Überschreitung der Sperrzeit durch den Juden
          Chaskil Zwiersynski, 25 Jahre alt, wohnhaft
          in Belchatow, Breslauer-Strasse 3.
          ————

                Am 16. 2. 1942 gegen 21,10 Uhr wurde der Oben-
          genannte in  der Breslauer-Strasse, südlich hinter den
          Häusern in Höhe des deutschen Friedhofes umherschleichend
          angetroffen. Auf Anruf, stehen zu bleiben, ergriff Z. die
          Flucht. Er wurde auf der Flucht erschossen.

                                          Meister der Schutzpolizei.

          Buch Nr 227/42
                Urschriftlich

                         dem Herrn  Bürgermeister u.Amtskomm.

                              in B e l c h a t o w

                zur gef. Kenntnisnahme übersandt.
                Belchatow, dem 17. 2. 1942.

                                          R e v i e r - L e u t n a m t
                                          u.Abteilungsführer.

                              ————O————

[Letter translated into Yiddish follows:]

Belchatow the 17/2/1942

Protection Police [*Schutz-Polizei*] –
Service Department
**Belchatow**
Diary no. 77/42

Stamp:
**The Mayor**
**Belchatow**
Received 20th Feb. 1942
No. 120/03

**Annoucement**

**Matter: The violation of walking in the street after the permitted time by the Jew Chaskil Zwierzynski, 25 years old, resident of Belchatow, Breslauer St. 3.**

On 2/16/1942 at around 9:10 p.m., the above-mentioned of Breslauer Street was discovered wandering around on the south side behind the houses above the German cemetery. When he was asked to halt, he began to run away. He was shot escaping.

**Roys**
Master of the Protection Police

**– 0 –** [sic]

Book – no. 227/42
Original

To the Mayer and Head Commissar

**In Belchatow**

Sent as a courtesy, on 2/17/1942

Ballerstadt
**District-Lieutenant**
**and Division Leader**

**– 0 –**

In fact this matter presented itself differently: the abovementioned Yecheskel Zwierszynski escaped from the Poznan Camps, returned home and hid in various places. On the evening that he was shot, he was actually at home. Someone let the Germans know, and they came right into his house. He was not shot in the German cemetery, but while he was trying to jump out of the window.

In the Poznan Camps, the Germans utilized a group of Belchatower criminal youths. They were installed as "*kapos*" [inmates in charge of work teams in a camp] and "*stube-dienst*" ["chamber-service" – inmates in charge of a chamber]. Because of their cruelty, these underworld people were absolutely no different than the German beasts. The Belchatower hairdresser, Szwarcberg, worked as a "*feldsher*" [an old-time barber-surgeon] in the Nekla Camp. He was the expert on all illnesses. He has hundreds of deaths on his conscience. He is guilty in the death of Fradl Wolfowicz's youngest son, who died at work. He is also guilty in the death of old Szjtnicki and his son Moshe. He sent people to work with broken ribs, with bones broken in two by beatings. A second *kapo*, Berish Fila, beat people violently. He broke people's hands and feet and then turned his victims over to the Germans to be sent to Auschwitz. He himself survived the war and wound up in Germany in the American Zone... [The following] distinguished themselves as murderers: Mayorek Nus, Melech Krawitski, Berish Grinberg, and Avraham Pila. They took everything that they owned away from the Jews of Belchatow, every package of produce that came from home. The unfortunate camp prisoners had to share every bite with them. They were the masters of the inmates' lives and deaths. Whoever tried to oppose them was reported and recommended for transportation to Auschwitz as having sabotaged the work effort. These louts broke the bones of Avraham Lipsycz and Asher Jakubowicz, because they didn't want to give away their food. Asher Jakubowicz died of these wounds while at work; Avraham Lipsycz was turned over for transportation to Auschwitz. The starvation in the camps was so impossible to endure that, ignoring the fact that people in the camps knew that stealing was punishable by shooting or hanging, they nevertheless tried to steal whatever they could and at least once be sated. For stealing a few potatoes in the Poznan-Wronczyn Camp, Yerachmil Szwarcberg, Welwel Walder, and two other Belchatower Jews, whose names are uncertain, were hanged. One of the four hanged succeeded in extricating himself from the noose on the gallows and was still alive, but the Germans shot him. Also hanged for trying to escape was Avraham Liszczanowski.

In the year 1942, three Poznan Camps were dissolved. The small number of surviving Belchatow Jews was sent to Auschwitz and Majdanek. There practically all of the 1,000 Belchatow Jews who had been transferred from the Poznan Camps died. Only a few people survived and they can be counted on one's fingers.

The liquidation of the rest of the Jews who remained in Belchatow began on the 11th of August 1942, at 6 o'clock in the morning. The whole town was locked in and surrounded by newly arrived killing squads and the local German gendarmes and police force. All of those who had tried the previous night to escape to Piotrkow were, for the most part, shot. The women, Zuchowski and Pilakowicz, were killed as they tried to escape into the woods. Hans Biebow, the hangman of the Lodz Ghetto, led the liquidation. He brought with him a division of the Lodz Jewish "Special Police" [SonderPolizei]. The local Jewish Belchatow police also helped. First thing in the morning, Itche Winter came into the tailor's factory and removed the Jewish policemen, who guarded the factory, and gave them the job of gathering all the old and sick people together on Zelower Road. There cars with Gestapo were already waiting for them and took them immediately to the Chemno death camp. These were the first victims. Thus started the final liquidation of the Jews in Belchatow.

When the Lodz Ghetto was liquidated in 1944, practically all of the Belchatow Jews who were in the Lodz Ghetto perished in Auschwitz. A large number of the thousand Belchatow Jews who had been in the Lodz Ghetto had died previously of starvation. In the Lodz Ghetto, Henoch Liberman, the well known Bundist activist and advisor on the Belchatow City Council, [also] expired from starvation. The evacuation in Belchatow lasted three days. The people, who it had been decided would go to Chelmno, were packed into the synagogue almost to the point of suffocation. In these overcrowded conditions, the Chasidic Jew, Avraham Yitzhak Farber, died. These people weren't given anything to eat, not even a sip of water. The cars went back and forth to Chelmno all day long. Even on the third day, Jews who had been discovered hiding were still being sent over. A group of Jews was left in Belchatow in order to clean out the Jewish houses of the possessions they had left behind. Afterwards, they were taken in an unfamiliar direction and every trace of them was lost. A small number of Jews succeeded in hiding during this time of liquidation and later escaping to Piotrkow, but very few of them remained alive.

————

After the Jews had been transported out of Belchatow, the Germans divided up the remaining Jewish possessions. The greatest part fell to those who ran the Lodz Ghetto, with [Hans] Biebow at their head. In the lawsuit against Biebow, which took place in Lodz after the war, it was actually shown that Biebow sent millions of dollars worth of Jewish possessions back to his "homeland." Whatever Jewish possessions remained were divided among the local Germans. This "master race" fought among themselves over every Jewish scrap. In a letter from the Mayor to the Land Office, he complains about this – – how difficult it is for him to accomplish this apportioning due to the squabbles among the Germans, and he requests that the Land Office relieve him of this duty. We have the following characteristic document from the Department Commissioner of Belchatow

Nr. 7455/42/3
510/04

201

20. August 1942

An Herrn
Reinhold O b e r m a n n - Lebensmittelgroßhandlung -
in B e l c h a t o w .

T/K.

Betr.: Verteilung der vorgefundenen Waschmittel im Lager des
jüdischen Ältestenrates.

Unter Bezugnahme auf die persönliche Rücksprache mit Herrn
Obermann und Herrn Semmler bezüglich der Verteilung der beim jüd.
Ältestenrat vorgefundenen Artikel, möchte ich Sie bitten die Verteilung am Samstag den 22. August von nachmittags 5 Uhr ab nach
beiliegender Liste vornehmen zu wollen. Die einzelnen Volksgenos-
sen sind verständigt. Jeder auf der Liste Aufgeführte erhält
gleichmäßig folgende Artikel ausgehändigt:
  2 Dosen Fix - 5 Paket Saponia - 5 Stück Gama Fix - 4 Stück
Gama Rex - 1 Paket Edelchlor - 1/2 kg. Malzkaffee und 1 kg. Soda.
  Der verbleibende Rest auf Grund Ihrer Aufstellung aus den
genannten Artikeln wird der NSV zur Verfügung gestellt. Im übrigen
bleibt es bei unserer Abmachung.
  Die 100 kg. Karbid werde ich gelegentlich abholen lassen.

Der Amtskommissar:

Bialum

—0—

20th of August 1942          no. 7455/43/3
                             510/40

To Herr
Reinhold Oberman – Wholesale Business of Products

In Belchatow

T/K

**Regarding:** Distribution of laundry products found in the warehouse of the Jewish Council of Elders.

In connection with a personal discussion with Herr Oberman and Herr Zemler regarding the distribution of the articles, which were found at the Jewish Council of Elders, – I want to ask that this distribution be accomplished on Saturday, the 22nd of August, from 3 o'clock in the afternoon on, according to the enclosed list. The comrades have agreed to this. Everyone on this list will be handed the following products:

2 boxes of Vim [dry cleanser similar to Ajax or Comet], 5 packets of Safoni, 3 pieces of Gamma Fix, 4 pieces of Gamma Rex, 1 packet of Eidchlor, 1/2 kilo of malt-coffee, and 1 kilo baking soda.

The rest of what remains, according to your records, will be disposed of by NSV [*National Socialistische Volkshilfe*, which was in charge of welfare, collection of clothing, etc.]. The other things remain, according to our agreement.

The 100 kilo of carbide, I will remove when I have the opportunity.

Department Commissioner:
**Trahner**

A few days earlier, on the 17th of August, a communication appeared signed by the Mayor:

"Enamel and zinc dishes will be for sale at the Catholic Church. The sale will take place on the 21st of August from 8 o'clock until 12. First choice is given to emigrated Germans and only afterwards to native [Germans]."

On the 19th of August, the Head Commissar told the Land Office what he had done with the furniture that had remained after the removal of the Jews.

"I am letting the Head of the Land Council know that I have decided, little by little, to sell the furniture that remained after the Jews' [departure], and to use what was unsuitable for sale as firewood, and to divide the rest among the National Socialists."

Another document of the same date lists precisely what furniture he divided among the National Socialists:

1. Kitchen cabinet                    11. Three sugar bowls

2. Three serving plates

3. Four cake plates

4. Five small bowls

5. Six soup plates

6. Ten supper plates

7. Twenty-eight cups and saucers

8. Twenty-two little plates

9. Five milk cans

10. Three coffee pots

12. A soup bowl

13. Five tin plates

14. Nine cooking pots

15. A samovar

16. Two stone pots [sic]

17. Two large bowls

18. Three pails

18. [sic] One grater

20. One egg beater

21. Two ladles

The Land Office then issued a special order that the Department Commissioner also be given furniture from Widawa, because unfortunately, a terrible pity on him, he didn't have the opportunity to procure any furniture, because there were practically no Jews left in Widawa. The Jews had been transported out of there as early as 1941.

The following Germans in Belchatow received furniture:

1. Pilts, Tatiana – a table for 5 marks;

2. Wizner, Emil – a bed for 5 marks;

3. Gut, Josef – a water bench [*wasser bank*]

4. Kubisch, Gustav – an armoire with two doors for 12 marks;

5. Krieger, Anan – a mirror for 6 marks.

    6.  Turbanski, Alfred – a box of coal for 2 marks

This is how they plundered, how the Jewish possessions, earned with blood and sweat, were given away or sold.

After the Jews had been transported, their synagogue was turned into a warehouse for straw. Later, the synagogue was turned over to the German peasant collective also to be used as a warehouse, and then, as is shown in a document dated June 19, 1944, issued by the financial office, permission was given to turn the synagogue into a sports gymnasium.

Belchatow was renamed – Belchetol.

———

After the Red Army liberated Poland and the war ended, the few remaining surviving Jews returned to Belchatow. Individuals came from the various camps, which were widespread across Germany and Poland. Individuals came from Auschwitz and Birkenau, near Auschwitz, from Theresienstadt, from Buchenwald, from Bergen-Belsen. They came tattered and torn, swollen from starvation and illness. Practically all of them wore the infamous "*pazhakes*" (striped garb), weak and sick, some of them even leaning on sticks. But in Belchatow they couldn't even find a roof over their heads. It is difficult to be certain about the number of Belchatow survivors: not all of them returned to their hometown. A few remained in the camps in German in the American and English zones. There are a few Belchatow Jews even in Sweden. Others succeeded in smuggling themselves into Eretz Yisrael after they had suffered the seven levels of hell in the last camps of Germany, Italy, and the like. In general, no more than 200 Jews of Belchatow survived Hitler's occupation. Perhaps another 200 Belchatow Jews returned from the Soviet Union. All told, no more than 500 Jews survived. That doesn't even amount to 10 percent of the former Jewish population of Belchatow.

There are now ruins in the place, where there such a lovely life blossomed. The synagogue lies in ruins. The land where the Jewish cemetery once was is destroyed – the land has been plowed under, and it is even difficult to see where the Jewish cemetery once was. With the headstones, the Germans paved the streets. Today, there is not even one Jew left in Belchatow. Several have settled in Lodz; the rest have dispersed across the world. This is how the

150-year-old Jewish settlement in Belchatow came to an end –torn out with its roots by the Hitler beast.

———

The Jews of Belchatow also contributed their share in the fight against Hitlerism. Belchatower Jews took part in the struggle against the Germans in the year 1939. Belchatower Jews took part in the heroic defense of Warsaw. They fought in the Red Army; they fought in the famous Kosciuszko Division, and they were also active in the partisan movement.

Josef Reich, a well-known community activist in Belchatow during the First World War, someone who had a hand in the development of cultural life in Belchatow, was exiled to Stolpce during the Hitler occupation. There he worked in the underground camp organization. He was in the partisan movement and fought in the partisan camp under the leadership of the well-known partisan, Hershl Pasesarski. Despite his age, he took part in all the heavy battles, which took place in the Stolpce region.

Now he is in Australia.

Moshe Levi, a Chassid who never had the slightest idea of how to hold a rifle, went into the woods during the liquidation of the Jews of Belchatow. He and another partisan went through Belchatow in 1944. The police noticed them and opened fire. Levi was critically wounded in a foot, which made it impossible for him to escape. He was captured alive and sent by the Gestapo to Lodz. For a while, he was kept in the hospital and then sentenced to be hanged.

A group of Belchatower [Jews] fought in the partisan camp behind Bialystok. They were known by the name: "The Suprasl Group." That was the town [Suprasl] where they were under the German occupation during the second half of the year 1942. This group earned a lot while organizing the partisan movement in the greater Bialystok area. The following belonged to this group: Hinde Kon, Chaim Kon, Moshe Kon and Lejbl Pudlowski. All three Kons distinguished themselves by exhibiting extraordinary bravery and heroism. All three come from poor, proletariat parents. Hinde, who as a child was very weak, actually exhibited the greatest endurance as a partisan. It appeared that she had a strong spirit in her weak body. When the liquidation of the Suprasl Jews took place on the 1st of November, she was the only one who escaped into the surrounding woods. She hid in a hay silo for two months during the worst frosts. If it weren't for the peasants of the hamlet Konno, who brought her some food, she would have died of starvation. She is among the first of the Bialystok region who went into the woods to fight the occupying forces. One had to have extraordinary strength to remain all alone in the woods during that time, without any contact with the partisan movement. Danger dogged one's every step. It was pioneering work, and it had to fall, of all people, to the weak, feeble soul, Hinde Kon. She looked around slowly; little by little she made contact with the neighboring peasants, who sympathized with the partisan movement. She made contact with the Russian partisan, Alexander, who also was very helpful in saving Jews who were hiding in the woods. For a time, he was the commander of the Judith Group (Judith was a famous heroine of the Bialystok Ghetto uprising). Thanks to Alexander and Hinde, the first Jewish partisan group was formed in the Bialystok woods. She procured the first arms by going into a deep lake and extracting a rifle, which came from the conflict between the Russians and the Germans, back in 1941. She blew up a train, and the locomotive was destroyed, and 12 tanks, and a great number of Germans soldiers were thereby killed. Another case shows her heroism, her cold-bloodedness, and her daring: one time, the Germans had surrounded the Suprasl woods, and a skirmish ensued between the Germans and the partisans. Since, according to their count, the Germans greatly outnumbered the partisans, the latter had to draw back. In the process, one of the partisans lost his rifle. Hinde Kon noticed this, and even without asking the commandant's permission, she returned, under a hail of German bullets, to the place and retrieved the rifle. However, she had to return alone by another way. This battle took place in the 15th district of the rugged "Bodzisker" woods. She stole out of the woods and ran across the field. The Germans shot after her. The partisans loved her very much because of her sincere goodness. During the hardest times, the winter of 1944, when the Jewish partisans in the Bialystok area were blockaded by the German soldiers, and there were casualties every day, it seemed already to be the end, and that no way out of this situation could be seen, Hinde Kon would come with warm, motherly words [of encouragement]. Indeed, that's what she was called: the mother of the Jewish partisans. She washed the partisans' laundry, cooked for them, darned and mended their clothes. When the partisan, Rivka Weiskowska was wounded with a dum-dum bullet [a soft-shelled bullet that expands inside the body] during a fight with the Germans and she couldn't move from where she lay, Hinde Kon did not leave her side for one minute. At one time, they were under heavy fire. Their deaths seemed imminent. Weiskowska pleaded with her to at least save herself. Hinde would not hear of it and did not leave her side. For her bravery, Hinde Kon was awarded the Grunwald Cross, one of the greatest distinctions in the Polish State.

Chaim Kon, who also played a large role in the history of the partisan struggle, was born in 1916. He was raised in the traditional Jewish way. From his earliest years, he exhibited a strong inclination to learn. The impoverished conditions of his family did not permit him to fulfill his dream. As a 12-year-old boy, he already must earn his own livelihood. He comes to Lodz in the year 1932; there he works in a store, but studies at the same time, preparing himself for matriculation exams. From 1933 on, he belongs to the Communist Youth Organization. He is also active in the Business Employees Union. He is arrested in the winter of 1935 for taking part in an illegal demonstration and is sentenced to one and a half years of prison. At the same time, his first literary efforts are published. He published his first poem about the hard life of a weaver in an anti-Fascist magazine "*Levar*". He also exhibits great talent in drawing. The outbreak of the war destroyed all of his plans. When the Germans marched into Lodz in 1939, Chaim and his sister and brother went to Bialystok, where he visits the textile school. During the German invasion in 1941, he escapes from Bialystok and hides for a time in the surrounding woods. From there, he goes to Suprasl and becomes the organizer of the Suprasl partisan group. When the Germans began to liquidate the Suprasl Jews, the Gestapo caught Chaim as he was trying to escape. He is sent to Bialystok with a group of Jews. On the 19th of November, the Bialystok camp is liquidated. Ten thousand Jews from the towns around Bialystok are loaded onto two trains and sent to Treblinka. On the way, near Lapi, Chaim and his brother, Moshe, and his wife, Ita Grosskop, jump off the train. His wife was killed on the spot. He and his brother drag themselves, cut up as they are, back to the Suprasl woods. On the 1st of January, Chaim steals into the Bialystok Ghetto and leads out a group of friends, 15 people. They were, however, attacked by the Germans and beaten. He and a few survivors manage to get back into the woods. In the woods, he is part of the leadership of the Suprasl partisan group. He takes part in all the hard fights, and fulfills his sister's mission. In the spring of 1943, he becomes a member of the partisan detachment "*Foroys*" ["Frontline"]. There, he edits the partisan newspaper along with Lunski of Bialystok. He led the operation in

Ogrodniczki. He went to Suprasl, killed the provocateur, Karabowicz, and didn't want to throw a grenade into the house, because there were small children inside. During the days of August, when the Bialystok Ghetto was in flames and every day the Germans attacked the partisans in order to prevent them from coming to the aid of the ghetto fighters and also to prevent them from giving asylum to the surviving ghetto fighters, in one such battle between the partisans and the Germans, Chaim Kon was hit by a bullet. He fell at a moment, when he had to man a machine gun in place of a fallen comrade. He was buried right on the spot where he fell in the Bialystok woods.

In 1947, his body was exhumed and was brought to Lodz, where he was buried near his father, who died of starvation in the Lodz Ghetto.

Moshe Kon was a martyr just like his brother Chaim. He was still practically a child when he left Lodz in 1939. He matured in the woods. The woods were his element. He almost became one with the woods. He never got lost. He had a marvelous sense of orientation in the woods. In general, that trait was something all three Kon children had in common, but Moshe Kon could find his way around the best. He moved freely about the woods without a map, without a compass, as if he were walking city streets. He looked as if he had been born in the woods. It was enough for him to walk a path once to know it well and for it to be permanently etched in his memory. In the woods, he was able to unearth the kinds of paths and trails that German feet would not find. He would carry out the most difficult spying assignments. It was known that if Moshe Kon was handling a surveillance mission, it would be successfully accomplished. In addition, he was an excellent machine-gunner. When the Red Army entered the Bialystok woods in July of 1944, Moshe led them over the river to a place which the Germans never expected them to be. This enabled the Red Army to enter the town of Suprasl almost without any casualties. The Jews of Belchatow, wherever they may now find themselves, can be proud that their shtetl [town] produced such heroes.

––––––––

1. The list can be found on page 479 [in the chapter "Documents of the Holocaust and Destruction" in this Yizkor Book]. [It indicates that it was made on September 7, 1940.]

2. See the document on page 490 [in the chapter "Documents of the Holocaust and Destruction" in this Yizkor Book].

[Page 456]

## "The Four Days of Horror"

### By Zohken Lieberman

### (Reworked by L. Podlowski)

### Translated from the Yiddish by Martin Bornstein

It began Tuesday the 11th of August 1942, at five o'clock in the morning. A host of foreign police divisions, as well as the local German gendarmes surrounded the town. All of the houses and streets were simultaneously being guarded, such that it was impossible to tear yourself out from there. The civilian German people also helped to remove the Jewish people from Belchatow, which they did of their own accord (free will).

Already a month or two earlier, when no one had imagined that the end was so near, a division of the border police was dispatched to the town. They carefully watched (paid strong attention) that no one should illegally cross the border, into the "Fatherland" (Germany), from the governed region (General Gobernia). The Jews of Belchatow, even when they saw how people were being driven, still believed that this was just one of the many German "drag-nets" (raids) that was perpetrated against the Jews of Belchatow, with the purpose of (catching and) sending them to the Posnan camps. They also built it up in our minds, such that we thought it would be (affect) just old people and not younger people, capable of working. Had it been otherwise, certainly a lot of people from Belchatow would have run away to the nearby woods. When we first saw the hellish scenes, that played themselves out on the streets, did we then understand how great our woe is, but by then it was too late to undertake anything.

I looked out from a crack from my house at number 14 Pabianice Street, and saw how the multitude of Jews were being driven, women with children and old people, they were met with slaps from guns, knouts (whips), sticks, and other instruments. We didn't even have time to dress ourselves, when we heard from our backyard the wild screams of "Everyone Out". Quickly the piece of bread was divided among all the family members. My mother in her haste put on my jacket. Everyone grabbed on the last minute what he or she could, and out we went to the backyard.

In the backyard area were already standing all of our terrorized turned out neighbors. We were pulled out to the street, and we were driven along with the rest of the population, to the old marketplace. At the location of the burned out houses, by the marketplace, there a few thousand Jews had already been driven together. One hears the cries and hiccups of children that are clinging to their mothers. They give the impression, like they would have a premonition, that a great tragedy was being pushed upon them. Everyone keeps themselves close to their relatives (near ones) almost as if to be able to be together in the last hour. A group of Jews were sent away immediately, without any selection, packed into vehicles being sent in the direction of the towns Zelow and Lask. There lies the road to travel to the Chelmno death camp. The remaining population was asked to place themselves in 2 lines. In one line were placed healthy people from 18 to 45 years of age, and all of the remaining people, that is grandparents, children, and the sick people were placed in the second (line). I was torn away from my parents. My sister-in-law Rivkeh Lieberman, who found herself together with her husband in the line of the healthy ones, was not able to bear the pain and crying of the children, went back over to them and perished together with them in the gas chambers of Chelmno.

The whole population had been driven to the synagogue courtyard. About 4,000 Jews were pushed into the synagogue. The people were packed in like herring ("sardines") and they were kept there in the synagogue for 3 days, children and old people without food and without water. There wasn't even the ability to breathe. The screaming and crying of the children was heard throughout the entire town. The Germans were standing outside and laughing. The healthy ones and young ones were standing exposed on the synagogue courtyard by the outside wall of the Talmud Torah (Yeshiva). A lot of them risked throwing over bread to those that the Germans were unable to push into the synagogue. There wasn't anyone that was badly beaten as a result of this. Sheva Rosenblat, who was holding a child by her breast, started to grab at one of the breads. Those people that were standing near her started jumping upon her. Everyone had bunched themselves together in one pile. People were tearing at and walking over one another. Sheva's child was suffocated on the spot.

Such scenes weren't so unique. We were standing outside pressed together in one heap. With grieving hearts we had to look upon these dreadful scenes. Twelve o'clock noon hour a German came to take out 200 men, from among those that were standing in the synagogue courtyard, in order to have them clean up the Jewish owned possessions and goods. My brother Joseph and I found ourselves in this group. While travelling by the synagogue courtyard, Hans Biebow, the hangman of the Lodz Ghetto held a speech for us, threatening and warning that by whomever they will find money or valuables, that person will receive (get) a bullet in the head. Of the 200 men only Abraham Granyk (Granick) reported anything. He showed where he had laying hidden valuables.

We were divided into groups of 20 and sent to the different parts of the town, to collect together (gather) whatever may be found in the Jewish homes. My brother Joseph and I belonged to the group that cleaned out the homes on Stercower (Stertzover) Street. We were guarded by gendarmes of the Lodz "Kripo". While we were at work a group of men in uniform approached us. To our amazement, it was a group of police from the Lodz Ghetto, that Biebow had brought with him to liquidate the Jews of Belchatow. A lot of Jewish policemen also helped to rob for themselves. We worked hard for the entire day without eating or drinking. After working, everyone had to undress completely naked, at the instruction of Biebow, and if something was found on someone, even only a piece of bread, that person was beaten at the direction of that murderer.

After the review we were once again sent to the right of the synagogue. This time we were not by the synagogue courtyard, but in front of the synagogue, where there was laying the robbed Jewish fortune. We laid ourselves down to sleep on top of the packages, but none of us were able to sleep.

On the second day the beasts once again pulled us off to work. My brother and I ended up in the group that had to clean up the tailor (cutting) shop that was in Dzalowski's factory. We carried out the new machines, which had formerly belonged to the Jewish bosses, and loaded them into vehicles. I used the opportunity, that I was designated to bring water for the group, and I went to take a look to see what had become of the Jews that were in the synagogue. I also wanted to know if my parents were still there, and as I came close I heard myself being called. These were my parents, who didn't have a place in the synagogue. I wanted to give them the 2 pieces of bread that I had. They didn't want to take it, because they said that in any event they were being sent off to their death. While I was standing there talking to my parents, and my heart was torn with pain with the sadness that was visible in my parent's eyes, a German ran in with a fury. He was holding a knout (whip) in his hand, and he right away gave it to me on my head. When I attempted to explain, that I was sent away for water for the workers in the tailor shop, he gave it to me again, and warned me that if he sees me again, I will have an end like that of all of the Jews in the synagogue.

After my return, they sent my group to clean the Piotrkower Street. A wagon traveled with us. Everything that we loaded upon it was driven to a place in front of the new magistrate. When we traveled by wagon past the synagogue courtyard, I jumped off from it, and once again went to see what was going on in the synagogue and synagogue courtyard, I once again ran into my sister Zlata and her child. I gave away to her the bread that I had. I was encircled by the women and children, that found themselves there, with tears in their eyes, asking me that I should also give a piece of bread for their hungry children. I turned my head away, almost so as not to see the pain of the hungry children. As I was just out of the synagogue courtyard almost rejoining my group, I saw from the distance that something was going on there. When I came closer I saw that the Germans were beating the people from my group. It was as a result of my being missing (from the group). I was afraid to go over there, while I would certainly not come out from their hands alive. I cut through Faivesh's house and back into my group without being noticed by the Germans.

After work, there was a repeat of everything that occurred yesterday. Once again we had to undress naked while being beaten. The second night we were sent to sleep in Machel Piotrkowski's house. On the first floor the brutes were sleeping, the Jewish Police from Lodz. Us (We) a group of 200 people were sent up to the attic. We lay pressed together without a drop of air, simply to be suffocated. It should be understood that even from the act of sleeping you were not able to derive anything. On the third day of our work we had a bitter day. Nine o'clock in the morning a massacre began. A German sadist came along and whomever he found he killed. He pushed out the eyes of Shaye Berkowicz (Berkowitz) and Abraham Wengliszewski (Wenglishewski). There were other shameful abuses, but I don't remember them precisely. My brother Joseph was beaten for such a long period of time till he lost consciousness. He also became deaf from the beating. We were on that day jealous of those that had already been sent away. At night we were sent (driven) to sleep in the synagogue. We did not find anyone there. Lying around there, there were different things that the people had thrown away. We believed that now the line was coming to (for) us. We were not able to fall asleep on the third night. Before our eyes were passing the nightmarish pictures of the last few days. We were filled with horror by it, that which transpired with the people we were close with and of them, as well as what we alone were awaiting. I became of the conviction that night, that there are (present) those moments when it is harder (more difficult) to die than to live.

On the fourth day, at noon time, the Germans called for everyone to give up their German Marks (currency). Those people that had Marks were asked to put them out separately. They numbered about 25 men. The Germans required 25 benches to be brought and all 25 men had to lie down upon them. The Jewish Police from the Lodz Ghetto lashed out upon them for so long, until the Germans told them to cease. After the execution (of the beating) everyone was put into 2 lines. Those that had good work, as tailors, shoemakers, and locksmiths were placed in one line and all the remaining ones, some 130 people, were placed in the second line. The tradesmen were sent to the Lodz Ghetto. They were a group of about 70 men. All of the remaining ones were the last Belchatow sacrifices that were sent to Lodz. Before we were sent out, we were still required to clean out the house where Moshe Luzer Podlowski had lived. We packed up everything from the house into trunks and brought it out to the street. Later they commanded that we carry the trunks on our shoulders and run with them. We ran with our last strength till we reached the place of Hillel the rope (knit-ware?) maker. There we were loaded onto vehicles, and together with the Jewish Police of the Lodz Ghetto, we were driven away to Lodz. With our departure was closed the last tragic chapter of the Belchatow Jewish Community.

---

*[Pages 463-476]*

# In the Years of the Holocaust

### By M. Kaufman*

### Translated from the original Polish by Andrzej Selerowicz**

**Edited by Jerry Liebowitz**

*[With translator's comments in italics]*
[Passages deleted from the Yizkor Book are in straight brackets.] **\***

Until the German-Russian war began in 1941, the Jewish population of Belchatow was integrated into the everyday life of the town. Craftsmen and weavers continued their work illegally, and when someone was caught, he bought himself free after paying a bribe. At night smugglers transported textiles to the Gouvernement [*the German administrative district in the central part of Poland, west of Lodz, under Nazi occupation*] and brought back shoemakers accessories such as leather, nails, pegs, and other things, tailors accessories, cigarettes, candles, in other words everything that was not available in our town. Jews displaced from surrounding villages snuck back to their former houses and smuggled butter, eggs, meat, as well as other agricultural products for us.

Thanks to the group of Jews mentioned above, the rest of us were able to survive, some by trading, some acting as middlemen. In other words, nobody was starving. The people sold everything that they possessed, willing to survive at any price. They knew that the future would be better, without fears or war, and they expected this new life and the end of the war very soon.

The smallest fact, every piece of gossip, was taken as evidence of the oncoming end of the war. [The rumors increased as much as the number of Volksdeutsche [*inhabitants who declared themselves to be part of the German people*] after 1 September 1939. Every story contained a high level of probability, coming from real life.] [*Ed: This passage, as all others in brackets, was deleted and does not appear in the Yizkor Book.*] For example, one German said (whispering in order to underline the importance of his message) that there had been a rebellion in Southern Germany. This rebellion meant that the end of the war was near.

Not to mention letters from Russia about Aunt Rosa, about a Messiah on a white horse, and different "uncles," which stood for Russians, who were about to arrive. This was the reason why nobody took to heart when he lost something. When a smuggler, for example, saving his life at the border at night from the hands of the thugs, had to throw away his goods, saying the next morning that he did not mind and went again as soon as he was able to collect new goods just to stay alive.

Once Stobiecki was caught as he was baking bread, and two "SchuPo-men" [*German policemen*] harassed him some 5 kilometers to the village where he had bought flour, throwing him for fun into water (they told him to dive in and catch the ducks). Afterwards they beat him so severely that he had to be carried home in a sheet. When he regained consciousness and was asked by neighbors how he was doing, he answered: "and we will survive anyway."

After the shochet [*ritual butcher*] Mlot was arrested, he was beaten severely, forced to drink a glass of denaturat [*a very strong alcohol not for consumption*], and was thrown into a shack, where he had to sit all night without any water and having terrible pains. The next day he was set free and returned to his work right away, because he wanted to survive.

Moszek Rozenblat, father of five, every day delivered fresh milk, butter, and chicken. No matter, summer or winter, he crossed the river on foot, although the water went up to his hips – completely wet in summer, and almost frozen in the winter time, shaking from cold in his frozen clothes, having wounds from the cold from crossing the river in the darkness. Nature kept alive this man who desperately held onto life but later perished through German culture with the help of gas at Chelmno [*a concentration camp*]. He did not stop trading, even when he was beaten and his hand was broken after he was caught carrying ducks. He did not even stop trading after being denounced and a dead calf was found at his place, for which he was again beaten and forced to clean the floor of blood using his own hat. He continued his work also after he spent half a year in prison. The saying "and we will survive anyway" was a kind of slogan which kept him alive even during the worst torture.

I could name many Jews who were turned by Germans into creatures, shapeless bodies and who until the very end still longed to survive the Germans. They will all remain anonymous because the murderers destroyed all archives, even their graves in the cemetery; [they all will be remembered in the chapter of the Holocaust of the Jewish Nation.]

[Every one of them was a human being with his life, thoughts, wishes, everyone wanted to survive those atrocities. How many times he had to struggle with death, being successful only due to his enormous will to live. Why the voice of revenge does not bring the heavens to explosion and a hail of damnation fall upon the nation of murderers and their helpers?]

The German-Russian war broke out [and, with this, new hopes arose. Unfortunately they disappeared very soon, right after the first Sunday. While listening to the "Sondermeldungen" [*special war report*] many Jews lost heart, but the passage of time also proved to be a good doctor. The German front moved forward], Germans became polite, and "Volksdeutsche" showed us how our future life would be: the Germans would stop killing us and start using us as a work force, because we were young and strong; Germany would be as big as the entire world, and the best evidence was the fact that the German/Russian front was moving forwards quickly, they have only to take Moscow and then the [*Russian*] government will give up, like in France. Then the time of reconstruction would come. [The evidence that we, Jews, could be useful in this was the fact that we had already repaired the whole street which had been destroyed in 1939, and that a building for the city hall was erected (and remains there even today). This building outlived all the Jews who built it, outlived all the "mister murderers" who relished in its rooms; and city hall still fulfills its purpose. All papers, all documents, were destroyed, and still this building and the ruins of the synagogue will remain as a monument at the graves of six thousand Jews who once lived in this town.] [*The ruins of the synagogue have since been removed.*]

[One did not have to wait long for the realization of the Volksdeutsch plans.]

Before the holidays, the authorities proclaimed that all male Jews between 18 and 40 years old must gather at the yard of the Klug factory. The only exceptions were men working as tailors and those who had permission to run a workshop. [*They produced goods for the army.*]

Nearly two thousand men appeared, accompanied by their wives, children, and fiancées, who gathered around the fence and tried to look through the smallest opening in it, fighting sometimes to have the chance to glimpse inside. The yard looked like this: in the middle a table was placed, and a woman sat there with two boxes in front of her with registration cards and yellow cards for those people who would be let free. In the distance some uniformed Germans stood like guests of honor; at an appropriate distance stood Jewish authorities, President Ehrlich and his advisers, Mr. Altman and Mr. Winter, as well as Dr. Basier from Piotrkow. The factory door was guarded by Jewish policemen and the gate in the fence by "SchuPo"-men [*German police*].

The inspection started at about 2 p.m. Naked men, carrying their clothes in their hands, came to the German doctors who ordered all healthy looking ones to be transported away. Meanwhile they had to wait in another room in the factory building. The others got red cards, evidence that its owner had taken part in the medical examination on that day (I do not remember the exact date). After the German commission left, the mongering started: Winter, Altman, Wengliszewski, not to mention the lesser ones who were part of the authorities, the police, the Grenzwache [*border patrol*], and other German agencies with their supervisors wandered around and took aside all of their relatives and acquaintances. But the poor mothers and wives, of those sons and husbands who did not have a chance to get free, cried and cursed at those who went in and out. The poor mothers knew that the person who left with Altman did not belong to his family at all, but an "uncle" bought for some 500 Reichsmarks [*German money*]. Before evening fell, the SchuPo broke up the crowd of women, because nobody could stand their crying and screaming any longer, and secondly, because the Jewish authorities felt the problems coming. How many were selected by the medical commission, I do not know. I only remember that after this mongering, 250 persons were sent to Poznan the next day.

Already after three weeks, new announcements with the same text were posted. This time, however, Jews did not appear so collectively like the first time. This transport had to be supplemented by a street raid, and finally a group of 450 was again sent to Poznan. Also this time, of course, they could not do without the mongering. Every German who was a member of the local hierarchy had his own Jew, through whom he got a part of the ransom for his freedom.

After the second group was sent away, the town looked changed. Logically enough that after sending away 700 Jews who almost all fed directly or helped to feed their families, hunger started to creep in under roofs of many houses. Now women and youngsters had to risk their lives not only to find enough food for themselves and their relatives, but also for the relatives who sent alarming pleas for help from the Lager [*German word for camp*]. Sometimes a mother saved up food during the whole week not eating anything and also taking away from the portion of 250 grams of bread given for her child, just to be able to send a package for her father or husband in a Lager.

Days and weeks passed slowly. Everybody lived out his problems trying with all his energy to keep himself and his family alive. Boys as of the age of 10 or so became heads of families, growing up very fast, finding out what is allowed and what is not, what has to be sent in a parcel to his father and how to pack the parcel in order that Germans would not discover food inside, but think it was old clothes. The news from the fronts via the Nazi propaganda began to become diluted. Newspapers with red-marked headlines became more and more infrequent. Jews again gained hope, although bad news about the Nazis brought about more beatings to our heads, backs, and cheeks, and the saying "and we survive anyway" gave new moral support.

All of a sudden, a public execution during Purim took place, bringing 10 victims: Taube, Baum, Feld, Wolfowicz, Ehrlich, Landau, Szapiro, Weiss, Lajzerowicz, and Pelzman. They were people of different convictions and social positions. All Jews who had to assist in the execution finally understood that they had to unite because they suffered as a unit, as a race unit. [They stood side by side observing this tragic spectacle, Zionists, Communists, and people from Bund and Mizrachi, party members and non-members, pious and free-thinkers, rich and poor, factory owner and worker.] Maybe suddenly the idea went through their heads that unified they would manage to tear off the head of the Hydra.

[There is however no fact or event which would be able to stop the wheel of history not even for a moment. That execution did not rescue Nazism from a defeat similar to all those executions taking part in the whole Warthegau [*the German administrative district during the occupation of Poland in which Lodz was situated*], in Zelow, in Lask, wherever Jewish communities used to exist.]

Before Pesach a message went around that again raids would be taking place. This was not an official proclamation, because Nazis knew that this time Jews would not appear in front of the medical commission. This was more gossip, which however made us pay more attention. Germans wanted to use some tricks, but they did not succeed one hundred percent. One day the management of the tailors union announced that current work permits would not be prolonged without a stamp from the "Arbeitsamt" [*Labor Office*]. In this way they wanted to gather all workers and to select a group for transport to Poznan. This did not succeed, because only a portion of the workers appeared, especially those who were safe anyway. The situation became tense, and rumors spread that if people did not show up, they would be shot. In fact, just the next day, a certain Gliksman who joined the crowd died from a bullet wound. Towards evening almost all police stations drove their members with weapons by truck outside of town. They wanted Jews to think that the policemen had been driven to other villages to make raids there and hoped that Jews would leave their hiding places and go back to their beds. But this was not successful, because this time the "hunted animals" were on alert. When the Nazis started a raid at midnight, they found only children and handicapped and older people. [That night Ickowicz and Cymberknopf were shot. But this all did not have any relevancy, because] the raid lasted three days and three nights, in the end using the Jewish police who had to bring five hostages each. On the fourth day, 400 Jews were sent away, and they had a tragic ending because they were mostly handicapped, old people, and children, who could not survive the hard work. [At the time that we were deported from town, almost no one from this group was still alive.]

[Dark clouds hung above the town.] Shortly after Pesach, like thunder from heaven, the news arrived about the deportation. [The question "where to and when" was asked by a thousand lips, longing for an answer which would be able to lighten the darkness and bring a piece of hope.] [*In the Yizkor Book*: No one knew where to.]

[I vividly remember those days when the "szpera" [*curfew*] was ordered in town. The first news about the deportation in Pabianice arrived, about how children were ripped away from theirs mothers and thrown onto trucks.] Neighbors and family members gathered in our apartment and wanted to make common plans, exchange information or simply unload their bitterness. [A young woman carrying a child said something that others were afraid to articulate. "Never," she said, "never will I give my child away, even if we have to jump together into the fire." She pressed the dark head of her child to her breast, and a stream of tears flowed from her eyes. Other women joined her crying quietly. To no avail the older women tried to calm her, saying that this was a sin and she was not allowed to talk like this and that God was merciful and would protect the Jews from Hitler as he once protected them from Haman. But all words of consolation coming from the lips of religious people or common optimists could not bring peace even for a moment to the completely shaken mothers. Their intuition told them that the end of their suffering in a very tragic way was approaching, without leaving anybody who would be able to remember them or to say a pray for their souls.] Deep sorrow overcame everybody who looked at the children becoming more and more afraid [*YB*: infected with fear].

It is difficult to describe what happened in our apartment during those three days. It is easy to describe the activities, deeds, and facts, even my own thoughts, but I would never find out what was in the hearts and heads of my mother and my other family members. What we did was actually opposite to what we thought, because everybody tried to stay calm and thereby influence the others. We carried out our everyday work, although it was hard to do so.

Despite all this we drew up a plan according to which everyone should act. My sister and I would probably stay in Belchatow in case of a deportation, because we had official work. My mother and the children would probably be deported. Based on those presumptions, she made rucksacks for my younger brother and herself, packed with the necessary underclothes, and sewed our address on them written on white sheets of fabric. For the child she made a bag which was put around his neck with a paper in it with his personal data. The poor children did not know what such bags were for and pranced with them around the yard. For me and my sister, mother hid some food under the roof which should help us in an emergency.

Additionally, we decided that our common address would become the address of our father in Poznan, and everyone should send letters there no matter where we were. After the war we should meet again in Belchatow.

Three days passed rich in happenings like centuries. The date of deportation was expected anytime. All of a sudden a good piece of news arrived like lightning, reaching all the places where a Jewish heartbeat. "The deportation was withdrawn." Many people thought about the meaning of this expression. Clear thinking was not possible when everyone was almost crazy with joy, when crowds of Jews gathered, despite the "szpera" [*curfew*], in the so-called "Judenstrasse" or in the yard of the Jewish Committee, trying to find out something more concrete and official about the quieted storm which hung over the town. Jews kissed each other, hugged, forgetting for a couple of hours all the differences between them, between the rich and the poor.

The "szpera" was withdrawn in the afternoon. There was, however, something which should not be forgotten and which somehow overshadowed the joyful mood which existed after the biggest danger, the deportation passed. This was the case of President Bodganski, a lawyer who was born, had studied and practiced in Piotrkow. Before the war, he married the daughter of well-known medical assistant Laskowski, Miss Andzia, who worked as a dentist in her private practice. During the Nazi occupation, many changes in the position of the President took place. After Ehrlich was hanged and Topolewicz stepped down, Bogdanski was appointed. During the entire period that he was in office, he tried with all his might to help people in their difficult existence, met delegations of workers, and debated with them about the slightest possible help.

[After asking the visitors to the soup-kitchen, he decided that the free soup served would be enriched with fat instead of margarine. He also wanted to establish a canteen like the one in Piotrkow, where one could get lunch for a minimal price, some five pfennig for larger families or 10 pfennig from a single consumer. Unfortunately he did not manage to realize all those plans due to the storm which broke out.]

On the first day of the "szpera" he rented a taxi for some thousand Marks to bring him and his family to Piotrkow. The cab driver, a German, brought them instead directly to the police station. After the Judenrat paid a ransom, they were not executed, only sent to Radogoszcz [*a concentration camp near Lodz*]. Among them were Bogdanski with his wife, old Laskowski with wife and his old mother, his son Szlamek with wife Pola Dykierman, who originally was from Radom, and their several months old baby, which she bore thanks to a big protection and money paid for in a clinic in Lodz, as well as Dawid Laskowski's wife, son of the old Laskowski, who at that time was in the Lodz Ghetto with an 11-year-old boy. All those listed above were transported to Radogoszcz by these murderers.

The President's chair was taken on by Topolewicz once again.

May ended and the summer arrived, time was quiet, no more raids for work camps. Although the Germans had not changed their tactics towards Jews, everyone was breathing easier. Even new facts of terrible torture did not disturb people. More and more cases of letting dogs loose on Jews. The Germans smiling, would say to the dog, "Du, Mensch, nimm den Hund" [*"You, human-being, grab that dog!"*]. Also murders became more common; for example, Zwierzynski was shot, after he escaped from the transport, hid in Zelow, and simply came home for a short visit. Borensztajn, who used to be a Hebrew teacher in "Yavneh" before the war, now earned money by giving lessons to children of richer people. One day he was caught hovering over a book with a child, and this was enough for the murderers to arrest him in the evening and shoot him on the way to the local prison, after having tortured him.

Also, Yossel Machabanski and his son were shot, in order to eliminate witnesses who could confirm that a German butcher had sold sausages to a Jewish woman who ran an illegal grocery shop. Moshe Zygmuntowicz, who was arrested carrying chickens, was beaten so long that he died after two days of torture, but still not confessing the names of the farmers where he bought the chickens.

All these facts could not darken the joyful atmosphere at that time as a message spread that the manager of the "Arbeitsamt" for the entire Warthegau was bribed. He came to us at the time when a raid was expected from Zdunska Wola where his office was. His arrival used to spread fear, but this time, however, he was literally welcomed. For furs, gold, diamonds, and similar gifts, he promised to bring our people from Poznan back to Belchatow.

[The will to be greedy was successful.] The first eighteen persons came back from the Lager towards the end of July. One can imagine what happened then in town. Everyone started selling everything he could turn to money, and this money flew to the boss through the cash shelter of the committee. The first eighteen persons came Friday before evening, and just the next Thursday came the second group of 70 people.

### A group of Belchatow Jews in the Poizner [Poznan] Camp
In the center sits Kalman Gelbart

This was another story. Actually a group of eighty should have returned, and for all of them the "Lagerfürhrer" [*camp manager*] had been paid. However, he kept ten men, demanding a ransom in the form of two pairs of shoes, two leather coats, and two clocks. This message about the Lagerführer's demand was brought by the people in the group that just arrived. Of course, the families of the remaining ten prisoners collected the needed ransom and sent Mr. Altman with these things to Poznan.

At the same time as Altman was on his way to Poznan, the mayor of Belchatow, who did not know anything about what had recently happened here, requested Altman's presence in order to discuss a matter. The mayor's anger was boundless when he found out that Altman was not there and when he learned of the purpose of his journey to Poznan. He called the camp immediately and ordered that the release of the people without his permission be stopped. After Altman's arrival, he was informed of the mayor's decision. With empty hands he returned to Belchatow on Saturday morning. In the afternoon, President Topolewicz was arrested, and, in the night from Saturday to Sunday, he was liquidated with a shot in the back of the head.

On Tuesday the 11th of August, at 4 o'clock in the morning, my uncle, with whom I worked at the shoemakers, woke me up. The first shift started at 5:00 am and lasted until 1:00 pm.

[The fog that morning could not block out the sun already coming up behind the roofs of the small houses. I left home without a coat and a cap, wearing only my workers shirt and trousers and carrying a bundle with shoemaker's accessories, such as a hammer, pincers, knife, and other things.]

In the street I noticed an unusual movement. [Something was in the air, but I was not able to say what. A German rode by us on a horse and answered our polite greetings. I am ashamed now, but I must confess that I presumed that a revolution had taken place in Germany. We all imagined that on a nice morning we would get up and everything would be over.]

In the workshop, also, where there were only a few men, we were discussing what each one had seen on the way to work [and analyzing the meaning of this information. Meanwhile newcomers added to our observations]. But suddenly we were interrupted by the news brought by Mr. Zylbergold, whose father was a gardener with the SchuPo. He said that Mr. Winter ordered him to go to the chief of the Jewish police, that all old and sick people and children should gather in Zelowska [*YB:* Zelower] Road. And then the happenings developed with the speed of lightening.

In front of us one SchuPo-man led with a whip in his hand a group of men, women, and children, old and young. Many of the workers went home to change clothes. My uncle also left, but I stayed because I was morally too weak to say goodbye.

At 7 a.m. trucks with trailers arrived from Zelowska [*YB:* Zelower] Road and stopped on both sides of Stary Rynek [*Old Market Square*]. We stood around helpless, not knowing what we were waiting for; some left for home, others for the factory. The general confusion which existed in the town also came over us. We were simply standing there and waiting.

Soon the manager of the factory arrived (a German) and told our supervisor (who was also a German), to get the keys and lock the building [*literally: shack*] and to send us to the devil. His order was followed. I was on the street and wanted to go home, but how? Between me and the other side of the street was a long row of German vehicles. At every one stood a driver armed with a weapon or at least a stick, club, or a knuckle-duster. We stood in a group without knowing which direction we should go. Someone called out, "Hop, Jude, hej" [*"Hey, Jew, come on"*], and this indicated the way. We had to run past Germans standing in a double row where we were beaten repeatedly, and out of breath we reached the yard of the synagogue.

I started looking for my people among the Jews who were gathered there. I could not find anybody, because these were mostly Jews from the outskirts of town. The Germans were afraid that if they started the action from the center, all those who lived on the periphery would flee and hide. They started their raid at night encircling the town, shooting those who tried to flee like hunting rabbits, and emptied one Jewish house after another. The people, half naked, were led to the synagogue yard. After the yard was full, the murderers led by Bibow arrived. It was silent, like at a cemetery, as he announced that those having documents or permission to work should go to the other side and form rows of five. Between us and the other side, Germans stood, checking all our documents, every single paper. The crowd jumped towards them, one pushing the other, showing their papers, afraid that the contingent soon would be full and they would have to continue roaming. The Germans created order right away. Two shots were fired towards the masses, and two dead bodies taught the people discipline.

After having shown my card, I was ordered to the other side; that means I was allowed to join those who, thanks to their work permits, could stay in town, according to circulating rumors. Standing in the row I was able to look around. The crowd had to form rows of two and was escorted outside. Dr Basier stood there with his wife, wearing a Red Cross armband. When he was supposed to form a row, his wife did not want to leave him. She kept coming back to him, despite being beaten with hands and feet. Finally she was allowed to stay with her husband, and both hugging each other left for the unknown.

While all this in the yard happened, while the fate of the people was being weighed, not knowing that they were going to their death, just peacefully standing together, happy not to be separated from each other, a girl with loose hair and torn skirt was brought in. Her appearance indicated that she had fought with the soldier who escorted her. I knew her. She was Miss Mendlewicz, about 17 years old, who came to Belchatow from Wielun during the occupation and who still traveled there earning money for her family from trading. I do not know how they found out she was Jewish. The soldier brought her in front of Bibow. His first question was, "Bist du Jüdin?" ["*Are you Jewish?*"]. "I don't understand," she answered in Polish. A loud slap to the face was heard. "Bist du Jüdin?" came the same question, and the same answer followed with the same reaction. This kind of conversation took so long until the Nazi became furious, hit and kicked her, and, when she was on the ground in spasms, he ordered that this piece of "sh__" be taken away from him and thrown on a truck.

[After the Germans counted 100 people,] we were escorted outside to the vans. They were high trucks, and we were supposed to get on through a hatch at the back. A large tumult started, because nobody knew how to climb onto the trucks, and, before we could think, we heard the sticks over our heads hitting people standing close together next to the truck. Even if someone managed to climb up, he was torn back down by those grabbing him trying to climb up.

[Not being aware of the risk involved,] I went to the truck at the side of the driver's cabin, climbed up over the wheel and got in, waiting until the truck was full, looking around the square.

Near the church fence stood those Jews who did not find room in the synagogue yard. Among them I expected to see my family. Using the knowledge of those who lived in our neighborhood, I discovered those from number 18, those from 20, all made to stand in this order. Then I saw number 22. At that moment my mother found my searching eyes and raised my 6-year-old brother into the air. He was saying goodbye to me, waving his hand. Unfortunately, this was the final farewell.

When the three trucks with trailers were full, the command to start was given. A Gestapo man got on every truck and ordered us to turn to the front for the journey, not leaning on sides, which could result in an accident. The transport started, first, second, third truck, and a taxi with some Gestapo policemen at the rear. After a two-hour drive we found ourselves on Balucki Rynek [*YB: Baluter Ring*] in the Lodz Ghetto. Here I [again] met my sister, who came with the same transport [because she had the documents for a tailor's workshop. What scenes of tragedy as brothers, sisters, and mothers discovered that nobody else had reached the ghetto. Jews from Balucki Rynek looked at us shaking there heads with pity; it is really hard to describe].

[All those happenings to which I was witness in the last couple of hours did not break my soul, my eagerness to live. I shook it all off like a dog leaving water, and with new energy I started my life under Ghetto conditions.

When I saw my desperate sister continuously telling me how my youngest brother looked when he woke up, and how he shook from the cold and fear while being dressed, or when she told me how my mother calmed everybody down, that this was all a new German trick, I was not able not to answer her.

Always when she started, heartbroken to remember our family, I calmed her down saying: We have to stay alive! If the war does not last long, we will see all of them – my father in Poznan; also my mother, who surely survived as I expected she would, a healthy woman, was deported for sure and we would meet them. If not, we have to stay alive to take vengeance for their deaths.]

Three years have passed since then. From Belchatow into the Lodz Ghetto, then Auschwitz, Flosseburg, Buchenwald and Theresienstadt – [all the time I was driven by the idea of vengeance. When finally the moment of paying back, when the groaning comes from under the soil and demands revenge, the mighty gentlemen in full dress and top hat spread their protective wings over those nests of vipers, which again multiply and will again poison the world with a new poison in the future. The hope which did not leave me during years of torture, and now brings me new energy to start a new fight, for once and for all the end of all those dark powers breeding this new nest of mean individuals. I am standing in the row of all those 44 million victims who should be addressed for the position of judges and those seeking vengeance and who overtake in their hands the steering wheel of government. Finally the gentlemen from Westminster Hall will speak their judgment, which will be fair for all those criminal Germans with heavy cleated boots covered with mud combined with the blood of innocent victims, will destroy the nest of those reptiles.] [*In the Yizkor Book, this passage ends as follows:* I have been dominated by one desire: survival, to be able to take revenge when the day of retribution finally comes.]

Lodz, 15 January 1946
[Narutowicza Street 29/37]

---

* From the Archives of the Jewish Historical Institute in [Warsaw,] Poland, catalog number 1413 [*written in Polish by Moniek Kaufman*] <u>retrun</u>

** [Editor's note: This chapter was originally written by the author, Mendel (Moniek, in Polish) Kaufman, after World War II, in Lodz, as one of many official Reports of Holocaust Survivors. Several years later, after he had settled in Israel, he was visited by his childhood friend, Jacob Meyer Pukacz (who had emigrated to Argentina in 1937). They found a copy of the original document in the archives at Yad Vashem and translated it into Yiddish for this Yizkor Book (with some deletions and minor changes that do not appear in this translation). Andrzej Selerowicz's translation is from the original document in Polish in the Archives of the Jewish Historical Institute, Warsaw, catalog number 301/1413. Mr. Kaufman now lives in Kibbutz Yafit, Israel, and has given permission for this translation.]

*** [Editor's note: The original report in Polish includes some passages later deleted and not included in the Yizkor Book. These are denoted with straight brackets in this translation.]

---

*[Page 477]*

# Documents of the Holocaust and Destruction

## (From the Jewish Historical Institute in Poland)

### Translated by Pamela Russ

Pabianice, March 30, 1940

The District Administrator of the Lask County
Department 30, Number 209/40

To Herr Mayor in Belchatow

Subject: Admission of the Jews in the Municipality.

With this, I am announcing that the admission of the Jews in the
Municipality (community office) is permitted from 11 until 12 o'clock.

I am requesting that you inform the people of your local community of this
ordnance.

Y.V. Sztenke

*   *   *

Belchatow, August 5, 1940

The Mayor of the City of Belchatow
Lask County
Number 2/771/40

To:
Herr Department Commissioner Berger
Zelow

Dear Comrade Berger:

I am making a private request. Is possible, that the brothers Borenstajn
(Jews) participated in the H'Y [?] football competitions in the H'Y [?] of
Zelow? Fourteen days ago, there was a competition between the two H'Y [?]
teams of Zelow–Belchatow and I heard afterwards that these two Jews were
playing. I ask that you find out about this and I will be grateful to you for
your reply.

Next, I have a personal question to ask of you: If I am not mistaken, not long ago, you purchased a "DKW" car in the Litzmanstadt [Lodz]. I would also like to acquire this, and would be very thankful if you wrote to me if you had any difficulties getting such a car. How high was the price? Is it quickly delivered? Did you have to put on new tires? Did you need a special permit?

Please reply to all these questions, and I send warm greetings, and Heil Hitler!

(Trahner)

*[Page 478]*

Belchatow, May 7, 1940
Number 1/628/40

### List of Jewish Tailors

| No. | Surname and First name | Street | Remarks |
| --- | --- | --- | --- |
| 1 | Rozenblum, Yidel | Breslauer Street, 2 | |
| 2 | Jakubowycz, Volf | General Litzman Street, 18 | |
| 3 | Jakubowycz, Khaim Ber | Breslauer Street, 6 | |
| 4 | Jakubowycz, Shloime | General Litzman Street, 5 | Women's tailor |
| 5 | Cincinatus, Shmuel | General Litzman Street, 9 | Women's tailor |
| 6 | Koltun, Moshek | | |
| 7 | Federman, Avrohom | Horst–Wessel Street, | Women's tailor |

|    |                              |                            |   |
|----|------------------------------|----------------------------|---|
|    | Itzik                        | 18                         |   |
| 8  | Novak, Dovid                 |                            |   |
| 9  | Zilberglat, Hershel          | Friezen–Platz, 5           |   |
| 10 | Luszczantowski, Shlomo       | Friezen–Platz, 5           |   |
| 11 | Adler, Moshek Shiye          | Friezen–Platz, 6           |   |
| 12 | Adler, Henokh                |                            |   |
| 13 | Moszkowycz, Dovid            | Friezen–Platz, 6           |   |
| 14 | Moskowycz, Yosek             | Friezen–Platz, 6           |   |
| 15 | Granek, Avram                |                            |   |
| 16 | Sztotlander, Shimon          | Friezen–Platz, 6           |   |
| 17 | Laske, Hershel               |                            |   |
| 18 | Szierzhant, Yisroel Yosek    | Friezen–Platz, 15          |   |
| 19 | Berkowycz, Yisroel           | Friezen–Platz, 20          |   |
| 20 | Berkowycz, Shimon            | Friezen–Platz, 17          |   |
| 21 | Jakubowycz, Yankel           | Paul–Gerhard Street, 11    |   |
| 22 | Frimowski, Moshek            | Horst–Wessel Street, 24    |   |
| 23 | Gliksman, Berek              | George–Schener Street      |   |
| 24 | Pila, Volf                   |                            |   |
| 25 | Pila, Yissokhor              |                            |   |

| | | | |
|---|---|---|---|
| 26 | Pila, Ezra | | |
| 27 | Jakubowycz, Shmuel | Hindenburg–Platz, 10 | |
| 28 | Zwierzhinski, Yosek Leyb | Hindenberg–Platz, 21 | |
| 29 | Piotrowski, Manuel | Pabianicer Street, 2 | |
| 30 | Brum, Shiye–Berek | Pabianicer Street, 11 | |
| 31 | Warszawski, Leizer Shiye | Horst–Wessel Street, 22 | |
| 32 | Jakubowycz, Noson Meyer | General Litzman Street, 6 | |

Belchatow, May 7, 1940

Trahner
Mayor

Round stamp:
The Mayor of the City of Belchatow
Completed

*[Page 479]*

Belchatow, September 7, 1940

### The stores, homes, and possessions of the additional Jewish residents in the city of Belchatow,
which were completely destroyed during the first days of
the month of September.

| Surname and first name | Streets Inhabited | |
| --- | --- | --- |
| | **Before** | **Now** |
| 1 Aranowycz, Zanwil | Narutowiczer, 35 | Friezen–Platz, 2 |
| 2 Borukhowycz, Zisla | Narutowiczer, 36 | General Litzman, 13 |
| 3 Berkowycz, Mordekhai | Pabianicer, 12 | Paul Gerhardt, 12 |
| 4 Benczkowski, Dovid | Narutowiczer, 21 | Lodzer, 31 |
| 5 Birenzweig, Shliama | Pabianicer, 12 | Lodzer, 38 |
| 6 Borenstajn, Golde Mashe | Pabianicer, 4 | Paul Gerhardt, 12 |
| 7 Brandwein, Meyer | Narutowiczer, 23 | Pietrokower |
| 8 Breitbart, Shmuel | Narutowiczer, 27 | Paul Gerhardt, 7 |
| 9 Breitberg, Itzik | Narutowiczer, 21 | Friezen–Platz, 21 |
| 10 Butkowski, Yisroel | Narutowiczer, 28 | General Litzman, 4 |
| 11 Khoinacki, Shmuel Zakan | Pabianicer, 2 | Horst Wessel, 16 |
| 12 Khoinacki, Dovid | Narutowiczer, 26 | General Litzman, 2 |
| 13 Cukerman, Avrohom | Narutowiczer, 36 | Lodzer, 28 |
| 14 Cimberknop, Yidel | Narutowiczer, 26 | General Litzman, 2 |

| | | |
|---|---|---|
| 15 Davidowycz, Alter | Narutowiczer, 35 | Tirpyder, 7 |
| 16 Davidowycz, Dobra | Pabianicer, 2 | Lodzer, 2 |
| 17 Davidowycz, Leybish | Pabianicer, 6 | Friezen–Platz, 2 |
| 18 Dobrowolski, Khaim Kassel | Pabianicer, 4 | Szlageter, 19 |
| 19 Dobrowolski, Shmuel | Narutowiczer, 30 | Paul Gerhardt, 9 |
| 20 Dobzhinski, Froim Aizik | Pabianicer, 8 | General Litzman, 5 |
| 21 Faivish, Moishe Mendel | Narutowiczer, 35 | Friezen–Platz, 5 |
| 22 Faktor, Avrohom | Pabianicer, 4 | Lodzer, 33 |
| 23 Feder, Shulem | Narutowiczer, 26 | Lodzer, 50 |
| 24 Pabianicer, Khil | Pabianicer, 4 | Paul Gerhardt, 9 |
| 25 Feld, Shulem Borukh | Pabianicer, 4 | Lodzer, 43 |
| 26 Gerszonowycz, Shliama | Pabianicer, 4 | Lodzer, 1 |
| 27 Glazer, Dvoire | Narutowiczer, 36 | Paul Gerhardt, 11 |
| 28 Goldberg, Khil Leybish | Narutowiczer, 24 | Paul Gerhardt, 9 |
| 29 Goldberg, Manuel | Narutowiczer, 23/24 | Paul Gerhardt, 23 |

*[Page 480]*

| Surname and first name | Streets Inhabited | |
| | Before | Now |
| --- | --- | --- |
| 30 Goldblum, Khaskel | Narutowiczer, 23/24 | Horst–Wessel, 13 |
| 31 Granek, Zalme–Yude | Narutowiczer, 35 | Adolf Hitler, 5 |
| 32 Grinboim, Mendel | Pabianicer, 6 | Paul Gerhardt, 13 |
| 33 Gutman, Binem | Narutowiczer, 34 | Friezen Platz, 10 |
| 34 Gutman, Khaim Yosef | Narutowiczer, 34 | Horst–Wessel, 13 |
| 35 Hertzkowycz, Golde Baila | Narutowiczer, 24 | Friezen Platz, 20 |
| 36 Hershberg, Reuven | Narutowiczer, 34 | Horst–Wessel, 23 |
| 37 Herzkowycz, Shabtai | Narutowiczer, 24 | Lodzer, 1 |
| 38 Jakubowycz, Khaskel | Narutowiczer, 21 | Paul Gerhardt, 5 |
| 39 Jakubowycz, Nekhemia | Pabianicer, 2 | Friezen Platz, 9 |
| 40 Jakubowycz, Leyb | Narutowiczer, 22 | Friezen Platz, 12 |
| 41 Jakubowycz, Mikhel | Narutowiczer, 36 | General Litzman, 13 |
| 42 Jakubowycz, Volf | Narutowiczer, 36 | Friezen Platz, 2 |
| 43 Janowska, Khava | Pabianicer, 4 | Lodzer |
| 44 Jakubowycz, Yoel | Narutowiczer, 23 | Horst–Wessel |
| 45 Jeruzalimski, Yorshim | Narutowiczer, 21 | Lodzer 15 |
| 46 Jeruzalimski, Hertzke | Narutowiczer, 21 | Friezen Platz, 12 |

| | | |
|---|---|---|
| 47 Jeruzalimski, Meilekh | Narutowiczer, 21 | Paul Gerhardt, 13 |
| 48 Yoav, Shmuel | Narutowiczer, 21 | Friezen Platz, 18 |
| 49 Kempinski, Itzik Mendel | Narutowiczer, 23/24 | Paul Gerhardt, 13 |
| 50 Kohn, Makhla | Narutowiczer, 36 | General Litzman, 2 |
| 51 Konsens, Moshek | Pabianicer, 6 | Hindenburg Platz, 23 |
| 52 Konsztam, Shura | Pabianicer, 2 | Lodzer 2 |
| 53 Koplowycz, Hersh | Narutowiczer, 32 | Tomaszow |
| 54 Kodzhol, Shiye | Narutowiczer, 36 | Friezen Platz, 4 |
| 55 Krysztal, Rakhmiel | Narutowiczer, 23/24 | Horst–Wessel, 11 |
| 56 Kuperwass, Shulem | Pabianicer, 4 | Horst–Wessel, 13 |
| 57 Kuper, Manuel | Narutowiczer, 35 | Paul Gerhardt 12 |
| 58 Lakhman, Berek | Narutowiczer, 26 | Friezen Platz, 2 |
| 59 Leyb, Shliama | Pabianicer, 2 | Lodzer, 2 |
| 60 Leizerowycz, Avrohom | Narutowiczer, 28 | Szlageter, 7 |
| 61 Leizerowycz, Yisroel | Narutowiczer, 32 | Schenerer, 46 |
| 62 Landau, Avrohom | Narutowiczer, 23/24 | Paul Gerhardt, 13 |
| 63 Lakse, Avrohom Sukher | Narutowiczer, 22 | Kielciglow |
| 64 Liberman, Henokh | Narutowiczer, 26 | Horst–Wessel, 8 |
| 65 Liberman, Dvoire | Narutowiczer, 26 | Lodzer, 27 |

| 66 Liberman Meyer | Narutowiczer, 34 | Paul Gerhardt, 14 |

[Page 481]

| Surname and first name | Streets Inhabited | |
| --- | --- | --- |
| | Before | Now |
| 67 Liberman, Aron | Narutowiczer, 34 | Horst–Wessel, 24 |
| 68 Liberman, Yakov Ber | Narutowiczer, 27 | Friezen Platz, 7 |
| 69 Librowycz, Avrohom | Narutowiczer, 26 | Horst–Wessel, 24 |
| 70 Likhtenstajn, Avrohom | Narutowiczer, 38 | General Litzman, 13 |
| 71 Lipinski, Hershel | Narutowiczer, 35 | Lodz, 26 |
| 72 Lipszyc, Avrohom | Narutowiczer, 23/24 | Paul Gerhardt, 13 |
| 73 Lipszyc, Leybsh | Narutowiczer, 30 | Adolf Hitler, 5 |
| 74 Lioszyc, Shimon | Narutowiczer, 23/24 | Paul Gerhardt, 13 |
| 75 Luszczanowski, Leyb | Pabianicer, 8 | Lodzer 8 |
| 76 Luszczanowski, Zanvil | Narutowiczer, 27 | Lodzer, 17 |
| 77 Landstajn, Esther | Narutowiczer, 35 | Litzmanstadt |
| 78 Makhabanski, Yosek | Pabianicer, 2 | Horst–Wessel, 13 |
| 79 Makhabanski, Lipman Zalman | Pabianicer, 2 | Lodzer, 43/45 |
| 80 Marczak, Khil | Narutowiczer, 33 | *nbsp; |
| 81 Medalion, Yehuda Leyb | Pabianicer, 41 | Horst–Wessel, 6 |

| | | |
|---|---|---|
| 82 Miller, Khaim Simkha | Pabianicer, 6 | Friezen Platz, 8 |
| 83 Moszkowycz, Dovid | Pabianicer, 6 | Friezen Platz, 6 |
| 84 Muszkat, Avrohom and Dvoire | Pabianicer, 8 | Paul Gerhardt, 13 |
| 85 Naparstek, Avrohom Khaim | Narutowiczer, 24 | General Litzman, 9 |
| 86 Novak, Hershel | Narutowiczer, 24 | Friezen Platz, 4 |
| 87 Perlmuter, Shliama | Pabianicer, 4 | Factory Street, 4 |
| 88 Pila, Khaskel | Narutowiczer, 23 | Friezen Platz, 3 |
| 89 Pila, Sukher | Narutowiczer, 23 | Lodzer 25 |
| 90 Pila, Nakhum | Narutowiczer, 29 | Paul Gerhardt, 13 |
| 91 Pila, Volf | Narutowiczer, 33 | Paul Gerhardt, 13 |
| 92 Pila, Volf | Pabianicer, 4 | Paul Gerhardt, 7 |
| 93 Puero, Meyer | Narutowiczer, 35 | Breslauer, 8 |
| 94 Plakhta, Leybish | Narutowiczer, 35 | General Litzman, 9 |
| 95 Polakowski, Surek | Narutowiczer, 35 | Lodzer, 9 |
| 96 Rogala, Hilel | Pabianicer, 8 | Lodzer, 8 |
| 97 Rotenberg, Khana | Narutowiczer, 4 | Factory Street, 2 |
| 98 Rotstajn, Aron | Pabianicer, 8 | Friezen Platz, 12 |
| 99 Rozenzweig, Shmuel Yankel | Pabianicer, 6 | Lodzer |
| 100 Rozensztok, Yosef and Laya | Narutowiczer, 25 | Paul Gerhardt |

| 101 Rozenblat, Yajov | Narutowiczer, 35 | Lodzer, 46 |
| 102 Rozenblat, Yosef | Narutowiczer, 35 | Lodzer, 46 |
| 103 Rozenblat, Moshek | Narutowiczer, 35 | Paul Gerhardt, 2 |

[Page 482]

| Surname and first name | Streets Inhabited | |
| | Before | Now |
| --- | --- | --- |
| 104 Rozenblat, Berek | Narutowiczer, 35 | Lodzer 46 |
| 105 Rozenblat, Zisman | Pabianicer, 12 | Lodzer, 31 |
| 106 Szczukocki, Avram | Pabianicer, 2 | Paul Gerhardt, 7 |
| 107 Szmulewycz, Moshek Aron | Narutowiczer, 24 | Lodzer, 9 |
| 108 Szmulewycz, Hersh | Narutowiczer, 30 | Adolf Hitler, 5 |
| 109 Szmulewycz, Noakh | Narutowiczer, 21 | Paul Gerhardt, 1 |
| 110 Szintenstajn, Alter | Narutowiczer, 22 | Horst–Wessel, 33 |
| 111 Taube, Moshek Aharon | Pabianicer, 8 | Horst–Wessel, 20 |
| 112 Veis, Henokh | Narutowiczer, 24 | Paul Gerhardt, 1 |
| 113 Warszawski, Avrohom | Narutowiczer, 23 | Friezen Platz, 20 |
| 114 Weber, Shliama | Narutowiczer, 26 | Horst–Wessel, 20 |
| 115 Wiszniewski, Khava | Narutowiczer, 32 | General Litzman, 8 |
| 116 Wolfowycz, Avrohom Sukher | Pabianicer, 2 | Lodzer, 2 |

| 117 Wolfowycz, Faige | Narutowiczer, 24 | Paul Gerhardt, 1 |
|---|---|---|
| 118 Wloszczkhowski, Ziskind | Pabianicer, 4 | Friezen Platz, 16 |
| 119 Wrublewski, Shliama Noson | Pabianicer, 4 | Lodzer, 50 |
| 120 Wiwiecki, Khaya Fraidel | Narutowiczer, 30 | Lodzer, 50 |
| 121 Zygmuntowycz, Moishe | Pabianicer, 12 | Lodzer 18 |
| 122 Zygmuntowycz, Nokhum | Pabianicer, 12 | Lodzer, 92 |
| 123 Ferster, inheritors (part of the factory) | Kosciuszko, 2 | General Litzman, 2 |

\*   \*   \*

Belchatow, November 16, 1940
The Mayor of the City Belchatow
Lask County
Number 821/40

To the Secret City Police
Litzmannstadt

Subject: The arrest of the Jew Jakubowycz Shmuel, Belchatow, the prison, and releasing him.
There lies a great suspicion on the Jew Jakubowycz Shmuel, that he is connected to the Jewish smugglers.

This notion was confirmed through his knowledge of and acceptance of the Jewish bands of smugglers.

*[Page 483]*

There is also a strong suspicion that Jakubowycz Shmuel allies politically with those elements who have already been delivered to the Gestapo.

Jakubowycz is known as a low swindler and has already been punished by the Polish government (with six months in jail) for false monies and false identity papers.

I ask the secret city police to investigate.

The Mayor
And District Administrator
Trahner

*  *  *

January 29, 1941
To
*Herr* Department Commissioner
Of the local Community of Sukhczyce

The Higher Council of the Jewish community in Belchatow presented me today with a bill of more than 222 Marks for putting Jews to work at cleaning the snow on Rasi–Konczyk Street. This bill mentions 222 work hours. With your permission, I am answering this issue of the Jews.

You can consider this work as an urgent, necessary job, and you are not obligated to pay the Jews an hourly rate of .80 Mark. Half of the usual payment of this would also be enough for them, as 40 pfennig. In case you find this cost too high, then I ask that you not pay this to the Jews, but to the city fund of Belchatow, because I have to bring in and organize additional workers.

The Mayor
Trahner

[Page 484]

Pabianice, February 1, 1941
District of Warta

The District Administrator
Of the County of Lask
Department 5/6

Postal stamp:
Of the Mayor of Belchatow
Received February 5, 1941 Number 1743/41

To:
Department Commissioner Trahner
In Belchatow

The manager of the Jewish tailors, Herr August, gave my employee Kehler, the two attached letters of Evangelist Pastor Gerhardt. In this letter, the pastor asks of Mr. August to employ Jews in the tailoring [business]. According to the claims of Mr. Kehler, Pastor Gerhardt is known in Belchatow for his Jew–friendly behaviors. This is confirmed through both of these letters. I ask of you to demand of Pastor Gerhardt that he show a distance to the Jews, as one demands of a German, especially of someone in such an honorable position.

(signature illegible)

\* \* \*

February 5, 1941

To: The District Administrator
Of the County of Lask
Pabianice

Following your letter of February 1, 1941, I wish to inform you that Pastor Gerhardt was informed of the message of your letter.

The Mayor
And Department Commissioner
Trahner

*[Page 485]*

February 3, 1941
To:
The Council of Elders of the Jewish Community
In Belchatow

The Jew ........... who lives on General Litzman Street, number 1, must empty the house within three days for Frau [Mrs.] Klarowski.

For the Jews .............. the following listed houses are available: on Shlageter Street near Czeszlyk, on Adolf Hitler Street near the bakery Senyor. Be in contact with Frau Klarowski.

The Mayor
And Department Commissioner
Trahner

*   *   *

February 18, 1941

To:
The Council of Elders of the Jewish Community
Belchatow

Subject: Organizing [cleaning]–service

Recently, every day, I see men and women of the Jewish community on the main streets, who are doing a so–called cleaning [organizing] service. Who set up this service in the streets of the city?

Why are the men wearing armbands?

What is their purpose?

A cleaning [organizing] service is only necessary in the Jewish tailoring, to take care of the material stock. In the city, this task is taken care of by the security police – service department.

In connection with this, once more I am stating that all those men and women who will be seen on those forbidden streets outside of the designated times, will be punished.

The Mayor
Trahner

*[Page 486]*

February 21, 1941

To:
The Council of Elders of the Jewish Community
Belchatow

Subject: Population statistics

By tomorrow morning, we have to have defined how many Jewish residents, men, women, boys and girls, there are in the city.

The city statistics must be presented by tomorrow morning to the Mayor's office.

The Mayor
And Department Commissioner
Trahner

* * *

Belchatow, February 24, 1941
County of Lask, District of Warta

The Council of Elders of the Jewish Community
In Belchatow
Department: Secretary 72/41
Subject: Population numbers

To:
Herr Department Commissioner
In Belchatow

We are herewith confirming that the general sum of the Jewish population in Belchatow is 5,197, comprising of the following:

| | |
|---|---|
| 1. Men from 8 years up | 2,377 |
| 2. Women from 8 years up | 1,128 |
| 3. Boys under 8 | 342 |
| 4. Girls under 8 | 350 |
| Total number of people: | 5,197 |

Chairman
H. Bogdanski

Round stamp:
The Council of Elders of the Jewish Community
In Belchatow

[Page 487]

March 25, 1941

To:
The Council of Elders of the Jewish Community
In Belchatow

Subject: Clean–up Work

The clean–up and maintenance work on General Litzmann Street must be done by Jews as of tomorrow morning. There must be 50 men available daily, who must do the work. Payment for the work will be calculated and adjusted per capita. The general cost for this work is 80 pfennig. But it must be stated that if few or more men think that they will just pass the time, these will receive absolutely no payment.

Daily work begins at 8 AM.

The Mayor
Trahner

\* \* \*

March 27, 1941

To:
The Council of Elders of the Jewish Community
In Belchatow

Subject: Cleaning the Factory Yard

The factory yard, around which exclusively Jews live, is in an extraordinarily filthy condition. I am ordering that a large ditch be dug in the factory yard, measuring at least one–and–a–half meters deep, into which all the garbage must be thrown. Then the entire area must be cleaned, the yards cleaned from refuse, ash, and so on. All of it must disappear. By April 1, the area must be in an orderly condition. I am holding the Elder Council responsible to carry out this order.

The Mayor
Trahner

[Page 488]

Pabianice
May 31, 1941

The District Administrator
Of the County of Lask T/Z

The Mayor of
Belchatow

Received on June 5, 1941
Number 2021/41

To: Herr Department Commissioner
In Belchatow

According to the instructions of the district school director, a collection must be made immediately of printed material within Jewish possession, as well as objects of Jewish culture of former Jewish communities. All this material must be collected by the party and its sections, as well as by the community and urban places. The amassed material must be brought to the "Institute of Research of Eastern Jewry" to Litzmannstadt, which itself is an affiliate of the college of the NSDAP [National Socialist German Workers' Party] that is raising the necessary material for the research. First, leadership of the county must be set up, where, until the next order, this will be carried out.

(signature is difficult to read)

*   *   *

Belchatow, July 2, 1941

To the Chairman
of the Jewish Community of Belchatow
In Belchatow

Subject: The final, new order in the Elder Council of the Jewish Community

The bad condition in the Elder Council of the Jewish community makes it necessary to instate a new order that must be put into place immediately:

As Chairman of the Jewish community, the following is assigned: Yakov Erlikh, and as his advisors, the Jew Vinter Tiszlermeister and the Jew Peretz Altman, Gerber.

*[Page 489]*

The work unit is set up as follows:

| | |
|---|---|
| a) work delivery | Shloime Topolewycz |
| b) supplies | Hendels Binem |
| c) bread distribution | Lipman Mendel |
| d) life supplies | Pakentrager Dovid |
| e) milk distribution | Pakentrager Moshek |
| f) financial administration | Zhukhowski Berek |

These abovementioned Jews are answerable to the chairman, and he – to the Mayor.

The Mayor
Trahner

*   *   *

To:
The Chief of Security Police – Service Department
Belchatow

With the request of giving over the orders into the hands of the Elder Council and to observe the changes.

The Mayor
Trahner

*   *   *

Belchatow, July 2, 1941

The District Administrator
of the County of Lask
Department: Z/T
Number ——

To the Herr Department Commissioner
In Belchatow

In addition to the regulations of the president of the government, according to which Jews are absolutely forbidden to leave their place of residence, I concur with this, that each exceptional permit must have my own personal consent.

TODT *

*trans. Note: The Todt Organization was a civil and military engineering group in the Third Reich from 1933 to 1945, named after its founder, Fritz Todt, an engineer and senior Nazi figure. The organization was responsible for a huge range of engineering projects both in pre–World War II Germany, in Germany itself and occupied territories from France to the Soviet Union during the war. It became notorious for using forced labor. Wikipedia*

[Page 490]

Pabianice
August 1, 1941

Four–cornered stamp:
The Mayor
Belchatow
Received August 7, 1941
Number 3586/41

To: Herr Department Commissioner
In Belchatow

Subject: The Classification of Frail and Sick Jews

The Herr President of the government ordered that these Jews must be
interned and placed into a special institution because they are crippled or
very sick (mentally ill, mentally deficient, paralyzed, and so on), and they
must be registered by name and by precise home address. This is
absolutely necessary, because these sick Jews must receive special nursing
care in an institution.

I require that this be announced at the latest on August 7, 1941.

Y.A.

County Counsel
(signature is not legible)

*   *   *

August 3, 1941

To:

The Elder Council of the Jewish Community
Belchatow

Subject: Reporting of the Frail and Sick Jews

According to the ruling of the director of the County Council, all the frail
and sick Jews who need to be interned in a health–care institution, must
be registered by August 5.

About the condition of the illness and the sick people, one has to immediately be in contact with the Department Commissioner. The conditions must be followed under all circumstances.

The Office Commissioner
Trahner

\* \* \*

*[Page 491]*

Litzmannstadt, August 18, 1941

The Government President
1–121/23–2

To: The Herren [plural of Herr]District Administrators of Ojesda
The Herren Chief–Mayor in Kolys, and
The Herr Chief of Police in Litzmannstadt

Subject: Sending sick Jews from the counties into the Litzmannstadt ghetto.

With reference to: My verbal orders to the County Administrator and Chief–Mayor, at the conference of the County Councils, 41/7/24.

In relation to the verbal bans at the conference of County Councils of 41/7/24, that does not permit to transport sick Jews from the city districts to the Litzmannstadt ghetto – I once again ban unequivocally transporting any sick Jews into the Litzmannstadt ghetto.

Also, it is impermissible, under any circumstances, to send any Jews with contagious sicknesses to the Litzmannstadt ghetto. In these situations, the Jews with contagious sicknesses will be isolated in their current place of residence, and with the appropriate isolation method, will not have contact with those around them. This is easy to do, in that a house where Jews are currently living must be evacuated and this building should be used exclusively for quarantining Jews with contagious conditions.

Signed by Ibelherr
Cofirmed:——signature    Government signature——

\* \* \*

Pabianice, August 25, 1941

The District Administrator
Of the County of Lask

Right–corner stamp:
The Mayor
Of Belchatow
Received: August 27, 1941
Number 3763/41

To: Herr Department Commissioner
In Belchatow

Sent in order to please acknowledge and take care of.

Y.A.
County Counsel

*[Page 492]*

Belchatow, August 28, 1941

The Head Commissioner
Of the City of Belchatow
Lask County

To:

The Head Commissioner
From the counties of Selow, Lask, Lutomiersk, Kleszczow
In Wiadawa and Khabielice

Subject: Lists of Jews

You have informed the District Administrator about your request, with regards to the records in your region, for a designated number of handworkers and craftsmen.

It is possible that in the coming days many interested people will present themselves to you and ask for work or a location [for work]. I ask that you support them with actions.

I am prepared to provide information about the worthiness and capacity of each interested person.

I would be very grateful if you could send me an exact list with numbers and other details of your Jews.

The Department Commissioner
Trahner

* * *

Belchatow, September 5, 1941

The Department Commissioner
Of the City of Belchatow
Lask County – Wartheland

To: The Elder Council of the Jewish Community
In Belchatow

Subject: Delivery of Workers

I have in mind to set up a larger cabinetmaking [workshop] right near the Jewish tailor workshop. For this reason, it is necessary that all the Jewish carpenters report.

Be in touch with Vinter, who knows all the craftsmen, carpenters, and polishers. With assistant workers [apprentices] I cannot accomplish very much, I need specialist workers who will work under the supervision and direction of carpenter Vinter.

The Department Commissioner
Trahner

[Page 493]

Pabianice, September 4, 1941
(Wartheland)

The District Administrator
Of the Lask County

Accounts of the County Community Fund:
Full accounts in the savings fund of the County of Lask in Pabianice
Postal–Cheque–account Breslau
Number 7228
Department DR ST / EP NR' To: The Herr Department Commissioner
In Belchatow

I am herewith returning the statistics I received the day before yesterday, and ask that these be completed according to my method of filling in the rubric: the number of people and the houses that are in consideration here. At the same time, I ask that you send me a copy and to do this always with this sort of work, because I must have a sample for the President of the Government.

Y.A.
County Counsel

Addendum 21

*   *   *

Belchatow, September 13, 1941

The Department Commissioner
Of the City of Belchatow
Lask County – Wartheland
Number 3955/41

To: District Administrator of Lask County
In Pabianice

Subject: The Concentration of the Jews.

Addendum: Statistics about the number of quarantined, with a copy.
Department of County Counsel.

I am herewith enclosing a list of the streets, and the number of those quarantined and [the number of] houses in the city of Belchatow, in order that the list should be useful for the concentration of the Jews.

The Department Commissioner
Trahner

\*   \*   \*

[Page 494]

Pabianice, September 16, 1941

The District Administrator
Of Lask County
DR ST / EP

Right–corner stamp:
The Mayor of Belchatow
Received September 18, 1941
Number 3997/41

To: Herr Department Commissioner
In Belchatow

The Department Commissioner Badeh in Kleszczow urgently demanded to transport the Jews from his area to Belchatow. I am looking at the first week of October to transport them to Belchatow. I ask that preparations be made for their quarantine. I will let you know of the exact day of the transport, and you will also receive an exact list of the individuals.

Y.A.
County Counsel
(illegible signature)

\*   \*   \*

Pabianice
September 17, 1941

The District Administrator
Of Lask County
D'R ST'/EP

Stamp:
The Mayor
Of the community of Belchatow
Received: September 20, 1941
Completed:
Actions:

To: Herr Department Commissioner
In Belchatow

Subject: The Summoning [amassing] of the Jews

According to a list of October 10, 1940, there are five Jews still found in your community. I am inquiring whether these five are still in your district. If not, please let me know where they have been taken. I am waiting for your report within a week.

Y.A.
(signature illegible)
County Counsel

For the duplicate of the original:

*[Page 495]*

Belchatow, September 22, 1941

The District Administrator
Of the City of Belchatow
Lask County – Wartheland

To:
Herr District Administrator of the County of Lask
In Pabianice

Subject: List of the Jewish population.
Department of Finance Office

In the official district of Belchatow, lives the following number of Jews:

| | |
|---|---|
| a) children under age 6 ... | 564 |
| b) employed Jews ... | 1,206 |
| c) unemployed Jews ... | 3,230 |

A list with the names of the employed Jews will be submitted as soon as it is completed.

The Department Commissioner
Trahner

\* \* \*

Belchatow, September 23, 1941

To Herr District Administrator of the Lask County
In Pabianice

Subject: Concentration of the Jews. Letter of 17, D'KH D'R ST / EP
In the community of Belchatow, village of Dobrzhelow, there are still 8
Jews. There are two men, two women, and four children – ages 21–8.
(signature illegible)
As a copy of the original.

\* \* \*

Pabianice, September 30, 1941
The Department Commissioner
Of the Lask County
D'R ST / EP

To: The Department Commissioner
In Belchatow

Subject: Concentration of Jews

I have instructed the Department Commissioner in Belchatow to …

[Page 496]

… transfer the eight Jews from the village of Dobrzhelow to Belchatow. He
will be in contact with you.

(signature illegible)
County Counsel

After having reviewed the Act!
a settlement is awaited and can be carried out.
Belchatow, October 3, 1941

The Department Commissioner
Trahner

\*   \*   \*

Belchatow, October 19, 1941

Police Office Belchatow
Lask County
Diary Number 1203/41

To:
Local Police Department
Belchatow

Subject: The Resettlement of the Jews from Dobrzhelow

On the morning of October 4, 1941, because of the local demand, the two Jewish families, Viener and Glik, were transported from Dobrzhelow number 25, Belchatowek Community, to Belchatow, and the Council of Elders was ordered to place them into homes.

The following persons belong to the Viener family:

Yakov Viener (husband), born in Belchatow, January 11, 1899
Ella Viener (wife), nee Horowycz, born in Zdunske–Wola, August 1, 1899
Moshek Viener (son), born in Belchatow September 27, 1920
Masha Vienerowna (daughter), born in Belchatowek, Feb. 13, 1924
And Rivka Vienerowna, born in Belchatowek, November 7, 1924

The following belong to the family Glikman:

Khaim Glikman (husband), born in Litzmannstadt, September 15, 1909
Rivka Glikman (wife), nee Horowycz, born in Zdunske–Wola, December 8, 1902
Avrohom Glikman, born in Litzmannstadt, July 11, 1933

Y.V. Urbas
From the Gendarmerie
As a copy of the original

[Page 497]

[German letter at top]

146/21

Belchatow, February 11, 1942

The Department Commissioner
Of the City of Belchatow
Lask County
Number 5418/42

To: Herr District Administrator Todt
In Pabianice

I am informing the District Administrator that yesterday evening, at 21:30, the two Jews Makhabanski – father and son, were shot as they tried to run away.

This episode, briefly, was as such: In a local butcher, sausages were always being stolen. It was almost impossible to capture the thieves. It is certain, even though they did not do this alone, that these two bought up all the meat and sold it for a profit. On the way to the prison, the two tried to flee and were then shot.

The Department Commissioner
Trahner

[Page 498]

## Belchatower Martyrs in France and Belgium

### Translated from the Yiddish by Martin Bornstein

The Belchatow Landslayt, who had in different times during the pre (eve of the) war years (had) settled in France and Belgium, also paid a dear price for the freedom of Europe, through their active fight against the Nazi occupiers.

The group of Belchatow immigrants in France and Belgium were home manufacturers and workers (laborers). The absolute majority of them were concentrated in Paris, where there even existed a Belchatow Union (Group), carved out from a section of the Piotrkower Lands(l)and-schaft.

In the bitter end of the beginning of the second world war the Belchatower, like all Jews, almost entirely (the entirety) registered of their own free will, in the French Army and actively participated in the war against Hitlerism.

Concerning (Not) all of the Belchatower that participated in the fighting, (both) those in the regular army and those that fought the opposition, there is not available precise reports (information).

We must therefore suffice with remembering one among them, that died for the holy name (G-d).

On the 4th of June 1940, as a fighter (soldier) of the French Army, Abraham Front, age 35, fell (was killed) by a German bullet, while in combat by the Belgian border.

He came from a poor working class family (parents) and because of the great need (poverty), that had existed in his house, from childhood on he wandered from different towns and countries (cities), from (in) Poland, immigrating later to Germany, and in the year 1931 he settled in France.

All around he worked hard to earn a piece of bread ("make a living"), and when the war broke out, he belonged to (was among) the first that of their own free will went (took) to fight.

On the 25th of November 1948, his body was moved from the fighting location (battlefield), where he fell, to a grave of the Jewish Volunteers in Paris.

When the Nazis occupied Paris, all of the Jews were deported from there, and among them also (were) the Belchatower, of whom only a (small) portion managed to survive to the liberation.

Among the deported Landslayt who perished you will find: Fischel Knop, Yechezkiel Pyulah, Yankel and David Tzintzinatus (Cincinatus), Shmuel Herzkowicz with his wife and children, Yossel Feltzman, Binem Gelbart, Aaron Pigulah, the once upon a time Belchatower Dozor Shaya Yidel Zeslawsky with his wife and children, as well as our landsman Liberman, Pinchas Meir's son, who was killed as a hostage, that was taken by the Germans in Paris.

Among the perished landslayt in Belgium we only know about Abraham Novak, a devoted artisan and activist of "The Jewish Solidarity".

After the occupation of Belgium by the Nazis, Novak went over to the underground, and after being caught by the Germans on the 5th of May 1944, in a bestial way he was murdered by the Gestapo in Brussels. His dead body was able to be buried on the Brussels Cemetery.

Also his wife, who faithfully helped him in his work, was deported by the Nazis and every trace of her disappeared.

Among the deported and perished Belchatower landslayt was also found Meir Knop, who was active in the organized workers life in Belgium.

## FROM A RUINED GARDEN

### The Memorial Books of Polish Jewry

Edited and Translated by
**Jack Kugelmass** and **Jonathan Bioyarin**
With Geographical Index and Bibliography by
**Zachary M. Baker**
Published in association with the
United States Holocaust Memorial Museum
Washington, D.C.
INDIANA UNIVERSITY PRESS
< http://www.indiana.edu/~iupress/ >
Bloomington and Indianapolis

[Page 501]

# Belchatov Without Jews

## Josef Reich

("From a Ruined Garden" pp. 244-246)

I feel oddly alien today in the town where I was born and raised, where I know each corner, each stone, where every house, every store reminds me of familiar people who lived, worked, and dealt here, scrimped and saved penny after penny, built a house for themselves, for children, for children's children. None of them foresaw the bitter fate of those for whom they struggled and built houses.

Here I stand in the marketplace and consider the house which is located right at the corner of Pabyanets Street. Here, a few steps up, was Hershl Plavner's store. I walk closer and am greeted with a bitter sight: now they sell holy pictures and crucifixes there.

I walk through the market and look at the stores of Yoysef-Leybish Grushke, Henekh Adler, Goldshteyn, and others. All of these shops have been taken by the new merchants.

I walk across to the other side of the marketplace and read the new signs on the stores. At one I read, "Village Cooperative," but underneath this inscription is still legible, insistent and accusing, an older inscription: "Tuvye Varshavsky."

Today is Monday, market day in Belkhatov. Once the market was jammed with people. Today, one can walk through quietly. The booths of the new merchants take up only a small part of the marketplace. Today, Belkhatov is like a large village. Of all the textile factories which were built by Jews, Orzhekhovski's is the only one still in operation; the others are idle and empty.

I look at Fraytog's factory. Various objects made of iron remain, the remains of the looms and other machines. I remember how my father used to talk about Perets Fraytog, how he had worked hard in his youth, carrying calves from the villages on his back, until he acquired money and built the factory.

A Pole complains to me that everything in town died along with the Jews, and there's no way to earn a living anymore. The Jews, he says, were resourceful and had initiative, and everything was busy around them.

The walls of the synagogue stand intact, but the windows are gone. Probably they were needed by the neighbors. The interior is utterly empty: the podium is gone, as are the Ark of the Torah, the lecterns, the benches. All that remains are the walls, empty, torn, and dirty. Everywhere there are broken, discarded boxes and dirt. 1n one place I saw a hole which has been dug, and next to it an iron pot. A Pole explains to me with a burst of jealousy that other Poles had dug up a treasure there, which had been buried in the pot under the floor.

The location of the cemetery was hard to find. I only managed to do so because the grain harvest was long past and the stalks no longer hid the bits of broken graves which lay like signs saying: Here lie the bones of generations of Jews, of our parents, brothers and sisters, and dear ones. Among the shards I recognized two pieces of my father's stone. When I returned a year ago, I saw another piece, which is now gone. Someone took it for sharpening scythes and axes.

On my way back from the graveyard, my eyes downcast, I found out where the gravestones had gone. The road to the Catholic cemetery from Startsev Street is planted with trees. There is a bridge just before the path, which was constructed out of gravestones. The path itself is also paved with Jewish gravestones.

In the meadow between Pabyanets Street and the woods flows a brook. In my days there were stepping-stones which we used to get across, while peasant wagons forded the stream.

Today there's a solid little bridge with massive supports, paved for a few dozen meters with Jewish gravestones. They have also been used to pave the sidewalks in various parts of town. They lie as if disgraced with their inscriptions in the Holy Tongue, with their engraved Psalms, menorahs, Jewish lions, and Stars of David. As they engraved these stones, the dust that flew from the stones consumed the lungs of my father and brother. How much effort and creativity they poured forth in order to find the right ornaments and inscriptions for each stone: for a young man, a broken tree; for a young woman, a broken candle; for a scholar, a bookcase and two deer; for a *Kohen*, two hands raised in reciting the priestly blessing, and so forth. Now these stones-torn out of their graves-stolen from the dead, with the holy inscriptions "Here lies" and "May the soul of this holy man be in paradise forever" are trodden by strangers' feet, and desecrated.

An article was printed in the central organ of the Polish Socialist party, *Rabotnik*, which concluded by stating that from being a dirty, isolated town before the war, Belkhatov had grown into a town that was both clean and cultured.

We would like to say to these "cultured people": you live in our homes, you sleep in our beds and you use our bedding, you wear our clothes-at least do *not obliterate our holy places!*

[Page 505]

# Polish Jewry

## Book Collection from the Central–Union of Polish Jewry in Argentina

### Editor: Mark Turkow

**Chief Publisher: Avraham Mitelberg**

**Translated from the Yiddish by Pamela Russ**

**Published until the present:**

1. *Mark Turkow:* Malka Owsziani Tells ... – sold out

2. *H.D. Numberg:* I.L. Peretz – sold out

3. *Grossman – Wiernik:* Treblinka – sold out

4. *Peretz Granetstein:* My destroyed City of Sokolov – sold out

5. *Yisroel Tabaksblat:* The Destruction of Lodz – sold out

6. *Zerubavel:* The Mountain of Destruction (Chapters of Poland) – sold out

7. *Elkhonon Ceitlin:* In a Literary House – sold out

8. *Dr. Kh. Szoszkes:* Poland – 1946 – sold out

9. *Z. Segalowycz:* Tlumaczka 13 – sold out

10. *M. Nudelman:* Laughter through Tears – sold out

11. *Dr. Meyer Balaban:* The Jewish City of Lublin – sold out

12. *Yisroel Efrat:* Homeless Jews – sold out

13. *Dr. Yakov Shatzki:* In the Shadows of the Past – sold out

14. *Dovid Flinker:* A House on Grzhibow – sold out

15. *Dr. Hillel Zeidman:* The Diary of the Warsaw Ghetto – sold out

16. *Children's Martyrology* (collection of documents) – sold out

17. *Khaim Grade:* Refugees (songs) – sold out

18. *Sh. Koczerginski:* The Partisans Are Marching! – sold out

19. *Frieda Zerubavel:* Wanderings (a refugee's drawings)

20. *Mordekhai Strigler:* Majdanek

21. *Yakov Leszczinski:* On the Edge of the Abyss – sold out

22. *Z. Segalowycz:* Burning Steps

23. *Avrohom Teitelboim:* Warsaw Courtyards

24. *Tanya Fuks:* Wandering through Occupied Regions

25. *Sh.L. Schneiderman:* Between Terror and Hope

26. *Leah Finkelstein:* The Story of Poland – sold out

27. *Jonas Turkow:* This Is How It Was... (the destruction of Warsaw)

28. *Sh. Izbahn:* "Illegal" Jews Split Oceans

29. *Yakov Pat:* Henokh

30. *Dr. Y. Kermysz:* The Resistance in the Warsaw Ghetto

31. *Simkha Poliakiewycz:* A day in Treblinka

32. *Mordekahi Strigler:* In the Factories of Death

33. *Avrohom Nakhatumi:* In the Shadows of Generations

34. *Yekhiel Leder:* My Home (poem)

35. *Yosef Wolf:* Reading Peretz...

36. *Tzippora Katzenelson–Nakhumow:* Yitzkhok Katzenelson

37. *Y. Hirshaut:* Dark Nights in Powiak

38. *Nakhum Sokolow:* Personalities

39. *Rokhel H. Korn:* Home and Homelessness (song)

40. *A. Almi:* Moments of Life

41. *Menashe Ungar:* Przysucha and Kotzk – sold out

42. *M. Bursztyn:* About the Destruction of the Unknown Person

43. *M. Kypnis:* One hundred Folk Songs – sold out

44. *Z. Segalowycz:* My Seven Years in Tel Aviv

45. *Dr. Kh. Szoszkes:* A World That Has Gone By

46. *Shloime Wago:* The Destruction of Chestokhow

47. *Avrohom Zak:* Years Wandering (songs)

48. *Sh. Izbahn:* The Karp Family (novel) – sold out
     (awarded by the Tzvi Kessel Literature Foundation, Mexico 1950)

49. *Dr. A. Mokduni:* My Memoirs

50. *R. Shoshana Cohen:* In Fire and Flames (diary)

51. *Y.Y. Trunk:* Yiddish Prose in Poland

52. *Janos Turkow:* Fighting for Life

53. *Yitzkhok Perlow:* The People of the "Exodus 1947" (novel)

54. *Pinkhas Bizberg:* Shabbath–Yomtovdig [Jewish holidays] Jews

55. *Shalom Asch:* Peterburg (novel)

56. *Shalom Asch:* Warsaw (novel)

57. *Shalom Asch:* Moscow (novel)

58. *Dr. Philip Friedman:* Auschwitz

59. *B. Rozen:* Tlumeczka 13

60. *Dovid Flinker:* In the Storm (novel) Volume I

61. *Dovid Flinker:* In the Storm (novel) Volume II

62. *Janos Korczak:* Little Moishes, Little Yosefs, Little Yisroels

63. *Mordekhai Strigler:* Factory "C," Volume I

64. *Mordekhai Strigler:* Factory "C," Volume II

65. *Khaim Grade:* The Glow of the Extinguished Stars

66. *Rivka Kwiatkowska:* From Camp, In Camp

67. *Yoel Mastboim:* My Stormy Years (memoirs)

68. *Eliyahu Trotsky:* Exile Germany

69. *Dr. Yakov Shatski:* Culture History of the Enlightenment – sold out

70. *Nakhman Meisel:* Once There Was a Life …

71. *Y.Y. Trunk:* Simkha Plokhta from Narkowa – sold out

72. *Yehuda Elberg:* Under Copper Skies

73. *Dr. A. Mokduni:* Foreign Countries

74. *Zygmunt Turkow:* Fragments of My Life

75. *Yehoshua Perlow:* Jews All Year
(winner of the Peretz Prize of the Yiddish Pen Club in Poland and
Literary Prize of the "Bund" in Poland, Warsaw, 1937)

76. *Yakov Leszczinski:* The Eve of the Catastrophe

## Soon to Be Printed and Published:

- *Daniel Czarny:* Vilna

- *Menashe Ungar:* Chassidus in Poland and Galicia

## Being Prepared for Printing:

- *B. Mikhalewycz:* Memoirs of a Jewish Socialist

- *Z.Y. Ankhi:* Reb Abba and Other Stories

- *Dr. Josef Tenenboim:* Galicia – My Old Home

- *Sh. Brianski:* Zhelekhow Faces

- *Mordekhai Strigler:* Fates

- *Rokhel Auerbach:* From Ringelblum's Archives

- *Yosef Reikh:* Memoirs of a Partisan

- *Dr. Yakov Wigodski:* Memoirs of the Years of Occupation

- *Dr. Gershon Levin:* The Book of My Life

- *Z. Segalowycz:* Fifty Letters

- *Sh. Berlinski:* Inheritance

- *Kodia Molodwski:* Once Upon a Time

- *Hershele:* Shabbath on the Stretch

- *Avraham Lev:* A Song after You

- *Gershom Boder:* Krakow

- *Moishe Zonshein:* "Jewish Warsaw"

———

*[Page 508]*

## Press Articles about the Book Collection

# Polish Jewry

### Translated from the Yiddish by Pamela Russ

\*

**Yitzkhok Berliner** writes about the book by Jonas Turkow, "Fighting for Life" ("Der Weg" [Yiddish newspaper], Mexico, August 12, 1950):

I read Jonas Turkow's book "Fighting for Life" in one breath.

The reason for this is not because of my reading habits but because the situations of these gruesome experiences, in reality, captivated me from beginning to end.

Just as in his first book, "That Is How It Was," in which Jonas Turkow so sharply describes life in the ghetto, the same thing is seen in "Fighting for

Life," as the writer was punished and bleeding as he wrote about his frightening experiences on the Aryan side of Warsaw and Province.

Experiences? – No! – This is not an appropriate or adequate word for these horrific things that the modern day Anusim [Hebrew: people who were coerced into something they did not want to do] went through.

To be on the Aryan side and to hide behind a Polish ID card, under the mask of an aristocratic moustache, under the constant fear of being discovered by the razor–sharp eye of a "Shmaltzovnik" [trans: pejorative Polish slang, referring to blackmailing Poles who protected Jews during the Nazi occupation], wandering from bunker to bunker, suffocating in hiding places, and trembling with each suspicious rustle in fear of being "informed" by the "friendly" Polish surroundings – all this means – playing your last card...

Playing the last card, after which, with your solitary life, you run away from the ghetto to "freedom" ...

Playing the last card with your own life and also with the lives of your wife and child...

*

How were they able to experience and live through all this, the "Janeks" (Jonas Turkow was called Jan Tatarkewycz on the Aryan side), the "Juzheks," the Dr. Bermans, the Dianas, the little Margaritkas, the Janinas, and the Anielas (the editor Rokhel Auerbakh)?...

You have to be physically and mentally strong to be able to conduct this fight for life, and – strong in morale, you had to be as well, in order to be victorious in this struggle...

And a strong morale Jonas Turkow did have ... so he actually was able to come out of that horrible chaos as a complete person ... Therefore, he was able to carry inside himself, and to tolerate and live through all the humiliations and debasements of the "goodhearted" Poles...

*

You think that Jonas Turokw gave his book a pretty simple title, "In the Fight for Life." But this expression, "In the Fight for Life," only gets its justice in Turkow's descriptions of his sufferings ... The well–known global expression

– "In the Fight for Life" – (La Luca por La Vida, in Spanish) is used by many nations, referring in general to the daily struggle of an individual to support himself and his household financially... and generally, for a class struggle. – The collective search to improve one's life circumstances.

This expression acquired a greater truth when it took on the name of Jonas Turkow's fight for life on the "free" side, outside the ghetto... when the actor, Jonas Turkow in reality played the difficult role of Jan Tatarkewycz... and he carried this role until the end of the final act...

If one is fighting for his life and survives these unequaled and incomparable struggles – physically intolerable struggle – mentally a miraculous fight – morally, one has to have a superhuman steadfastness and resilience in oneself that does not permit you to bend or break with any oppositional horrors.

If you lose yourself, you become an "Emilke" (a Jewish woman in Turkow's book who lives as a Pole in Warsaw).

*

The woman mentioned, "Emilke" (Emilia the Kosower), was so steeped in her role as an Aryan woman, that the surrounding Poles began to think of her as one who belonged to their nationality ... and she herself began to waiver ... until she became a business partner to the so–called goodhearted Pole, Theodore Pajewski, who saved Jews from the ghetto – according to the instructions of the Polish underground – and at the same time he negotiated and cheated with unfortunate lives and with the last few groshen [pennies] of the hidden Jews on the Aryan side...

Emilke used to look for houses for the disguised Jews with "good faces." But that's how she used to deplete these condemned people until their last groshen, to their greatest danger...

How far did they, these dissidents of humanity and nationhood, go with their perverse behavior?

It is necessary to present a situation from Turkow's book, where he describes in all its nakedness, these morally weakened people of the Emilke type:

"And the second sister, Emilke, added:

" 'I never had anything good come from the Jews. If not for the Poles, my sister and I would long be buried in the ground. When the war will end, I will not have any contact with a Jew...

" 'Our hearts were bleeding (this was recounted by Jonas Turkow – Y.B.) when we constantly heard this topic and the "beautiful expressions" about Jewish women, to which were later added the cynical observations of Theodore Pajewski.

" 'When the author Rokhel Auerbakh (Aniela) came to us, we told her about the propaganda that the Kosowo sisters were putting out. Rokhel Auerbakh smiled, and told us that we should be careful with Emilke Kosower, because this is a terrible person and we had to be very vigilant with her...

" 'When Rokhel Auerbakh left, Emilke says to Theodore: 'I don't understand. Why are you letting her in here? You have to forbid her to come here. She can bring a tragedy upon us here.' 'You're right,' Theodore replies, and then he turns to me. 'If she comes here again, then you, Yanku (Turkow's Aryan name – Y.B.) tell her that I don't want her to come to me because the neighbors are already talking anyway that Jews are coming to me...

" 'I won't tell her that,' I reply. 'And you do not need to tell her that either because she belongs to the underground organization. Just like she has been coming to you until now and no one has been thinking that she is Jewish, no one will even thing that she is guilty.'

"After that discussion, I was afraid to present to them my sister–in–law Ruzhe Blumenfeld as a Jew. When she came to us, I introduced her as Frau [Mrs.] Doctor Stepa – one of the most important activists in the Polish underground. With that, she earned their highest respect." (page 204)

Fortunately, these Emilkes were few in the martyred lives of the Jews in Poland under the Nazis and also under the Poles and Ukrainians. The Jewish people held themselves proud and strong against all the stumblings, and accepted the pains with heroic and indescribable stoicism.

*

This is how Jonas Turkow came to play in a theater with his own life on the stage of reality...

The planks [of the stage] shook under his steps... and each minute he thought the stage would break under him...

Nearby and behind the scenes, were fellow performers, with terror and patience in their sad eyes ...

The crowded room – on the Polish street – was filled with murderous faces... judgemental, sharp looks, would eat away at him ... insecurity hovered over the entire theater – Poland ...

He tried to hide himself behind the foreign stage make–up and in a foreign language and – he played his role beautifully...

Jonas Turkow performed in a theater under a strict rule of the horrors of life...

A terrible theater play!...

————

About all issues related to the Book Collection
"Polish Jewry"
contact:
**Union Central Israelita Polaca**
Pueyrredon 667 – Buenos Aires

# בעלכטאָו

## Belchatów Memorial Book

## List of Pictures

### Captions translated by Martin Bornstein

**[ note that the page numbers below refer to the pagination of the original Yizkor book, not this translation ]**

# INDEX

The page references in this index are for this English translation

## C

## D

# T

www.ingramcontent.com/pod-product-compliance
Lightning Source LLC
Chambersburg PA
CBHW062018090426
42811CB00005B/891